THE LIFE AND MYSTERIES OF THE
JUNGLE

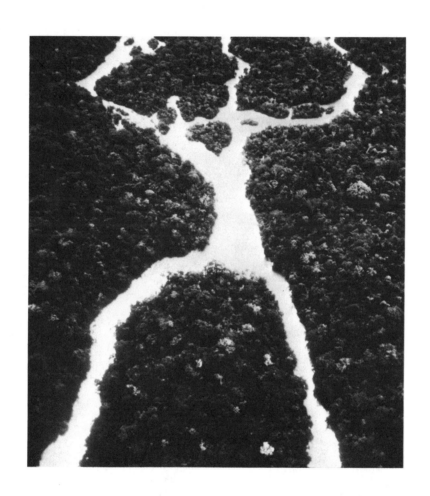

THE LIFE AND MYSTERIES OF THE
JUNGLE

Edited by Edward S. Ayensu

Crescent Books, New York

Consultant: **Dr P. Whitfield**

Text: **Dr Michael Lock**
Professor P. W. Richards
Dr D. M. Stoddart
Dr Bryan Turner
Dr T. C. Whitmore

Illustrations: **Richard Orr**
Michael Woods

Jungles was conceived, edited and designed by Marshall Editions Limited, 71 Eccleston Square, London SW1V 1PJ

Editor: **Jinny Johnson**
Art Editor: **Mel Petersen**
Assistant Editor: **Rosanne Hooper**
Design Assistant: **Linda Abraham**
Researchers: **Pip Morgan**
Jazz Wilson
Libby Wilson
Picture Research: **Visual Research Services**
Production: **Hugh Stancliffe**

© 1980 Marshall Editions Limited

First Edition

First published in the United States of America in 1980 by Crown Publishers, Inc., under the title *Jungles*.

Inquiries should be addressed to Crescent Books, distributed by Crown Publishers, Inc., One Park Avenue, New York, New York 10016.

Printed and bound in Spain by Printer industria gráfica sa Sant Vicenç dels Horts, Barcelona D.L.B. 25415-1980

ISBN: 0-517-451506

"The most critical issue of our time, indeed of all human history, is the unprecedented biological destruction involved in the massive and accelerating loss of tropical forests. Dr Ayensu's book introduces us to the mysteries, complexities and fragility of the biological treasure-trove known popularly as jungles. The book sounds a clarion call to the rescue and should be required reading for anyone taking global citizenship seriously."

Dr Thomas E. Lovejoy
Vice-President for Sciences,
World Wildlife Fund

The most mysterious of all natural worlds

Encounters with jungles are endlessly surprising. Even I, born and raised in the humid tropical zone of West Africa, and a lifelong student of the jungles of Asia, Africa and Latin America, still feel a stranger in this type of vegetation; at every outing the forest shows a different face, with that first sight of intricate vines indicating an awaiting tangle of interwoven relationships.

Epiphytes and parasites seem to have commanding roles among communities of jungle organisms. The eye adjusts to the low light levels, and mosaics of hue reveal the exquisite nature of animals and flowers that depend on filtered light to exhibit their radiance. The buzz of symphonic music made by bees and wasps, with percussion from the crackling vegetation, always disturbs the visitor's nerves. And where snakes, bloodsuckers and other crawling organisms abound it is hard not to feel fear. Here then, is mystery, excitement, unimaginable diversity; the essence of the magnificence of nature.

The area covered by jungles or tropical rain forests is just one twelfth of our planet's land surface; yet jungles contain more than half of the earth's fauna and flora, which is estimated to be ten million species. Our current knowledge shows that, for example, 70 to 85 per cent of the nearly one million species in the insect world are confined to the tropics.

Most jungle happens to be located in the economically disadvantaged countries, where medical improvements coupled with improving pre- and post-natal care continue to contribute to excessive population growth—paradoxically the greatest single impediment to social and economic progress. Naturally the developing countries look upon their forests as resources to be exploited in pursuit of industrial and economic independence.

But during the past half-century mankind has been steadily foreclosing on the future of the jungles. We are currently witnessing a dramatic escalation in the destruction and transformation of rain forests into cleared land and timber; the rate of removal is now estimated at 150,000 square kilometres a year. After deforestation comes the devastation of erosion, with deep, meandering gullies washing away layers of top soils that took millions of years to accumulate.

Who is going to suffer most for these seemingly senseless acts?

I would not suggest that the world's vegetation should be untouched; rather that there should be judicious management, and that endangered plant and animal species should be conserved in appropriate areas for future study. For here are inestimably important genetic resources with large potential to increase the value of our foods, medicines and industrial products. A number of individuals, forward-looking governments and non-governmental organizations now share these concerns, questioning the processes which, in the name of development, cast doubt on the survival of a sprawling variety of organisms.

This book comes at an appropriate moment to recap on the state of our knowledge of the tropical rain forests, whose structure and inhabitants are even now so little understood. Here are the facts of this majestic habitat. And here are the questions that make the jungle the most mysterious of all natural worlds.

Professor Edward S. Ayensu
Smithsonian Institution, Washington D.C.

What is jungle?

Steamy morning mists rise from the rain forest at Gogol, New Guinea, on a series of ridges stretching to the skyline.

Jungle . . . . the word conjures up images of a steamy, mysterious, impenetrable forest with extraordinary plants and fierce animals. Derived from the Sanskrit word *jangala*, jungle was originally applied by Anglo-Indians to any impenetrable vegetation. Today it is the popular term for tropical rain forest, the world's most complex natural community.

Seen from space, the three main regions of rain forest lie as a sombre green girdle around the equator. They are frequently shrouded in cloud, and merge to the north and south into monsoon forests. Tropical rain and monsoon forests together occupy about 4.3 million square miles (11.1 million sq km), just over half the world's forests. About two fifths of their extent are rain forests.

Unlike the monsoon forest, where the climate has a fairly marked dry season, tropical rain forest occurs where the climate is hot and wet all year round. The steamy heat is ideal for plant growth, and so it is not unusual to find more than 100 different sorts of big tree on a single acre. Some species are common, but a few are so rare that they may be known only from a single tree. Trees make the framework of the forest, with the biggest commonly reaching a height of 150 feet (45m). The giants have trunks reminiscent of cathedral columns, which are often fluted or buttressed at the base. Beneath them are medium-sized trees, and on the forest floor miniature trees, only a few feet tall, live permanently in deep shade.

The forest interior, occasionally flecked by sunlight, is open and easy to walk through. Along roads and rivers, however, the jungle edge is a dense tangle of sun-loving climbers. It is these fringes that have created the popular impression of impenetrability and danger. Big, woody climbers hang down within the forest, each with a crown as big as a small tree at the canopy top. Other shade-loving climbers cling to tree trunks; those of the lower levels, many of which are ferns or aroids, may have huge leaves. Epiphytes, plants which grow on other plants and have no connection with the ground, depend on the forest frame. Some species are adapted to the moist, dark, forest interior; others, especially orchids, are sun-loving, and drape limbs and boles of trees in the top canopy.

Another characteristic of the tropical rain forest is that it provides many habitats for animals, ground-dwellers and tree-dwellers. This animal diversity is further enhanced by interdependence with plants. Flowers may be specialized for pollination by birds, bats or insects. Many fruits are adapted for animal-dispersal. Some mammals are attracted to the plants' bright hues and strong smells; birds to their vivid, contrasting hues; bats to trunk- or branch-borne flowers and fruits; and fish to fleshy fruits hanging over streams.

Plants familiar in cooler parts of the world as small herbs exist as huge trees in the jungle. Tree violets reach 80 feet (24m) in Malaya, and milkworts grow even taller. However, many rain forest plants have been unable to adapt to unfavourably cold or dry climates and have no temperate cousins. Thus the nutmegs are found only in tropical rain forest (Malaya has 54 kinds) and the great family of the Brazil nut is confined to the New World tropics.

Man has long obtained many commodities, timbers, medicines and spices, from the jungle. First he traded with indigenous tribes, some of which lived off wild food but needed to barter for salt. But as trade developed with temperate civilizations, Western man eventually penetrated to the source of these highly prized goods. Different nations then began to vie for control of the supplies and, as the jungles were explored, scientists were amazed at the richness and exuberance of jungle life and the astonishing complexity of its functioning.

In the past quarter century tropical timbers have become a major trade commodity and more land has been needed for agriculture to support burgeoning tropical populations with rising expectations. Today the jungle is being destroyed despite its widely recognized scientific, aesthetic and commercial value. It is still not known whether mankind has the ability to conserve adequate fragments of these grand forests to ensure the survival of their splendour for future generations.

Where are jungles?

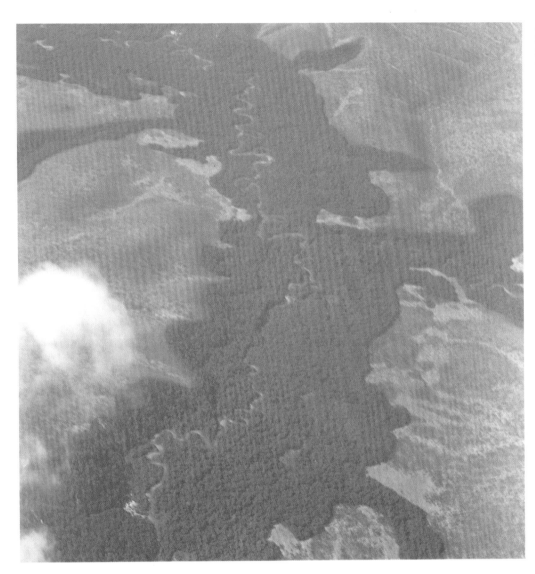

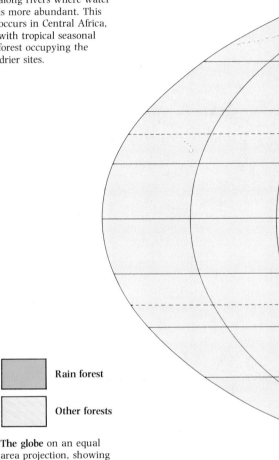

At its fringes, tropical rain forest sometimes penetrates seasonal climates as gallery forest along rivers where water is more abundant. This occurs in Central Africa, with tropical seasonal forest occupying the drier sites.

▆ Rain forest

☐ Other forests

The globe on an equal area projection, showing the land with a natural covering of closed forest.

The equatorial girdle of tropical rain forest is not continuous but occurs as three main blocks. Over half (56 per cent) lies in the Neotropics, mostly in the great basins of the Amazon and Orinoco rivers, extending westward to the flanks of the Andes. It is replaced by tropical seasonal forests in the northeast bulge of Brazil. About a quarter (26 per cent) is located in the Asian tropics, centred on the Malay archipelago, with patchy extensions into continental Asia. Africa has the third great rain forest region, about one fifth (18 per cent) of the total area. It is concentrated in West and Central Africa, the Zaire [Congo] basin and the shores of the Gulf of Guinea, but does not reach across the whole continent. Each main block has outliers which look tiny on a world map, but which actually are extensive, with their own fauna and flora.

Besides the huge Amazon-Orinoco forest, there is in the New World a discrete belt along the Atlantic coastal mountains in Brazil and one on the Pacific coast of Ecuador and Colombia, reaching up through Central America to south Mexico on the Caribbean shore of the American isthmus. In Africa there are small patches of rain forest on some of the

mountains of East Africa, mainly in Tanzania, and an isolated, curious forest on the west coast of Malagasy; there is also forest on the Mascerene and Seychelle Islands in the Indian Ocean.

The Asian rain forest block is broken by areas of seasonal forest on some of the islands in the centre of the Malay archipelago and in peninsular Thailand, but it then continues into Burma and Assam and along the coast of Indochina into southern China and the island of Hainan. There are disjunct small blocks on the western Ghats of India and in southwest Sri Lanka. Eastward, it extends through the Solomons, New Hebrides and Fiji archipelagos into the Pacific; southward, there are two small areas on the Queensland coast of Australia.

Tropical rain forest merges at its edges into one of two other kinds of forest. In southeast Brazil, on the Asian continent, in Burma and Assam and the eastern coast of Indochina, on the eastern coast of Australia and on the islands of the southwest Pacific, tropical rain forest changes steadily with increasing latitude to subtropical rain forest, which has different flora and structure. Among the trees

found here are many belonging to families better represented in the temperate regions of the world. This change happens roughly in accord with decreasing mean temperature and increasing annual variation in day length, though why some plants are better adapted to subtropical than tropical conditions is not known. Epiphyte and climber species also change. It is thought that forest structure alters subtly and gradually because of these differences in species composition. A sharp boundary must, therefore, be arbitrary. Subtropical rain forest is included in most reckonings as a localized, limited extension of tropical rain forest.

The other, and more widespread, type of boundary occurs when tropical rain forest blends into tropical seasonal, or monsoon, forest. Viewed from above, this looks like a patchwork, with rain forest dominating the most favourable sites—that is rain relief slopes, or the banks of water courses, or where the soil is either more fertile, deeper, or has better water retention. Different types of monsoon forest, often with an increasing percentage of deciduous trees, occupy habitats of increasingly severe drought. There is a complex interaction between

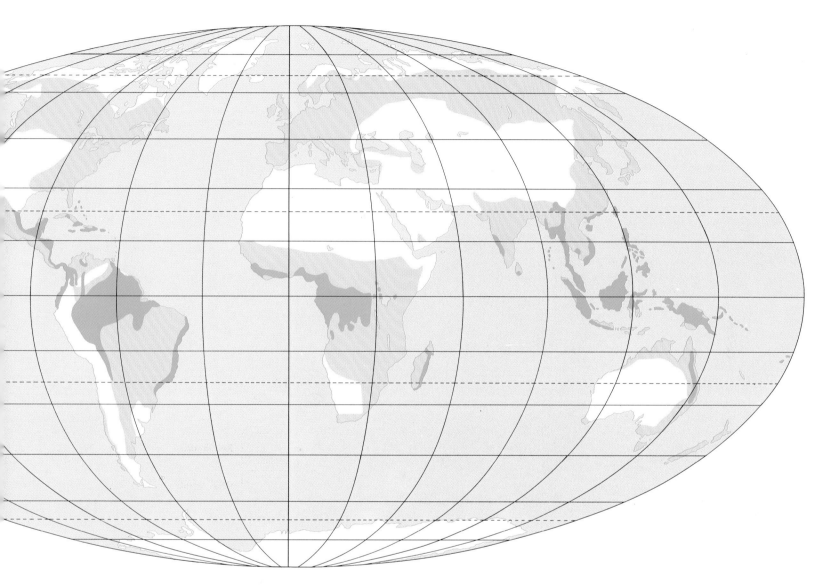

the extent of drought and other characteristics of the site, so that the same kind of forest may occur on different rocks in places with different degrees of drought.

In addition, the mosaic of the two types of forest is rendered more complex by the extent to which man has altered it. Seasonal forests are highly inflammable in the dry season. Rain forests do not easily burn, although they may be eroded by degradation at their edges. In Java, for example, fire has played havoc with the monsoon forest, whether it was used for hunting, for pleasure, for pestering neighbours, for clearing land, for making land passable or for converting forest to pasture.

It is the seasonally dry tropical forests in Middle America, Sri Lanka and Indochina which have harboured the great tropical civilizations of the past. The trees in these forests could be removed by fire and the seasonal drought halted the build-up of agricultural pests and diseases. From these seasonal forests come teak, sal and the subtropical pines which are so important in world commerce. The rain forest has not sheltered complex civilizations, but nevertheless its gifts to man are copious.

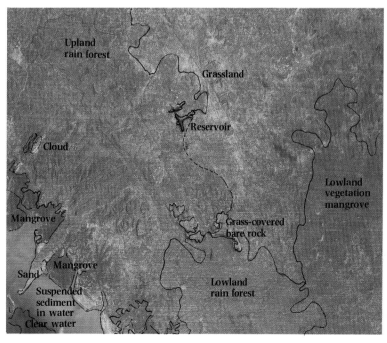

Satellite imagery has become available in the last decade to assist in mapping vegetation cover and land use. These are not conventional photographs but images constructed from sensors which record the amount of energy reflected in each of four wave bands. Here, data from each band has its own coloration, and all four bands are superimposed to give an image in which forest appears red and water blue. The scene, *left*, is part of Guinea, West Africa, and shows a mosaic of forest and grassland. Upland, lowland and mangrove forest can be distinguished in this image, each with its own subtle internal variations.

Jungle variations

There are many different kinds of tropical rain forest. The kind with the greatest diversity of species, complexity of structure and stature is the forest of comparatively dry lowland sites on 'normal' tropical red or yellow clay-rich soils. It has the greatest number of different commercially useful plants and is the main source of rain forest timber. Not only is it of paramount interest to naturalists, but it is also the kind of jungle which is most rapidly being destroyed.

In the lowlands there is a range of other types of rain forest on soils periodically or permanently waterlogged or inundated. There are also forests which grow on limestone soils, over ultrabasic rocks and on sandy soils. Finally, there is a series of different types of tropical rain forest found at increasing altitudes in the mountains. All these major categories are called forest formations.

The main formations of wet sites are mangrove forest, developed under the influence of salt water, freshwater seasonal forest and permanent swamp forest. In Asia and in small areas of northern South America, another type of formation, peat swamp forest, appears in places where dead plant matter becomes waterlogged and, instead of decaying, accumulates as peat. Many swamp forest trees have flying buttresses, or stilt roots, and specialized breathing roots which provide aeration for the plant parts below the water-table. Swamp forests are typically of simpler structure and are less rich in species than dry land forests.

The forests on limestone and ultrabasic rocks have species able to tolerate harsh conditions. For example, limestone sites are prone to periodic desiccation and plants show adaptations to withstand this. These forest formations are not extensive but are highly distinctive.

Sandy soils are freely draining, poor in nutrients and usually podzolized (that is with a hard iron or humus 'pan' layer at some depth in the profile). They support a forest formation known as heath forest. Characteristically, this is a dense forest of pole-like trees, in which a considerable amount of direct sunlight is able to penetrate to ground level. It lacks emergent trees and has an even canopy top with a greyish-green hue. The average leaf size is smaller than in other lowland forests. Heath forests are subject to drought because of the coarse, freely draining soil, but it is not yet known to what extent their highly distinctive features are an adaptation to withstand occasional water deprivation or shortages of mineral nutrients. Myrmecophytes, or ant plants, and, in Asia, pitcher plants are widespread in this formation, as they are able to supplement the nutrients obtained from the soil by their unusual methods of feeding. Heath forest areas are drained by tea-hued streams bearing humus in suspension. Their greatest area is in northwest Amazonia, drained by the Rio Negro.

In the mountains of the humid tropics the crests of ridges and the upper slopes are clothed by a small-leaved forest of even canopy which is similar to heath forest in both physiognomy and species composition. Known as the upper montane rain forest, it forms above the level of persistent cloud. The trees, whose crowns are gnarled, are commonly swathed in a dense covering of mosses and liverworts. Because of the richness of these epiphytes, the term 'mossy forest' is also applied. Many ridge crests have periodic droughts, but the degree to which either these or mineral deficiency control this forest is unknown. The upper montane forest gives way to a zone of very short trees known as elfin woodland. Above, on the highest mountains, a

low, scrubby forest with even smaller leaves occurs, the subalpine rain forest. Below the mossy forest, on all but the smallest mountains, lies lower montane rain forest. This is usually sharply bounded, although it merges gradually downward into lowland rain forest from which it differs in floristic composition more than structure.

These major categories of rain forest are found in all parts of the tropics. They are recognized by their structure and features, but their species composition is totally different from continent to continent. The formations are not homogeneous, as they show subtle variety in both structure and species which is seldom sharply bounded. Lowland forest on any land is the most complex forest, but different kinds of heath forest and peat swamp forest are now known to exist.

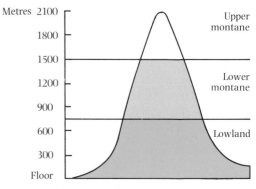

On wet tropical mountains there are three main rain forest formations according to altitude. The exact elevations of change depend on the size of the mountain. In Malaya on small mountains, boundaries lie at about 2,500 and 5,000ft (750 and 1,500m) but on the central massif of New Guinea they are at about 5,000 and 10,000ft (1,500 and 3,000m).

Above a certain height, mountains in the humid tropics are covered with clouds most of the time. Within this foggy belt the trees are draped in epiphytic liverworts, mosses or occasionally, as at Chiriguana 6,500ft (2,000m) up in the Colombian Andes, lichens. This so-called mossy forest drips with water nearly all the time. Some mossy forests are low and stunted, others, as at Chiriguana, are of considerable stature.

Mangrove forest, *left*, is swamp forest which develops on land regularly inundated by salt water. One tree family, Rhizophoraceae, which can tolerate the conditions, predominates. The wide-spreading stilt roots typical of many mangrove trees, enable the plants to obtain oxygen from the air rather than the waterlogged soil.

This Sarawak heath forest, *far left*, is called *kerangas*—a native term meaning 'place unsuitable for rice'; its sandy soils are too infertile for agriculture. Heath forest is even more delicately balanced with its physical environment than other rain forest ecosystems and is easily degraded to grasslands or open scrublands by felling and burning. It has its own characteristic flora.

The Americas

Of the regions of tropical rain forest in America, the Amazonian jungle, one of the great wild places left on earth, is by far the largest. There are two other regions, the Chocó forest and the Brazilian Atlantic coast forest.

The Chocó rain forest lies on the northwest coast of South America, between the Pacific and the foothills of the Andes in Colombia. This is one of the wettest parts of the world, with rainfall of over 236 inches (6,000mm), in a few places exceeding 393 inches (10,000mm) per annum. A poorly known region, it is rich in plant and animal species, many of which occur nowhere else. Southward, the Pacific coast rain forest just reaches into Ecuador. Northward, it runs up through Panama (the Darien

forest) and the Caribbean side of the American isthmus as far as southernmost Mexico.

On the Atlantic coastal range of Brazil lies a second block of rain forest, also with unique plants and animals. The region is heavily populated, and, as a result, there has been much clearance for agriculture. Little undisturbed forest remains.

The third block, the Amazon-Orinoco rain forest, is the largest jungle area in the world. The Amazon lies mainly within Brazil, though at its western flank Bolivia, Peru, Ecuador and Colombia share the forested headwaters. To its north lies the Orinoco basin, which is largely in Venezuela. The northeastern part of this forest extends into Guyana, Surinam and French Guiana.

Ambitious schemes have been devised to exploit the mineral wealth and timber of the Amazon basin. Roads are being built to penetrate its vastness. On the Mato Grosso fringe, in the south, parts have already been converted to cattle ranches. Maps of the Amazon forest are only now becoming available, as the area has been too big to survey conventionally. The development of aerial radar photography which penetrates clouds has recently provided pictures of the forest cover. Most of the different rain forest formations are represented in Amazonia.

The Amazon river itself carries a greater volume of water than any river in the world. Every day during maximum flood one-fifth of all the river water

on earth flows into the Atlantic Ocean from the Amazon. Second only to the Nile in length, the Amazon is joined for its entire length by tributaries which are themselves major waterways, some even larger than the Mississippi. The main rivers flood annually and are flanked by permanent or seasonal swamp forest. The western part of the Amazon zone experiences scarcely any seasonal climatic changes; the eastern portions are much more seasonal.

The most important world crops of Amazonian origin are Para rubber, *Hevea*, which is widespread, and cocoa, *Theobroma*, restricted to the western Amazon. Other well-known exports include mahogany and Brazil nuts. At present, the Amazon forests provide little of the world's hardwood.

For a stretch of 2½ miles the Iguzu Falls cascade over the lava formations cut by the Rio Iguzu. The misting waters plunge 210ft (64m) into the Rio Parana below. Dense tropical jungle covers this part of the Parana plateau, near the border between Brazil, Paraguay and Argentina. Rainfall is constantly high in this area, keeping the turbulent waters of the falls at full swell.

Overgrown by jungle, ancient Mayan temples were hidden for years.

Amerigo Vespucci (1454–1512)

The extraordinary wealth of plant and animal life in the Amazon basin has attracted explorers and scientists since the dawn of the sixteenth century. In 1499–1500 Amerigo Vespucci crossed the mouth of the Amazon river, but it was a Spanish navigator, Vicente Pinzón who first sailed up part of it in 1500. The first European to navigate the length of the river was Francisco de Orellana, who in 1541 floated 1,700 miles in a small boat with 60 men—an extraordinary feat.

In the mid-eighteenth century, Charles de la Condamine made the first scientific study of the Amazon, and Friedrich von Humboldt mapped the connection between the Amazon and the Orinoco. Many other pioneers followed during the nineteenth century, some impoverished enthusiasts. Naturalists Alfred Wallace and Henry Bates earned threepence for each insect collected on their Amazon travels, yet their researches proved invaluable.

The 1800s brought two husband and wife teams. Henri and Olga Coudreau mapped the larger Amazon tributaries, while Louis and Elizabeth Agassiz made detailed observations of the wildlife. This century, ex-President Theodore Roosevelt led an expedition which added 900 miles of river to the map. In 1925, Colonel Percy Fawcett set out to explore the unknown, wild jungles of the Mato Grosso. He disappeared without trace.

Louis Agassiz (1807–1873)

Naturalist Henry Bates explores the jungle.

Africa

The rich African rain forests satisfy the pygmies' every need, including the luxury of palm wine. They scale the tree with natural agility and tap the palm to extract a liquid sap. This is then fermented to produce a potent drink for festive occasions.

Still one of the least urbanized areas in the world, the Congo (Zaire) basin in equatorial Africa is largely covered by tropical rain forest. Forests extend up on to the flanks of the mountains to the east and along the coast of the Gulf of Guinea to the northwest. They are bounded by high mountain vegetation to the east; elsewhere in the lowlands they gradually merge into seasonal tropical forests, open woodland and savanna. The Congo river itself is at least 2,700 miles (4,350km) long and is the second longest river in Africa.

In West Africa, a narrow coastal belt of humid climate gives way to progressively drier, more seasonal climates in the north. The vegetation also changes, from that typical of rain forest on the coast through to that characteristic of desert in the Sahara.

During the Ice Ages Africa is believed to have had a much drier climate, which considerably reduced the size of the rain forests. The present southern Congo forests grow over the desert sands of the Kalahari, presumably having extended on to them in the current Interglacial. Even today, the jungle climate is somewhat seasonal. The lowland rain forests with the least seasonal climates in Africa are comparable in structure and physiognomy to the eastern, more seasonal parts of the Amazon and to the narrow, slightly seasonal fringe of the Asian rain forests.

Most of the African rain forests probably have fewer tree species per square mile than the rain forests of Asia and the least seasonal parts of America, and are more uniform in composition over large areas. The corner of the Gulf of Guinea, Cameroun and Gabon, and the eastern fringe of the Congo forests differ, however, with rich flora and many localized species of plants and animals.

Beyond the main rain forest block, in East Africa, lie small isolated patches of species-rich montane rain forest. These are fast disappearing because of clearance for agriculture and firewood. On the east coast of Malagasy there once lay a narrow belt of lowland rain forest, abundant in plants and animals. To its north and east, there were small areas of rain forest on the Seychelles and the Mascarene Islands. They have now largely disappeared or been greatly altered.

Although most of the different kinds of tropical rain forest are found in Africa, heath forest hardly exists and peat swamp forest has not yet been recorded there.

In West Africa, many of the rain forests have been disturbed by man. Only a few hundred years old, they are rich in African mahoganies and other important commercial species. Eventually, however, these valuable trees die and are replaced by those of lower commercial value. In some nations the forests approach exhaustion or, as in Nigeria, the internal market consumes the whole harvest. Central Africa remains only lightly exploited.

The main world crop plant derived from African rain forests is oil palm. It has long been cultivated by villagers for their own use as well as for a cash crop; there are also some large commercial oil palm plantations.

Hugh Clapperton
(1788–1827)

Heinrich Barth
(1821–1865)

Paul Belloni du Chaillu
(c 1831–1903)

Pierre Savorgnan de Brazza
(1852–1905)

Cameron and his followers crossed countless rivers while exploring tropical Africa and freeing slaves. As Livingstone's successor, he mapped Lake Tanganyika and travelled across the equator.

Exploration of the West African coast began around 450 B.C. over 2,400 years ago, when the Carthaginians and Phoenicians sailed down the southern Atlantic. In 1352, Ibn Batuta, a remarkable Muslim explorer, travelled to Timbuktu and the river Niger, which he called the Nile.

Detailed exploration of the coast, however, began in earnest in the fifteenth century when the Portuguese gradually worked their way southward until Bartholemew Dias finally sighted the Cape of Good Hope in 1487. It was not until 1788 that explorers began to probe inland to rediscover Timbuktu and explore the river Niger. In 1796 the Scotsman, Mungo Park, after escaping from some Moorish captors, finally reached the Niger, which he explored for 80 miles, discovering that it flowed eastward. His second expedition to the Niger in 1805 proved a disaster. All 40 of his team died of fever, attacks or drowning.

Undaunted by such hazards, another Scotsman, Hugh Clapperton, set out with two companions and reached Lake Chad and Nigeria in 1823. On his second expedition in 1827, Clapperton died, leaving Richard Lander to continue his work. Lander and his brother John, in spite of being imprisoned and robbed, made their way to the Niger delta.

In 1828 Rene Caillié, disguised as an Egyptian Arab, was the first man to return alive from Timbuktu, though disappointed with his findings. German scientist Heinrich Barth spent from 1845 to 1853 exploring the Chad and Nigeria regions, and published invaluable accounts of the area and its tribes. Equally accurate information on pygmies and gorillas was gathered by Paul Belloni du Chaillu, although it was treated with scepticism at the time. In the 1870s Pierre Savorgnan de Brazza, a Franco-Italian, visited Gabon and the Congo. Perhaps most remarkable of all was Mary Kingsley, who made two voyages in the early 1890s while African territory was rapidly being divided between the colonizing powers.

Southeast Asia and Australasia

The great archipelago which connects Southeast Asia to Australia is the hub of the tropical rain forest in the Far East. In contrast to both Africa and America, there is no great continental land mass, as no place is more than a couple of hundred miles from the sea; the region is also much more mountainous, with many peaks and cordilleras.

The Malay peninsula and the western islands of Sumatra, Java and Borneo lie on the Sunda continental shelf, an extension of Asia. In the east, New Guinea and its attendant islands lie on a second shelf, the Sahul, which extends from Australia. Wallace's line is the name of the biogeographical boundary which separates these two distinctive regions. Both shelves have been dry during the low sea levels of the Ice Ages of the last two million years. The rain forest animals of Sundaland are Asian; those of the Sahul shelflands are of Australian affinity. There are also important though less extreme differences in plant life.

All the major kinds of tropical rain forest occur in the Far East; in particular, there are extensive heath forests and huge areas of peat swamp forest in Sumatra, Malaysia and Borneo.

An important difference between forests of the west and east is the abundance of trees belonging to the family Dipterocarpaceae in Sundaland. Dipterocarps occur in all kinds of lowland and in lower montane rain forest. They are most diverse in dry land rain forest, such as in parts of Borneo and the Philippines, where they dominate the upper canopy. Their grandeur and stature plus their wealth in plant and animal species have made the dipterocarp forests the peak of evolution anywhere on earth.

In the eastern part of the region, dipterocarp species are less common; the forests are not so tall or rich in species. The southern outlying rain forests of Queensland, Australia, and the eastern outliers of the Solomon and New Hebrides archipelagos are no more abundant in species nor taller than some temperate forests. On New Guinea, main bastion of

the eastern rain forest block, instability of the land due to landslides on the steep, immature mountain slopes, frequent earthquakes and volcanic activity has a profound effect on the forests. Malaysia, Borneo and Sumatra in the western bastion are much less prone to catastrophic disturbance.

Southeast Asian dipterocarp forests today supply the largest number of tropical hardwoods to enter international trade. By the end of the century, most of the dipterocarp forests are likely to have been felled. Besides this modern trade in timber, the Asian rain forests have long provided many other valuable commodities: rattans, climbing palms, for cane furniture; diverse tree fruits, including the durian, rambutan and mangosteen; gutta percha; jelutong, the base of bubble gum; gambir for tanning; gamboge dye; Manila copal and other gums and resins (dammars). World crops which originate from this region are sugarcane (New Guinea), bananas (wild throughout; commercial varieties from the western bastion), citrus fruits (in the

forests of the continental fringe) and teak (from adjacent monsoon forests of Thailand and Burma).

There is evidence that during the Ice Ages the mountain treeline and various belts of montane rain forest were lowered. But there is not yet proof that the lowland rain forests of Asia were forced to contract to form a number of separate blocks of rain forest. This contrast with the rest of the tropical rain forest belts, if real and not just due to incomplete knowledge, may result from the more humid, maritime climate and the abundant mountains whose foothills always tend to be relatively wet.

Today, the Asian rain forests are disappearing quickly, as their giant hardwoods are being felled to provide timber and to make room for plantation agriculture as well as that of the migrating populations of shifting cultivators. Hopefully, the nations of Malaysia, Brunei, Indonesia, Philippines and Papua New Guinea, which lie at their heart, will be able to conserve representative fractions of jungle for posterity.

The majestic towering rain forests on this Malaysian shoreline are part of the belt of jungle which extends through the Malay archipelago from Sumatra to New Guinea. These Asian forests are perhaps the grandest of all and have the greatest diversity of plant and animal life. The intricacies of this complex ecosystem are only just beginning to be explained, but because the forests harbour many trees with great commercial value, they are fast disappearing before their secrets are fully known.

Marco Polo
(c 1254–1324)

Vasco da Gama
(c 1469–1524)

Sir Thomas Stamford Bingley Raffles
(1781–1826)

The tangled undergrowth and swamps of Burma did little to deter pioneers in their explorations.

Southeast Asia was a flourishing trading centre long before the first Europeans arrived. Indian seamen began trade as early as the sixth century B.C. and by A.D. 200 the Chinese had established trading stations all along the island coasts. By the thirteenth century, China was regularly exchanging silk, bronze and pottery for the highly valued spices, gold, tin and wood from the Asian islands.

Marco Polo was the first European to travel extensively in Asia, visiting Sumatra in 1292 while in the service of Kublai Khan, and later Java, Burma, Siam and Ceylon. Several European travellers followed, taking the Persian Gulf route. The Chinese, however, made the first well-documented voyages to Southeast Asia in the early fifteenth century, when the Portuguese were only just beginning to edge down the west coast of Africa. Cheng Ho commanded seven huge expeditions—60 400-foot ships carrying 28,000 men set out on the first trip to Java, Sumatra, Burma, India and Ceylon.

It was not until 1498 that Vasco da Gama, the Portuguese navigator, opened the new sea route to India from the west, round the Cape of Good Hope, and across the Indian Ocean. Within 50 years the Portuguese had established trading stations in India, Ceylon, Malaysia and south China. In the early sixteenth century, the first European reached the Spice Islands. Italian soldier Ludovico de Varthema studied and reported on nutmeg and cloves in the Moluccas before venturing on to Sumatra. The Spanish staked their claim to the Philippines in 1564 but the Portuguese trading empire soon began to collapse as Dutch and English competition arrived at the start of the seventeenth century.

Exploration continued throughout the seventeenth and eighteenth centuries, although warfare and colonial rivalry flared. With the nineteenth century came the scientific explorers. Sir Stamford Raffles, an enthusiastic amateur naturalist, made scientific and historical studies, particularly about Java and Sumatra, while officially an administrator for the British East India Company. Alfred Russel Wallace, the British naturalist, contributed immeasurably to European knowledge of the area when he travelled to Malaysia in 1854 and spent eight years making detailed studies of many species including the giant flower rafflesia, the orang-utan, and birdwing butterflies.

The genesis of jungles

For about a hundred years, biologists have claimed that the present world distribution of plants and animals is inexplicable unless continents have drifted. How otherwise could marsupials and the plant family Proteaceae, for example, be present in both South America and Australia? But earth scientists have only recently taken this contention seriously.

In the last two decades there has been a revolution in earth sciences, and continental drift powered by ocean floor spreading, is now an established fact of earth history, questioned by few. The distribution of plants and animals in the tropics today is strongly influenced by movements of this sort which have occurred over the last 140 million years. At first there was a great southern land mass, Gondwanaland, and a northern one, Laurasia. Between about 140 and 120 million years ago Africa, South America and Antarctica plus India and Australia began to split apart. India then split off and moved north, and about 55 million years

ago collided with Asia; today it continues to underthrust the Asian margin to form the Himalayas and the Tibetan plateau. The southern land masses continued to drift apart, and about 53 million years ago Australia split from Antarctica. Only 15 million years ago collision of the northern and southern continents occurred to form the Malay archipelago.

But it is still impossible to perceive details. One major drawback is that not enough is known about how the climate has altered during this long period. Something is known, however, about the climatic fluctuations of the last two million years, the Pleistocene period, during which Glacial and Interglacial episodes have alternated, with profound effects on the ranges of tropical organisms. It has recently been discovered that the main effect of Glacials on the tropics was to make the climate drier and more seasonal and to lower sea level by perhaps up to 650 feet (200m). Interglacials, such as we live in today, are times of high sea level and a more

moist, equable tropical climate and they occupy only a fraction of the last two million years.

The extent of the tropical rain forest is now believed to have waxed and waned with the climatic fluctuations. Today it is probably as widespread as it ever was. There is good evidence that during Glacials the tree line on tropical mountains, and the different layers of mountain rain forest, were lowered. Fragmentary evidence suggests that at the same time in the lowlands, tropical seasonal (monsoon) forests and savannas gained in area.

Research on these historical questions is now in full swing. Only the main outline has been established so far, but already the views held of the tropical rain forest until recently have changed profoundly. The rain forest, and its component plants, can no longer be regarded as an archaic, stable relic of an early phase of flowering plant evolution, with its fabulous richness of species due to that fact; the next decade should see exciting discoveries on the true course of its evolution.

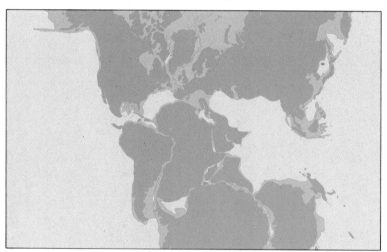

Glacial

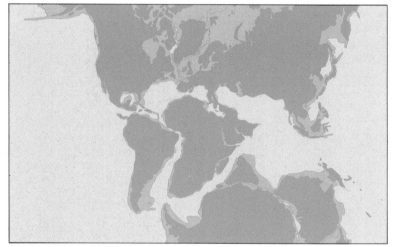

Present day

■ Extent of glaciation

■ Extent of glaciation

During Ice Ages, polar caps have extended and the highest mountains in the tropics have had icy summits, some of which do not exist today. Water is locked up in the ice so the sea level is lowered. Global mean temperatures and rainfall are also lowered. Tropical areas with seasonal climates become more extensive. Constantly humid, non-seasonal climates contract, and with them the rain forest. As an Ice Age diminishes, humid climates, and with them the rain forest, expand.

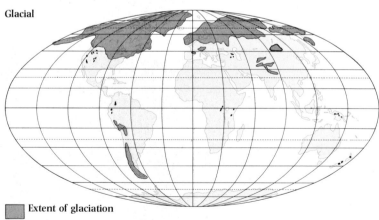

Warm, wet Interglacial   **Cooler, drier Glacial**   **Warm, wet Interglacial**

In the Interglacial periods rain forests are at their maximum. In Glacial periods rain forest contracts because of the encroachment of more seasonal vegetation, and the boundary between rain forest and montane forest is lowered.

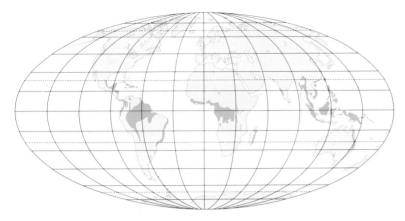

The drift of continents during the last 140 million years, *below*, has influenced the distribution of plants and animals in the tropics. As past coastlines were different, the maps show coastlines and the true continental margin at the edges of the fringing continental shelves.

[Present-day rain forest]

Alfred Russel Wallace (1823–1913), British naturalist who, at about the same time as Charles Darwin, independently developed the theory of evolution by natural selection.

Like many of the great nineteenth century naturalists, Wallace began as an amateur. After a four year trip to the Amazon exploring and collecting specimens to sell, he set off for the Malay archipelago in 1854. For eight years he travelled all over the islands, astounded at their natural wealth. He amassed many specimens, particularly of beetles, and in one year in Borneo collected about 1,000 species of beetle.

The discovery for which he is most remembered is named after him—Wallace's line. This imaginary line dividing two continental shelves is one of the sharpest, most dramatic biogeographical boundaries in the world. Wallace realized that islands such as Bali and Lombok, so close that they are in sight of one another, had strikingly different animals, and recognized this as the boundary of Asian and Australasian fauna. The division is believed to be due to the collision in the East Indies of the two continents 15 million years ago.

In 1862 Wallace returned to Britain and wrote a number of books including *The Malay Archipelago* (1869).

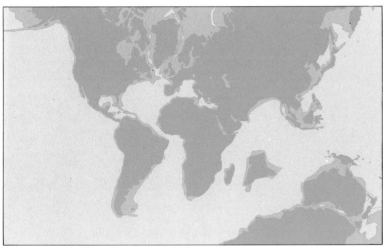

Most pollen, when it reaches the ground, is consumed by soil invertebrates or broken down by bacteria and fungi. In certain airless conditions, such as are found in bogs or lake bottom sediments, pollen can persist, essentially undamaged, underground. In these locations the successive layers of laid-down sediments retain the pollen characteristic of the time of their deposition. As progressively deeper sediments are sampled at a location older and older pollen samples are reached.

Luckily most pollen grains are genus- or species-specific in shape and size—the plant that produced them can be identified purely on the basis of pollen appearance. So, if the pollen types in successively deeper portions of a sediment sample are carefully identified and counted, a relatively clear picture of the vegetation types which produced them can be built up. These vegetation types represent the plants around the sample spot at a series of times back into the past.

In the example illustrated, the boring was made at a spot which is today in a rain forest. Rain forest pollen predominates in the boring down to a depth corresponding to 8,000 years ago. At about that depth the pollen types change abruptly and in deeper layers savanna plant pollen makes up the bulk of the samples. This evidence shows that between 10,000 and 8,000 years ago the sample area was in a savanna region. About 8,000 years ago the rain forest/savanna boundary moved across the sample spot and from then on the area remained within rain forest vegetation.

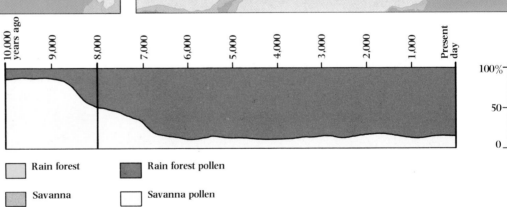

☐ Rain forest	☐ Rain forest pollen
☐ Savanna	☐ Savanna pollen

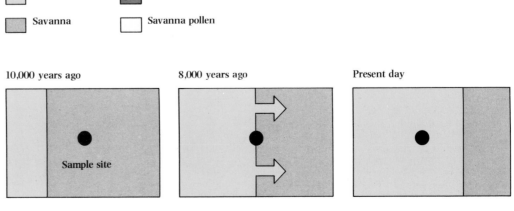

10,000 years ago

8,000 years ago

Present day

Sample site

The climate of the rain forest

Tropical climate is thought of as always hot and always wet. Certainly there is little temperature variation throughout the year. The difference between the hottest and coldest months is much less than that between night and day. High on tropical mountains hot days are followed by cold nights, often with frost. The relatively high cloud cover as well as the high humidity tend to keep the daytime temperatures down—33 degrees centigrade (91°F) is unusual. The high humidity, however, does make the climate of the tropics feel hot, sticky and uncomfortable.

The subtropical zones, with seasonal rainfall, are much hotter than the equatorial zone, particularly just before the rainy season and at its start. Isolated rainstorms clear the dust from the air on these first rainy days, which are interspersed with cloudless days when temperatures of 40 degrees centigrade (104°F) are common. But the humidity in the subtropics is usually lower, and so the level of discomfort is no greater than at the equator.

Most of the rain in the tropics falls as short, heavy showers. Sometimes low cloud and light rain will persist all day, but the more usual pattern is a warm, sunny morning with rapidly increasing cloud, culminating in a heavy afternoon shower which cools the air before evening. During these storms, which do not last more than a few hours, an inch or two of rain is likely to fall. But if the rainfall continues, large daily totals result; 10 or even 20 inches (50cm) may fall within 24 hours, accompanied by thunder and lightning, and by strong squalls of wind which break branches and at times also fell trees.

The approach of such a storm is spectacular. Large, threatening black clouds build up, the wind drops and everything is still. Even the birds are silent. Flashes of lightning streak across the darkened sky, and occasionally the distant roar of the rain is heard between the claps of thunder, although normally these follow one another in a continuous roll. A cool wind arrives in a great rush and roar, quickly followed by the rain, which lashes down and soon begins to drip through the forest canopy. At the height of the storm, it is difficult to see more than a hundred yards ahead. The rain often stops as suddenly as it began with perhaps a light drizzle continuing for a while. Wisps of mist drift from the canopy and the jungle birds gradually start to call again.

Few places in the tropics are continually wet; even in the wettest areas there are predictable breaks in the rains, when fewer storms occur, or even dry spells lasting two to three weeks. During these times, the forest plants must survive on the water stored in the soil from earlier rains; they use their few deep roots to draw on these reserves when the root-filled surface layers of the soil become dry. Such short, dry spells are important in triggering flowering and fruiting of forest plants.

The climate recorded by a meteorologist is that of the open ground. To study the microclimates in which most jungle animals and plants live, however, tall towers have been built in the depths of the forest equipped with instruments for recording wind velocity, temperature and humidity at different levels. These towers have been especially useful in providing information about the transmission of yellow fever, a fatal disease before inoculation against it became available. It is caused by a virus spread from forest-dwelling monkeys to man by mosquitoes. The data gathered from these towers have led to an understanding of the movements of the mosquitoes from the canopy, where the monkeys live, to man on the ground. Such towers have been built in Panama and in Uganda.

Measurements from towers have shown that the amount of wind decreases enormously from the

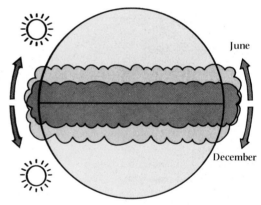

The world's climate is controlled by the apparent movement of the sun. The noon position of the sun moves every day because the earth's axis is not at right angles to the line joining the sun and the earth. Thus the sun makes a pendulum swing between the Tropic of Cancer and the Tropic of Capricorn. It is directly overhead at the equator on March 20/21 and September 22/23 (equinoxes) and reaches the Tropic of Cancer (22°N) at June 21 (summer solstice) and the Tropic of Capricorn (22°S) on December 22/23 (winter solstice). When the sun is directly overhead, it penetrates the thinnest possible layer of atmosphere so the maximum of solar energy reaches the ground below, producing high temperatures. As the hot air rises from the earth, it expands, cools and forms cloud. Yet this belt of cloud always follows about a month behind the sun because the ground and atmosphere take time to heat up. As a result, there is a constant broad band of mixing cloud between the tropics which falls as rainstorms. As shown in the Meteosat pictures, the equatorial forests of Africa are covered with raincloud both at June 21, *left*, and December 22/23, *right*, when the sun reaches both extremes. The satellite also shows how the forested regions along the equator and around Liberia are rainy most of the year, the latter because of moist winds from the sea.

canopy to the ground. For every metre of air movement at two metres above the ground, there are 30 metres in the lower canopy, and 120 metres above the canopy (40 metres above the ground). The understorey is therefore a still environment, where delicate flowers and large insects can exist without being battered by strong winds.

The highest as well as the lowest temperatures have been recorded above the canopy. Not only do the leaves and branches prevent the sun's energy from reaching the ground, they also trap heat in the lower layers of the forest during the night. As a result, the range of temperature is greatest above the canopy and least in the understorey. The humidity of the air remains high day and night in the understorey, rarely falling below 95 per cent. Above the canopy there are much greater fluctuations, both from night to day and from one day to another.

Measurements of this kind demonstrate how important it is to collect data right inside the forest where the animals and plants live, rather than in convenient clearings or at the forest edge. To apply results of measurements obtained outside the forest to describe conditions within it, would give a totally false impression.

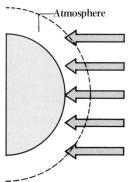

Some solar energy is usually absorbed by the atmosphere, which becomes hot; dust and clouds also reflect rays back into space. At the equator, however, where the sun is more or less overhead, the rays hit the atmosphere at right angles and so pass through the minimum of atmosphere. The equator is heated more than anywhere else on earth.

The equatorial regions receive more energy from the sun in a year than the rest of the world. The sun is always more or less overhead at midday and the days barely fluctuate from 12 hours of daylight. To the north or south the summer days are longer and winter days are shorter. This means that on a cloudless summer day, London or even Spitsbergen (near the north pole) receives more solar energy than the equator. This seasonal high input of energy is offset by short winter days, reducing the annual level of solar energy well below that of the equator. At Spitsbergen, the sun never rises during the middle of winter, so no energy is received. Jungles need the constantly high level of energy from the sun for photosynthesis.

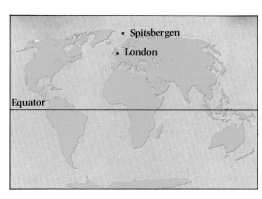

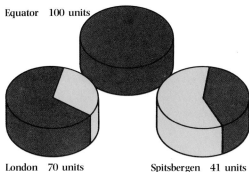

Equator   100 units

London   70 units   Spitsbergen   41 units

Rain forests exist in the tropics wherever there is sufficient rain. The lowest level of rainfall required to maintain a jungle is 80in (2,000mm) per year There is no upper limit as the habitat thrives on moisture. The even distribution of rain throughout the year is generally more important than the total volume. There is, however, an exceptional forest in Sierra Leone where the 120in (3,000mm) annual rainfall compensates for an intense three month dry season. Normally forests with dry seasons are vulnerable to fire. The level of evaporation is also vital as true jungle can only flourish if rainfall exceeds evaporation.

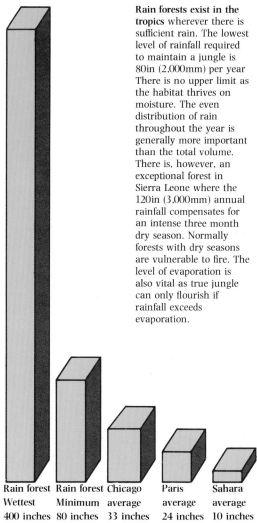

Rain forest	Rain forest	Chicago	Paris	Sahara
Wettest	Minimum	average	average	average
400 inches	80 inches	33 inches	24 inches	10 inches
per year	per year	per year	per year	per year

Soil: the life support

Soil is the thin, vital skin of rotted rock which covers the surface of the earth. It supports the earth's vegetation, which in turn affects the development of the soil, but, more importantly, supports all terrestrial animal life.

Soil develops from rocks by weathering processes. Water falling on rock can eventually break off fragments, but flowing water, charged with abrasive rock particles, is extremely destructive. The sun, as it heats and cools rocks, causes particles to become detached from the surface layers. Winds bearing sand grains erode rock. Known as mechanical weathering, all these processes break down large rock masses into small particles.

Perhaps of more significance in the tropics are the chemical means of weathering. Water slowly dissolves rock, but if it is slightly acidic because it contains dissolved carbon dioxide, then it is even more effective. Some soil minerals are much more difficult to dissolve than others. In the temperate regions, for example, silica (quartz or silicon dioxide) is the most resistant mineral, and because of its great abundance, is the most common residual mineral in soils. It also forms the bulk of sand deposits. Silica is insoluble in cold water, but as the temperature of water rises, it dissolves more easily. In the tropics, as

water percolates through the soils, a great deal of silica is removed. But since it is present in such vast quantities in the original rocks, it is still common in the soils.

Other minerals, such as aluminium oxide and iron oxide which are also plentiful in soils, do not become much more soluble as temperatures rise, and therefore are found in substantial amounts in tropical soils. This accumulation of aluminium oxides helps explain why so many of the world's reserves of aluminium ore (bauxite) are in the tropics. Pure aluminium oxide is white, but iron oxide is reddish or yellowish, and gives the tropical soils their distinctive red or yellow hue.

Soil is part solid, part liquid and part gas. The solid fraction makes up between 40 per cent and 60 per cent of the volume of the soil; it is composed mainly of fragments of rock, ranging in size from boulders and pebbles to the minute pieces which make up clays. The rest, the pore space, contains either gas or water, the relative amounts varying from time to time. The gas, or soil air, is like the atmosphere in composition, but contains more carbon dioxide because of the respiration of roots and other living things. The liquid, or soil water, is not pure, but is a solution containing minerals and

organic substances, some of which can be taken up as nutrients by the plant.

Most tropical soils have developed on ancient land surfaces that have been exposed to weathering for millions of years. By temperate standards they are extremely deep. The unweathered rock may be covered by 1 to 200 feet (30cm to 60m) of weathered material, from which at least some of the mineral nutrients have been removed by percolating rain water. Of those which are left, a high proportion is not in the soil, but held in the plants. This has obvious dangers. If man clears the forest by cutting the trees and burning them, a sudden rainstorm can wash away the ash, and with it the mineral nutrients which were stored in the plants. There are some tropical forest soils which are not poor in nutrients, however; forests in Indonesia, and in parts of Central and South America, are occasionally sprinkled with volcanic ash. This finely divided unweathered rock is a source of mineral nutrients.

In temperate regions large areas of soil have developed since the last Ice Age, either on material eroded out and deposited by glaciers, or on older soils which were thoroughly mixed by the freezing and thawing of ice within them. As a consequence, they are relatively rich in nutrients.

Of the mineral nutrients which plants need from the soil, the most important is probably nitrogen fixed as ions like nitrate. Elemental nitrogen occurs abundantly in the air, but is unreactive, and so is often in short supply in forms which plants can use. In jungles, nitrogen comes from the decomposition of organic matter, and from the air either through the activities of blue-green algae and bacteria, some of which live on leaf surfaces, or from the combination of nitrogen and oxygen during the intense heat of lightning flashes. When plant material is burned, much of the nitrogen is lost to the air. Within the plant, nitrogen forms part of many essential chemical compounds, including proteins.

Another vital element needed by plants is phosphorus. It originates in the soil as a result of the weathering of rocks, but is always scarce. Within the plant it is used in many vital compounds including the nucleic acids DNA and RNA and the vital energy transfer molecule ATP.

The third essential element, which also results from rock weathering, is potassium. Plants require a great deal of it for normal rapid growth and enzyme activity. In addition to these elements, there are about twenty others which are also vital to a plant but which are not usually in short supply.

All the material which falls on to the soil surface in a jungle is quickly decomposed by soil animals and plants. Much of the initial breaking up and incorporation of the litter into the soil is done by termites, though earthworms also play a valuable role. Fungi, present in enormous numbers, and bacteria are responsible for the eventual breakdown of most of the organic matter. Many of the fungi form associations with the roots of the trees; it has been suggested that these associations or mycorrhizas lead to the direct transfer of mineral nutrients released by the activities of the fungi to the roots, instead of their release into the general soil solution and subsequent uptake by roots.

Although the soils of tropical forests are deep and ancient, they are often fragile. If the protective layer of vegetation is removed, they can easily be eroded. Sadly, this fact is frequently overlooked when forests are cleared for agriculture. The original forest inhabitants practised shifting cultivation, leaving a clearing after a year or two and allowing it to regenerate and replace its soil nutrients over many years before clearing the area again. But modern schemes call for continuous cultivation, and often this is not sustainable without large and expensive inputs of fertilizer.

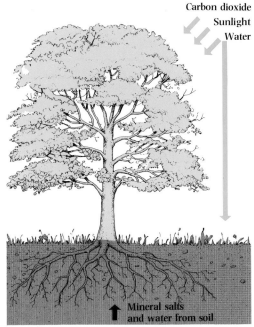

Carbon dioxide
Sunlight
Water

Mineral salts and water from soil

To survive and grow, a plant needs water and dissolved mineral nutrients from the soil, and carbon dioxide and oxygen from the air. It needs sunlight to unite carbon dioxide and water to make sugars.

The distribution of roots and the nutrients they seek differs greatly between temperate and tropical soils. In temperate zones, most soils have developed on material either deposited or reworked during the last Ice Age, which ended only 12,000 years ago. Soils have effectively been weathered only since then and are still relatively rich. In the tropics thousands of years of high rainfall have produced deep soils from which most of the nutrients have been removed. Analyses reveal that the nutrients contained in the vegetation often exceed the amount in the upper soil layers. Removal of large amounts of forest vegetation thus involves removal of a significant part of the nutrients in the ecosystem. In jungles most of the nutrients—and roots—are near the surface where plant litter is decomposing and releasing them. In temperate forests nutrients are more evenly distributed, as are plant roots.

The eroded banks of a jungle river reveal deep soil and shallow tree root systems. The soil has developed on soft riverine deposits of silt and sand (alluvium) and no hard rock is visible. The rapidity of the erosion has prevented the development of the curtain of foliage which usually conceals the banks of tropical rivers.

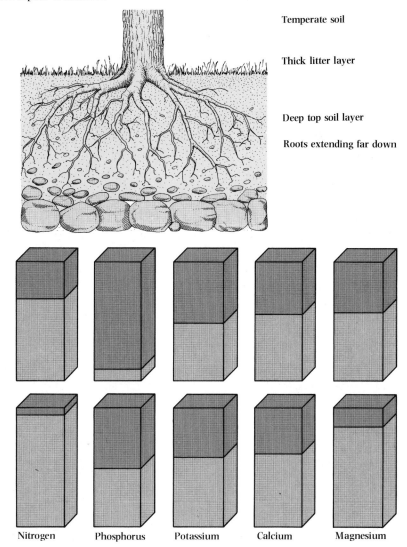

Tropical soil

Thin litter layer

Shallow top soil layer

Roots mainly in surface layers

Unweathered rocks only at great depths

Rain forest

% of nutrients in vegetation

% of nutrients in soil

Oak woodland

% of nutrients in vegetation

% of nutrients in soil

Temperate soil

Thick litter layer

Deep top soil layer

Roots extending far down

Nitrogen   Phosphorus   Potassium   Calcium   Magnesium

The dynamics of the forest

No forest is static. There are always some trees growing while others are decaying or falling. Basically, a forest-growth cycle starts from a gap phase, passes through a building phase, as colonizing trees grow up, to attain a third, or mature, phase.

No entire forest undergoes such a clear-cut cycle. At any one time the forest is a mosaic of these different phases of the growth cycle. The coarseness of the mosaic depends on what causes the gaps. Some parts of the humid tropics—such as the Caribbean and the northern Philippines—are prone to cyclones which fell great swathes of forest. In seismically active and mountainous New Guinea, landslides are frequent and gaps are huge. In regions such as Malaya and Amazonia this type of extensive catastrophic damage does not occur. Instead, gaps usually develop as individual trees decay of old age or a small group is blown over by the wind which accompanies a local thunderstorm.

The trees which colonize big gaps have seedlings which are well-adapted for growth in bright sunlight, high temperatures and relatively low afternoon humidity. Such species compete strongly with each other for light, and typically grow fast or die if overtopped by other trees. They are often called pioneers because they must colonize big gaps and cannot perpetuate themselves in their own shade. These trees could be considered forest nomads, as they are always seeking a new home in which to survive.

In a small gap seedlings or saplings already present will flourish. They can tolerate low light and require the higher relative humidity and lower temperature of the forest interior. The conditions of a big gap would kill them. They differ from pioneer trees because they are able to perpetuate themselves *in situ*, and so do not need cataclysmic disturbance. The structure of a forest formed by these species is more complex and has less tendency to groups of the same-sized trees.

Many pioneer trees are small and short-lived; they are soon replaced by shade-bearing species. Others live many decades and reach large size. It is these which are of great forestry importance, partly because they have characteristics which make them easy to grow in plantations, but also because their pale soft wood makes them commercially valuable. Balsa, native to South America, is probably the best-known rain forest pioneer tree.

Forests have different layers of trees, but this layered structure has also to be considered in terms of the forest-growth cycle. The deep, narrow crowns of the building phase forest form a different vertical pattern from the broad crowns of the mature phase. A forest of pioneers recolonizing a big gap tends to be single-layered and even-aged; it has a different vertical and population structure from a similar area of forest formed in a series of small gaps. In the former, the big trees have no small individuals waiting to replace them. In the latter, the big trees commonly do have juveniles. Forest dynamics thus provide a key to understanding the structure, floristics and economic potential of rain forests.

A profile of a lowland forest in Brunei shows the mature phase and the building phase (centre) of the forest-growth cycle. The young, growing dipterocarps in the building phase have deep, narrow, unbranched crowns in contrast to the broad branched crowns of the mature trees. The stratification also differs between the phases.

- *Shorea laevis*
- *Shorea glaucescens*
- *Shorea parvifolia*
- *Hopea bracteata*

In the African jungles, *Musanga cecropioides*, *left*, is a common pioneer tree. Its counterparts in Asia and the neotropics are *Macaranga* and *Cecropia* respectively. These pioneer trees must have light and can only establish themselves in the open. Once established they are fast-growing, forming stands along roadsides, on land slips and in other big gaps. They are fairly short-lived and are replaced by other species of tree which grow up beneath them.

Forests are a spatial mosaic of patches of trees at different stages in their lives. A gap is formed, trees colonize that gap and build a mature canopy.

A single tree has fallen, destroying others as it fell to create a long, narrow gap in which the aerial environment is similar to the forest interior but more brightly illuminated. Competition below ground between roots is temporarily reduced, and the decaying killed plants release nutrients at ground level and below. These changes stimulate seedlings and saplings already present to grow, and eventually the high canopy is restored.

A small gap has been created, *right*, by one fallen tree. This gap will rapidly be colonized by existing seedlings.

The life of the jungle

The whole jungle from the top of its canopy to the roots of its trees is a living and dynamic entity—a sort of superorganism. The multitude of plants and animals do not simply live *in* the jungle, they *are* the jungle. All the living organisms have been moulded by the same climatic regime and each is more or less dependent on the others.

Jungles have two outstanding characteristics. First, the total bulk of plant and animal matter supported by each square yard is enormous and many times larger than on any other square yard of the earth's surface. Second, the diversity of animal and plant forms is far higher than in any other habitat. These characteristics make the jungle unique. The total mass of living matter and the enormous diversity of life together produce a wild profusion of specific niches for animals and plants. In this scaffolding of life it is usually the plants which provide microhabitats for particular specialized animals rather than vice versa.

The jungle floor is virtually bare of plants, and the gloom is relieved only by the occasional shafts of sunlight which penetrate the canopy. At higher levels there is more light, more vegetation and more animal life. In this respect the layered structure of the jungle is similar to that of the sea—in both, life is concentrated in the upper layers. While many animals in the jungle feed on and live in the canopy and understorey, others feed on the fruits, nuts and leaves which fall to the jungle floor. In an area of Central American jungle 16 species of bird feed on the ground, mostly on insects; 75 species live in the understorey and 130 in the canopy. Birds are primarily tree-dwelling, which may bias this analysis, but the same sort of distribution occurs in mammals.

Although layered, the jungle is not cakelike with each layer strictly defined and self-contained. Most plants do have a characteristic habitat—although many must grow through other levels to reach their mature habitat—but this is not always true of animals. Insectivorous birds forage high in the canopy one moment and on the floor the next, and there are numerous other examples. But many creatures are highly adapted to life in a particular layer or habitat and are seldom found outside it. The three-toed sloth, for one, is so well adapted to life in the trees that it can no longer walk on the ground. In general, animals with specialized diets are found only in the part of the jungle where their food grows, while those of more catholic tastes are found in a number of places.

The jungle is a complex system in which each organism has its appointed place according to its specific adaptations. Yet the fate and survival of each is intricately linked with every other's and ultimately with their living conditions.

The layers of the jungle

All plant communities are made up of layers; only the simplest, such as duckweed floating on a pond, have a single layer. Even a lawn has two layers— grasses stand above a lower layer of mosses. In a temperate woodland there are usually four layers: trees, shrubs, herbs (field layer) and mosses (ground layer). Since jungle trees are often taller than those in temperate woodlands, it is possible to distinguish three layers just among the trees. Thus the jungle itself is made up of six layers: emergent tree, canopy tree, lower tree, shrub, field and ground— lower tree, shrub and field are grouped together as understorey in the following pages.

In order to study the layers of a jungle, foresters and ecologists construct a profile diagram. First, they select a typical patch of jungle and mark out a strip, 15 to 30 feet (4.5 to 9m) wide and 200 feet (60m) long. They clear smaller shrubs and herbs and measure the positions, heights and canopy shapes of each tree, as well as identify the individual trees. Then they plot out the results on paper to produce the profile diagram. In architectural terms, this is an elevation of the forest strip, condensed from its original width on to the paper.

Normally, three layers can be recognized. Highest is the emergent layer, formed of forest giants which rise well above the rest of the trees. Below them is the main canopy, composed of flat-crowned trees, which, together with the emergents, make up a complete canopy. Beneath the main canopy are smaller trees, often with vertically elongated crowns, which constitute the lower tree layer.

Any arrangement of the jungle into layers, however, is not obvious at a casual glance. In reality, there is almost continuous greenery extending from the top of the canopy to the bottom of the understorey, with sparser foliage between the understorey and the ground. A true section of jungle is not often seen; the margins of roads, rivers and clearings quickly acquire a lush growth of climbers which obscure the normal jungle structure. Within the jungle, the layers are linked by the stems and foliage of lianas; these are generally omitted from profile diagrams, which are likely therefore to exaggerate the clarity of the layers.

Some of the irregularities seen in profile diagrams, and the problems of recognizing layers consistently, can be attributed to the fact that the jungle is always changing. When an emergent tree falls it brings down other trees with it, and forms a gap where light reaches the ground and allows young trees to grow. A portion of a profile diagram lacking a canopy probably marks such a gap, but fifty years hence the canopy will have closed over the gap once again.

The layered structure of the jungle is the key to its fantastic richness, because the layers provide innumerable tiny and discrete habitats. Epiphytes, for instance, may grow on the outer branches of the canopy trees in full sun, on the main branches, on the trunk, or in the shaded crown of an understorey tree, or even in the gloom of the shrub layer. Thus, the initial complexity of the framework of trees breeds a further complexity in the plants and animals which depend on them.

The giants of the jungle are the emergent trees. Their trunks thrust up through the canopy and their huge crowns of branches spread out well above the rest of the trees. Although, as the uppermost layer, they enjoy first share of the sunlight, they must also endure high temperatures, low humidities and strong winds. But all emergents must start their lives in the markedly different conditions of the lower layers of the jungle.

The broad crowns of the main canopy trees fill the gaps between the emergents, and with them form a continuous cover. The spreading branches, the upper parts of the trunk and even the twigs provide habitats for orchids, bromeliads and lichens. The canopy trees are often densely interwoven and bound together with large woody climbing plants.

Smaller trees with vertically elongated crowns lie beneath the main canopy. Some are young trees which will eventually reach the canopy. Others are small, slow-growing trees which have reached their full size.

The shrub layer contains young canopy trees but there are also small, mature woody plants. Many are miniature trees with crowns of large leaves and, sometimes, showy flowers.

Seedlings and scattered herbs (soft-stemmed plants) make up the sparse field layer.

The floor of the jungle has a thin carpet of dead and rotting vegetation.

Rivers slice through the jungle, admitting light which encourages the growth of dense foliage along their banks.

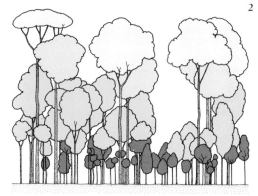

Dividing the jungle into layers is helpful when describing jungle structure, but it may not always be easy to define precisely where one layer ends and another begins, except by drawing arbitrary height limits. The clarity of layers varies greatly, as profile diagrams show. In profile (1) one tree species is common and forms a distinct canopy layer. Profile (2) shows a more usual situation; layers are present but are less easily distinguished. No section of jungle is ever quite like any other.

	Humidity	Rainfall	Max temp	Min temp	Temp fluctuation	Windflow
Emergent	● ●	● ● ● ●	● ● ● ●	● ● ● ●	● ● ● ●	● ● ● ●
Canopy	● ●	● ● ● ●	● ● ●	● ● ●	● ● ●	● ● ●
Lower tree	● ● ●	● ● ●	● ●	● ●	● ●	● ●
Shrub	● ● ●	● ●	●	●	●	● ●
Field	● ● ● ●	●	●	● ●	●	●
Floor	● ● ● ●	●		● ●	●	●

The jungle canopy is like an umbrella, intercepting both sun and rain. As a result, the layers of the jungle do not all share the same climate—they have different microclimates. At the top of the canopy there is strong sun, plenty of wind, and daily variation in humidity and temperature. On the sheltered floor of the forest the air is still, humidity is always high and the temperature varies comparatively little. At most, 2 per cent of the sunlight falling on the canopy reaches the jungle floor—some as flecks of sunlight and some as a greenish light transmitted through and reflected from the canopy leaves. The lack of light makes the jungle floor a difficult environment for plants.

The nature of the plants

The tropical rain forest is the realm of the woody plant. Soft-stalked plants (herbs) play a minor role among the trees, shrubs and woody climbers. One reason for this dominance of woody plants is the constancy of climate; little change in temperature and moisture through the year means that growth can be continuous. Such constancy of climate has also excluded other plant types, such as those with bulbs and tubers which help plants to resist spells of drought, from occurring in the jungle. Likewise, there are no suitable temporary habitats in the dark forest undergrowth for annual plants, which grow, flower and seed quickly, passing most of the year as seeds.

The jungle is enormously diverse. Unlike temperate zone woodlands in which there are only a few readily distinguishable tree species, a couple of acres of ground in the jungle may contain hundreds of plant species and scores of different trees. In fact, it may take considerable time just to find two trees

The complex plant life of the jungle is divided into groups of plants which make similar demands on their environment. Most plants have chlorophyll, and can make their own food if water, carbon dioxide and light are available. Among these plants are trees, shrubs and herbs, all of which are strong enough to support their own weight. There are three other groups which have chlorophyll but need a support to grow on: climbers, epiphytes and stranglers. Climbers, often large and woody in the jungle, root in the ground but cling to trees for support. Epiphytes are not rooted at ground level but grow on the trunks and branches of trees. Stranglers start life as epiphytes then send roots down to the ground. Two other groups lack chlorophyll and depend on other sources for food: parasites extract food from other plants; saprophytes feed on rotting material.

⬤ Has chlorophyll   + Self-supporting

◯ Lacks chlorophyll   − Needs support

belonging to the same species. Rainfall seems to be one factor behind this diversity. Generally, the wettest forests are the most diverse.

The plants belong to many different families, which also increases diversity. In the northern temperate zone, the majority of the trees belong to the oak family (Fagaceae), maple family (Aceraceae) or birch family (Betulaceae). In the jungles many families are represented. Some, such as the Dipterocarpaceae, which are so important in the forests of Southeast Asia, are unknown in temperate countries.

To cope with such enormous diversity, botanists and ecologists have divided the species of plants into groups called synusiae, whose members make similar demands on the environment. For example, the climbers, which have chlorophyll and can therefore make their own food, but which need other plants to support them, make up one synusia. Trees, herbs and shrubs are others.

Why should the tropical forest be so diverse? First, it is an ancient ecosystem. Tropical forests have existed for many millions of years. During the drastic climatic fluctuations of the last million years, jungles have expanded in wet periods and shrunk in dry ones, but the splitting of large areas of forest into small isolated blocks may have contributed to species richness. Two populations of a single plant species may slowly become different if separated; when conditions change and they again come into contact, interbreeding may no longer be possible, and two species are eventually established instead of one.

Second, the very diversity of the forest is self-perpetuating. Many different tree species provide many different bark types on which varieties of epiphyte can grow. In addition, a single large tree offers distinct epiphyte habitats on the vertical, deeply shaded trunk, the horizontal main branches and the dry, brightly lit outer branches.

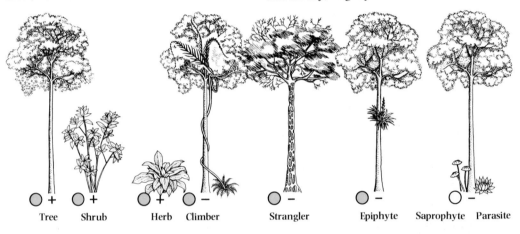

Tree   Shrub   Herb   Climber   Strangler   Epiphyte   Saprophyte   Parasite

Violets and pansies are familiar small plants in temperate regions of Europe and North America. In the jungle, members of the same family, Violaceae, are large woody plants. One South American species, *Rinorea*, grows 25 to 30ft (7.5 to 9m) tall.

Violet

30ft (9m)

Rinorea

Plant species are also classified according to the position of their buds, *right*. This again emphasizes the dominance of woody plants in the tropical forest. The contrast between temperate and tropical forest is striking, even though trees form the bulk of plant material in each case.

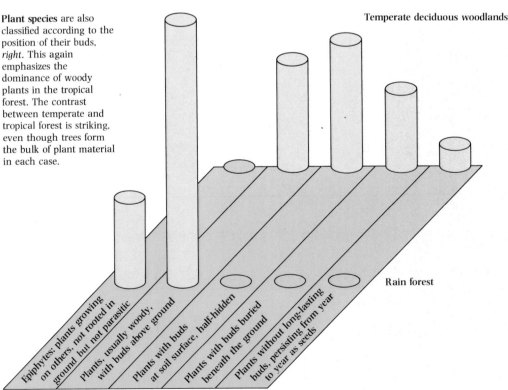

Temperate deciduous woodlands

Rain forest

Epiphytes: plants growing on others, not rooted in ground but not parasitic

Plants, usually woody, with buds above ground

Plants with buds at soil surface, half-hidden

Plants with buds buried beneath the ground

Plants without long-lasting buds, persisting from year to year as seeds

The luxuriance and variety of the tropical rain forest is demonstrated in this fragment, *right*. Members of several synusiae—trees, shrubs, and climbers—are evident. The *Cecropia* tree in the centre suggests that this forest has been disturbed. *Cecropia* trees are characteristic of the secondary forest which springs up after primary forest has been cleared or damaged. The varied leaf forms of the shrubs and small trees are also characteristic of secondary forest. In the lower layers of primary forest, leaves are much more uniform in their size and shape.

1. Trees
2. Young tree (*Cecropia*)
3. Liana
4. Epiphytes
5. Shrub

Dominating the forest

The tall trees of the emergent layer dominate the jungle; their entire crowns frequently clear the canopy. But they are not, as is commonly believed, the world's tallest trees. The tallest species of tree is the coast redwood, *Sequoia sempervirens*, with a tallest measured example of 366 feet (111m). The tallest non-conifer is *Eucalyptus regnans*, which also holds the record for the tallest individual tree at 375 feet (114m).

Within the tropical rain forests, particularly those of Africa and South America, trees more than 200 feet tall are rare. The only authentic measurements of trees exceeding this figure come from Southeast Asia, where the tallest rain forest tree is the tualang, *Koompassia excelsa*, which has been reliably recorded at 272 feet (83m). At least four other Southeast Asian tree species have been recorded as exceeding 200 feet (60m).

A common myth about the tropical rain forest is that the tallest trees occur in the wettest forests. Studies in both Africa and South America have shown that this is not true, perhaps because too much of the soil nutrient store is washed away in the wettest climates. In fact, the biggest trees are usually located in drier and often seasonal forests.

The form of the towering jungle trees is remarkable. Their trunks hardly taper until the first branches are reached, but then they break up immediately into a number of huge limbs which support a dome-shaped crown. In Malaya a *Balanocarpus heimii* tree had a girth of 27 feet 6 inches at 4 feet above the ground and a girth of 23 feet at 88 feet above ground, where the branches began.

The age of these huge trees is difficult to determine. In temperate regions trees grow quickly during the summer, but slowly during the winter. Their wood is marked by a series of rings, each representing a year's growth, and it is easy to count these and discover an individual tree's age. But in the tropics, growth is either continuous or, if periodic, the growth periods do not necessarily occur once a year.

If the girth of a tree is measured regularly, however, it is possible to find out the average annual increase. To estimate age, the girth of a mature tree is divided by its average annual increase. Growth probably does not continue at the same rate throughout the years, however, and so ages obtained by this method are likely to be underestimates. *Balanocarpus heimii*, according to calculations based on this method, can reach 1,400 years of age.

Another way to determine age is to date the heartwood of the tree by radiocarbon analysis. *Shorea curtisii*, another tall Malayan tree, has been shown by this method to be at least 800 years old. But none of these ages approaches the 4,000 plus years achieved by the bristlecone pines, *Pinus longaeva*, of the mountains of California. Thus it would appear that the giants of the tropical forest are no older than some trees in the forests of northern Europe and North America. So another myth—the great age of jungle trees—is exploded.

At intervals the jungle canopy is dramatically broken by an emergent tree branching above its solid greenery. Tropical rain forest trees and temperate forest trees are thought of as having very different shapes at maturity. While this is partially true, our view is influenced by the many fine temperate trees which have grown up in the open, and therefore branch close to the ground. Because of the crowded growing situation, a rain forest emergent tree can branch only at the top of its long straight trunk.

The world's tallest trees are found in the warm-temperate parts of the world, but the tropical rain forest does have its giants. Illustrated are the two largest tree species and a giant tree from each jungle area. These tall jungle trees are among the heaviest living things in the world.

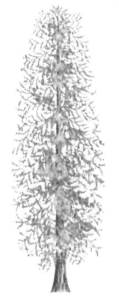

The 100ft (30m) trunk of an African mahogany tree accounts for two-thirds of the tree's weight.

The all-time record as the world's tallest tree at 375ft (114m) is held by *Eucalyptus regnans*.

The Californian coast redwood, *Sequoia sempervirens*, is 366ft (111m) tall.

The tualang, *Koompassia excelsa*, of Southeast Asia, is the tallest known rain forest tree species.

An African mahogany, *Entandrophragma cylindricum*, is claimed to reach 200ft (60m).

One of the largest South American jungle trees is *Dinizia excelsa*. It may reach 200ft (60m).

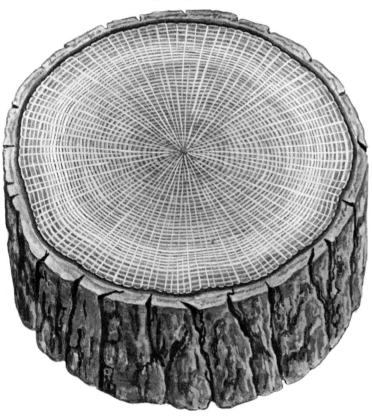

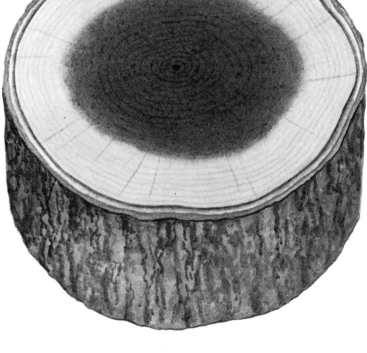

Clear, annual growth rings are seen in a cross-section of a northern European oak tree. These rings are formed by the seasonal activity of the cells which form new wood. In the spring these make a number of large, water-conducting vessels; later in the year the cells are smaller and have relatively thicker walls. Because these rings of large vessels are formed regularly each year in response to the changing seasons, the age of the tree can be discovered by counting the rings. Only occasionally, when, for instance, the first leaves are all eaten by caterpillars, is a double ring formed in one year. The bark of the oak is thick and furrowed. Its function is partly protective, but its inner layers include the sugar-carrying cells.

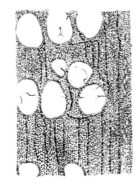

A cross-section of the rain forest tree sapele, *Entandrophragma cylindricum*, shows no clear growth rings. Although the wood-forming cells may show rhythmic activity and may produce rings in the wood, these are often discontinuous and are not annual. Counting them does not reveal the age of the tree. However, the number of rings is certainly related to age and, given trees of known age to start from, they can be used to ascertain age. The big water-conducting vessels are scattered through the wood, separated by smaller water-conducting cells and by thick-walled strengthening fibres. The bark of the African mahogany, as in many rain forest trees, is fairly thin. The reasons for this are not known.

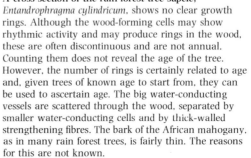

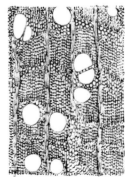

35

The giant trees

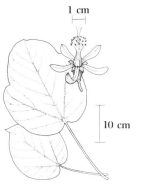

An attractive tree, *Cavanillesia platanifolia* grows in the jungles of Central America. It is particularly distinctive when covered with its mass of small red flowers.

Found throughout the jungles of West Africa, *Triplochiton scleroxylon* can be 200ft (60m) high. The timber is both exported and used locally.

A Southeast Asian tree, *Shorea curtisii* soars above the jungle canopy, reaching a height of 220ft (70m). *Shorea* is an important timber species.

The giants which form the sparse emergent layer of the tropical forest must be able to stand on their own in a harsh and difficult environment. Although they began life in the damp shade of the understorey, at maturity they live above the other trees, fully exposed to the relatively high temperatures, strong winds and low humidity found above the shelter of the canopy. The leaves that they bear when adult are smaller and tougher than those they have as young trees. In addition, the leaves often have a thick, outer waxy layer which helps reduce water loss, a useful adaptation for the dry atmosphere in which the trees live at the top of the tropical rain forest.

Many emergents have winged fruits which rely on the wind to carry them to new sites. Above the canopy, air movement is at least 100 times greater than in the understorey, and 10 to 20 times more than in the main canopy. Consequently, a seed's chances of dispersal are much greater if it falls from an emergent tree than from a tree in the canopy or understorey.

Consideration of three typical emergent trees, one from each of the major jungles, explains what these giants of the forest are like, how they grow and reproduce and the usefulness of their timber and products to man.

Indigenous to Southeast Asia, *Shorea curtisii* belongs to the family Dipterocarpaceae, named for the two wings that support their fruits. The genus *Shorea* contains many forest trees of this region; it was named after Sir John Shore who was Governor-General of India, 1793–8. The species name honours Charles Curtis, a botanist and plant collector who ran the Penang Botanic Garden at the end of the last century. *Shorea curtisii* is found throughout the Malay Peninsula, and also in Sarawak, Brunei and Sabah on the island of Borneo.

A huge tree, attaining 220 feet (70m) in height and 22 feet (7m) in girth, *Shorea curtisii* tends to grow on ridges, mainly between 1,000 and 2,500 feet (300 and 750m) in Malaysia, but lower in Borneo. The towering trunk may rise for 90 feet (27m) before the first branch appears, and it supports a huge cauliflowerlike crown. The greyish-brown bark is deeply fissured by vertical cracks. The leaves, which are spear-shaped with long tapering tips, have a greyish bloom on the underside; the shade of the leaves makes this dominant forest tree easily recognizable from the air.

The creamy flowers of *Shorea* are small, only $\frac{1}{2}$ inch (1cm) across, and each is composed of five petals spreading out in a starlike pattern. The sepals grow enormously after flowering, forming the wings which help to disperse the nut held between them. *Shorea curtisii* produces a timber similar to that of other *Shorea* species; together the woods are known as meranti and are important, valuable commercial hardwoods.

Although not the largest of South American emergent trees, *Cavanillesia platanifolia* is distinctive and impressive when in flower. Native to Central America, from Panama south to Colombia and Peru, it is known locally as *cuipo* or *lupuna colorada*. The generic name commemorates Antonio José Cavanilles, director of the Madrid Botanic Garden at the beginning of the nineteenth century; the specific name refers to its large lobed leaves, which are similar to those of the plane or sycamore tree (*Platanus*). The trunk, slightly swollen at the base, is thick yet smooth, like the leg of a huge elephant. Small, thick buttresses and raised ridges grow around it every few feet. It supports a huge, umbrella-shaped crown.

The leaves of *Cavanillesia* fall once a year, and during this period small red flowers are produced. Each flower is only 1 inch (2.5cm) across, but in a mass they are impressive, enhancing the whole tree. The fruits that follow are more remarkable; each has a central seed with five radiating wings. The whole fruit is about 5 inches (12cm) in diameter. Even though the tree looks strong and heavy, its wood is extremely light when dry, and has been suggested as a substitute for balsa, also a rain forest tree.

Called *wawa* in Ghana and *obeche* in Nigeria, *Triplochiton scleroxylon* grows throughout the forests of West Africa, from Guinea to Zaire. It is rarer in the wettest forests. Reaching 200 feet (60m) in height and 22 feet (7m) in girth, this emergent has large winglike buttresses running many feet up its trunk. The grey bark is fairly smooth, but is fissured in old trees. The crown is frequently irregular in shape, with large maple-like leaves.

About 1 inch (2.5cm) across, the flowers have purple-based white petals. The generic name, *Triplochiton*, means three layers and refers to the sepals, petals and staminodes (sterile stamens) which make three coverings over the ovary. The fruits, which tend to be formed at intervals of several years, are winged and so are blown about by the wind. Seedlings seem to grow best in clearings and gaps. Despite the specific name, which means hard wood, the timber from this tree is soft, light and easy to work. It is much in demand in Europe, and locally is used to make dugout canoes. Even the buttresses of this tree are trimmed and made into doors.

The unbroken canopy

Seen from an aircraft, the canopy trees form an undulating green carpet, their crowns closely inter-laced and often bound together by woody climbers. A more usual view of these trees is from below, their tall straight trunks towering up from the jungle floor. They are often devoid of branches and twigs for the first 60 to 80 feet (18 to 24m), and then suddenly break up into several huge branches which spread out almost horizontally before them-selves dividing to form the flattened crowns of the canopy.

Many of the largest species develop buttresses at the base of their trunks, while some of the smaller trees are supported on a strange pyramid of stilt roots. The bark of some canopy trees is thin and smooth; near the ground it may bear a sparse covering of mosses and lichens, but the sheltered parts between the buttresses frequently have dense growths of moss or patches of delicate filmy ferns.

Below the vault of the upper canopy are many medium-sized trees. Some are young and, given luck and space, they will eventually reach the canopy. Others are smaller at maturity, and have elongated crowns which fill the gaps between the large, flat crowns of the main canopy trees.

In the temperate regions, a forest which con-tains more than 20 species of tree would be considered rich and unusual. It is more common for one species to dominate, as in a beech forest or an oak forest. In the tropical forest, on the other hand, there may be hundreds of different tree species in the same area.

Since the species are so numerous in the tropical forest, problems of identification arise. Not only are there several species in a small area, but they are likely not to be well known. Even in the often-travelled parts of the jungle, species are constantly being discovered. A major worry of botanists and conservationists is that forests are being destroyed so quickly that many species will be extinct before there is an opportunity for them to be examined and described, let alone screened for possible useful applications.

A more practical and immediate problem in identification is that of inaccessibility. The leaves, flowers and fruits which would help in classifying a species are in the crowns of trees perhaps fifteen times the height of the average man. To bring them down, guns, catapults and trained monkeys have all been used. At ground level there may be only a scatter of fallen flowers, or a congregation of butterflies sucking the juices of fallen fruits to indicate a tree of potential interest.

An experienced forester, however, can usually recognize a tree from the characteristics of a slash through the bark to the wood, made with a machete. This shows the hues and textures of the inner and outer bark, which are generally distinct-ive. The cut may 'bleed' white latex, or, less commonly, a red ooze. If these methods of identifi-cation fail, a tree can be felled. This task is not so easy, even with the help of a chain saw. When the trunk is severed, a tree may remain upright, held by its neighbours and guyed to them by the ropelike stems of woody climbers.

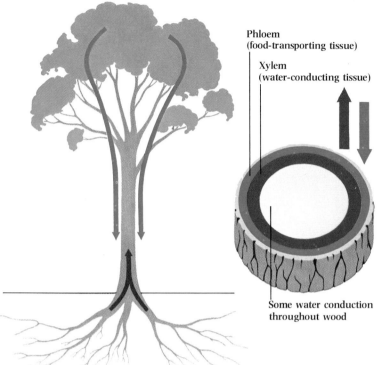

Phloem
(food-transporting tissue)

Xylem
(water-conducting tissue)

Some water conduction
throughout wood

The materials a tree needs to build itself are made in the leaves from carbon dioxide and water, using light energy from the sun. These food materials, such as sugars, are moved about the tree dissolved in water. The foods travel in the phloem, food-transporting tissue which forms the inner layers of the bark. Water, used for photosynthesis and constantly evaporating from the leaves, is taken up from the soil by the tree roots. It is carried up to the leaves in the xylem, a porous tube-filled tissue which forms the central woody part of the tree trunk.

Identification of jungle trees is a problem as most branch only at canopy height, perhaps 80ft (24m) from the forest floor. Many trees can be named by looking at the bark and cutting a small piece of it with a machete. The outer bark can be distinctive; that of *Diospyros sanza-minika* is hard, brittle and black like chips of coal. The inner bark may be an unusual hue, like that of *Enantia polycarpa*, called *sikadua* (gold tree) by the Ashanti of Ghana. Milky latex may flow out (*Ficus*) or ooze out in droplets (*Mammea africana*). Some barks have a characteristic smell; that of *Maesopsis eminii* smells of cold roast chicken. Using all these points, together with the pattern of the bark and the trunk shape, most of the common jungle trees can be named.

Diospyros sanza-minika, top left; Ficus, top right; Enantia polycarpa, bottom left; Mammea africana, bottom right.

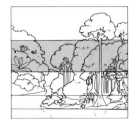

Canopy

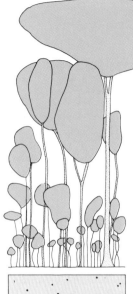

Striking canopy diversity is characteristic of the tropical rain forest. The profile of a small section of forest, *left*, demonstrates this diversity, even though it excludes all plants less than 10ft (3m) tall. Among the 31 individual trees in this patch of forest 26ft by 59ft (8m by 18m), there are 20 different species.

A monkey's eye view of the jungle canopy is seen from a walkway built between two tall trees, *right*. This canopy is characteristically diverse, made up of many different trees, each with subtly different leaves. Canopy walkways have been built in several jungle areas and give completely new insight into a world previously viewed only from below, or at a distance from aircraft.

Buttresses—wings or flanges spreading out from the base of the trunk—and stilt roots are seen in many jungle trees. There have been many theories as to their function, but it is now generally agreed that buttresses help to keep the tree upright against the force exerted by the wind, and also spread the great weight of the tree over a larger area. These ideas are supported by the fact that on the soft soils of swamp forests, relatively large numbers of trees have buttresses and stilt roots. However, many forest trees function perfectly well without buttresses. Foresters dislike buttresses as they complicate the felling of a tree. As some buttresses are 15ft (5m) high, it is necessary to build a platform above them from which to cut through the trunk.

39

Foliage of the canopy

In contrast to the great variety in size and shape of the leaves of temperate woodland trees, the leaves of tropical forest trees are strikingly similar. The majority of the canopy trees have leaves which are smooth, shiny on both sides, and resemble those in the laurel family.

The leaves of many rain forest species are of similar size and taper to a point, the so-called drip-tip. Although there is no obvious reason for the uniformity of size, a plausible explanation does exist for the constant shape. A number of tropical forest leaves, particularly in the lower canopy and under-storey, last a long time, often more than a year. Tiny lichens, algae and mosses (epiphylls) grow on moist leaf surfaces, eventually covering them and shading the photosynthetic cells with their own. But a leaf which is smooth-surfaced and pointed will shed water quickly after rain, discouraging the growth of epiphylls. This theory is supported by two observations. Plants in the damper understorey have more uniform leaves and longer drip-tips, and leaf points tend to be longer in the wettest forests.

Conversely, the leaves of emergent tree species are much more varied in form, and often have little in the way of a drip-tip. They are also often smaller and thicker than leaves of trees at lower levels; this fits them for the less humid environment where they live.

Many trees, especially in the drier forests, are deciduous, that is, they lose their leaves each year. The leafless period frequently lasts a month or less, and some species exhibit leaf replacement; they shed the old leaves and grow a new set simultaneously. The intervals between leaf sheddings are usually regular, but often do not coincide with a calendar year. *Terminalia catappa* changes its leaves every six months, both in its native Malaysia and also in West Africa, where it has been introduced. A tree of *Koompassia* in Malaysia replaced its leaves every 12.7 months over a period of several years. It is hard to see how such timing could be stimulated.

Contrary to expectations, evergreen trees in a tropical environment do not continuously produce new leaves. Instead leaves are produced in flushes of new growth. All the shoots suddenly grow and make several new leaves at once, waiting for many months before repeating the process. New leaves appear quickly, and are likely to be brightly hued, soft and floppy. One explanation for this pattern of leaf replacement is that it helps the leaves to avoid being eaten. If leaves grew all the time, leaf-eating creatures that preferred new, soft leaves would always have food. Thus their numbers would increase and they would damage most of the succulent young leaves. But a big flush of leaves after a long interval satiates the few leaf-eaters which have survived on the old leaves, and allows most of the new leaves to expand unscathed.

Just as leaves are produced at long intervals, so are flowers, possibly for the same reasons. Besides producing splashes of brilliance throughout the jungle canopy, simultaneous flowering and fruiting ensures that at least some of the resulting seeds are not eaten, and so will survive to bring forth another generation.

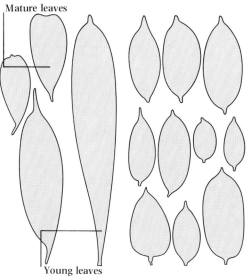

Mature leaves

Young leaves

Jungle canopy leaves are alike in size and form. The pointed tips and hairless surfaces may encourage rapid drainage after rain and prevent growth of lichens and mosses on these long-lasting leaves. Leaves of young and mature trees of the same species often differ in size and form because of the different conditions they encounter in understorey and canopy.

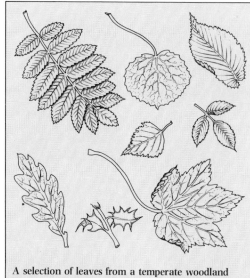

A selection of leaves from a temperate woodland shows much greater diversity. Since these leaves are shed every year, they do not require mechanisms to prevent lichens and mosses growing on their surfaces.

Silk-cotton trees flower simultaneously in a Trinidadian forest, *right*. Many tropical forest trees have this habit of flowering together, which could have several advantages. Individual trees are often widely scattered in the diverse canopy; simultaneous flowering greatly increases chances of successful cross-pollination. Moreover, trees which flower together fruit together. If the trees were to produce fruits and seeds all year round, the animals which feed on them would have a constant food supply and would allow few seeds to escape. Simultaneous fruiting at long intervals tends to swamp the animals with food, allowing plenty of seeds to survive and germinate.

Delicate young leaves of a canopy tree brighten the undergrowth, contrasting sharply with the deep green of the mature leaves. Young foliage of jungle trees often shows two peculiarities. First, new leaves often hang down limply, only stiffening as they darken and mature. Second, on some trees the new leaves are red, white or even blue. Both features are rare outside the rain forest and are not fully understood. The drooping of the new leaves may relate to their rapid growth; they reach full size first, then add strength. The unusual pigments may shield the chlorophyll in the delicate leaves, or may signal the presence of compounds which make the otherwise juicy, attractive leaves distasteful.

The canopy's seeds and fruits

Like all plants, canopy trees must reproduce. Many, however, flower and fruit at irregular, often long, intervals. It is not known what triggers the flowering; in some species it seems to occur after short, dry periods, yet there is no apparent reason why other species suddenly burst into flower. Whatever factor may have caused the flowering, it usually affects all the individuals of one species in an area, so that there is a good chance of cross-pollination. Many canopy trees are pollinated by insects, but birds and bats also play a valuable role.

The seeds of most plants have some kind of mechanism to take them away from the parent. Generally, the offspring do not grow close to the parent, because competition for light and water is intense. And conditions change; the seed which produced the parent may have germinated in a clearing which no longer exists. The neighbourhood of the parent is a dangerous place; seed-eating birds and insects tend to congregate there.

Seeds can be dispersed by wind, animals or water. The latter is only useful if it is moving, and even then, spread is often in one direction. Although the lower layers of the jungle are still, many large trees have wind-dispersed seeds. *Ceiba pentandra*, the silk-cotton, has seeds covered in silky fluff that can travel long distances. The seeds of some leguminous trees, such as *Newtonia*, have flattened seeds with a marginal wing. Mahoganies, such as *Khaya* and *Entandrophragma*, have winged seeds, though the wing of the latter is just at one end, causing the seed to spin as it falls. The seeds of the liana *Strophanthus* have a parachute of hairs on a long projecting stalk. The minute seeds of orchids can also be dispersed by wind like dust.

Animals are the most important seed dispersers in the jungle. About 70 per cent of tree species in the forests of Ghana have fleshy fruits; their seeds are hard and resistant to digestion, and pass unharmed through animals. When the fruits are ripe, fruit-eaters such as monkeys, hornbills, toucans and fruit bats feast in the trees, and then scatter the seeds in their droppings. On the ground, tapirs, gorillas and elephants eat the fallen fruits.

Once a seed has been dispersed, it has to germinate and establish itself successfully. The forest undergrowth is a hostile environment for this. There is intense competition above ground for the small amount of light that reaches the forest floor, and below ground, for water and mineral nutrients. To grow, plants employ two strategies. One group produces large seeds in comparatively small numbers. The food reserves in each seed allow it to establish and sustain a large seedling. This remains in the understorey, growing very slowly perhaps for many years. If a tree falls, and makes a gap with more light and less root competition, then the seedling can take advantage of the change.

The alternative, adopted by many quick-growing species, is to produce innumerable tiny seeds. These do not germinate in undisturbed forest, probably because the composition of the light in the understorey inhibits them. But once a clearing is made, the seeds begin to germinate. Both strategies involve a waiting game; in one case as a seedling, in the other as a seed.

The seeds of jungle trees are dispersed in many ways. A few, like those of *Hura*, are contained in fruits which explode and hurl out the seeds. Others rely on wind to blow them away from the parent. The fruits of *Dipterocarpus* spin and are supported by greatly enlarged sepals. The seeds of *Enkleia* fall with a piece of stalk on which are two small leaflike bracts. These make the seed spin and slow its fall. There are also large fleshy fruits containing hard seeds which are fed on and dispersed by animals—avocado, durian and *Balanites* are examples.

Enkleia

Newtonia

Strophanthus

Melanorrhea

Durian

Entandrophragma

Avocado (*Persea*)

Koompassia

Hura

Balanites

Rubber (*Hevea*)

Dipterocarpus

Piptadeniastrum

The single-seeded fruit on a dipterocarp tree spins to earth in a Malaysian forest. The long wings are formed from two of the five sepals which increase enormously in size as the fruit develops. Suspended between these wings, the seed is borne away by the wind and escapes the competition of its parent. The vicinity of the parent can be dangerous for the seed; seed-eaters gather there, or a caterpillar falling from the parent tree can devour a whole seedling. But wind dispersal also has risks; the seed may land in a totally unsuitable environment.

Richard Spruce (1817–93) British botanist who made an extensive study of the plant life of the Amazon jungle.

Richard Spruce was an outstanding amateur botanist who began by collecting plants, particularly mosses and liverworts, on the moors of his native Yorkshire. He was commissioned by leading British botanists, including Sir William Hooker, director of Kew Gardens, to study tropical plant life in South America.

In 1849 Spruce arrived in South America. In 17 years he travelled the length of the Amazon, explored the Orinoco and Negro rivers and journeyed to Venezuela, Peru and Ecuador. Despite illness, attacks by Indians and other hardships, Spruce amassed a collection of 7,000 important plant specimens. He also recorded 21 Amazonian languages and mapped three previously unexplored rivers.

His health finally shattered, Spruce returned to England and spent the rest of his life working on his plant collection. His books include a work on liverworts, *Hepaticae of the Amazon and the Andes of Peru and Ecuador*, which remains a classic.

Animal-dispersed seeds are common in jungle plants. Usually these seeds are hard and formed inside a fleshy fruit. When the fruit is unripe, it is green—thus camouflaged among the leaves—and scentless. As it ripens the green skin usually changes to yellow, orange or red, and the flesh softens, becomes sweet instead of sour and often develops a strong scent. The attractiveness may be increased by a contrast between fruit and seed; black seeds often hang from red fruits or red seeds stand out against yellow flesh. Animals are attracted by the scent and appearance of the fruits and feed on them. As the seeds are too tough to digest they pass through the animal unharmed.

The dark understorey

The myth of 'the impenetrable undergrowth' of the jungle originated from accounts written by early explorers, travelling along jungle rivers by boat. The forest does present an impenetrable wall of foliage along the riverbanks because it is here that the river creates a gap; this allows sunlight to reach the forest floor and accelerate plant growth. But break through the wall and there lies a gloomy but by no means impenetrable world, the forest understorey. Although there are tree trunks and the twisting ropelike stems of the lianas, these can be negotiated fairly easily.

The understorey is a difficult environment for plants. Only 2 to 5 per cent of the sunlight that falls on the canopy reaches the understorey; the rest is intercepted and partly absorbed by the leaves of the canopy trees and lianas. Isolated flecks of sunlight reach the forest floor, but most of the light is reflected from, or transmitted through, leaves, and tends to have a strong greenish tinge.

Plants rely mainly on the red and blue ends of the light spectrum for photosynthesis, so this reduced light, from which much of the red and blue has already been absorbed, is not as useful to them as direct sunlight. Furthermore, the wavelengths just beyond red are sensed by plants, and particularly by seeds, upon which they have a strong inhibitory effect. These 'near infra-red' or 'far-red' wavelengths are transmitted by the canopy, so that the light in the understorey is relatively richer in them than sunlight. When a clearing is made by man, or by a fallen tree, direct sunlight streams down to the ground and allows the waiting seeds to germinate.

In addition to altering the quantity and quality of the light reaching the understorey, the canopy reduces air circulation. The air in the understorey hardly moves, and the humidity is always high. Temperatures, although not as extreme as they are above the canopy or outside the forest, are still high and fluctuate little. These factors make the understorey an uncomfortable, sticky place for man from temperate regions.

Despite the difficult growing conditions in the understorey, it is well populated with seedlings of the canopy trees. True shrubs—woody plants with several stems from ground level—are rare, but tiny single-stemmed miniature trees, up to 10 feet (3m) high at maturity, are common. Dwarf palms, of similar habit, are often found in South American and Southeast Asian forests.

Other low-growing plants that tend to be well-represented in this environment are ground herbs —soft-stalked plants—especially those belonging to the arrowroot (Marantaceae), the ginger (Zingiberaceae), the acanthus (Acanthaceae) and spiderwort (Commelinaceae) families. Many of these herbs have a similar appearance; their leaves are broad, with long, pointed tips, and they are often reddish beneath, with a matt green upper surface. Perhaps both these features help the plants absorb the little light that is available. Plants such as *Calathea*, *Fittonia* and *Maranta* (prayer plant) that grow wild in the jungle understorey have become popular houseplants.

The top of the canopy is in full sunlight. By the time light reaches the forest floor all but 0.2 to 2 per cent has been absorbed by the vegetation, so understorey plants must survive on little light. The quality of the light is also affected. The green matter in leaves, chlorophyll, absorbs red and blue light—this is why leaves appear green. Thus the most useful parts of the available sunlight have already been used by canopy plants before it reaches the lower layers of the rain forest.

The deep green leaves of a huge member of the arrowroot family dominate the understorey of this Sumatran rain forest, *below*. The broad, thin leaves form the maximum light-absorbing surface from the minimum of material. The arrowroots (Marantaceae) are familiar from the culinary use of the starchy roots.

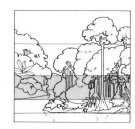

Shrub   Miniature tree

Dwarf palm   Herb

The main types of plant found in the understorey—
apart from seedlings of canopy trees—are shrubs,
miniature trees, dwarf palms and herbs.

Flowering in the understorey can be spectacular. The
cone-shaped inflorescence of the ginger, *Zingiber
spectabile*, is made up of overlapping shell-like bracts
which protect the flower buds until they are ready to
open. Each flower lasts only a day. A miniature tree,
Pycnocoma macrophylla, displays a showy mass of
brilliant white flowers, *below*. These appear from its
terminal rosette of leaves and enliven the darkness of
the understorey.

Flowering in the understorey

To reproduce in the peculiar microclimate of the forest understorey, plants have evolved certain features. Grasses and sedges are normally wind-pollinated, but in the almost windless understorey this is unlikely to occur. To attract pollinating insects, therefore, some species, such as *Pariana* in the New World tropics, have developed large, showy, yellow stamens, while others exude nectar. The West African forest sedges in the genus *Mapania* have grown whitish scales around their flowers, and are visited, and thought to be pollinated, by slugs.

The deep gloom of the understorey creates problems even for the insect-pollinated plants because the flowers are difficult to see. To overcome this, some plants flower at night, producing large, white, strongly scented flowers to attract moths for pollination. There are others which produce flowers on their trunks and large lower branches instead of bearing them on small leafy twigs. Known as cauliflory (stem-flowering) this habit is common among understorey trees and shrubs.

In addition to making the flowers conspicuous, cauliflory has other possible advantages. As plant establishment is difficult in the forest, a large seed with copious food reserves has a better chance of producing a self-supporting seedling than does a tiny seed. But large seeds need large fruits to produce and house them, and it is only with difficulty that large fruits can be carried on slender branches. If they are carried on the trunk and larger branches, however, they can easily be supported.

The cocoa tree, *Theobroma cacao*, for instance, is cauliflorous; its small white flowers are borne on special parts of the trunk and lower branches called cushions. When a flower is pollinated, it grows quickly, the stalk lengthens and thickens, and after four to five months the pod is up to 12 inches (30cm) long and weighs about a pound (400–500gm). It contains 20 to 70 large seeds which, when fermented and dried, are the cocoa beans of commerce. Such fruits would damage slender twigs.

Many understorey shrubs synchronize their flowering so that all the individuals of a species in an area flower within a few days. This timing obviously improves the chances of cross-pollination, as a pollinating insect is likely to visit more than one plant in a short time. Some species of coffee, including the most commonly cultivated species *Coffea arabica*, produce flower buds which develop to a limited extent and then stop. They remain like this until heavy rain falls, which stimulates development to start again, and within a week to 12 days all the flowers open simultaneously. In other shrubs rain, or the sudden fall in temperature which nearly always accompanies heavy tropical rain, stimulates the production of flower buds rather than their development.

Despite the spectacular gregarious flowering which sometimes takes place, and the conspicuousness of flowers borne on trunks and branches, the understorey often seems a remarkably flowerless place. Many species probably flower only after long intervals, perhaps not every year, and perhaps only when conditions are ideal.

Flowers and fruit sprout from tree trunks and large branches in many understorey trees—the phenomenon of cauliflory. Flowers that grow on the tree trunk, like the cocoa flowers, *far right*, are probably more obvious to pollinators than if they were among foliage. The flowers will also attract different insects from those in the canopy. Another advantage of cauliflory is that fruit can be large, like the breadfruit, *right*. The fruit is well-supported by a sturdy trunk and the tree can produce large seeds with plenty of food reserves to establish the seedling in the relative darkness of the understorey.

The bright, tubular flowers of a species of *Heliconia* distinguish the plant in the understorey and attract pollinating hummingbirds and butterflies. Both these creatures have vision which extends into the red part of the spectrum, and flowers pollinated by them tend to be red. *Heliconia* is a relative of the banana.

Open country   Rain forest

The broad leaves of rain forest grasses, *left* and *above*, are quite unlike the familiar slender grasses of open country. Instead they are similar to the ordinary leaves of other understorey plants. Grasses are usually pollinated by the wind, but in the still jungle understorey many grasses have turned to insect pollinators. Some have bright floral parts to attract insects, and nectar to reward their efforts.

47

The sombre forest floor

So little light reaches the jungle floor that virtually no plants can survive there. Despite travellers' tales of 'thick layers of rotting vegetation', only a thin layer of decaying leaves hides the underlying soil. The continuous rain of dead leaves, flowers and twigs from the upper layers of the forest does not accumulate, but is rapidly decomposed. A fallen leaf becomes unrecognizable after only two to three months.

The main decomposers are fungi, living abundantly but largely unseen in the soil and litter, feeding by destroying plant tissue. Most of the time they exist as networks of tiny threads, but sometimes they form cottony wefts among rotting leaves. When conditions are right these threads interweave to form a strong structure, the familiar fungus, or mushroom, which appears above the ground. It can be of many shapes and bright or sombre. On gills beneath the cap of the mushroom, some threads produce beadlike growths at their tips. These develop a thick protective wall and form the dustlike spores which blow in the wind and disperse the fungus.

Devoid of chlorophyll, fungi do not feed by photosynthesis. The threads penetrate plant tissue and secrete substances which can break down the toughest plant materials to give simple foods such as sugars, which the threads absorb. Some fungi, however, weave threads into a mat around a living plant root, obtaining substances, particularly sugars and those containing nitrogen, which are to be found in the root. The root, in turn, takes up a supply of the minerals absorbed initially by the fungus. This symbiotic association, in which both partners benefit, is a mycorrhiza, and is enjoyed by many trees in the world's tropical forests.

Fungi, living as they do on dead material, are known as saprophytes. There are a few flowering plants on the jungle floor which also have no chlorophyll and obtain all their food in the same way. Saprophytic plants are small (few are more than 8 inches (20cm) tall) and most are so inconspicuous that they are easily overlooked, and therefore thought to be rare.

Among the sparse population of plants on the jungle floor is a parasite of jungle lianas, *Rafflesia arnoldii*, which bears the world's largest flower. The rafflesias and their relatives are among the most complete parasites known. Only their flowers appear outside their host; the rest of the plant lives inside, between the wood and the bark. Another parasite, whose rose-red flowers are a common sight among the fallen leaves of the African jungles, is *Thonningia sanguinea*. Although the jungle floor appears to be a dark, gloomy area, it is full of life, mostly dependent on the rain of litter from above. Many floor plants are invisible for most of their lives except for occasional spectacular flowering and fruiting.

A cluster of fungi grows out of a rotting tree trunk lying in leaf litter on the jungle floor. The few living leaves are gradually covered by epiphylls—tiny lichens which grow on the leaf surface.

The spectacular fruiting body of a fungus, *Dictyophora duplicata*, occasionally thrusts up from the jungle floor. For most of the year it is invisible, living as a mass of tiny threads in the surface layers of soil and feeding on the litter from trees. The thimble-shaped tip carries a foul-smelling liquid containing reproductive spores. The liquid attracts flies which then disperse the spores.

The starlike flower of *Thismia* pushes out from the rotting leaves which provide its food. *Thismia* is one of the few saprophytic flowering plants. These plants do not have chlorophyll, so cannot live by photosynthesis. Instead they feed on decaying matter. Most are jungle plants as the continuously warm and moist climate of these regions allows decay—and saprophyte growth—throughout the year.

The giant flower of *Rafflesia* is the largest single flower known, and can be up to 3ft (90cm) across. It is the only visible part of a plant which is an internal parasite of the roots of jungle lianas in Southeast Asia. The flower bud arises inside the root of the host plant. It then breaks through to the outside and enlarges, finally appearing on the ground surface. The huge fleshy flowers smell of rotting meat which attracts pollinating flies—essential for the plant's reproduction, as male and female flowers are produced on different plants. Inside the fleshy fruits are tiny hard seeds.

49

The riverbank's wall of foliage

In the openings created by rivers and streams sunlight is able to reach ground level. Then trees, shrubs, climbers and herbs take advantage of the light and form dense walls of greenery. To the river traveller, this seems to form an impenetrable barrier. But beyond this mass of foliage, the forest understorey is much more open.

The plants which grow beside rivers face certain difficulties. Roots, like all parts of a plant, need oxygen to survive. About 65 per cent of soil is made up of air-filled spaces between the particles of earth and these can usually provide enough oxygen. But if the soil is very wet, and unable to drain freely, the spaces become filled with water. Oxygen moves 10,000 times more slowly through water than through air, and when the soil oxygen has been used up by roots, bacteria and fungi, it cannot be replaced quickly. The soil then becomes anaerobic, or devoid of oxygen. Under such conditions, other kinds of bacteria thrive and produce foul-smelling and often poisonous substances such as hydrogen sulphide, with its smell of rotten eggs. How can the roots of swamp plants survive in this soil?

All plants have air spaces between their cells, but in swamp plants the spaces in the stems and leaves are so large that they join together to form air canals through which oxygen can pass to the roots. There are some swamp trees whose side roots grow upward into the air instead of downward into the soil. In the aerial parts of these roots small pores, lenticels, allow oxygen to enter the air spaces of the roots so that the plant can breathe.

Plants that grow beside fast-flowing jungle streams encounter different problems. The waters can rise quickly and submerge them, or rapid currents can easily tear off leaves and branches. But many of these plants have long, narrow leaves which offer little resistance to the water, and so survive. Plants of several different families, including palms, have leaves of this type, which suggests that they are of real advantage.

A number of riverside plants in the jungle produce seeds which float and are spread by the flowing water. Others have seeds or fruits with fleshy coats. Fish digest the fleshy part, leaving the seeds ready to germinate, perhaps way down the riverbank, far from the parent.

Although the waters of streams and rivers form a separate but related ecosystem from that of the jungle, both are subject to the same climatic conditions—rainfall throughout the year and continuous warmth. In the slow-flowing rivers and backwaters of the Amazon basin there are many submerged water plants. Other water plants, like the famous giant water-lilies, *Victoria regia*, are rooted in the river bed but have floating leaves and flowers at the surface.

In the fast-flowing rocky streams of the same area are found the mosslike members of the family Podostemaceae—flowering plants with no real leaves or roots, just a lobed stem clinging to the rocks. When the water level drops and exposes the plants to the air, small flowers appear from these stems. Similar plants are found in jungle streams of Africa and Southeast Asia.

Leaves of the giant water-lily, *Victoria regia*, float on a jungle backwater in Brazil. These enormous leaves are up to 7ft (2m) across. The pale, cream flowers of the lily open at night and some of the flower parts heat up through biochemical reactions. This distils a strong scent which attracts beetles to pollinate the flowers. Indians gather the pea-sized water-lily seeds and grind them into flour.

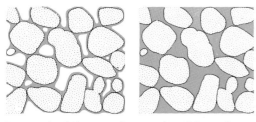

In **normal soil** the spaces between the solid particles are filled by air. There is some water on the particle surfaces and in the smaller pores. Plant roots obtain oxygen from the air spaces. In waterlogged soil, all the spaces between soil particles are filled by water and little oxygen is available for the plant roots.

Aerial roots

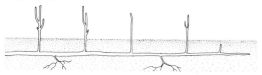

The roots of swamp plants cannot get the oxygen they need from the wet soil. Many have specialized roots, pneumatophores, which grow up into the air. Spaces inside the roots are connected to the outside by pores which allow oxygen to enter the roots.

The Swiss cheese plant, *Monstera deliciosa*, a familiar houseplant is one of the great family of aroids (Araceae). These plants thrive along jungle rivers where there is light and constant water supply. *Monstera* clings to tree trunks by climbing roots.

A broad, forest river breaks the jungle canopy and allows in light, *above*. Plants respond by producing a green wall of foliage along the riverbank, giving rise to the myth of the jungle's impenetrability.

Narrow-leaved palms are growing along this Southeast Asian jungle stream, *below*. Such leaves offer little resistance to rushing water and escape damage when the riverbank floods after heavy rain.

51

The animals

Almost limitless opportunities exist for the vertebrate animals living in the various layers of the tropical rain forest. Dominating the canopy, tall trees and their interwoven branches host epiphytes of all kinds. Flowers bloom year round in these aerial gardens and attract bats as well as birds to their sweet nectar and energy-rich pollen. The luxuriant understorey below provides innumerable walkways and hideouts for creatures that spend their lives either hiding from larger predators or looking for prey themselves. Lower down, on the forest floor, leaves and thickets make an excellent refuge for very small animals and serve as a rich source of food. Usually winding its way through this part of the jungle is a quietly flowing river, alive with myriad life forms.

To exploit these opportunities the animals need specialized features. The three-toed sloth, for example, could not spend its entire life hanging upside-down beneath the forest's branches without its curious, hooklike feet. Styles of locomotion are the most prolific of jungle adaptations. Except for birds, the only vertebrates capable of true flight are the bats. But frogs, snakes, lizards and mammals have evolved membranes that enable them to glide from one place to another. Many primates, as well as some anteaters, pangolins and a porcupine, have prehensile tails which function as another limb. The primates use their tails for rapid and agile passage through the branches, while anteaters use them for holding on to a tree as they tear at an ant or termite nest with their claws.

Though the general characteristics of the jungle habitat are the same everywhere, the way in which its inhabitants have adapted to them varies from one continent to another. The monkeys of Africa and Southeast Asia are born without prehensile tails and, as a result, they move by running along the upper surface of the branches, or by swinging beneath them.

Many jungle animals demonstrate parallel evolution: two unrelated species develop to the point where they resemble one another because they are doing the same job, even though they occur in two distinct geographical regions. Thus the forest hog in Africa is mimicked by the peccary of South America, and the pygmy hippopotamus of Africa by the capybara of South America. The drifting apart of the continents caused dislocation in the spread of certain types of animal, but others have evolved to take their place. The present distribution of some jungle animals reflects the past movements of the earth's crust; the presence of the tapir in both Southeast Asia and South America suggests that it originated somewhere in the African/Indian region, but reached South America when the continent was joined to Africa.

Unfortunately, the very adaptations which enable animals to live in the jungle may yet prove to be their downfall. As the forests are disturbed by man these specialized creatures cannot adapt fast enough to the new conditions. The animals do not simply live in the forest— they are an integral part of its complexity. Their unique and bizarre characteristics help to make the rain forest the most fascinating and mysterious of all the world's habitats.

Mona monkey,
Cercopithecus mona

Schmidt's white-nosed monkey,
Cercopithecus ascanius schmidti

Diana monkey,
Cercopithecus diana

De Brazza's monkey,
Cercopithecus neglectus

Moustached monkey,
Cercopithecus cephus

Redtail,
Cercopithecus ascanius ascanius

Owl-faced monkey,
Cercopithecus hamlyni

The treetop dwellers

Moving around among the thin branches of the tallest jungle trees is a problem, a reason why few vertebrate animals other than birds inhabit the trees that emerge above the main canopy. Those that do manage do not spend all their time there but come down to lower layers from time to time. Creatures found in the emergent trees are generally small and light, in keeping with the fragile branches.

An exception to this rule is the proboscis monkey, found among the mangrove swamp jungles of Borneo where the emergent trees are firm and rigid and do not grow to enormous heights. The proboscis monkey, *Nasalis larvatus*, is a sturdy animal—a male weighs up to 50 pounds (22 kg)—and lives in groups of one or two adult males, two to five females and several young. The troop roams through the swamps feeding on mangrove shoots and the young leaves of the pedada tree as well as fruits and flowers. But for much of the day the monkeys apparently sunbathe up in the emergent trees. At night, too, they seek the haven of the treetops to foil predators such as the clouded leopard—their main enemy.

Proboscis monkeys are remarkably agile. They have long tails of up to 30 inches (76cm) but use them only as counterbalances. With the aid of long fingers and toes they run along branches or swing from one to another. They will launch themselves across a gap in the trees using a supple branch as a springboard. Landing safely depends on the accurate integration of hand and foot, but, if surprised or startled in the treetops, a proboscis monkey may drop 20 feet on to a sturdy branch.

Little is known of their social life, but proboscis monkeys are thought to be territorial. Males have large pendulous noses—the origin of their vernacular name—and are very vocal. As the monkey makes its hard 'honking' noise, the long nose straightens out. Females can make the honking noise, but are usually quieter than males. The monkeys mate in the trees at any time of the year, and give birth to a single offspring. Even birth takes place up in the trees.

Living among the emergent trees of the New Guinea jungle is the tiny pygmy or feathertail glider, *Acrobates pulchellus*, a marsupial mammal related to the greater and sugar gliders of Australia. To solve the problem of travelling from tree to tree, the pygmy glider has a flap of skin, a patagium, strung between the front and rear limbs. The animal extends its limbs, and thus the skin flaps, which gives it sufficient lift to glide smoothly forward and downward. The tail, which is fringed with stiff hairs and strongly resembles a feather, provides directional stability. The tail's light structure is essential for these tiny creatures—adult males are about 3 inches (7.5 cm) long. A furry tail would be too heavy.

Pygmy gliders feed on insects, and the nectar and flower buds of the tallest forest trees. They may come down to lower layers but are extremely vulnerable to predators when on the forest floor. Among the treetops their nocturnal and secretive life-style seems to protect them.

The aptly named proboscis monkey, *Nasalis larvatus*, is an agile inhabitant of the emergent trees. The male's nose is extraordinarily long and bulbous, but the female's is less pronounced, changing little from infancy. Proboscis monkeys are now an endangered species and have proved difficult to keep in captivity. Studies on their long-term survival are now being carried out in Kalimantan, Indonesia.

The tiny pygmy glider, *Acrobates pulchellus*, from the forests of New Guinea and the northern tip of Australia, is no bigger than a shrew. It lives high among the eucalyptus trees, feeding on sap and insects. During the day many gliders pack into one tree hole nest lined with shredded leaves; like many small mammals, gliders are active at night. The pygmy glider is depicted on the Australian one cent piece and the 75 cent stamp

The wing of the pygmy glider is nothing more than a fold of skin stretched between the wrist and the ankle of the animal. When front and hind limbs are moved, the size of the membrane and the angle of attack alters. Cinematic studies of small mammals gliding show that directional stability is given to the flight by the actions of the hind legs and tail. As the glider comes into land, the hind legs are thrust downward, thus increasing the angle of attack of the membrane and gaining the animal extra lift. The pygmy glider's tail resembles a feather with stiff hairs projecting laterally from the centre. Muscles change the angle of the hairs so altering the width of the tail.

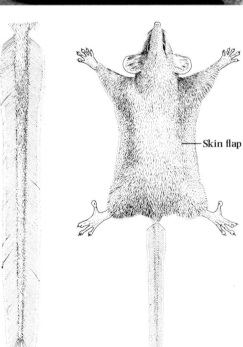

Skin flap

The foot of the pygmy glider is adapted for safe landing. Fingers and toes are deeply divided to allow good independent action. At the end of each digit is a short but sharp hooklike claw, useful for finding a grip on even the smoothest branch. The finger and toe pads are enlarged and their surface deeply scored, again to aid grip. Such adaptations are vital as pygmy gliders land on large branches that they cannot clasp with their tiny hands and feet.

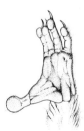

Clinging to the canopy

The mesh of interwoven branches of the forest canopy is the home of animals specially adapted for clinging to and grasping trees. Hands and feet are adapted as well as tails, but a long, prehensile tail is not an essential, as a successful group of canopy dwellers—the sloths—demonstrates. Sloths have little or no tail, and cling to branches with their hooklike claws. These odd, unkempt-looking creatures get their name from the fact that they never move fast—a mother sloth was observed to travel at a speed of 15 feet an hour when hurrying toward her baby! Undoubtedly though, their slow tempo of life helps to protect them from predators, as they do not catch the eye of jaguars and harpy eagles, both of which prey on sloths given the chance.

There are seven types of sloth—five have three digits on each hand and foot, and two have just two digits—all found only in the jungles of Central America and Amazonia. Adults are about 2 feet (60cm) long and weigh 9 to 16 pounds (4 to 7kg). Sloths have a curious physiology—their body temperature fluctuates with that of their surroundings to a marked degree. This feature is thought to be primitive, pointing to their ancient origin. Most of their relatives, the giant ground sloths of the Tertiary, became extinct quite recently, and only the specialized sloths, anteaters and armadillos survive today as three tips of a once enormous iceberg.

The sloth's 3-inch long claws function primarily as hooks to allow the animal to spend much of its time hanging upside-down from the branches of trees. The claws are also useful for pulling down twigs of *Cecropia* and hog plum so the sloth can feed on the leaves. The three-toed sloth feeds mainly on these two plants, which makes it a difficult animal to keep in captivity, but the two-toed sloth eats the leaves and fruits of a wide range of plants. Surprisingly, the sloth can wield its claws as weapons with considerable speed and skill if roused. Forest tribesmen do not often hunt the sloth, partly because of the injuries it can inflict, but also because a sloth does not drop to the ground when wounded or killed. The claws continue to cling by reflex action, and it seems that a dead sloth will only drop to the ground when decomposition of its body is quite advanced.

Sloths spend almost all their lives up in the canopy, but once a week the three-toed sloth, genus *Bradypus*, descends to the base of its tree to defecate. Using its stumplike tail as an auger, the sloth digs a

The sloth's hair grows toward its spine so that it sheds the rain when upside-down. In the continual dampness green algae grow in grooves in the hair, giving the sloth a greenish tinge, and thus camouflage. Moths lay eggs in the hair and the caterpillars seem to feed on the algae.

Magnified hair

Although members of the group Edentata—without teeth—sloths have 16 to 20 peglike teeth. These are not covered with enamel so wear down quickly, but continue to grow throughout life.

The smallest anteater, the dwarf anteater, *Cyclopes didactylus*, is about the size of a squirrel. Well equipped for its life high in the trees, it has a prehensile tail and specialized feet for climbing.

The foot of the dwarf anteater is well adapted to life in the trees. A downward padlike projection from the heel provides a rigid 'stop' against which the digits and claws can press when the foot is tightly clasped. The pad is made of springy connective tissue and is attached to a pair of projections from the supporting bone. Smaller pads positioned at the base of the claw on the digit itself allow grip to be maintained without the claw being involved—an important point, as the claw needs to be kept sharp for smashing ant and termite nests.

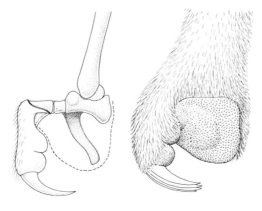

The hands and feet of sloths are long and thin, and the digits are bound together with elastic connective tissue. The digits—two or three depending on species—are covered by a layer of skin and hair. The long sharp projecting claws cannot be moved much relative to the hand, and so make a permanent hook for the sloth to cling to the trees by. The sloth remains upside-down even when asleep.

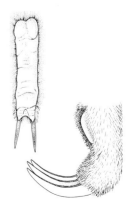

shallow hole into which it drops its stool. After covering it, the sloth climbs back up into the canopy. Two-toed sloths, genus *Choloepus*, defecate while hanging on branches, and tend to use the same spot each time. On the ground a sloth cannot stand properly or walk, but lies with all four limbs sprawled out helplessly. On a flat surface it can use its strong claws to drag the body slowly forward. Strangely enough, though, these arboreal creatures are excellent swimmers and move well in the jungle rivers.

Females give birth hanging in the trees. One infant is born which is about one-twentieth of its mother's weight, and crawls up the mother's abdomen with the help of its well-developed claws. For about two months it stays concealed in the shaggy fur and feeds on its mother's milk. After about five or six months the young sloth leaves its mother and wanders off to start its own life. Female sloths breed for the first time when they are about two years of age.

A relative of the sloth is the dwarf or pygmy anteater, *Cyclopes didactylus*, which is found from Mexico to Trinidad, Brazil and Peru. The dwarf anteater, like its cousins the giant anteater and the tamandua, is specialized for sucking up ants and termites, and has no teeth. Instead it has a long sticky tongue and a muscular gizzard in the stomach to grind up insects. The dwarf anteater is well adapted for life in the trees, with a strong prehensile tail from which it can suspend its whole body, and knifelike claws which tear through the tough nests of tree termites with great efficiency. To defend itself from predators, the dwarf anteater can lash out with these claws; the vulnerable young ride on mother's back for protection. The dwarf anteaters gather most of their food at night, although they will sometimes emerge during the day. Like the sloth, they are slow and sluggish in their movements.

Sloths and anteaters are found only in the jungles of Central and South America and have no real counterparts in Africa and Southeast Asia, other than the leaf-eating monkeys and scaly anteaters or pangolins. Neither the monkeys nor the pangolins show such extreme adaptations to their niche in life as the sloths and anteaters. To be of ancient lineage is not necessarily to be of inferior design, and the healthy stocks of these animals are a clear testament to the success of their arboreal, jungle life-style.

Upside-down is the sloth's typical posture. Never moving more than one limb at a time, the animal's progress is both slow and graceful. A three-toed sloth has nine neck vertebrae—two more than is usual for mammals—which allows it great flexibility when turning its head.

The forest acrobats

With the aid of arms twice as long as the body, gibbons swing effortlessly from branch to branch in the densely tangled jungle canopy. Both gibbons and orang-utans use this method of locomotion, brachiation, which allows them to live and move high in the trees even though, as great apes, and close cousins of man, they are tailless. Although both will come down to the forest floor to search for insects and roots, their movements are awkward and shuffling there. In the trees their poise is superb.

There are six or seven species of gibbon in the genus *Hylobates*, all living in Southeast Asia, from Burma in the west to Borneo in the east. Males and females are much the same size and weigh 11 to 18 pounds (5 to 8kg). Their great characteristics are the dangling arms about twice the length of the trunk; even the legs are 30 per cent longer than the trunk, making them relatively as long as man's. Elongated curved fingers make the hands ideally suited to act as grappling hooks. The gibbon's thumb is more deeply cleft than that of any other ape, including man, and is connected to the wrist bone with a ball and socket joint rather than a hinge. This system allows the thumb a high degree of mobility—essential when the gibbon is racing through the trees. To prevent distortion of the trunk during the swinging movements, the rib cage is extremely solid; and the lumbar, or lower spine, is short and relatively inflexible.

Gibbons live in small troops of a mated pair and up to four youngsters, and defend their territories by shouting at others that come too close. The most vocal gibbon is the Hoolock—the name is onomatopoeic—and both males and females make the warning calls. Within its territory the troop searches for fruits, leaves, buds, flowers, eggs, insects and other small invertebrates. A troop is easily frightened by the appearance of any large terrestrial species, but the only serious enemies are large eagles which attack adults and young alike.

Orang-utans (the name literally means 'jungle-man') come from Borneo and Sumatra. They are much larger than gibbons at about 5 feet (1.5m) tall; an old male may weigh up to 220 pounds (100kg), but females are almost half the size of males. With its armspan of about 8 feet (2.4m), the orang-utan can cover large distances quickly, sometimes crossing small gaps by launching itself from one branch to another and climbing and walking on branches as well as brachiating. The thumbs are tiny, and play no part in gripping the branches. The fingers are massive and strong.

If a small fruit needs to be peeled, the orang-utan holds it between index and third finger while teeth and lips work deftly at the peel. Each night the orang-utan builds a nest in the trees, breaking and bending branches and scattering leaves as bedding. They sleep much like humans, on the side or back, often with an open hand under the head.

In Southeast Asia gibbons are still quite abundant, but the orang-utan is severely threatened by the destruction of primary jungle for timber and agricultural land. They are fairly easy to breed in captivity, so there is no need for fresh captures, but there are probably fewer than 5,000 left in the wild.

The agility of the female orang-utan, *Pongo pygmaeus*, is not hindered by an infant clinging tightly to her fur. The orang-utan's feet are as useful as its hands in climbing, but to travel fast they use the brachiation technique, swinging hand over hand through the trees.

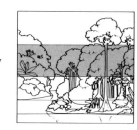

The infant and juvenile orang-utan has no trace of the huge flaps on each side of the face which characterize adult males. The youngster has an appealing moon face.

When sexually mature and forced to leave its family, the male orang's fatty flaps start to develop. Newly mature females do not have these flaps, but they do develop a fatty chin and throat flap at this time.

Fully adult males have a flap which completely surrounds the face, stretching from cheek to cheek. This seems to be a secondary sexual characteristic which signifies the social status of the individual.

With an armspan of about 7ft (2.1m) gibbons swing through the trees extremely fast. They use this brachiating form of movement more than any other ape. On occasion the gibbon will even let go with both hands and 'fly' perhaps 20ft (6m) to the next branch or tree.

When swinging from tree to tree the gibbon rarely, if ever, uses its feet for grasping, but a 'rowing' action of the legs helps to propel it to the next handhold.

The hand of the gibbon, *right*, is elongated and slender with a thumb deeply divided from the index finger; this gives flexibility, useful when climbing. The orang-utan's hand, *far right*, is strong, but with shorter fingers in relation to its palm and a short thumb.

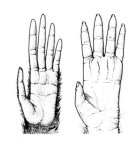

The extreme length of its forelimbs is the main feature of the gibbon's skeletal structure. As they touch the ground when the gibbon stands upright, the animal often carries the arms above its head out of the way. The bones of the wrists and fingers are also greatly elongated. Although apparently skilful acrobats, gibbons often break their long limb bones, as examination of their skeletons shows. The fact that gibbons continue to move with agility on three limbs while breaks mend is further testament to their outstanding abilities.

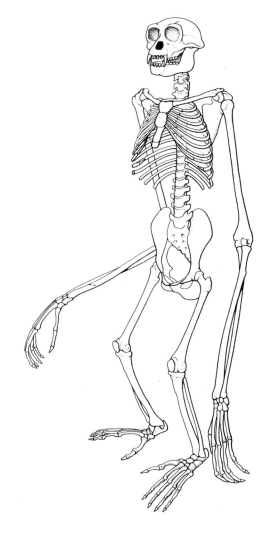

The fifth limb

The largest of the New World prehensile-tailed monkeys, the howler monkey, gets its name from its extraordinary vocal abilities. Howlers live in troops of up to 20 animals; each troop has its own territory. To defend the boundaries of their territory, the monkeys shout and roar at neighbouring troops in voices that can be heard several miles away. The howler monkey's voice is amplified by an expanded larynx which acts as a resonating chamber. The bulbous larynx, covered with a thick beard, gives the monkey's head a bulky appearance.

A prehensile tail is a fifth limb, a well-designed and useful tool for many tasks from climbing to holding food. A variety of jungle animals have prehensile tails, including a tree-living porcupine, but the mammals with the most highly developed tails are the South American monkeys. (Inexplicably, the African and Southeast Asian monkeys have evolved without this adaptation.) The prehensile tail, a continuation of the backbone, has a central core of bony vertebrae which are joined together in a much more flexible fashion than those of the back. They are bound together with ligaments, and the muscles of the tail are attached to the vertebrae by strong tendons. As the muscles at the base of the tail contract, the tail tip curls around and can be used as a hook. In the spider monkey, *Ateles geoffroyi*, for example, the prehensile tail may be one and a half times as long as the body, and longer and thicker than the legs. A slender, wiry animal, the spider monkey is undoubtedly the most acrobatic of the New World monkeys. It uses its powerful tail as adroitly as its arms and legs as it moves swiftly through the forest.

The prehensile tail is flattened rather than cylindrical. The underside is naked and its skin is tough, similar to that of the human palm, and crisscrossed with a network of fine grooves. These grooves, or 'dermatoglyphics', resemble the fingerprint patterns on human fingers and serve the same function, that is, to increase friction. Each monkey is thought to have its own characteristic dermatoglyphics. But, unlike the human hand and fingers, the underside of the prehensile tail is not well endowed with sweat and sebaceous glands.

The woolly spider monkey and the woolly monkey are two other South American monkeys with well-developed prehensile tails. The hands of all these monkeys are adapted too; the thumb, and, to a lesser extent, the great toe, have become reduced in size. In the woolly spider monkey, for example, the thumb is reduced to a fine scalelike flake. Thumbs are of little use to animals that spend much of their lives swinging from branch to branch, a form of locomotion known as brachiation. Yet the gibbons, the most pronounced of all brachiators, have long, thin thumbs that strongly resemble fingers. Both evolutionary adaptations, however, result in a hooklike hand. As a consequence, most prehensile-tailed monkeys use their tails as a fifth limb, for holding and gathering their food—fruits, nuts and shoots.

The South American monkeys spend most of their lives high in the trees, rarely venturing to the ground. Although marvellously adapted for an arboreal life, they are not without their enemies. The harpy eagle feeds primarily on juveniles, which may be caught unawares more easily than adults, and human forest tribes who highly prize the flesh of the spider and woolly monkeys kill them with blowpipes, spears and arrows. Sometimes the woolly monkey lessens its chances of escape by gorging itself when food is plentiful. This tendency is reflected in the monkeys' Brazilian name, *barrigudos*, meaning 'big bellies'.

In the jungles of Africa, monkeys are without prehensile tails. They have adapted well, however, to their forest habitat. Their long, bushy tails provide directional stability as well as balance, and their well-developed thumbs and great toes enable them to run along branches and leap across wide gaps between the canopy trees with amazing precision.

A type of anteater, the tamandua, *Tamandua tetradactyla*, has a fully prehensile tail which at 22in (55cm) long is as long as its body. The tail does not have any pads or ridges for grip. The tamandua tears open ant and termite nests with its sharp claws and then scoops up the escaping insects with its long, sticky tongue. These anteaters live in the jungles of Central America, Bolivia and Brazil.

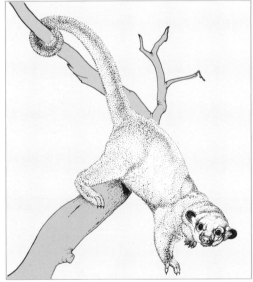

The South American kinkajou, or honey bear, *Potos flavus*, is related to the raccoon but spends almost all its life in the trees. When the kinkajou reaches out for ripe fruits, or perhaps a wild bees' nest, it is supported by its prehensile tail—a baby animal can hang by its tail at only seven weeks. Kinkajous live alone in nests in hollow trees, but large troops may congregate in trees bearing ripe fruit.

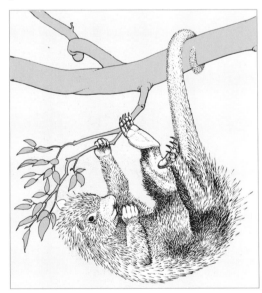

A tree-living porcupine, *Coendou prehensilis*, inhabits the jungles of Central and South America. Its main adaptation is the long, prehensile tail, which curls upward rather than downward as in most other prehensile-tailed animals. The upper part of the tip of the tail is naked and has a calloused pad for extra grip. Tree porcupines live in small groups and lead inoffensive lives, feeding on shoots and leaves.

The agile spider monkey lives in the Brazilian jungles. Its strong, prehensile tail can support its entire weight, allowing incredible reach. Its five-legged appearance earns the monkey its common name.

The black and white colobus, *Colobus polykomos*, is one of the most elegant of African monkeys. Its plumed tail is not prehensile but acts as rudder and parachute to control the monkey's great leaps.

When swinging through the trees the spider monkey uses its hands like hooks to catch on to branches. Thumbs are unnecessary for this action and have become mere stumps. This lessens manipulative ability, but the monkey can hold fruit in its tail and pick off the shell with its teeth. The sensitive tip of the tail is patterned like human fingertips to increase friction and aid grip.

61

Fliers and gliders

The first vertebrates to try true flight 180 million years ago were reptiles with rib-supported wings. Today there are no reptiles capable of true flight—defined as sustained passage—but there are several species which can glide from a higher to a lower place. There are some mammals that glide, and a frog. The ability to glide adds a new dimension to an animal's life in the jungle canopy, for not only can it escape from predators more effectively, but it can also search for food over a wider range.

Gliding requires a winglike membrane which, in its simplest form, may be only a fold of skin projecting from the side of the body. Several mammals have this type of wing, or patagium, attached to the wrist and ankle. They use subdermal muscles to pull the wing away when it is not in use, but, when ready to glide, they relax these muscles and extend their limbs, thus allowing the membrane to spread to its fullest extent. Tail action, together with small movements of one or more limbs, provides the animal with directional stability. The flight membrane of flying frogs—the webbing between the toes—is similarly uncomplicated.

A more complex arrangement is found in the Malaysian flying snakes. These tree-dwelling species do not possess a special membrane, but they do have the ability to pull in their ventral surfaces, flatten out their ribs and slightly rotate their scales to produce a concavity that traps a cushion of air beneath them as they glide. By making lateral 'swimming' movements, these snakes are able to steer. At the end of its 'flight' the snake makes a sudden upward flick of the head which ensures a safe, smooth landing on to a tree or branch.

The 'flying dragons' of the South Pacific islands possess the most complex type of membrane. These lizards have a series of elongated, mobile ribs, covered with a tough skin, which project from the sides of their bodies. When a lizard is feeding or resting, the wings are folded away. When it launches itself off a tall tree, strong muscle action extends the ribs and holds them rigid. Such a system is aerodynamically sound because there are many small muscles associated with the wing which can change its trim during flight. This adaptation allows the lizard to travel long distances as well as perform complicated banking and rolling manoeuvres in the air.

Fossils found in England dating back to the late Tertiary period (some 180 million years ago) show that reptiles had rib-supported wings at that time. The flying dragons of today probably resemble those first flying vertebrates.

True flight, however, demands membranes that can be flapped by muscular action to provide lift. In the bats, the membrane is formed by the arm and four of the five digits. For flapping flight, strong chest muscles are needed to pull the wings downward, and this necessitates a rigid thoracic chamber and a big keeled breastbone. The manoeuvrability of tiny forest bats as they swoop and twist in pursuit of minuscule insects indicates how well their wings can be controlled. Bats and birds are the only vertebrate animals to feed on the wing; the many gliding species use their fascinating though limited powers of flight primarily to try and escape their predators.

The flying lemur or colugo, *Cynocephalus variegatus*, can glide distances of up to 443ft (135m) with a loss of altitude of 40ft (12m).

Female colugos sometimes use their flight membrane as a cradle for their young. These Southeast Asian animals are nocturnal, emerging from their nests at dusk to feed on fruit, buds, flowers and leaves. To ensure safe landing after gliding, the colugo's short toes are armed with sharp, recurved claws. Colugos are agile climbers.

Few snakes have developed the technique of gliding flight, even though many live in the trees. The paradise tree snake, *Chrysopelea pelias*, will 'fly' not only to escape the clutches of hawks and eagles, but also to speed through the jungle canopy in pursuit of its prey.

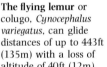
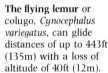

As a flying snake launches itself from a high point, it contracts its ventral surface and at the same time swivels the ribs upward and the lateral scales outward. While the snake glides as far as 160ft (50m), it holds its body stiffly but steers itself by 'swimming' movements.

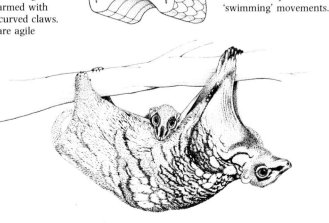

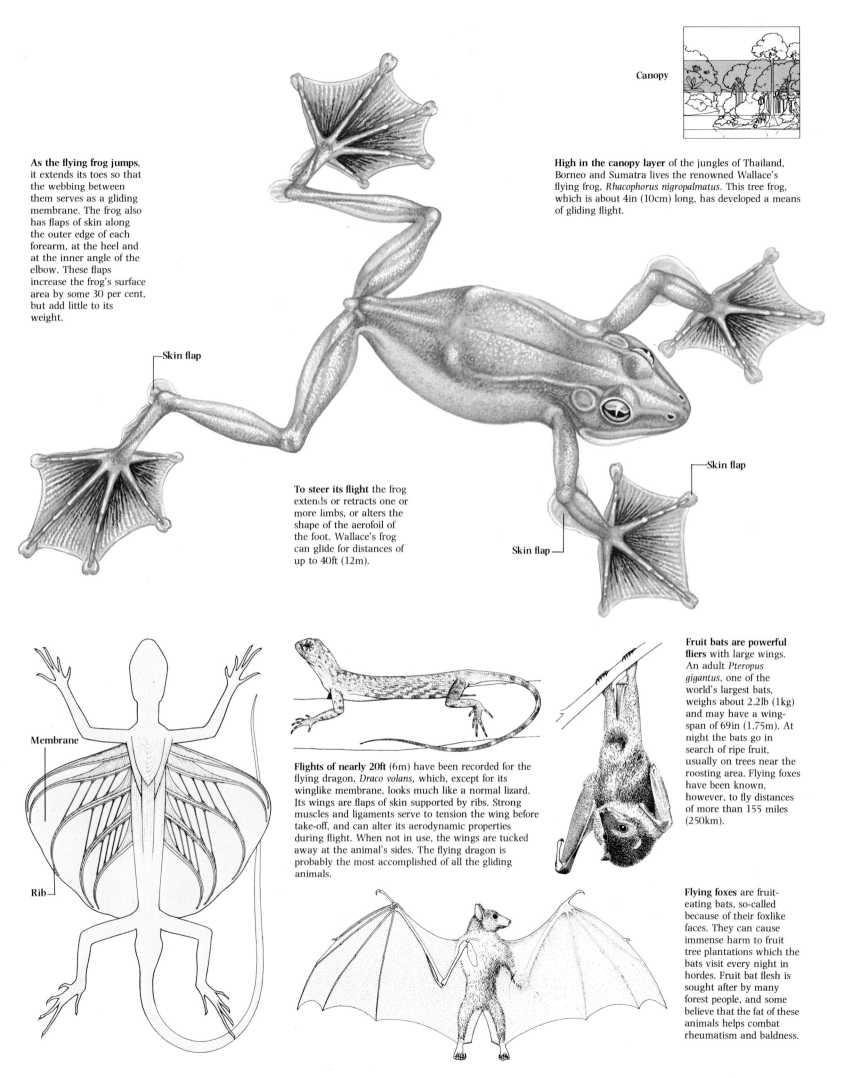

As the flying frog jumps, it extends its toes so that the webbing between them serves as a gliding membrane. The frog also has flaps of skin along the outer edge of each forearm, at the heel and at the inner angle of the elbow. These flaps increase the frog's surface area by some 30 per cent, but add little to its weight.

Skin flap

To steer its flight the frog extends or retracts one or more limbs, or alters the shape of the aerofoil of the foot. Wallace's frog can glide for distances of up to 40ft (12m).

Canopy

High in the canopy layer of the jungles of Thailand, Borneo and Sumatra lives the renowned Wallace's flying frog, *Rhacophorus nigropalmatus*. This tree frog, which is about 4in (10cm) long, has developed a means of gliding flight.

Skin flap

Skin flap

Membrane

Rib

Flights of nearly 20ft (6m) have been recorded for the flying dragon, *Draco volans*, which, except for its winglike membrane, looks much like a normal lizard. Its wings are flaps of skin supported by ribs. Strong muscles and ligaments serve to tension the wing before take-off, and can alter its aerodynamic properties during flight. When not in use, the wings are tucked away at the animal's sides. The flying dragon is probably the most accomplished of all the gliding animals.

Fruit bats are powerful fliers with large wings. An adult *Pteropus gigantus*, one of the world's largest bats, weighs about 2.2lb (1kg) and may have a wing-span of 69in (1.75m). At night the bats go in search of ripe fruit, usually on trees near the roosting area. Flying foxes have been known, however, to fly distances of more than 155 miles (250km).

Flying foxes are fruit-eating bats, so-called because of their foxlike faces. They can cause immense harm to fruit tree plantations which the bats visit every night in hordes. Fruit bat flesh is sought after by many forest people, and some believe that the fat of these animals helps combat rheumatism and baldness.

The fruit bats

Bats have always been associated with evil and witchcraft by some cultures but for others they have been objects of worship. This carved bat god is from Mexico and is at least a thousand years old.

As night falls over the tropical rain forests, bats emerge from their roosts in tree holes, under bark and vines and prepare to take to the wing. Except for a few species that feed on fish, on blood and on other bats, these mammals—the only ones capable of true flight—divide into two main feeding types: insect eaters, and flower and fruit eaters. The jungle, with trees flowering and fruiting all year round,

makes an ideal home for the latter types of bat.

Some bats simply feed on the whole fruit. They have a well-developed sense of smell that enables them to find a single ripe fruit among many unripe ones. The common bat *Carollia perspicillata*, indigenous to the jungles of Central and South America, detects exactly when bananas, guavas and plantains ripen. As a result, the natives who depend upon these fruits for a livelihood have to cut them while they are still green. Even if the fruits are stored inside a hut, the bats may seek them out. Using their teeth to crush the fruit, the bats drink the juice and swallow the soft pulp. Pronounced palatal ridges and a muscular tongue help fruit-eating bats extract all the juice from the waste; they compress the fruit skins and any large pips into peanut-sized pellets and spit them out.

Other types of bat feed on the nectar and pollen of flowers. In fact, some species of tree previously pollinated by birds are now pollinated primarily by bats. In the Old World plant family *Bignoniaceae*, the direction of change is from birds to bats, although in the related family *Bombacaceae*, the trend is in the reverse direction.

Those trees which rely upon bats for pollination and seed dispersal have evolved scents to attract them. Unlike the sweet, heavy odours which attract insects, these scents are musty, or even reminiscent of mammalian sweat. The guava, for example, smells strongly of butyric acid, a constituent of meat.

In general, bats are drawn to flowers that are drab, bloom at night and produce copious quantities of nectar and pollen. Many of these flowers even have rigid petals which the bats use as landing

platforms. All are large and strong enough for the bats to be able to insert their heads without fear of the flowers collapsing. When sucking the nectar and eating the pollen, the bats use their hooklike thumbs to grasp the flowers. Other bat plants have flowers massed into a ball-like inflorescence. In the West African dawadawa tree, *Parkia clappertoniana*, for instance, golfball-sized inflorescences of two thousand flowers each are produced after the leaves fall; these are a particular favourite of bats of the species *Epomophorus gambianus*. While hovering in front of a flower head, a bat usually gets pollen on its chest, which it transfers to the stigma of another inflorescence, thus effecting pollination.

Pollen- and nectar-feeding bats are adapted to their specialized diet. All have long tongues tipped with soft, threadlike outgrowths; these function like an absorbent paintbrush. In the three-inch-long bat *Megaloglossus woermanni*, the tongue is more than an inch long, allowing it to reach nectaries in the deepest tubular flowers. Since a bat does not need to chew this type of food, its teeth are small and weak. In most species of nectar bat, the teeth are capable of crushing the softest pulp, but cannot crush fruit.

Although the number of bats is second only to the number of rodents in the world, their shy and secretive habits mean that knowledge of their biology is fragmentary. On the whole they are useful creatures. Undoubtedly, the existence of many of the tree and plant species found in the tropical rain forests depend upon the pollinating ability of these specialized fruit- and flower-feeding bats.

One of the smallest fruit bats, the West African bat *Megaloglossus woermanni* is 3in (7.5cm) long. It feeds on nectar and pollen which it extracts from flowers with its long bristly tongue.

By night bats search for food and by day they sleep hanging in trees or caves. Many species of fruit bat are gregarious and roost in groups of hundreds of individuals on one tree. At first young bats travel with their mother all the time, but later they remain in the roost while she hunts.

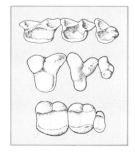

The teeth of fruit bats reflect their diet. Bats feeding on nectar and pollen have small, weak teeth, *top*. Fruit and nectar feeders have poorly developed teeth with low cusps, *middle*; those feeding on fruit only have broad flat molars and well formed incisors, *bottom*.

The long-tongued bat, *Glossophaga soricina*, of Central and South America has a rough-surfaced tongue which, when protruded, is longer than the bat's head. As the bat probes a flower for nectar it collects pollen on its chin and neck. When it visits the next flower some of this pollen is transferred, and pollination is accomplished. In return the plant produces copious amounts of nectar.

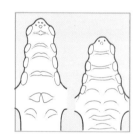

On the roof of the mouth of a fruit-eating bat are several horny ridges against which the muscular tongue presses fruit. The ridges function like a juice strainer and allow the bat to spit out only the fruit skin and pips. The ridge pattern varies according to the species.

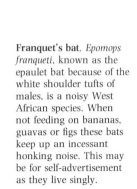

Franquet's bat, *Epomops franqueti*, known as the epaulet bat because of the white shoulder tufts of males, is a noisy West African species. When not feeding on bananas, guavas or figs these bats keep up an incessant honking noise. This may be for self-advertisement as they live singly.

65

The camouflaged killers

The cats—some of the most beautiful of all the forest creatures—live in the jungle understorey. Representatives of the cat family are found throughout the world except in the Arctic and Antarctic wastes, the Malagasy Republic and Australasia. They are excellent climbers, although many spend a great deal of time on the ground tracking and stalking their prey. Cats are exclusively meat eaters and, while a starving cat will not walk past some carrion, all prefer to hunt for their food. Small cats, such as the South American margay, prey on small rodents, birds and lizards; large species such as the jaguar, attack brocket deer, tapir and other large game. Since each species of cat occupies its own feeding niche, several species may be found in the same jungle.

Cats have always occupied a special place in man's culture and affection. Two thousand years before the birth of Christ, the ancient Egyptians entombed mummified cats with the bodies of their princes and kings, and from 850 B.C. the people of the Amazon worshipped a feline deity. Effigies of the jaguar and the puma adorned the carvings of their sarcophagi, and the power of 'el tigre' is still strongly felt by many jungle tribes. In the east of Bolivia, where the jaguar is common, young men have to kill a specimen single-handed, armed only with a wooden spear, before they may become warriors.

Unfortunately, modern man has developed a new cat cult that has brought many species to the brink of extinction. Fur coats made of ocelot skins were selling for $40,000 in Munich in 1979; these prices will inevitably rise as the animals become scarcer. Stricter enforcement of wildlife legislation makes smuggling more profitable—in 1977, 2,770 jaguar skins entered the United Kingdom from Brazil to be made into coats that only a few people can afford to buy. Although legislation is reducing the number of these majestic creatures killed each year, the real danger is that their present populations are so low that males will soon be unable to find females for breeding. Despite the fact that most species of cat breed well in captivity, anyone who has seen big cats in the wild will know how pitiful they look behind bars.

Cats are top predators—that is, the big species and most of the small are without enemies, at least as adults. They kill when they need to eat; an adult jaguar, for example, needs about one peccary a week, while a nursing female needs more. This means they must occupy an area in which sufficient food will be found for a family's needs. A female jaguar holds a territory of up to six square miles; a female margay requires just a tenth of that.

Man's stock of domestic animals is always vulnerable to marauding attacks, and this provides justification for cat-hunting expeditions. Stockmen are blind to the fact that cats are beneficial to man—they kill rodents and other small animals that spread disease and compete for grass. Hopefully, the spirit of enlightenment that is burgeoning in Europe and North America will continue to flourish before greed and irresponsibility destroy the world's jungles.

Dubbed the clouded leopard, *Neofelis nebulosa*, because of the indistinct edges to its spots, this rare Southeast Asian animal spends much of its life hunting and sleeping up in the trees.

The spotted coats of jungle cats work with the dappled forest light to deceive the eye of their prey. Rudyard Kipling wrote about these in 'How the Leopard got his Spots' (*Just So Stories*). Plains-living cats like the lion have lost their spots, although traces may still be seen in the young.

The ocelot or painted leopard, *Felis pardalis*, lives in the Central and South American jungles. It measures up to 40in (1m) long with a 20in (50cm) tail and is capable of killing peccaries, deer and large rodents.

The **golden cat**, *Felis aurata*, lives only in the forests of West Africa. It is about twice the size of a domestic cat and preys on birds and small antelopes.

The **two-spotted palm civet**, *Nandinia binotata*, of equatorial Africa, is a nocturnal hunter, feeding on small rodents, birds and lizards. Civets will also eat fruit, which they hold in their forepaws while sitting up on a branch.

The **servaline genet**, *Genetta servalina*, is a long-tailed member of the mongoose family which lives in the West African jungles. It spends its day in a tree hole, emerging at dusk to hunt tree-roosting birds.

One of the rarest of the cat-sized African carnivores is the linsang, *Poiana richardsoni*. It is about 13in (33cm) long with a tail as long as 15in (38cm). Natives use the skins of linsangs to make medicine bags.

The largest cat in South America, the adult jaguar, *Panthera onca*, weighs between 155 and 300lb (70 and 135kg) and is up to 6ft (1.8m) long, excluding the tail. It is more heavily built than the Asian leopard and has black markings inside its spots. The name jaguar is derived from the Indian word '*jaguara*', which means 'animal that overcomes its prey in a single bound'. A means of attack favoured by the jaguar is to wait high in the branches and then to drop silently on the back of its prey. The jaguar also eats fish, and will sit dangling the tip of its tail in the water. When a fish rises to inspect the lure the jaguar quickly scoops it up.

Clamberers and climbers

Amid the jungle understorey branches, with their lacework of galleries and runways, many animals with limbs adapted for climbing and grasping have found their home. The animals best suited to this part of the forest tend to be small and light, although some, such as the tree kangaroo, and the larger cats, such as the jaguar, are restricted by their size to the thicker branches.

Prehensile tails, so effectively used by canopy-living monkeys of South America, are seldom found in understorey animals. Indeed, some of the most successful creatures of this habitat, the lorises, are tailless. The majority of species, however, have tails that are often long, bushy and distinctively marked, such as those of the coati and several species of lemur. The aye-aye and the tree kangaroo have tails almost one and a half times as long as their bodies. All these creatures use their tails as counterbalances when they are leaping from branch to branch or when they are sitting eating. The aye-aye, like the tree squirrels in the temperate forests, wraps its tail around its body when sleeping, presumably to keep warm.

The understorey animals have hands and feet adapted, in varying degrees, for grasping. The species which spend most of their lives in the trees, such as the lorises, have the most specialized feet; those which often forage on the forest floor, such as the coati, have relatively unspecialized ones. Digital mobility in the loris's hand has been sacrificed in favour of a pincerlike grip. Special muscle fibres in the limbs, and an enhanced blood supply to these regions, enable the loris to grip on to things for long periods. Slow lorises, *Nycticebus coucang*, can hang by just one leg while they feed.

In contrast, the short-legged, stout-bodied coatis simply have large, strong claws that enable them to secure a hold. Extremely agile, they throw out their limbs as they race through the forest almost as if they were grappling irons. Similarly, the hands and feet of tree kangaroos show little modification from those of their grassland cousins; they are almost equally at home on the ground and in the branches. Their claws, however, are sharp and massive like crampons, and the soles of their hands and feet are particularly rough to provide maximum friction for gripping branches.

Essentially arboreal, the majority of primates live in the understorey, with just a few of the larger species inhabiting the forest floor. Some groups, such as the lemurs, are found only in the Malagasy Republic (Madagascar), although fossil deposits reveal they once roamed African forests. Freed from competition with monkeys, lemurs have been able to survive on this island, but, sadly, the populations of several species are threatened as forests are cleared for agricultural development. The understorey primates are never numerous, for most are carnivores or omnivores, and thus need to roam over a large area to find sufficient food. Since they are the prey of many cats, hawks, eagles and snakes, these forest primates have become nocturnal, and developed excellent night vision. The main threat to their survival is man's encroachment upon their jungle home.

One of the most bizarre primates, the aye-aye, *Daubentonia madagascariensis*, lives in the forests of the Malagasy Republic. The aye-aye's most curious feature is the enormously long third digit, with which it extracts insect larvae from decaying wood. Natives fear the aye-aye—one touch is said to cause death.

When first discovered, the aye-aye was thought to be a rodent because it has large, chisel-like incisor teeth. Having located a burrowing grub by smell and sound, the aye-aye gnaws away the wood and extracts the morsel with its long middle finger.

Living in the jungle belt of Africa, the potto, *Perodicticus potto*, belies its cuddly appearance—a row of horny spikes between its shoulders can be turned on any would-be aggressor. The potto's hands are modified for grasping, with a strong stubby thumb.

Handsome, lemurlike primates, sifakas, *Propithecus verreauxi*, have long, silky fur and dark, hairless faces. Their habit of sitting with their open palms stretched out to the sun has given rise to the legend that they are sun worshippers.

The loris's resemblance to a clown so struck the Dutch sailors who first encountered this animal that they called it by the Dutch name for clown—loeris. The startled look of the loris is caused by its huge forward pointing eyes and prominent facial markings. The modified hand, *right*, allows an astonishingly powerful grip which can be maintained for long periods. Lorises are up to 16in (40cm) long and feed on small mammals and birds, berries and shoots.

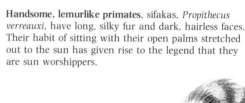

Tree kangaroos live in the New Guinea forests. They are quite large for tree-dwelling animals— *Dendrolagus ursinus* measures up to 32in (81cm) with a tail of 38in (96cm). They feed on fruits and leaves and, like the ground kangaroos, have pouches.

Bands of as many as 40 coatis, *Nasua nasua*, roam the forests of Central and South America seeking birds, lizards, frogs, insects, fruit and berries. Coatis have long mobile snouts with which they probe into narrow cracks in the trees in search of food.

Amphibians and reptiles

Living in the jungle understorey in South America are tiny frogs which have in their body a poison so strong that one millionth of an ounce of it can kill a dog. These arrow-poison frogs, Dendrobatidae, are one dramatic example of the huge variety of reptiles and amphibians in the jungle.

Although reptiles have waterproof skins and are not restricted to damp places, amphibians readily lose water from their bodies and so must live in moist, dark areas. Jungle is ideal. They must lay their eggs in water; first, for protection, as the eggs do not have shells, and second, for the aquatic tadpole stage. The arrow-poison frogs lay two or three eggs in a wet place, though not actually in water. When the young hatch, they climb on to their father's back for transportation to the forest understorey. There he deposits his charges in a water-filled bromeliad whorl. As these tiny ponds are also used by insects, there is plenty of food for the developing tadpoles.

Other frogs have reacted to the vulnerability of their eggs in different ways; in Darwin's frog, *Rhinoderma darwini*, the male takes the newly fertilized eggs into his mouth and protects them in a throat sac until they develop into tadpoles.

For the reptiles—lizards, chameleons and snakes—the forest understorey presents other threats: chief among these are eagles and predatory mammals such as coatis. Most of these vulnerable reptiles are camouflaged to some extent; they are either dappled brownish-orange, as some chameleons, or bright green, as the Papuan tree python, *Chondropython viridis*. Tree snakes tend to give birth to living young, unlike the ground-living snakes, which lay eggs. Although there are fewer offspring produced this way, each has a greater chance of survival if it can remain within its mother's body for the early part of its development.

Cryptic camouflage, in addition to protecting jungle reptiles against predatory attack, serves another equally important purpose—making them invisible to their prey. Several tree snakes mimic twigs and branches in form as well as hue, and even sway from side to side to simulate the effect of air movement. Geckos resemble tree bark to the extent of having raised knobs on their skin that resemble irregularities in the bark. Their camouflage is so realistic that insects and small vertebrates are unaware of the danger that threatens them as they approach these lizards. In fact, most tree-dwelling reptiles catch their prey by remaining invisible until the moment of their surprise attack. In the chameleon, the ability to assume a cryptic disguise has been greatly refined. As the light on the reptile changes, so does the shade of the animal's skin.

Nearly all arboreal reptiles have prehensile tails. For the tree snakes, this adaptation allows them to shoot out for almost their whole length when striking at a prey. Arboreal frogs have special suction pads on their feet which enable them to cling to the underside of shiny leaves. Geckos also have suction pads on their feet which help them to climb. With specialized features such as these, both amphibians and reptiles have been able to adapt remarkably well to life in the jungle understorey.

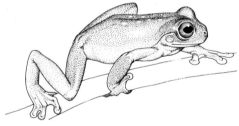

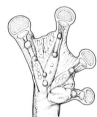

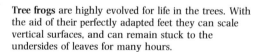

Tree frogs are highly evolved for life in the trees. With the aid of their perfectly adapted feet they can scale vertical surfaces, and can remain stuck to the undersides of leaves for many hours.

Arrow-poison frogs deposit their developing tadpoles in the pools of water inside bromeliads. To extract the poison from these frogs for use on arrow tips, South American Indians hold the frogs over flames until the poison oozes from the skin. The poison, called batrachotoxin, acts on the heart and the nervous system.

Each digit of a tree frog's foot has a disklike suction pad. The pad is supported by a piece of cartilage, the shape of which can be changed by muscular action. The surface of the pad is covered with cells which secrete a sticky mucus.

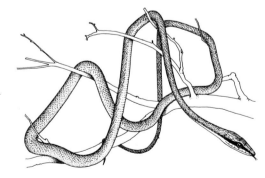

The vine snake, *Thelotornis kirtlandii*, of West Africa hangs motionless among the twigs of understorey trees watching for prey. It darts out to snatch a lizard, frog or insect. The snake is well concealed by its cryptic coloration and angular pose and has only to wait for prey to approach.

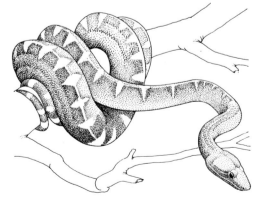

The emerald tree boa, *Corallus caninus*, of Amazonia is a constricting snake; it has no poison but strangles its prey—small rodents, young birds and, occasionally, lizards—with its muscular coils. Its bright green skin conceals it among the foliage from predators such as the harpy eagle.

In 4/100ths of a second a chameleon shoots out its tongue, traps an insect and returns it to its mouth. The prey has no chance of escape. The tip of the chameleon's tongue is split. At the moment it grasps prey, muscular action forces the parts together in a pincerlike grip.

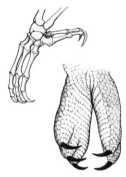

The feet of the chameleon are adapted for grasping branches. Each foot is like a clamp with two toes on one side and three on the other ensuring a firm and steady hold.

A chameleon can lighten or darken its skin almost instantaneously. This ability to camouflage itself is vital for its role both as predator and prey, but the chameleon also changes shade for purely physiological reasons. In bright sunlight when the temperature is high, the chameleon's skin lightens and, like all pale surfaces, reflects heat. As the day wanes and temperature and light intensity decrease, the dark pigment cells expand and the skin darkens. Like this, the body absorbs as much solar radiation as possible. But if danger threatens at any time of day, this process occurs in seconds.

Spinal nerve — Spinal cord

Pigment cells

The network of pigment cells controls the chameleon's camouflage system. These chromatophores expand and contract when stimulated by messages travelling along the spinal nerves from the spinal cord and the brain. Patterning occurs when one group of cells is more stimulated than another.

The mouth cavity of the chameleon can be seen as an open-ended cylinder. With tongue and central tongue bone retracted, the hyoid horns are rocked forward. Flanges on the horns hold the tongue. To fire the tongue, the three muscle blocks contract, protruding the central tongue bone and rocking back the horns. This frees the tongue from the restraint of the flanges. The tongue muscle contracts, shooting the ever-narrowing tongue along the tongue bone.

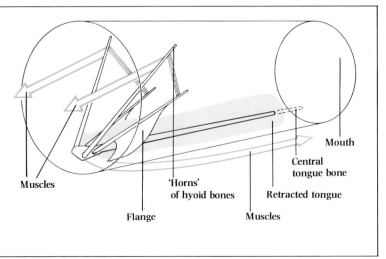

Muscles

'Horns' of hyoid bones

Flange

Muscles

Mouth

Central tongue bone

Retracted tongue

The foragers

For animals prepared to root for their food, the forest floor provides a lush home. Literally millions of ants, termites, spiders, land crabs, beetles, molluscs, earthworms and many other invertebrate animals live on or near the soil surface. And there is an abundance of roots, tubers and rhizomes, as well as above-ground shoots to tempt those whose diet is strictly vegetarian. Digging for food takes time, however, and while an animal is searching among the leaf litter for a tasty morsel, it is vulnerable to a surprise attack from a jaguar, puma or tiger. A few species have evolved effective means of defending themselves, but several of the larger species, such as the peccary and the giant forest hog, can survive only by feeding in groups, with one or

two individuals acting as sentries. Although small, rat-sized animals are not free from attack either, they can hide in crevices under roots and other vegetation until danger has passed.

Among the rooters, the chief adaptations relate to the specific diet of the individual species. Insectivores, such as the moon rats of Southeast Asia, tenrecs of the Malagasy Republic and the armoured shrews of the Congo, are the least specialized. These creatures have many teeth—a primitive condition that allows them to feed on a mixed diet of invertebrates from earthworms to land crabs, and occasionally fish. All tend to have spiny hairs, but they are not as well-armed as their more familiar relatives the hedgehogs.

A number of specialized anteating mammals feed largely upon one of the most common forest-floor invertebrates—the termite. In South America some anteaters have pursued their quarry up into the trees and have become adapted to an arboreal life, but the biggest, the giant anteater, is still a floor dweller. This remarkable animal is as much as 6 feet (1.8m) long. It collects its insect food with a long tongue coated with sticky saliva.

Other disparate forms that have stayed on the forest floor have come to look alike superficially because they exploit the same food source. They exemplify 'evolutionary convergence'. Principal among these are the armadillos of the New World and the pangolins of the Old World. Both animals

The **white-lipped peccary**, *Tayassu pecari*, lives deep in the Amazon forest. Bands of 50 to 100 peccaries of both sexes and all ages roam slowly through the jungle sniffing out underground bulbs and shoots. They will also kill and eat snakes, and are said to be unaffected by the venom of the bushmaster snake.

The **striking black and white body** of the Malayan tapir, *Tapirus indicus*, camouflages it in the forest by breaking up its outline. All young tapirs are patterned with stripes and spots which conceal them from predators in the same way. These markings disappear as the tapirs mature.

The **giant forest hog**, *Hylochoerus meinertzhageni*, is the largest wild pig and weighs as much as 600lb (275kg). Herds of 15 to 20 hogs search the West African forests for bushes and shoots. The hogs are feared for their unpredictable tempers and the Terekis warriors greatly prize shields made of giant hog hide.

The **giant armadillo**, *Priodontes giganteus*, from eastern Amazonia is the only truly jungle-dwelling armadillo. This animal is 4ft (1.2m) long, weighs up to 100lb (45kg) and is one of the most powerful diggers in the animal kingdom. The curved claws on its front feet are the largest found on any animal today. The armadillo uses these claws to dig for its food—worms, larvae, beetles and termites.

have armour-plated backs, massive fore-claws and long, thin snouts. The pangolin has no teeth, but possesses a tongue up to 12 inches (30cm) long. It scoops up insects with its tongue, then swallows them whole. The armadillo has more teeth than any other land mammal—up to 100. However, the armadillo's teeth often wear out before the animal is old, and they appear not to be particularly functional. Even though the armour-plating devices of the two creatures differ in appearance and structure, they serve the same protective purpose.

Swine in the Old World feed primarily upon underground tubers, roots and fungi, but pigs are not native to the New World. In the Amazon jungle they are replaced by two species of peccary. Pigs

and peccaries are close relatives, each having adapted to a similar set of conditions in different parts of the world. Both have shovel-like snouts that can be used as powerful diggers, both live in large herds, and both are equally unpredictable in behaviour.

One of the strangest of the jungle rooters is the tapir. There are three species in South America and one from the Malaysian and Sumatran jungles. All belong to the same genus (*Tapirus*) and provide evidence that the American and Asian continents were once joined together by the Bering Strait landbridge. Although they originated in the northern hemisphere when its climate was tropical, tapirs are restricted today to two widely separated

places that were formerly part of a continuous distribution. All tapirs have rounded, sturdy bodies and tapering snouts, ideal for easy movement through the jungle vegetation. They are surprisingly good swimmers and spend much of their lives in or near water. Unlike peccaries, tapirs live singly or in pairs.

In every part of the world's jungles, hogs, peccaries and tapirs are used as a major source of meat and skins by native tribes. But modern man and his projects are threatening to destroy these, along with all other floor-dwelling animals of the jungle, by cutting down the rain forests and clearing the land for farms and ranches. Their habitat is fast disappearing.

The moon rat, *Echinosorex gymnurus*, is one of the foulest smelling of all animals. Rat is a misnomer as these animals are insectivores, not rodents. They measure about 16in (40cm) from nose to rump and feed on snails, worms, insects and land crabs.

Tenrecs are found only on the island of the Malagasy Republic. The tailless species, *Tenrec ecaudatus*, lives in the jungle and mangrove swamps. It emerges from its burrow at night and, using its long mobile nose, searches for its food —insects, worms and plant shoots.

With its long tongue and snout the giant anteater is highly specialized for feeding on ants and termites. Powerful claws on its front feet are used for ripping open the insects' nests; the anteater keeps its claws sharp by walking on its knuckles with the claws held well out of the way. The mother carries her young on her back.

The herbivores

Sunlight has little opportunity to filter down through the thick canopy of leaves to the jungle floor, so plant growth there is severely retarded. As a result, most of the herbivorous mammals that live on the rain forest floor are small and lead retiring lives. In constant danger of attack from leopards and jaguars, these creatures escape by leaping high into the air just as a predator attacks. There are a few larger species, such as the okapi, *Okapia johnstoni*, of West Africa, and the elephants of the African and Asian jungles, which are specifically adapted for feeding on the understorey layer while standing on the forest floor. Perhaps the lowland gorilla, *Gorilla gorilla*, of West Africa is best able to enjoy both the forest floor and the understorey. Although it spends its life on the ground, it climbs into the understorey to feed and occasionally sleeps in low trees.

No large herbivores feed directly on the forest floor, as there is insufficient plant growth to support them. Elephants, okapis and jungle cattle, such as the Malaysian banteng require huge amounts of food each day. Known as bulk feeders, these

animals are not fussy about the quality of the food they eat, since their stomachs are adapted to cope with the toughest and most fibrous materials. In complete contrast are the small herbivores of the forest floor that have adapted to the low overall level of primary production by becoming highly selective in what they eat. These concentrate feeders search for the highest-quality foods—usually buds, growing tips, fruits and fleshy roots—and thus make up in high-energy foods what they miss in bulk. To enable them to nip out the right piece of a chosen food plant, they use their small, delicate mouths and sensitive lips. If they eat a piece of leaf or fibrous twig by accident, they are able to reject it quickly with their lips and tongue. Animals of this type are found in jungles throughout the world.

In the bulk feeders, the chief physical adaptations are designed for obtaining food from above their heads. The okapi, for example, has an elongated neck and a particularly long muscular tongue, with a rough, scale-like surface to enhance its efficiency as a kind of bill-hook. The elephants

have long trunks and short necks. The trunk, which is derived from the nose and the upper lip, is sensitive and strong, enabling the elephant to choose a single ripe fruit from among many unripe ones, or to lift up a fallen tree trunk. Elephants tend to eat fibrous, woody plant material; they tear down whole branches and then eat them. The banteng, though a dweller of the forest edge as well as the jungle proper, is more like the okapi because it prefers twigs and leaves to branches. It does not need any special feeding adaptations for its less specialized life, but it does have an extremely long tongue.

Like most monkeys and apes, the gorilla uses its hands for grabbing food—nuts, berries, fruits, shoots and leaves. Even though its fingers are thick and stubby, the gorilla manages to remove skins and pips with its lips and teeth, supplementing its hands. Gorillas generally gather their food in the trees and consume it on the ground. Each species of forest floor herbivore has adapted its method of feeding so that it can function well in an area of low biological activity.

Gorillas live in troops of up to 40 individuals, but 15 is a common number. A troop includes one adult dominant male, several other males, females and young. Although they roam over a large area, their slow progress allows time for grooming and play.

The largest of the great apes, the adult male lowland gorilla may be nearly 6ft 6in (2m) tall and weigh up to 660lb (300kg). The hair is black and coarse, becoming silver-grey on the back of an old male. Gorillas are quiet, docile animals unless wounded or cornered, when they can fight ferociously. Their only natural enemies are leopards.

Until 1901, the existence of the okapi escaped the notice of African explorers, although it had been hunted by pygmies for centuries. Sir Harry Johnston, Governor of Uganda and the discoverer of the okapi, thought it was related to the zebra because of its size— 5ft 6in (1.7m) at the shoulder and 6ft 6in (2m) from head to rump. Indeed, the okapi's stripes serve the same purpose as those of the zebra—to break up the outline and conceal it from the eyes of its main enemy, the leopard. Adult males, however, have short, fur-covered horns like giraffes, and these, with features of the teeth and skull, indicate that the okapi is an aberrant, jungle-dwelling type of giraffe. The okapi feeds on understorey vegetation with the aid of a tongue so long that it can also be used to clean the eyes and eyelids.

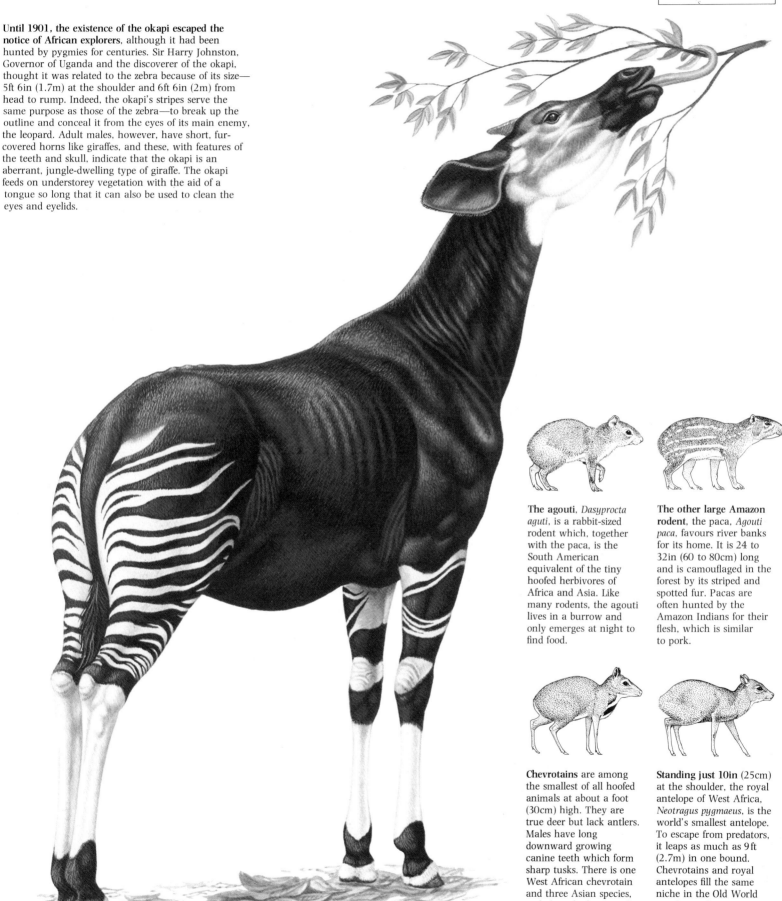

The agouti, *Dasyprocta aguti*, is a rabbit-sized rodent which, together with the paca, is the South American equivalent of the tiny hoofed herbivores of Africa and Asia. Like many rodents, the agouti lives in a burrow and only emerges at night to find food.

The other large Amazon rodent, the paca, *Agouti paca*, favours river banks for its home. It is 24 to 32in (60 to 80cm) long and is camouflaged in the forest by its striped and spotted fur. Pacas are often hunted by the Amazon Indians for their flesh, which is similar to pork.

Chevrotains are among the smallest of all hoofed animals at about a foot (30cm) high. They are true deer but lack antlers. Males have long downward growing canine teeth which form sharp tusks. There is one West African chevrotain and three Asian species, including the lesser Malay chevrotain.

Standing just 10in (25cm) at the shoulder, the royal antelope of West Africa, *Neotragus pygmaeus*, is the world's smallest antelope. To escape from predators, it leaps as much as 9ft (2.7m) in one bound. Chevrotains and royal antelopes fill the same niche in the Old World jungles as the agouti and paca do in the New.

Killers at ground level

The word jungle suggests a place seething with aggressive, dangerous predators, but this is a misconception. Nowhere are predators numerous, and many of those that do live in the jungle are seldom seen. Forest floor snakes lie curled up and partly buried in the detritus of fallen leaves and twigs. They do not hunt often because, as they do not maintain a constant body temperature, they are not obliged to burn up stored food continually for the energy to stay alive. Predatory mammals are more in evidence. They hunt for food more frequently than snakes, as they must keep their body temperature constant.

A number of medium-sized and large herbivores live on the forest floor—prey for the large understorey cats. The truly ground-living predators, such as the bush dog and the bushmaster snake, concentrate on smaller mammals, mostly rodents, as well as frogs, toads and lizards. The venomous bushmaster will even tackle small deer. It finds its prey with a pair of heat sensors on its head. These organs detect heat rays and enable the snake to locate an object that is warmer than its surroundings. Even deprived of sight and smell, a pit viper can hunt successfully by this method. It can detect changes in temperature of as little as 0.005 degrees centigrade—the heat emitted by a mouse some 6 inches (15cm) away from the snake.

In general, the floor-living carnivores do not have feet adapted for clinging and grasping, because they rarely climb trees. The sloth bear is an exception, with digits armed with long curved claws that can tear open termite and other insect nests, as well as dismember a rodent or a bird easily. Generalized carnivores, such as the grison and the tayra, which belong to the same family as the weasel, stoat, otter and badger, have remarkably unspecialized feet. Among nature's greatest opportunists, they feed on whatever prey they can catch. Their feet have hard, rough pads and strong short claws, similar to those of a dog. They have jaws and massive teeth that are powerful enough to kill young deer.

Whenever man has employed animals to help him hunt, he has turned to the carnivores. The jungle people of South America, for instance, tame young tayras and grisons, and then use them to flush rabbits and agoutis out of the thickest cover. In Chile, where grisons are found at altitudes of more than 4,000 feet (1,200m), they are trained to flush chinchillas out of cracks and crevices. In Guatemala, the tayra is called *perrito ligero*, meaning 'little swift dog', and is used to flush out small game. The natives believe the tayra has magical powers, and eat shavings of its penis bone, the baculum, as an aphrodisiac.

All the forest floor inhabitants have shy, retiring natures and are rarely seen. Only if threatened by man, or accidentally startled, will they unleash an aggressive attack—often fatal.

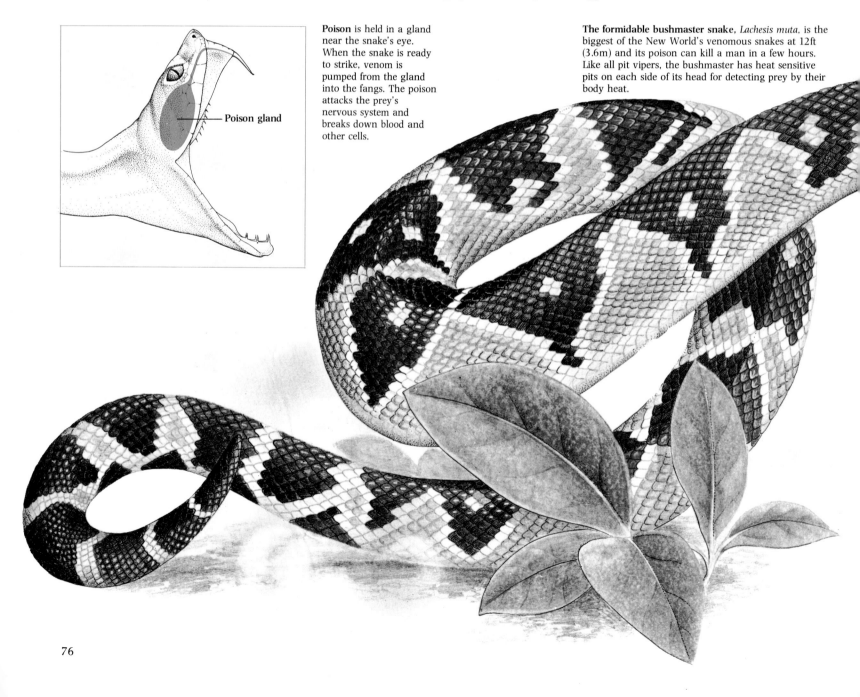

Poison is held in a gland near the snake's eye. When the snake is ready to strike, venom is pumped from the gland into the fangs. The poison attacks the prey's nervous system and breaks down blood and other cells.

— Poison gland

The formidable bushmaster snake, *Lachesis muta*, is the biggest of the New World's venomous snakes at 12ft (3.6m) and its poison can kill a man in a few hours. Like all pit vipers, the bushmaster has heat sensitive pits on each side of its head for detecting prey by their body heat.

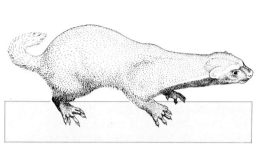

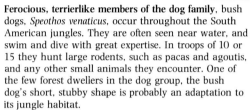

The grison, *Galictis vittata*, looks like a cross between a skunk and an otter. It is not restricted to jungle habitats, and occurs over much of Brazil. Grisons are very much at home in the water and feed on frogs and worms, as well as many ground-living animals; they generally hunt at night. Grisons live in groups of perhaps six individuals in a burrow. They do not dig their own homes, but take over burrows abandoned by agoutis.

The sloth bear, *Melursus ursinus*, lives in the tropical rain forests of southern India and Sri Lanka. Although they will feed on carrion, eggs and small reptiles, sloth bears are best adapted for feeding on termites. They protrude their lips into a tubular shape and use them like a vacuum cleaner to suck up termites, making a noise that can be heard 200yd (180m) away. These bears, which weigh up to 300lb (135kg), are agile climbers if disturbed.

Ferocious, terrierlike members of the dog family, bush dogs, *Speothos venaticus*, occur throughout the South American jungles. They are often seen near water, and swim and dive with great expertise. In troops of 10 or 15 they hunt large rodents, such as pacas and agoutis, and any other small animals they encounter. One of the few forest dwellers in the dog group, the bush dog's short, stubby shape is probably an adaptation to its jungle habitat.

The snake locates its prey by swinging its head from side to side to expose the heat organs to the heat emitted by the prey animal. The amount of heat decreases with distance from the prey, so the point between equal heat levels perceived by left and right pits is the direction in which to launch an attack.

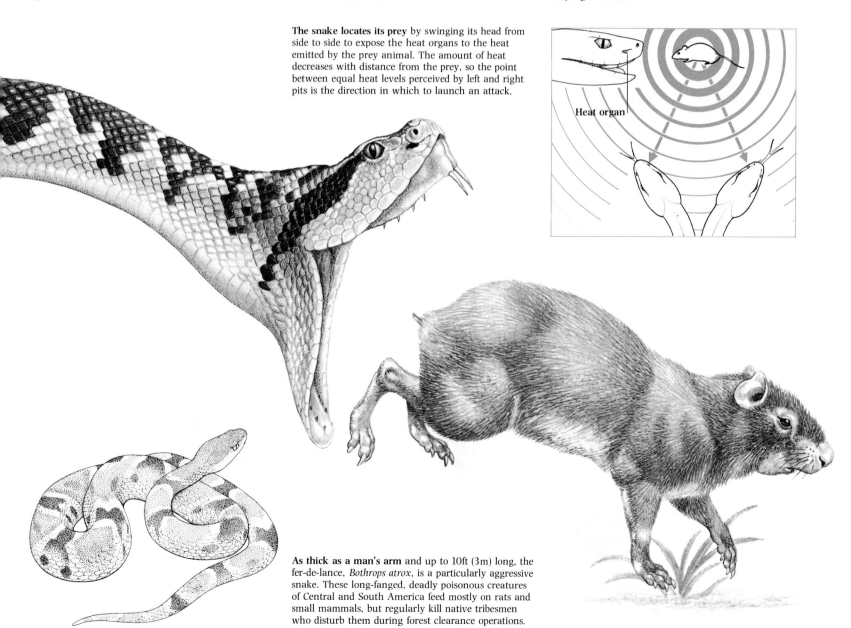

As thick as a man's arm and up to 10ft (3m) long, the fer-de-lance, *Bothrops atrox*, is a particularly aggressive snake. These long-fanged, deadly poisonous creatures of Central and South America feed mostly on rats and small mammals, but regularly kill native tribesmen who disturb them during forest clearance operations.

Creatures of the river

The rivers and streams which drain the world's jungles are home for a number of reptiles. Some, such as the anaconda, the world's largest snake, and the freshwater crocodiles, are feared by man; most lead quiet lives, partially submerged beneath the river's surface, feeding on fish, invertebrates and, in the case of turtles, plants.

The larger crocodiles and caimans lie in wait for a thirsty forest hog or a paca. In the water their enormously powerful tails give them almost un-believable grace and precision of movement, and their attacks are usually successful. Crocodiles seldom attack on dry land.

The riverside jungle tribes have long feared and respected the crocodiles of the Old World and the caimans of the New World. In the region of the Fly River of Papua New Guinea, the freshwater croco-diles, *Crocodylus novaeguineae*, traditionally pre-sented a threat to the natives whose bow-and-arrow and spear-hunting expeditions had little effect on the reptile populations. Once firearms were introduced, they no longer represented a menace. Female crocodiles lay about 30 eggs each year, of which more than 25 are normally eaten by monitor lizards or predatory birds. Under a government-assisted farming scheme, hatchlings are collected in the wild and brought into fenced stockades. Fed on fish and offal, the young crocodiles grow quickly. They are slaughtered for their skins when they are three years old. Although this farming has reversed the social and nutritional decline of the natives, it has had the unfortunate effect of stimulating world demand for crocodile skins and thus encouraging illegal poaching in other parts of the world.

In the rivers of South America are several species of turtle. Some, such as the matamata, *Chelys fimbriata*, are too small to serve as food for humans, but others (such as the seven species of Arran turtles, *Podocnemis*, from the Amazon basin) are large and palatable. The giant Arran turtle, *Podocnemis expansa*, is one of the largest turtles in the world and can weigh 110 pounds (50kg). In 1799 the naturalist Alexander von Humboldt esti-mated its population at more than one million on the lower Orinoco. Today it is much less numerous, but still abundant.

For the people of the várzea, the seasonally flooded area of the Amazon basin, turtle raising is a more attractive proposition than cattle raising. A one-acre lake of *Podocnemis* turtles can produce 440 times more meat annually than a one-acre cattle pasture (22,000lb/acre/year vs. 50lb/acre/year). Female giant Arrans are among the most fertile turtles, laying up to 150 eggs a year. Generally the hatchlings, but sometimes the eggs, are collected by the tribesmen and transported to semipermanent lakes, where they are supplied with aquatic plants and dead fish (even the most herbivorous turtles like to eat some animal flesh). There is a danger that the supply of turtle meat will create a new demand and so encourage indiscriminate hunting of adults.

Such husbandry schemes show what a rich asset the river is to the jungle people; with careful management it can provide them with a valuable and renewable resource.

The rivers and streams that flow through the jungle are rich in aquatic life, particularly those in Amazonia, *above*.

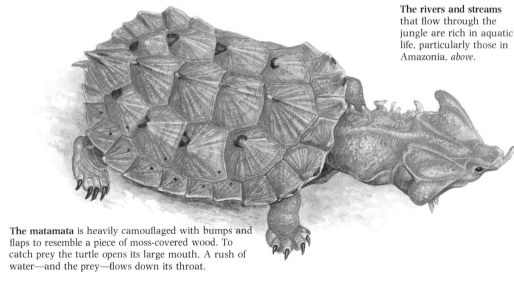

The matamata is heavily camouflaged with bumps and flaps to resemble a piece of moss-covered wood. To catch prey the turtle opens its large mouth. A rush of water—and the prey—flows down its throat.

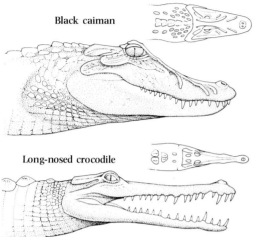

Black caiman

Long-nosed crocodile

The **Amazon black caiman**, *Melanosuchus niger*, is the New World equivalent of the long-nosed crocodile, *Crocodylus cataphractes*, of Africa. Both can grow 15ft (4.5m) long and will attack man. Their normal diet is of aquatic mammals and the jungle-dwelling creatures which drink at the water's edge. These two species of crocodile are the largest lizardlike carnivores in the world's jungles. Many jungle crocodiles, including the black caiman, are now extremely rare.

Mary Henrietta Kingsley (1862–1900) British traveller and writer who explored extensively in West Africa.

Mary Kingsley was an adventurous and enlightened woman. The niece of novelist Charles Kingsley, she had a studious interest in science.

Her first journey to West Africa, made on her own, lasted from August 1893 to January 1894. She sailed down the coast to Loanda, travelled from there overland through unexplored regions, and visited Kabinda and Matadi on the Congo River. Later in 1894 she made a second journey to West Africa. She travelled through the dangerous rapids of the Ogooue River in a canoe, and then journeyed in unexplored cannibal territory, posing as a trader. On her return she wrote a number of books, among them *Travels in West Africa* (1897).

Unlike many Europeans of the time, Mary Kingsley was insistent that the customs and views of the Africans should be respected, and believed that they should be allowed to govern themselves, albeit under European direction.

Lying partially submerged in the river, the spectacled caiman, *Caiman crocodylus*, waits for an unsuspecting but thirsty pacu or peccary. Originally found only in the Amazon and Orinoco basins, spectacled caimans now live in the swamps of Florida. These populations are thought to originate from pet baby caimans released by their owners when they become unmanageable.

The anaconda kills by strangulation. It rapidly winds around its prey, keeping a tight hold on the neck so the victim cannot bite back. The prey is asphyxiated in under a minute.

The largest snake in the world is the anaconda, *Eunectes murinus*, of the Amazon jungle. The longest recorded specimen is 37½ft (11.4m) although explorers have fantastic accounts of anacondas measuring 140ft (42m).

Creatures of the river/2

Whether a river is fertile or not depends largely upon the quality of the soils it flows through. If the soils are productive, the water will be teeming with fish, and local tribes can rely on it for their staple food. In places where rich rivers regularly flood, such as the seasonally flooded várzea area of Amazonia, the wealth of the river is transferred to the land, which in turn will yield abundant plant life. If the soils are poor, the river will provide little and the natives must go into the forest to look for food. The Rio Negro in Brazil, a deep, black, turbid river, is so sterile that the indigenous Indian population can use it only for transport.

Native tribes tend to hunt the largest river creatures and leave the smallest alone. In Amazonia the pig-sized capybara, *Hydrochoerus hydrochaeris*, the world's largest rodent, is a favoured food of many tribes. It spends most of its life in the river,

eating water plants, but comes out on to dry land to graze on lush bankside vegetation. In the forests of West Africa the capybara is replaced by the pygmy hippopotamus, *Choeropsis liberiensis*, which is sought with equal zeal by the pygmies. River people eat a wide variety of fish and have developed many hunting techniques to catch them. They poison fish with toxic jungle plants, shoot them with bows and arrows, or catch them with hand nets.

Humans are not the only enemies of fish; the largest otter in the world, *Pteronura brasiliensis*, which may reach over 6 feet (1.8m) in length, competes with the natives of northeastern Amazonia for food. Respected for its fish-catching ability by the Xingu river people, it is even kept by some of them as a pet. Nearer the coast, these gentle, playful creatures are themselves the targets of hunters' weapons, as their dense, soft pelts are highly prized.

Life for the river people is not without its hazards, for the water harbours many dangerous creatures, such as the electric eel, *Electrophorus electricus*, and parasitic catfish. In the Amazon the chief threat comes from the piranha fish. There are several carnivorous species, ranging in length from 12 to 20 inches (30 to 50cm), and each is equipped with vicious teeth. Since they usually swim in shoals of several hundred, any animal they attack stands little chance of surviving. Not all species of piranha are dangerous predators, some feed only on plants. One of these, the pacu, *Colossoma occulis*, is valued as a food source.

Despite these noxious animals, river people have a more secure life than their forest-dwelling counterparts. The bounty of most jungle rivers means that human population density is greater along their banks than elsewhere in the forest.

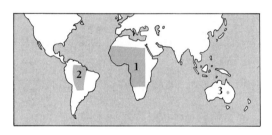

Protopterus aethiopicus

Lepidosiren paradoxa

Neoceratodus forsteri

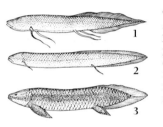

The powerfully jawed, air-breathing lungfish of today are the remnants of a group that flourished in the Devonian age which ended approximately 345 million years ago. Three distinct species remain and are distributed across the southern continents of the world in rain forest regions: one in the Amazon basin, one in West and Central Africa and one in two particular rivers in northern Queensland, Australia.

Manatees are aquatic mammals sometimes known as sea cows. Their nearest living relatives are elephants. The African manatee, *Trichechus senegalensis*, lives in the rivers of the West African rain forests feeding on water plants.

The river dolphin or bouto, *Inia geoffrensis*, lives in the Amazon and Orinoco rivers. These 3ft (10m) long mammals travel singly or in pairs searching for fish. Boutos are not hunted by the Indians as they are thought to be bewitched.

The candirú, *Vandellia cirrhosa*, is a parasitic catfish. About 2in (5cm) long and as slim as a match, this fish penetrates the gill chambers of larger fish; with its sharp teeth it starts a blood flow on which it feeds. The candirú also attacks man. Mistaking the underwater urination of the swimmer for the respiratory water flow of a fish, the candirú enters the urethra. It becomes lodged there by the barbs which normally help it stay in gill chambers. If it is not removed the victim dies.

The Amazonian capybara, *far left*, and the West African pygmy hippo, *left*, are ecological equivalents even though the former is a rodent and the latter a pig. Both feed on aquatic and bankside vegetation. The capybara is the more aquatic—it has partially webbed feet. At 3 to 4ft (90cm to 1.2m) long the capybara is the largest rodent in the world today.

River

The most lethal of predatory freshwater fish, the red piranha is 14in (35cm) long. Each fish can only bite off a thimbleful of flesh from the prey at a time but, because piranhas attack in shoals of hundreds, even a large animal such as a cow is devoured in minutes. The red piranha, *Serrasalmus nattereri*, is among the most ferocious of piranhas.

Alexander von Humboldt (1769–1859), German explorer and naturalist whose travels and researches laid the basis for the modern study of physical geography.

In 1799 Humboldt, with the French botanist Aimé Bonpland set out to make a scientific exploration of South America. They spent some months in Venezuela and then made a marathon 1,700 mile journey up the valley of the Orinoco River. Humboldt collected 12,000 botanical specimens and observed a fascinating range of wildlife. He investigated rubber, learned the secrets of curare, and made a detailed study of the piranha and the electric eel.

Despite the rigours of this journey, the two men went on to explore the sources of the Amazon and study the cold Peru Current—now named the Humboldt Current.

In 1808 Humboldt settled in Paris to work out and publish his conclusions. His *Personal Narrative of Travels to the Equinoctial Regions of America* (23 vols.) describes in accurate detail the wildlife of South America.

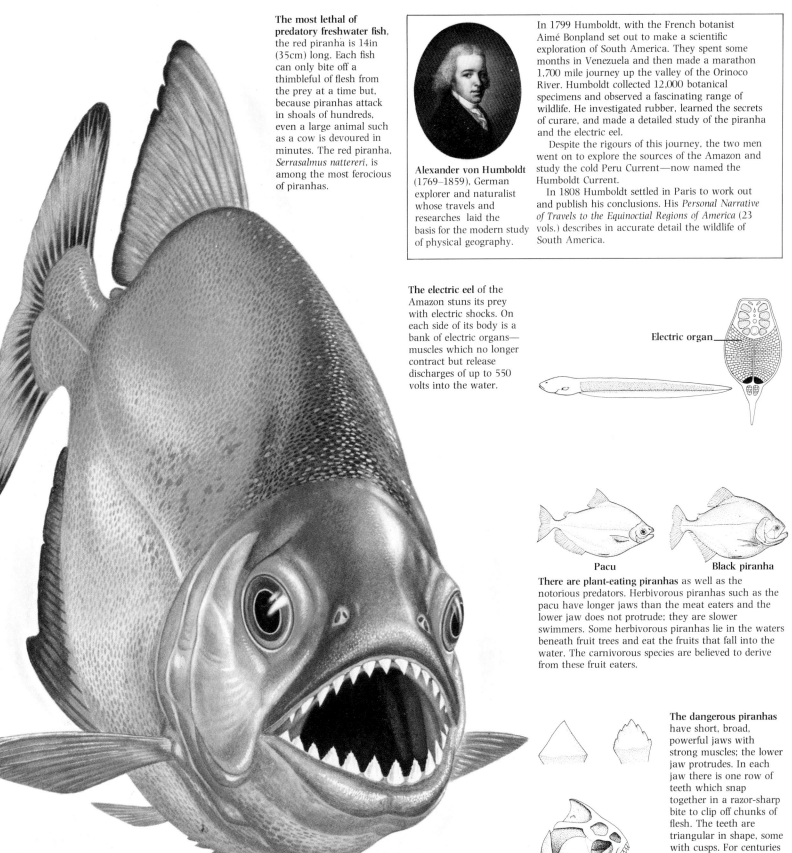

The electric eel of the Amazon stuns its prey with electric shocks. On each side of its body is a bank of electric organs— muscles which no longer contract but release discharges of up to 550 volts into the water.

Electric organ

Pacu   Black piranha

There are plant-eating piranhas as well as the notorious predators. Herbivorous piranhas such as the pacu have longer jaws than the meat eaters and the lower jaw does not protrude; they are slower swimmers. Some herbivorous piranhas lie in the waters beneath fruit trees and eat the fruits that fall into the water. The carnivorous species are believed to derive from these fruit eaters.

The dangerous piranhas have short, broad, powerful jaws with strong muscles; the lower jaw protrudes. In each jaw there is one row of teeth which snap together in a razor-sharp bite to clip off chunks of flesh. The teeth are triangular in shape, some with cusps. For centuries South American Indians used piranha jaws for cutting almost anything from hair to wood.

The birds

No other habitat in the world has so many brilliantly plumaged birds as the tropical rain forest, yet even the most iridescent feathers are difficult to spot in the dappled sunlight and dense vegetation. As a result camouflage, so important for insects living among the leaves, is not usually necessary for jungle birds. Most species have developed gaudy feathers and found other means of protecting themselves against attack. Toucans, quetzals and parrots are large, and their strength protects them from many predators. Hummingbirds, sunbirds and pittas fly off with great speed if danger threatens.

The most extravagantly beautiful of all these birds, the birds of paradise, have a bewildering variety of dazzling plumages. So fantastic are these birds that their discoverers believed them to be from Paradise, as nothing on earth resembled such brilliance. This runaway evolution occurs because the threat of predation is so low that there is no harm in sporting bright feathers.

The larger jungle birds communicate with one another by song—if the whistle of the guan, the booming of the trumpeter or the harsh cackling of the cassowary can be described as song. Smaller birds produce sounds with such a strange, haunting quality that it is often impossible to ascertain where the sound originates. Some of nature's finest ventriloquists, bower birds and pittas, are found in the tropical jungles.

Although jungles differ, and those of each continent contain distinct flora and fauna, there are many instances among the fauna of convergent evolution: unrelated bird species which not only perform the same ecological role but also look alike. Thus the fruit- and berry-eating toucans of South America and the hornbills of Africa and Southeast Asia are unrelated but closely resemble one another physically and in their habits. The ecological pattern of the bird fauna is the same in all jungles, although species differ.

Because of the dense vegetation through which they have to fly, jungle birds tend to have short, broad wings. Many species have adapted to climbing—the trogons, parrots, toucans, puffbirds and woodpeckers have pincerlike feet, with two toes pointing forward and two backward. Others, such as the curassows, are reasonable fliers but more agile climbers, even though their feet are unspecialized.

Jungle tribes have long exploited the bird fauna for food and for their feathers. Species such as the quetzal were captured alive by the Aztecs and Mayas, who prized their long tail feathers. But once these had been removed, the birds were released. During the last century milliners practised no such conservation, and so many species were hunted to the brink of extinction. Today, the major threat comes from the cage-bird exporting industry; large parrots can fetch as much as a gold watch. Ironically, the species with the least to fear from modern man are those which, because of high natural predation, have never evolved the glorious plumages for which the jungle birds are famed.

Red-billed toucan,
Ramphastos tucanus

Channel-billed toucan,
Ramphastos vitellinus

Saffron toucanet.
Baillonius bailloni

Rainbow-billed toucan.
Ramphastos sulfuratus

Swainson's toucan,
Ramphastos swainsonii

Cuvier's toucan,
Ramphastos cuvieri

Toco toucan,
Ramphastos toco

Toucans and hornbills

Toucans with bills as bright as rainbows and their African and Asian counterparts, the hornbills, are showy residents of the tallest jungle trees. Other fruit-eating birds, the sombre imperial pigeons of Malaysia and the Philippines, also roost there, and birds from lower layers use these emergent trees when moving from one area to another.

Instantly identified by their large beaks, the toucans of the Amazon forest and the hornbills are superficially alike but not closely related. Both groups have the same basic bill shape for feeding on fruits and berries. Why such an apparently clumsy structure evolved is a puzzle. These bills are certainly useful for reaching berries on thin, weak twigs which would not support the bird's weight, but a slender bill would suffice. The beaks may look formidable—in some toucans the bill is longer than the bird's body—but they do not deter a determined predator. Instead they may serve as a flag to aid in species and mate recognition. When sleeping, the toucan lays its huge bill along its back, covering it with its tail.

Toucans are so-called from the word *toucano* the name given them by the Tupi Indians of Brazil. They are 12 to 24 inches (30 to 60cm) long and make their nests in high natural tree holes which they enlarge by removing rotten wood. Gregarious birds, toucans move about in groups of a dozen or so. They are weak fliers and merely glide short distances between trees. The tail, unlike that of most birds, moves up and down during flight.

Hornbills are larger—about 2 to 5 feet (60cm to 1.5m) long. The beak is like the toucan's, but bears a casque, a horny outgrowth along the top of the bill. They have well-developed eye lashes—an unusual feature among birds. More omnivorous than toucans, hornbills supplement their fruit and berry diet with insects, tree frogs, eggs and the nestlings of other birds.

Hornbills move over the jungle in small groups; they have loud but unmelodious voices—the casqued hornbill of Africa sounds like a braying donkey. Hornbills fly well but noisily because of the air which rushes through the gaps in their wings between the primary feather quills. These gaps are usually covered by other feathers, coverts, but in the hornbills these small feathers are greatly reduced.

The hornbill's casque is usually a light, honeycomb structure with plenty of air spaces. It probably acts as a resonating chamber to amplify the bird's calls. The Asian helmeted hornbill is an exception. It has a solid casque of ivory, red on the outside, yellow inside, much in demand for carving into snuff boxes and buckles. The long tail feathers of many hornbill species are also prized, particularly by the natives of Borneo, who make use of them in rituals. Young hornbills hold their tail feathers upright when in their tree hole nest so that they can fit inside it. Even if the young birds are taken out of the nest their feathers remain upright.

The helmeted hornbill and others in Southeast Asia are endangered species. African hornbills are revered and surrounded by superstition, and thus in less danger.

The toco toucan, *Ramphastos toco*, uses its apparently clumsy bill with great dexterity. With the tip of its bill it can reach small fruits and berries, pluck them and toss them into the throat. Chunks of larger fruit are bitten off with the serrated edge of the bill, worked down to the tip and knocked back into the mouth. The toucan occasionally eats insects, spiders and birds.

Female

Male

The black and white casqued hornbill, *Bycanistes subcylindricus*, lives in the rain forest of Africa's Ivory Coast. Its large striped casque is just one example of the wide variety of hues and shapes to be found among hornbill beaks.

Female

Male

The male black casqued hornbill, *Ceratogymna atrata*, from West Africa, has a unique cylindrical casque, which almost masks the huge upper mandible. Its call, amplified by the casque's resonating chamber, carries for half a mile.

The great hornbill, *Buceros bicornis*, from Southeast Asia, is the largest hornbill in the world, at 5ft (1.5m) long. Its feathers often have a yellowish tinge from the bright yellow oil from the preen gland which the bird smears over its feathers during preening. The hornbill's nesting habits are unique. The female nests in a tree hole which she walls up with mud, faeces and other material brought to her by the male. She leaves only a narrow slit through which the male delivers food.

The horny casque surmounting the huge bill gives the hornbill its name and its top-heavy appearance. This growth is deceptively light: it is composed of a 'honey-comb' of bony cellular tissue enclosed in a shell of horn.

Captive in her nest, the female moults. By the time the appetites of the young are too great for the male to satisfy, her flight feathers are regrown, so she breaks out of the nest to help him. The nestlings rebuild their mud wall.

Eagles, the top predators

Large eagles are the top predators in the jungle's emergent layer. The sheer height of emergent trees protects their inhabitants from most other forest predators. The world's largest and most powerful eagle, the harpy eagle, lives in the Amazon forest; the slightly smaller monkey-eating eagle, now a rare bird, inhabits the jungles of the Philippines; and the beautiful crowned eagle dominates the African forest tops. All three eagles occupy the same ecological position in the jungle; thus their structure and biology are also similar.

As in most hawks and eagles, the female harpy is larger than the male. She weighs about 20 pounds (9kg) and is about 3 feet (90cm) long from head to tail. One of the most remarkable features of this eagle is the size of its feet—about the size of a man's hand and tipped with lethally sharp, curved claws. Once these feet grasp their prey, it has little hope of escape.

The harpy's shortened and broadened wing profile is an adaptation to its forest top environment. With its rounded wings, the harpy can generate sufficient lift to move almost vertically through the forest. When flying between the trees, the short wings give the harpy great agility as well as speed. It does not soar over the landscape, as do many other eagles. Instead, it moves from tree to tree in short flights, looking and listening intently for the sounds of suitable prey, particularly monkeys and sloths. For this purpose, its grey coloration is particularly effective, making it inconspicuous while it is searching. Both the monkey-eating and crowned eagles have similar hunting and flight patterns, although the latter frequently hunts in the lower levels of the forest and sometimes even at ground level, taking such prey as bushbuck and antelope.

The nests of all these majestic birds are alike. Together, male and female eagles build large, irregular platforms of twigs in the branches of emergent trees. Because these nests may be 150 feet up, there have been few observations of parental and nestling behaviour, but it is known that the harpy lays two eggs at a time and may nurture its young for a couple of years.

The eagles have a variety of calls. Young harpy eagles make high-pitched screams which mount with increasing hunger, and short screams when they receive prey. Adults scream at a lower pitch and make soft croaking noises. The African crowned eagle has a shrill call but the monkey-eating eagle makes a weak whistling sound.

The harpy eagle preys mainly on capuchin monkeys, sloths, opossums, coatis and tree porcupines in the treetops and occasionally agoutis on the ground. It may also kill macaws and snakes.

The harpy eagle, *Harpia harpyja*, of South America, is the largest and most ferocious of the world's eagles. Its mottled plumage and double crest blend in with the bark and foliage so well that the prey is often shocked into plummetting to the floor in its effort to escape. The agile harpy may chase a monkey through the trees at speeds of 50mph (80kmph), until it finally kills with its massive claws. Feeding is leisurely. The harpy carefully removes the fur of its prey with the bill before eating, and will often take several days to consume one monkey. When a young eagle receives prey from the parent, it goes through the motions of killing the already dead animal, repeatedly grasping at it with its powerful talons.

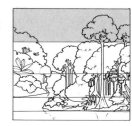

A few fast wing beats and a glide precipitate the harpy through the forest. When hunting it makes short trips, listening intently for monkey calls.

Strange wailing cries reverberate through the Philippine jungles as the monkey-eating eagle takes to the wing, occasionally soaring above the canopy.

Conspicuous black and white barring characterize the African crowned eagle in the air, particularly during its noiseless, undulating flight display.

All from the emergent layer, these eagles are similar in design. Their short, broad wings and long, spatular tails equip them aerodynamically for the forest chase. Their huge claws are deadly weapons. The head crests and camouflaging plumage facilitate their method of stalking, rather than diving at their prey.

The Philippine monkey-eating eagle, *Pithecophaga jefferyi*, is slightly smaller than the harpy, but an equally successful predator of large forest animals, particularly flying lemurs. It also raids villages for dogs, pigs and poultry. The bird's ferocity is mirrored in its narrow, sharply hooked bill and its piercing blue eyes, which are slightly hooded by the spiky crest. This eagle only rears one eaglet a year and is in grave danger of extinction due to forest clearance, hunting and traffic to zoos.

The crowned eagle, *Stephanoaetus coronatus*, is the largest African monkey-eating eagle. At 30in (76cm) long it is smaller than its South American and Philippine counterparts, though still a formidable bird of prey. It soars above the canopy and also hunts lower down, often dragging its prey to the ground to eat. The crowned eagle builds a large platform-style nest of twigs just above the canopy. A pair may spend up to three months constructing the nest, which lasts for many years as other pairs add to it. One is recorded as in use for 75 years. The only bird of its kind to have legs feathered to the toes, this eagle also carries a regal crest.

The strong, sharp talons are hooked so as to stab inward as the foot closes around its victim. As the eagle flexes its leg, the grip of the foot tightens with deadly force, crushing the prey within its grasp. The foot can adjust to grip different sizes of prey with equal power.

The nectar feeders

With their darting movements and fantastic aerobatics, tiny iridescent hummingbirds and sunbirds are nature's avian showmen. Both feed on the nectar of flowers. Hummingbirds (family Trochilidae) are distributed throughout North and South America; their ecological equivalents, the sunbirds (family Nectariniidae) occur only in Africa, Asia and the northern part of Australasia. When the canopy is unbroken, these tiny birds feed on the flowers of the giant trees, but when a clearing has been made, either by man or by a falling tree, they feed among the luxuriant understorey which quickly develops. All are highly specialized for removing nectar from flower heads.

Since many flowers are too delicate to support a perching bird, these nectar-feeding birds often hover in front of the individual flower while carefully probing it with their long bills. This demands high-precision flying, which can be achieved only by small birds with high power-to-weight ratio. (If an average-sized man produced as much power as a hummingbird, relative to his weight, his work output would be equivalent to 40 horsepower.) Carrying limited reserves of fuel because of their size, hummingbirds and sunbirds have to feed frequently —every 10 to 15 minutes during active periods—to support their high power output. (If an average-sized man were to match the work output of a hummingbird, he would need a daily energy intake of 155,000 calories, which he could obtain from 370 pounds of potatoes or 130 loaves of bread.)

In the jungle, where the temperatures are high, hummingbirds do not have to use much energy to maintain their body heat. But in western Amazonia, in the foothills of the Andes, where the night-time temperature may be very low, these birds do not attempt to keep warm, or else they would deplete their meagre flight reserves. Instead, they have evolved a means of allowing their body temperature to drop each night rather like hibernation.

Nectar feeding is not a one-way process. By producing copious, high-energy nectar, a flower entices a bird to visit it. Since the nectaries are normally located deep within the recesses of a flower, a bird has to brush against the anthers of the flower to reach them. The bird goes on to another flower and the pollen grains on its bill and feathers are rubbed off on to the stigma, thus ensuring pollination.

Pollination is so important to plants that flowers have evolved which are specifically suited to the biology of the pollinating animals. Flowers pollinated by birds are usually odourless but bright. Birds seem to be drawn to red flowers more often than to those of other shades. Since hummingbirds and sunbirds fly just in the daytime, they flock only to flowers which are diurnal.

Most hummingbirds are only a few inches long and the smallest, the bee hummingbird, is little larger than a bumble bee. Their rapid flight—up to 40 miles per hour (65 kmph)—tends to keep them clear of predators, so they do not need to be camouflaged. With sunbirds, the glossy jewel-like hummingbirds are among the most brilliantly plumaged birds in the world.

The hues of birds are produced in two ways. First, by pigments—melanin makes black, brown, grey and beige; carotenids make reds and yellows. Second, by structure—interference coloration produces the iridescent sheen of hummingbirds and others. The feather barbs are arranged like the slats of a tiny venetian blind so that the light bouncing off each slat splits into its spectral components to give iridescence. There are over 300 species of hummingbird with a wonderful variety of bright, glossy plumage.

Sword-billed hummingbird,
Ensifera ensifera

Frilled coquette,
Lophornis magnifica

White-tipped sicklebill,
Eutoxeres aquila

Marvellous spatuletail,
Loddigesia mirabilis

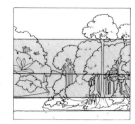

The needlelike bills of hummingbirds are specifically adapted for the types of flowers they visit. The bill fits snugly into the flowerbell, enabling the bird to reach the nectar at the base. Some species, such as the sword-billed, have a long pokerlike bill for probing tubular flowers; others have hooked bills or short, pointed bills for exploiting the smaller, more open flowers.

Hummingbird nests, built entirely by the female, are a delicate 'cup' of woven feathers, fibres, twigs and spiders' webs. Many nests are surprisingly resilient and some even watertight.

Nectar-feeding birds have long sensitive tongues, which extend beyond the bill tips. The tongue rolls into two tubes, separated at the tip, through which the bird sucks nectar. In hummingbirds the tongue is often flattened to a spoon-shaped tip. Nectar-feeding birds also occasionally lassoo insects with their muscular tongues to supplement their diet.

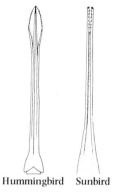

Hummingbird   Sunbird

Sunbirds occasionally hover while they feed, but more often find a strategic perch. Some species perform gymnastic feats, sometimes bending over backward to gain access to the nectaries. The bill is slender and curved to the shape of the flower type the bird feeds on, and it is often serrated toward the tip. Sunbirds build hanging 'tear-drop' shaped nests.

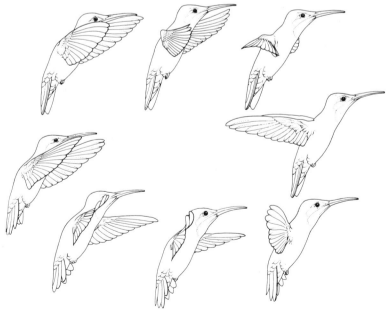

Hummingbirds have very rapid wingbeats (often as many as 100 per second) to maintain their hovering flight. A special sternum and muscular arrangement enables the bird to hold its body vertical and to move its wings to and fro in a figure of eight motion. This creates a lift force on backward and forward strokes.

The spectacular parrots

Alexander the Great probably brought the first tame parrots to Europe from the Far East. Their present popularity as pets makes them the most familiar of tropical birds. Constant activity and raucous voices make parrots the noisiest of all jungle animals—especially when they mass in flocks of more than 500. More than 100 species inhabit jungle regions—most in South America and Australia, fewer in Asia and Africa.

Most parrots have a vivid plumage, with green one of the dominant hues. Although the plumage is striking, it is the feet and the beaks of these birds which show the most important adaptations to forest life. The feet are zygodactylous—that is, two toes point forward and two point to the rear—thus enabling the parrot to establish a vicelike grip on branches. Short legs give the bird added stability while climbing and perching.

A parrot uses its beak to climb to grasp a higher branch while moving its feet forward. The beak is specifically adapted for cracking nuts, such as the tough-shelled Brazil nut; the complex pivoting bones of the skull let the upper part move as well as the lower. Its scissorslike cutting edges are immense—tough aviary wire is no match for a large, powerful macaw.

Parrots are hole-nesting birds, choosing safe sites in tall jungle trees. Courtship is simple: the male may bow a few times before the female, and then flick his wings and wag his tail. Some of the lories, such as *Lorius lory*, expose the underside of their wings. The male then feeds the female regurgitated food shortly before copulation. After mating, the female lays two to four pure white eggs on to the floor of the tree hole—most parrots do not line nests. The female alone incubates the eggs, during which time she is fed by her mate on regurgitated food. After an incubation period of three weeks, the naked, helpless young hatch. For the first few days the female feeds the chicks on a creamy paste of regurgitated food. After about a week, the male helps her until the young can fend for themselves. In many species, the young remain with their parents until the next breeding season.

The quick intelligence as well as the beautiful coloration of parrots is bringing about their downfall. For centuries the tail feathers of macaws have embellished the headdresses of the Jívaros, Carajas and other forest tribal chiefs, who kill small numbers with blowpipes or poisoned arrows. Sometimes parrots are captured alive, relieved of two or three tail feathers and released.

Recently, animal dealers have penetrated Amazonia, seducing tribal people away from the traditional agriculture by offering substantial rewards for captured parrots. But when the parrot population is impoverished and the traders move on, the Indians experience extreme hardship. In the United States the demand for parrots as pets has pushed up the price of a single hyacinth macaw to around $8,000. Although this trade is illegal, local authorities seem unable to prevent it. This, with the destruction of the primary forest habitat, poses a serious threat to these beautiful birds, many species of which are unlikely to survive the decade.

The scarlet macaw, *Ara macao*, at 36in (90cm), is the largest and one of the most spectacular of South American parrots. The imposing build of the macaws gives them some immunity from predators—a possible reason for their evolution of gaudy plumage.

The parrot's hooked bill is a massive nutcracker. The hinged upper mandible can be raised to allow precise positioning of the nut in the beak. The thick, knobbled tongue steadies the shelled nut, while the lower mandible rubs off the husk.

Among the most agile of climbing birds, parrots have short, muscular legs and clamplike feet with two toes pointing forward and two back to ensure an iron grip. Some parrots hang upside down for hours so sure are they of their foothold. Many species use one foot as a 'hand' to hold the food up to the bill, and show a marked tendency to use the left foot.

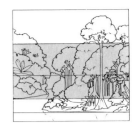

The eclectus parrot, *Eclectus roratus*, is one of the world's most beautiful parrots. The female is particularly sought by milliners for her rich blue and red feathers, but is now protected by law in New Guinea. The male has mainly green plumage.

As it veers and twists in the air the rainbow lorikeet, *Trichoglossus haematodus*, gives full exposure to its kaleidoscopic plumage. Its broad, splayed tail may act as a brake, slowing the normally rapid flight of this brilliant bird.

Rainbow lorikeet

Dusky-orange lory

Double-eyed fig parrot

Mealy parrot

Black-capped lory

Blue-crowned hanging parrot

Golden parakeet

The black-capped lory, *Lorius lory*, from New Guinea, is distinguished from the lorikeets by its short tail, bulky form and slow flight. The male's crimson and gold underwing is used in display.

The blue-crowned hanging parrot, *Loriculus galgulus*, from Malaya, is the size of a robin, and sleeps hanging upside down from a branch, like a bat. It nests in tree holes, which, unlike most parrots, it lines.

The dusky-orange lory, *Pseudeos fuscata*, from the New Guinea area, is a noisy, gregarious bird. It feeds on nectar and pollen from flowering forest trees, snipping open the base of the flower to gain access.

The double-eyed fig parrot, *Psittacula diopthalma*, from New Guinea and north Australian rain forests, feeds on figs. A noisy parrot in flight, its shrill calls are mostly heard around dusk.

The golden parakeet, *Aratinga guarouba*, from the Brazilian jungles, has striking golden plumage with bright green flight feathers, which blend in with the forest surroundings. It feeds on nuts, fruit and berries.

The mealy parrot, *Amazona farinosa*, from Central and South America, gets its name from the powdery bloom which covers its greenish-yellow plumage. At times it ventures from the deep forest to raid crops.

91

Birds of paradise

In 1522, when the survivors of Magellan's circum-navigation expedition brought back a few skins of the lesser bird of paradise, the Spanish court was so struck by the incredible beauty of these birds that it decided they must be from Paradise. In fact, they are highly adorned relatives of the crows and starlings. At home in the jungle canopy, these unspecialized omnivores eat fruits, insects and spiders. Some use their strong claws to tear into dead bark in search of food. Undoubtedly, they play a role in the spread of figs and other fruit trees.

Found only in the densely forested areas of Papua New Guinea, northern Australia and some associated islands, these small birds have evolved ornate plumages. Before the introduction of European cats and dogs, there were no natural predators, except for a few reptiles, such as the Papuan tree python; thus there was no pressure to develop camouflaging coloration. Instead these birds have become nature's most flamboyant, capable of putting on stunning visual displays.

Only the male birds have the striking plumage for which the group is famed; the feathers of the females are dull. The fabled displays of the males (for the benefit of the females) enhance the visibility of whichever part of their plumage is most exaggerated.

Several species, such as the greater bird of paradise, king bird and blue bird, display by hanging upside-down underneath the branches; this enables them to show off to maximum advantage the underside of their wings and patches of breast feathers. Their vivid hues are produced by a combination of pigments, and structural modification of the feather barbules which distort the reflection of light to give an iridescent sheen.

Little is known of the breeding biology of the birds of paradise. The female builds a well-constructed nest, usually of pandanus leaves and palm fronds, about 12 to 30 feet (4 to 10m) above ground in a dense thicket. It is left unlined. After laying two to four eggs, the female incubates them for three weeks.

Breeding between species frequently occurs; at least 19 hybrids have been reported. Since hybridization is rare in nature, these cases seem to indicate that all the birds of paradise are closely related. The hybrids appear to have been the results of indiscriminate selection, with the display of one species attracting another. The strict adherence among birds of paradise to different altitudes and forest zones prevents more than minimal overlapping of species.

The natives of New Guinea have long used the feathers of these birds for their sunburst headgear, particularly the blue breast feathers of the blue birds and the golden rain of the greater bird's tail. The populations can withstand such a modest level of exploitation, but several species came close to extinction during the nineteenth century when their feathers were in great demand by milliners. Although the export of plumes is now officially banned, poaching continues and this, along with the clearance of the primary forest for agriculture, threatens the existence of the birds of paradise.

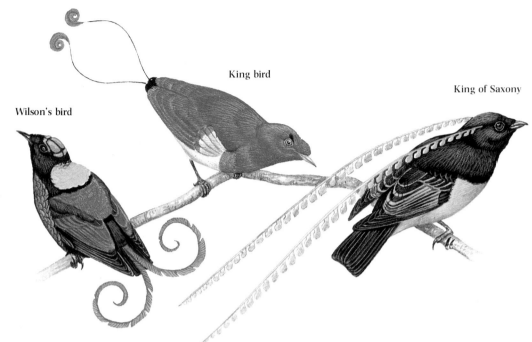

Wilson's bird

King bird

King of Saxony

A fabulous variety of tail plumes exists among the birds of paradise. Wilson's bird of paradise, *Diphyllodes respublica*, has two coiled tail plumes of steely blue which are held at right angles to the body during courtship display. The king bird, *Cicinnurus regius*, often called the 'money' bird, is graced with a lyre-shaped tail tipped with two metallic green 'coins', as well as a fan-shaped plume on each shoulder. The King of Saxony, *Pteridophora alberti*, has two long plumes, growing from its head, which flap up and down as the male bounces during display. As the excitement mounts, he points the plumes at the female and calls softly.

The feathers of Count Raggi's bird, *Paradisaea raggiana*, are the most popular among the natives for head-dress decoration. During display, the male calls loudly, claps his wings over his back and lets the plumage cascade forward and downward.

Canopy

Understorey

A dramatic 'upside-down' display is performed by the blue bird of paradise, *Paradisaea rudolphi*. While hanging, the bird fans out the triangular shield of velvety black breast feathers and allows the tail wires to fall into a graceful curve. With metronomic precision, the bird then swings its deep-blue tail feathers. These catch the light and reflect myriad hues, hypnotizing the female. The whole display is accompanied by a low grating call peculiar to this species. After the breeding season, the bird moults its tail plumes, which regrow for the next season.

93

Quetzals and curassows

For splendid plumage the quetzal, or resplendent trogon, from the mountain jungles of Central America, has few equals. This brilliant emerald and crimson bird is the national emblem of Guatemala and gives the name to their unit of currency. The Mayas and Aztecs used the quetzal's tail plumes in their ceremonies and worshipped the bird as god of the air. They linked the quetzal with the serpent god Quetzalcoatl, god of civilization, and its feathers symbolized spring vegetation.

The quetzal is the most famous of the trogons, a group of birds common in both Old and New World rain forests. They populate the lower levels of the canopy and are perhaps a foot long. Male trogons have soft breast feathers of red, orange or yellow, and back and wing feathers of metallic green or bronze. The females' plumage lacks the brightness and flamboyance of the males'.

Trogons nest in tree cavities, often using the same holes as ants or wasps to lay their two or three eggs. These solitary birds eat insects and fruit and berries. The quetzal is partial to the fruit of *Ocotea*, a member of the laurel family, which it swallows whole, regurgitating the large stone later. It will also eat small frogs, lizards and snails.

At home in the tropical forests of South and Central America are a range of birds, pheasantlike in appearance, belonging to the family Cracidae. The largest of these are the turkey-sized curassows. Guans tend to be smaller, usually under 5 pounds (2kg), and are more arboreal than the curassows, which eat various fruits on the forest floor. The chachalacas, named after their call, are the smallest of the cracids.

The cracids are highly mobile, moving quickly through the canopy and understorey. With their large, powerful feet, they are adept at running along branches. Curassows climb to a high position in the jungle, then launch themselves with a few wing beats into a long, descending glide. Curassows feed primarily on fruit—often when it is still hard and unripe. They also take buds, leaves and occasionally insects and small frogs.

Strong and chickenlike, the beak of the cracids is often surmounted by a shiny cere. In many species, the males have a bright, hard knob on the base of their bill, as well as wattles and crests of feathers on their heads.

Curassows and guans nest in the trees. They build untidy nests of twigs and leaves in which they lay two or three eggs. The chicks develop quickly. On hatching, they have functional wing feathers and grasping feet, and are soon ready to leave the nest and roost on branches. Within three or four days, they are able to fly. Both parents feed the chicks and keep them under their wings while they roost. The family group stays together, along with other families, to form a mixed age flock.

Famed for their highly variable, often raucous song, curassows utter cries ranging from a whistle to a pumping, booming noise that carries well through the jungle. Only the males sing, but females do make low-pitched notes; male birds have extremely elongated windpipes that may contribute to the loudness of their song.

The rare and beautiful quetzal, *Pharomachrus mocinno*, was revered by the Aztecs and Mayas who plucked its 2ft (60cm) tail feathers to use in their ceremonial dress. The quetzal normally sheds and regrows its tail feathers after each breeding season.

Relief of plumed serpent god – Olmec, Mexico

The god Quetzalcoatl was linked with the quetzal by the Aztecs and Mayas and symbolized as a serpent with quetzal feathers. He represented the forces of good and light and was finally consumed by divine fire, the ashes becoming birds.

Canopy

Understorey

The black curassow, *Crax alector,* has no facial wattles but is crowned with a curved head crest and performs the most complex courting display of any curassow. The male struts in front of the female, picks up a feather or twig, and dashes it violently against his back, accompanied by a champing sound. He then noisily claps his wings together, convulsively gulps air and sings a booming song. All cracids build rather small nests of loosely joined twigs and leaves, but the curassows differ in that only the female broods.

The razor-billed curassow, *Crax mitu,* of the Amazon jungle, has an ornamental bony casque projecting from the bill; both bill and casque are bright red and compressed into a high 'razor' edge. The bird also has scarlet legs.

The male wattled curassow, *Crax globulosa,* has a large scarlet knob and wattles, which develop at sexual maturity together with the black crest of curved feathers. The female is drab with a small red or yellow cere.

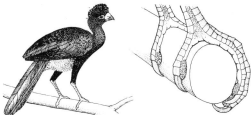

Curassows have large, strong feet and well-developed hind toes, which enable them to run nimbly along the branches. Their long, thick toes and curved claws provide a firm grip and stability even on narrow branches. The quetzal's feet, however, are weak and have a unique toe arrangement. Two toes point forward and two backward, as in many perching birds, but the first and second toe instead of the first and fourth point backward.

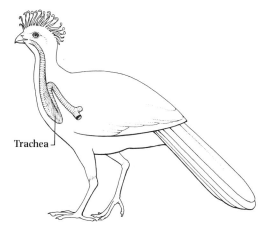

Trachea

An elongated trachea is a feature of male curassows. This looped windpipe—and air chambers in the neck—may serve to amplify the curassow's song. The song is both a means of attracting a mate and threatening other males. It ranges from a loud booming in many species to a leisurely whistle adopted by the wattled and yellow-knobbed curassow. The female lacks the specialized 'bagpipe' trachea and emits a muffled rumble.

Hawks, owls and vultures

Jungles are commonly believed to house the biggest, most spectacular organisms. While this could be disputed in many instances, it is true of birds of prey. During the day the biggest eagles seek their quarry—monkeys—in the emergent and upper canopy layers; at night the largest owls, the eagle owls, use the canopy as their hunting ground. There are also many smaller hawks that live and hunt in the jungle.

The eagle owls, named because of their superficial resemblance to eagles, have large heads and flattened faces with eyes directed forward, giving them stereoscopic vision. Like all owls they have the ability to turn their heads around through at least 180 degrees. Unlike the other birds of prey, owls have well-developed auditory powers; their ears are often asymmetrical, which enhances the differences in the strength of sound collected by each ear. By analyzing these differences the owls can accurately locate their quarry. The ear tufts of eagle owls and horned owls are purely ornamental and do not coincide with the ears themselves.

As owls hunt at night and locate their prey primarily by sound, their own movements must be as soundless as possible. Although they are not fast fliers, owls have large wings cushioned with soft, downy feathers that make their flight noiseless and allow them to take victims by surprise.

The equatorial jungles of Africa contain several eagle owls of the genus *Bubo*. The largest, Shelley's eagle owl, *Bubo shelleyi*, is about 2 feet (60cm) long. Its plumage is barred, making it difficult to see in the dim, dappled light of the jungle canopy. Fraser's eagle owl, *Bubo poensis*, up to 18 inches (45cm), has an orange-yellow face, and the Akun eagle owl, *Bubo leucostictus*, similar in size to Fraser's, has a weaker build and is mainly insectivorous. The Philippine eagle owl, *Bubo philippensis*, has dark orange feathers above and paler ones below, instead of the usual sombre brown.

The jungle canopy is frequented by several other owl genera collectively referred to as wood owls. The spectacled owl is a wood owl indigenous to the Amazonian jungles and is 16 to 19 inches (40 to 48cm) long. It preys on small mammals and large insects.

A range of forest hawks or falcons inhabits the tall forest trees of Central and South America. In contrast to most falcons they have short, broad wings and longish tails which provide the aerial mobility necessary to chase prey through the jungle vegetation. One example is the ornate hawk eagle, which catches curassows and guans so frequently that it is often known as the curassow hawk.

African rain forests house several species of hawk. Cassin's hawk-eagle feeds in the canopy on birds and squirrels, but also occasionally soars above the jungle in typical hawk fashion. The African long-tailed hawk often ventures out from the canopy to attack poultry in African villages.

Scavengers are also carnivores, but do not kill for their living. Jungles are not such good hunting grounds for vultures as the open grasslands, but one species, the king vulture, does fill the scavenging niche in the South American forests.

The barred forest falcon, *Micrastur ruficollis*, is adapted for life in the dense forest. Its short, broad wings and long, flared tail allow the bird to twist agilely between the entangled branches with supreme control. It frequently hunts at twilight, its large ear openings enabling it to locate prey by sound.

The peregrine falcon, *Falco peregrinus*, is adapted for the open country. Long, narrow wings with pointed tips, and a short tail give this bird swift, soaring flight, which would serve no purpose in the dense vegetation of the rain forest. Once an abundant species, this large, streamlined falcon is now rarely seen.

Shelley's eagle owl, *Bubo shelleyi*, perches on a high branch watching for prey. Armed with powerful talons, it silently pounces on the victim.

Owls' flight feathers are designed for silent flight. The 'frayed' leading edge smooths the air flow over the wing and the fringed rear edge muffles the sound.

The spectacled owl, *Pulsatrix perspicillata*, from South America, is so named because of the white rings of feathers around its eyes. It is also known in Brazil as 'knocking owl' as its call resembles the woodpeckers' hammering. It preys on small mammals, birds, crabs and small insects. It nests in tree holes.

Owls' eyes are adapted to nocturnal hunting. They are tubular and forward-facing, giving binocular vision. The overlapping fields of vision judge distances well, while the large ultra-sensitive retina enables the owl to see in dim light.

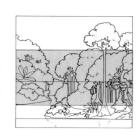

Canopy

Understorey

Cassin's hawk-eagle, *Spizaetus africanus*, never ventures out of the deep jungle. This rare African bird preys on squirrels and smaller birds.

In the dense forests of the Congo lurks the African long-tailed hawk, *Urotriorchus macrourus*, waiting to pounce on unsuspecting canopy birds and small mammals. Its exceptionally long, graduated tail speeds its flight as it swoops down on its prey, which it strangles to death in an unrelenting grip. This powerful hawk is well-adapted to a forest life-style with its short broad wings, and its attractive chestnut and black plumage merging discreetly with the trees.

The garish facial markings of the king vulture, *Sarcorhamphus papa*, brand it the world's most spectacular bird of prey. It is the only vulture to live in the rain forest. Prey is hard to see from a canopy seat, so the vulture relies on smell to detect food, often seizing stranded fish from river banks. At large carcasses in clearings other birds give way to the king, which has the most powerful bill of any American vulture. Unlike most vultures, it is thought to kill reptiles and mammals.

Bowerbirds and cocks-of-the-rock

The forest floor becomes a stage for the spectacular communal displays of bowerbirds, manakins and the cocks-of-the-rock. The bowerbirds (family Ptilonorhynchidae) of Papua New Guinea and northern Australia, are closely related to the birds of paradise and are often found in the same vicinity. Manakins (family Pipidae) and cocks-of-the-rock (family Cotingidae) occur only in Central and tropical South America. The African jungles are devoid of any ground-displaying birds, probably as a result of chance rather than any particular environmental factors.

The displays of these birds, as well as those of many gamebirds of the northern temperate region, are the domain of the males. Known as leks, these all-male shows serve two purposes. First, they provide a forum in which each male can assess his dominance against that of his peers—an important factor in species in which just a small number of males are allowed to breed. Only male bowerbirds that own a bower will breed, and consequently there is great competition for bower sites. Bowers are not constructed indiscriminately but in traditional places, and there is much raiding and counter-raiding of partially finished ones during the building season. Second, the leks attract the females for mating purposes. Often the glitter of many males displaying at once exerts a stronger influence on the females than the display of a single male and encourages her to watch.

In all these communally displaying species, the sexes come together only for mating. Once inseminated, the females leave the arena to build nests, lay and incubate the eggs, and feed and guard the young until they are fledged. In human terms this seems an unfair division of labour, but it does emphasize a fundamental biological difference between the roles of the sexes among these species. The male, however, can be relieved of parental duties only if the female is capable of raising the young herself and can gather adequate food for them. Then the male is free to devote his energies to those activities which will most enhance his sexual appeal to other females.

In all birds which perform these displays, males and females are strikingly different in appearance. Female manakins and cocks-of-the-rock lack ornate plumage, but the males have showy feathers.

Similarly, female bowerbirds have dull brown plumage while the males are adorned with yellow and golden feathers. Some, such as McGregor's bowerbird, *Amblyornis macgregoriae*, and the orange-crested, striped gardener bowerbird, *Ambly-ornis subalaris*, even have dramatic feather crests of stunning beauty.

During the displays, all the birds make noises to attract the females as well as intimidate the other males. The male bowerbird accompanies his movements with a complex ventriloquial and imitative call, while cocks-of-the-rock make snapping noises by rapidly closing their bills. Manakins produce a whirring sound by flapping their special vanelike wing feathers.

Some cocks-of-the-rock exhibit strange display movements after bobbing and puffing themselves up like farmyard cocks; they may go into deep trances, standing still for four minutes. They then jump high into the air. These displays are well known to the Jívaro Indians of western Amazonia, who imitate the birds' prodigious leaps in their ceremonial dances.

To draw more attention to their activities, these ground-displaying birds scrupulously clear their arenas of twigs, leaves, dead flowers and other debris. Some manakins even bring one or two special twigs to sit upon when they are not singing and fluttering up and down above the females. The dances and activities of these jungle floor birds are among the most interesting and impressive courtship displays in the avian world.

The male regent bowerbird, *Sericulus chrysocephalus*, is a striking iridescent black with golden yellow head, neck and flight feathers, and a light yellow iris. The female is an olive-buff shade.

The thrush-sized golden bowerbird, *Prionodura newtoniana*, lives in the rain forests of northern Queensland. It is golden yellow all over, except the wings which are olive. The female is dusky brown washed with olive.

McGregor's bowerbird, *Amblyornis macgregoriae*, is pale olive-buff and light fawn. The male is crowned with a spectacular yellow-orange crest which is highly prized by Papuan tribes for ornamentation.

As the breeding season approaches, the male regent bowerbird constructs an avenue by planting twigs in the ground to form two walls about 4in (10cm) apart. He sometimes paints the twigs white with a mixture of chewed vegetable pulp and saliva, using a wad of leaves for a brush. He also collects bright berries, shells, and feathers which he constantly rearranges in the bower as he hops around, trying to attract a female.

The golden bowerbird builds a 'maypole' bower. First, he constructs one 'pyramid' of twigs around the base of a tree to a height of up to 6ft (1.8m), then a smaller one around a nearby tree trunk. He strews the intervening space with moss and uses a bridging root as a perch. The bird tends the bower throughout the year, most regularly during the breeding season, and may ornament it with clusters of fruit and flowers.

McGregor's bower is characterized by a mossy, saucer-shaped platform which is so tightly woven with moss, ferns and tiny twigs that it can be rolled up and removed in one piece. It is often decorated with lichen-covered sticks, tassels of insect silk, pieces of white fungus and small piles of seeds. It may have a narrow rim. In the centre there is usually a sapling with a 'maypole' of twigs up to 2 ft (60cm) high around it.

Floor

The vivid crest of the male cock-of-the-rock conceals its bill when held fully erect. By slow head movements the bird shows first one side of the crest then the other during display.

Cocks-of-the-rock, *Rupicola rupicola,* display to each other at their communal lek, which is a cleared arena on the forest floor. The males leap into the air and display to one another by head bobbing, bill snapping, wing flicking, feather whirring and the fanning of the tail to an accompaniment of resonant calls. Females, who are dull brown with no 'helmet' crest, visit the lek only briefly, purely for mating.

Pheasants and junglefowl

Since the beginning of recorded history man has domesticated pheasants and spread them around the world. These familiar birds stem from a handful of species living in the jungles of Southeast Asia, from India eastward to Borneo and Sumatra. Their presence in the rain forests of the Congo—the western limit of the pheasant population—seems to indicate that the group evolved when the continents of Africa and Asia were closer together than they are now.

Pheasants, as well as peafowl, argus pheasants, peacock pheasants and junglefowl, spend most of their lives on the forest floor, where they feed on a wide variety of foods, including seeds, fruits, berries, insects and even occasional small mammals. They are all capable of flying, but do so only when threatened. Their large bulky bodies make a normal avian existence difficult.

Pheasants never migrated to the western hemisphere; in the jungles of South America their place is taken by the handsome curassows and the awkward tinamous. Superficially, tinamous resemble pheasants, with the same general feather coloration, but they are more solidly built. In fact, their closest relatives appear to be the ostriches. They are well adapted for running, with strong legs and feet, but will take to the wing if threatened. Their flight is weak and often punctuated by collisions with branches and trees.

Male and female tinamous look alike, though the female is slightly larger. In the pheasant family, however, males are always larger than the females, and are also more showily dressed. Lustrous ocelli, or 'eyes', composed of bands of blue and purple feathers adorn either the tail or the wings of the peafowl, peacocks and argus pheasants. This unusual plumage feature is displayed during courtship and inter-male rivalry.

Pheasants have been described as the world's most aggressive birds. When disputing a territorial boundary, two males will fight with intense ferocity, leaping into the air and slashing out with their backwardly projecting heel-spurs.

The junglefowl, from the dense, dark rain forests of the Orient, nave had a greater impact on man than any other species: the four species represent the ancestral stock from which domestic chickens are descended. Although there has been intense selective breeding for docile behaviour, and enhanced fecundity, modern chickens retain many features of the wild junglefowl. The crow of the red junglefowl, *Gallus gallus*, for example, closely resembles that of the farmyard rooster. In addition, the fleshy comb on top of the junglefowl's head has passed down to the domestic stock without modification. Ornithologists do not know to which part of the pheasant family the junglefowl are most closely related; in details of anatomy and behaviour they remain isolated. They will interbreed with most types of pheasant, but their hybrid offspring are infertile.

The junglefowl and pheasants are hunted both by tribes and predators for their tasty flesh. With the exception of the rare Congo peacock, these forest floor-dwellers exist in abundance.

The red junglefowl, *Gallus gallus*, of the Oriental jungles, is the ancestor of the domestic chicken. The junglecock is very aggressive and uses his sharp spurs to deliver ferocious attacks on any rival who threatens his sovereignty. His courtship 'waltzing' display is as elegant as his fighting is ferocious. He bows before the hen of his choice, stretches one wing and gently strums his foot against the flight feathers as the wing sweeps round, producing a vibrating 'harplike' sound. The male is predominantly black, bronze and red, and adorned with comb, lappets and a ruff. The female, who is slightly smaller, is a mottled brown and does not have spurs or ornamental feathers.

The domestic chicken is similar to the junglefowl in appearance and in courtship display, although it is much less aggressive. The female, unlike her wild counterpart, sports a comb and lappets, and lays considerably more eggs. Both the wild and domestic species have arched and compressed tails.

The Congo peacock, *Afropavo congensis*, is the only pheasant native to Africa. A single feather found in the head-dress of an Ituri forest native led to the discovery of this short-tailed pheasant. The female incubates the eggs but the male looks after the young, taking them under his wing at night.

Vieillot's crested fireback, *Lophura ignita rufa*, is one of the largest jungle pheasants at 27in (68cm) long. The erect crest of racquet-tipped feathers, the long legs and iridescent plumage lend these birds a regal air. During courtship the bird rubs its wings along the ground and makes a deep ventriloquial bubbling sound.

The crested argus pheasant, *Rheinartia ocellata*, from Indochina and Malaysia, has the longest feathers possessed by any bird. The tail feathers are 5ft (1.5m) long and, when fanned out during courtship display, present a richly illuminated bowl of hues to the female. For a large bird, this argus has a slender bill and legs.

The great tinamou, *Tinamus major*, from Amazonia, is adapted for ground dwelling and is almost flightless. It has thick legs and massive feet which, like its relative the ostrich, have almost lost the fourth toe. When danger threatens, the tinamou crouches low. The male incubates the eggs in a clutch often laid by several hens. The large eggs are beautiful and highly polished.

Peacock pheasants, *Polyplectron emphanum*, have highly decorative tail feathers which, when raised during courtship, closely resemble the peacock tail display. They are shy, secretive birds which hide in the dense jungle undergrowth, yet they emit loud cackling-laughing calls and whistles in courtship.

A jungle chorus

Many travellers to the world's jungles are struck by the incredible noises that begin at nightfall, continue throughout the night and reach fever pitch by dawn. Sound as a mode of communication is particularly well developed in jungle animals, for the general darkness of their habitat severely limits visual communication over more than a few yards. Although there are some exceptions, jungle-floor animals are usually bright, as their surroundings make sombre concealment coloration unnecessary. Their coloration is important in courtship displays, when the male is close to the female and trying to impress her.

Some of the strangest forest sounds are made by birds, especially those species which spend much of their lives on the ground. New Guinea's largest endemic birds, the cassowaries, *Casuarius casuarius*, are completely flightless. They are more often heard than seen, announcing their presence by a loud, deep booming which changes to a harsh cackling and croaking. These large birds, whose nearest relatives are the Australian emus, may stand as tall as a man and weigh about 100 pounds (45kg).

Surprisingly light on their feet, cassowaries seem to melt into the forest thickets with great ease if enemies are near. They are pugnacious creatures and dangerous to men if cornered. Their attack consists of a powerful forward kick in which the inner toe is thrust outward. These birds are so strong that they can slash open a soft-bodied vertebrate with a single kick.

For many of New Guinea's tribes, such as the Ceram, cassowaries represent a cornerstone in their economy. They are hunted by the natives with bows and arrows for their delicious flesh. Ironically, the Ceram tip their arrows with the sharp, strong claw from the inner of the bird's three toes. In addition, in the Wahgi Valley the local inhabitants 'farm' cassowaries in stout wooden stockades, plucking them regularly for their hairlike iridescent feathers, which they use to adorn their ceremonial head-dresses. The natives also highly prize the quills which sprout from the vestigial wings; they put these through the nose for decoration, or bend them into circles and use them for earrings. Even the long leg bones are made into spoons or scrapers.

Resonating throughout the Amazonian forest are the calls of the male trumpeters. These birds, similar in size to domestic chickens, live in large flocks deep within the forest. Even though they can fly, and build their nests in tree forks and other safe places above the ground, trumpeters feed almost entirely on the ground, searching for fruits, berries, seeds and insects. If danger threatens they run quickly to the safety of a dense thicket. The females look exactly like the males, and the sex of an individual can be confirmed only by observing its behaviour. The male takes the lead in courtship.

The Southeast Asian equivalent of the Amazonian antbirds, the jewel thrushes, or pittas, are readily distinguished by their distinct trilling, whistling and rolling calls. These brilliantly plumaged, stocky little birds search for small invertebrates, as well as vertebrates, on the jungle floor, carrying snails to anvil stones to crack them. Their diet also includes berries, fruits and seeds.

The cassowary, native to the rain forests of New Guinea, nearby islands and northern Queensland, is closely related to the emu. This large, flightless bird, enveloped in a cloak of black plumage, may be as tall as 6 ft (1.8 m) in the largest species. The helmetlike horny casque has been thought to act as a protective shield as the bird crashes through the undergrowth, but it is more likely that both the casque and gaudy neck wattles play a part in the bird's social behaviour.

Like all pittas, the banded pitta, *Pitta guajana*, from Southeast Asia, is capable of fast flight in spite of its short tail, stout body and forest floor habitat.

With its stocky build and quaint habit of breaking snail shells open against a favourite stone, the pitta superficially resembles the thrush. This shy, multi-hued bird blends in subtly with the undergrowth, where it moves around with long easy hops. Its distinctive ventriloquial call makes it even more difficult to locate. It feeds at night, mainly on insects, with a few seeds and berries from the forest floor, and takes its own weight in food each day. The pitta builds a rather untidy nest on or near the floor.

The grey-winged trumpeter, *Psophia crepitans*, is a gregarious bird which lives in dense flocks on the floor of the South American jungle. It owes its common name to the loud, trumpeting call emitted by the cock during the breeding season to threaten others in the flock. While calling, the bird opens and shuts its beak; the back feathers are raised which exaggerates its hunchbacked appearance. Trumpeters enjoy bathing in shallow water.

103

The water birds

With their great river systems and adjacent low-lying areas that are frequently flooded, the rain forests make a suitable habitat for certain ducks, bitterns, rails and herons. In this environment they are able to feed in and beside the rivers, and nest in the nearby tall trees.

One of the aquatic birds native to the jungles of Central and South America is the muscovy duck, a familiar farmyard and ornamental duck. A close relative of the muscovy, the white-winged wood duck, *Cairina scutulata*, is found in the Southeast Asian rain forests. Both species are omnivorous, eating insects, molluscs, small fish and reptiles. Pugnacious fighters, the muscovy and the wood ducks have well-developed, clawed feet and bony knobs at the angles of their wings which they use to advantage during battle.

Tiger herons nest in trees close to small streams and rivulets. The striped pattern in their plumage helps make these shy, secretive birds inconspicuous. They feed on small fish, crabs, frogs, snakes and insects.

The sunbittern is a relative of the heron family. There is only one species and it is restricted to the South American jungles, particularly to the banks of streams, where it feeds on frogs, insects and other small animals. The Amazonian Indians often keep the sunbittern with their domestic poultry.

Perhaps the most bizarre of the rain forest birds is the hoatzin. It inhabits the more open parts of the jungle, alongside large rivers and lakes in South America. Pheasantlike in appearance, it has a slender body, long neck, and a small head crowned by a ragged cluster of stiff feathers. The hoatzin feeds primarily on mangrove and arum leaves with the aid of its powerful beak. Its wings are large but the breast muscles are weak, and consequently it is a poor, laborious flier. As its feet are poorly developed the hoatzin moves through the vegetation in an ungainly fashion, using its wings and tail as stabilizers and supports.

Hoatzins move in flocks and nest in colonies. Their nests are untidy and are always built of twigs in trees overhanging water. In contrast to the parents, the young hoatzins are adept at moving nimbly among the branches. They have well-developed feet as well as beaks adapted for climbing. A unique feature in the juveniles is the presence of two hooked claws on each wing, with which they cling to branches.

Claws

The hoatzin, *Opisthocomus hoazin*, from South America, earns its nicknames 'gypsy' and 'smelling pheasant' from its ungainly, bristly crest and strong musky smell. This primitive-looking bird builds an untidy twig nest overhanging the river, so that, if threatened, its young can drop into the water and swim to safety. Hoatzins are poor fliers and use their wings more for support when climbing and perching than for flight. The top-heavy appearance of the hoatzin is caused by an enlarged digestive tract—necessary to deal with the tough mangrove and arum leaves eaten by the adult.

An extra pair of claws at the bend of the wing gives the baby hoatzin greater stability when climbing. These are lost as the bird matures.

The muscovy duck, *Cairina moschata,* a native of the Latin American jungles, is a vicious fighter despite its soft, velvety-black mien. Selective breeding by man has produced a fat, speckled domestic species.

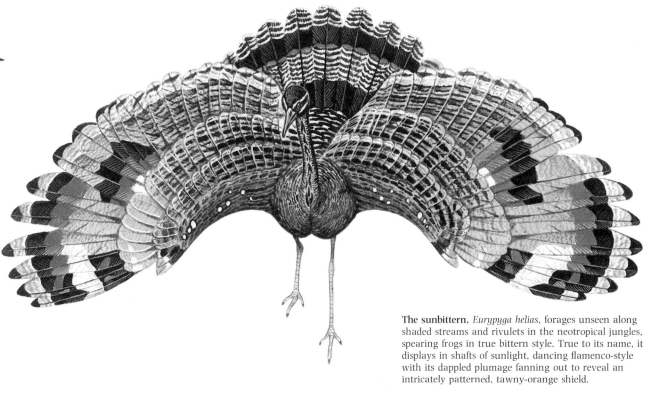

The sunbittern, *Eurypyga helias,* forages unseen along shaded streams and rivulets in the neotropical jungles, spearing frogs in true bittern style. True to its name, it displays in shafts of sunlight, dancing flamenco-style with its dappled plumage fanning out to reveal an intricately patterned, tawny-orange shield.

The white-crested tiger heron, *Tigriornis leucolophus,* from West Africa, is the only heron to live entirely in the rain forest. Unlike other herons, it grasps rather than spears fish in the water with its long, finely serrated bill. Like other herons, the tiger heron uses patches of powder-down, formed by disintegrated feathers, in preening to remove fish slime from its body.

The pearly forms of egrets and ibises often speckle the forest-bordered rivers of the American tropics. They breed in colonies in the trees, and come out into the water to feed on fish, insects and crustaceans. This rich habitat satisfies the needs of many tropical birds adapted both to forest and aquatic life.

The insect feeders

The world's jungles, teeming with insect life, are populated by birds able to exploit this abundant food resource. One technique of insect-feeding birds is to make swift darts from a vantage point and catch prey on the wing.

Motmots, experts in this technique, live in the Central and South American rain forests. The rufous motmot sits for long periods without moving, but is quick to seize suitable prey. After a successful capture, the motmot returns to its perch, where it impales the insect on the branch before eating it. Both the male and female excavate a tunnel in which to nest.

Tunnel nests are also dug by another insectivorous group, the puffbirds (Bucconidae) of the Amazonian jungles. Like the motmots, these small birds sit motionless on branches, but are alert to passing insect life. Close relatives of the puffbird are the jacamars (Galbulidae), also inhabitants of tropical South America. Although much the same size as puffbirds, and with similar long, pointed bills, these birds are markedly different. The jacamar's electric iridescent plumage and slender form contrast with the puffbird's buff feathers and chunky shape. While the puffbird tends to be sluggish and silent, the jacamar is energetic and vocal.

The jacamar makes a fine display while catching prey, since it takes the brightest dragonflies and butterflies on the wing. Constantly on watch, the jacamar darts out, grasps the insect and, with its prey fluttering in its long slender bill, returns to its perch. There it hammers the insect rapidly and loudly for some minutes, until the wings fall to the ground. It then eats the insect's body. Some jacamars also feed on small, inconspicuous insects.

Of the two groups of birds named flycatchers, the ones from the Americas, the tyrant flycatchers, are more primitive and are thought to have had the same ancestors as the cotingas and manakins. Although the Old World species have the same life-style, their origins are different. All flycatchers are insectivorous, and many catch prey in the air by making short sallies from a vantage point. The Old World flycatchers are attractive, brightly plumaged birds, especially the paradise flycatcher of Southeast Asia, which has long tail feathers and an erect crest. The tyrant flycatchers are comparatively drab, with green and brown feathers.

Perhaps the most specialized order of insectivorous birds are the potoos, nightjars and frogmouths, all with enormous gaping bills and long wings. The potoo (Nyctibiidae) resembles the flycatchers in its hunting methods—it darts out from its perch to catch moths, fireflies and other insects in its huge mouth. A nocturnal hunter, the potoo spends much of the day perched in a strange, vertically elongated pose on a tree stub. Excellent camouflaging plumage combined with this pose makes the bird appear part of the tree. Incubating its eggs, the potoo assumes the same camouflaging posture, but faces into the tree trunk. Nestlings too adopt this pose.

The potoo's plaintive cry, heard at dusk and dawn and by moonlight, is the source of its Trinidadian nickname 'pour-me-one'.

The potoo, from South America, is a master of camouflage. Its mottled, lichen-hued plumage and rigid, upright pose make it hard to distinguish from a tree stub. The potoo flies silently, making short, nocturnal sallies to catch insects, the long wings and tail presenting a hawklike silhouette. The huge, owl-like eyes are firmly closed by day. Its capacious, fleshy mouth is armed with a projecting tooth.

The rufous-tailed jacamar, *Galbula ruficauda*, is a familiar representative of these vibrant, vocal birds from southern Mexico and Brazil. The glittering green, copper and gold plumage, the swordlike bill and vitality of the jacamar are reminiscent of the hummingbird. The jacamar, however, is entirely insectivorous, and pursues showy insects, which it captures in mid-air and beats against its perch before swallowing.

The rufous motmot, *Baryphthengus ruficapillus*, at 18in (45cm) is the largest of these New World birds. Motmots are characterized by their racquet-tipped tails. Originally the bare shaft is covered with weakly attached barbs, but these gradually fall out during preening. A perching motmot often swings its tail pendulum-style or tilts it sideways.

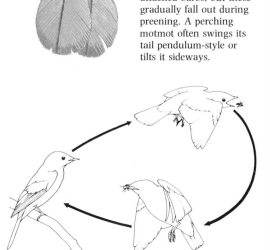

Flycatchers seize insects in mid-air with short, swift darts from a look-out post. The bill is broad with a wide gape, and surrounded by stiff bristles to facilitate the snapping up of insects. Many tropical flycatchers build neat, cup-shaped nests in the forks of trees, and lay clutches of up to three eggs. The black-naped monarch, *Hypothymis azurea*, *right*, is a Southeast Asian flycatcher.

The insect feeders/2

Antbirds, foliage gleaners and woodpeckers are among the many birds that prey on the millions of insects crawling over the jungle floor or living in the trees. The technique of these birds is different from the flycatcher's 'on the wing' method, but equally efficient.

The soberly plumaged antbirds (family Formicariidae) of South America are diverse in shape, behaviour and feeding habits. Some, such as the white-faced antcatcher, hunt in small groups specifically for ants and termites in the understorey; others, such as the black antwren, look for insects in the lower canopy.

The best known antbirds, however, are those which have an opportunist association with the marauding bands of army ants which roam the jungle floor. While most creatures flee in the path of a foraging column of thousands of army ants, the antbirds take advantage of the scramble to capture spiders, scorpions and insects disturbed by the ants. They do not eat the ants themselves.

When an antbird discovers an ant column, it sings, attracting other antbirds to the site. Several different species of antbird will attend an army ant column, and a hierarchy develops in which the largest species or individual supplants subordinate, smaller species in choice foraging positions. These frustrated subordinates will often resort to robbing the army ants of their captures. The best foraging positions are branches just above the advancing column. From its perch the antbird darts down to seize a fleeing creature and bounces back with its prey.

Particular arboreal adaptations enable the woodcreepers, from Latin America, and the woodpeckers, with a worldwide distribution, to remove insects from wood. Between 8 and 15 inches (20 and 38cm) long, woodcreepers have strong, stiff tail feathers which they use as supports during climbing. Though their bills are strong, they forage by moving spirally up a tree, extracting insects from crevices. Woodcreepers are also attracted to ant columns by the songs of antbirds.

Woodpeckers dig into bark and wood to winkle out burrowing insect larvae. Their tails act as struts, supporting them below, while their feet, whose toes end in strong, curved claws, anchor them to the tree.

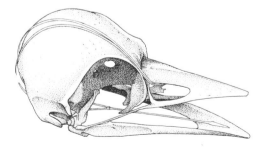

Woodpeckers feed by chiselling into tree bark with their solid bills. The hammering motion is powered by strong neck muscles, and the long wormlike tongue is operated by flexible skull bones. The hard tip of the tongue may be spear- or brush-shaped to capture insects, or coated with sticky saliva to mop up ants.

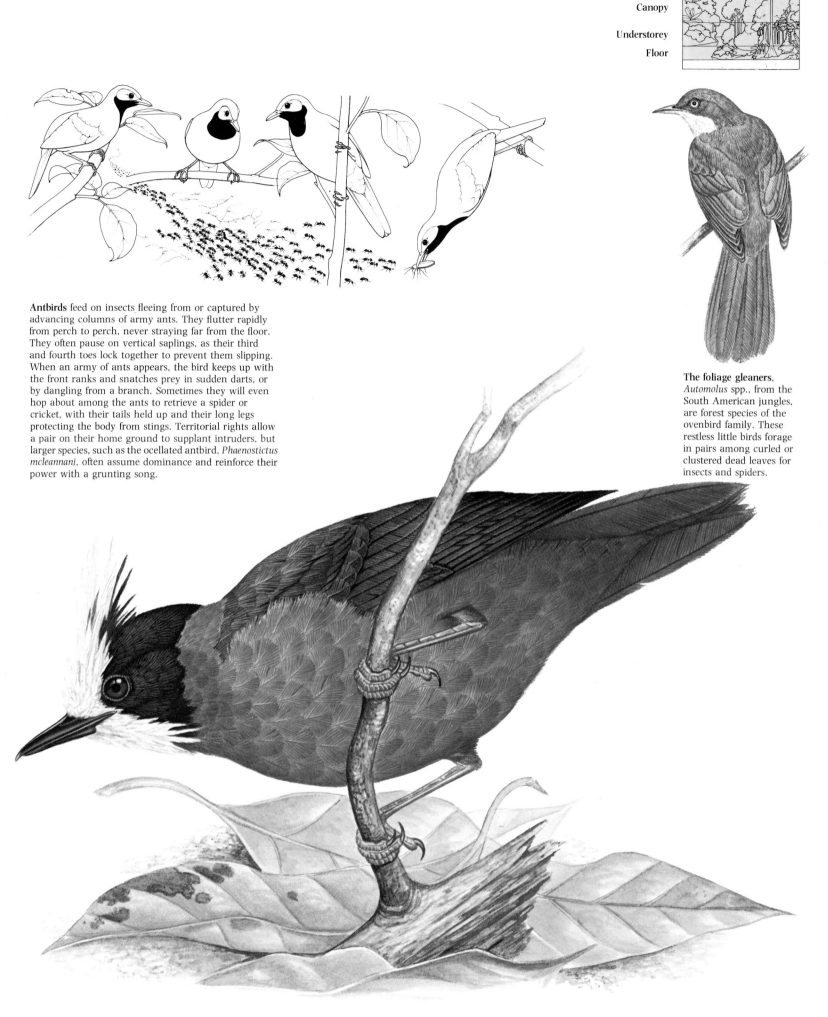

Antbirds feed on insects fleeing from or captured by advancing columns of army ants. They flutter rapidly from perch to perch, never straying far from the floor. They often pause on vertical saplings, as their third and fourth toes lock together to prevent them slipping. When an army of ants appears, the bird keeps up with the front ranks and snatches prey in sudden darts, or by dangling from a branch. Sometimes they will even hop about among the ants to retrieve a spider or cricket, with their tails held up and their long legs protecting the body from stings. Territorial rights allow a pair on their home ground to supplant intruders, but larger species, such as the ocellated antbird, *Phaenostictus mcleannani*, often assume dominance and reinforce their power with a grunting song.

The foliage gleaners, *Automolus* spp., from the South American jungles, are forest species of the ovenbird family. These restless little birds forage in pairs among curled or clustered dead leaves for insects and spiders.

The insects and invertebrates

Sixty per cent of all known plant and animal species in the world are insects, and almost half of these are beetles. About one million insect species have already been described, and there may be twice this number still to be discovered. Recent Canadian research suggests that, because of the relatively crude methods used to detect new species, many may be missed, and there could be as many as ten million insect species.

One reason insects are so diverse and tremendously successful is that their basic structure is highly adaptable and their organ systems can take on roles for which they were not primarily designed. For example, the stings of bees, some ants and wasps are derived from the egg-laying apparatus; the sounds of cicadas and some cockroaches are amplified or produced by the respiratory system; and the silk of lacewing larvae is secreted from the excretory organs.

Most insects are small—the most common size is about $\frac{1}{4}$ inch (3–5 mm)—and this has enabled them to occupy a vast range of micro-habitats that would be unsuitable for larger species. Their nervous system is highly developed, allowing complex behaviour such as social life, and is capable of a high level of discrimination of the environment. Insects can appreciate subtle differences in the landscape, and so identify microhabitat boundaries.

As the lifespan of an individual insect is so short, there is no need for it to learn to adapt to new conditions. Any benefit would be too short-lived. Instead, it is the genetic changes which are important, and these can be made quickly because of the short generation time. Insects are, for example, easily able to acquire a resistance to insecticides, not because they have adapted to the toxin, but because there is a change in the genetic composition of the population of the insect species.

Throughout their long evolution, insects have been interacting with every kind of flowering plant. Since more than half of all insects are herbivores, many of these plants produce toxins or distasteful compounds to discourage them. Because of their short generation time, however, certain insect species develop the metabolic reactions to detoxify these defence compounds. New species are often created as a result of the continual innovation and experimentation in this plant/herbivore conflict.

The great productivity and luxuriance of the jungles provide not only a wealth of different types of food for insects, but also a wider range of micro-habitats for them to colonize. The specialized relationships between plants and their herbivores are multiplied for all the different plant species. These are similar to the battles which develop between predators and their prey. In temperate regions the struggle for life is directed against the climate; in the jungle the struggles are between organisms. Jungles are also rich in invertebrate species.

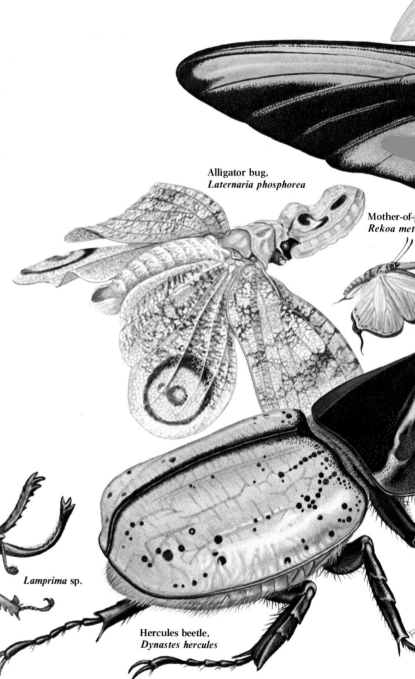

Alligator bug,
Laternaria phosphorea

Mother-of-p
Rekoa meto

Lamprima sp.

Hercules beetle,
Dynastes hercules

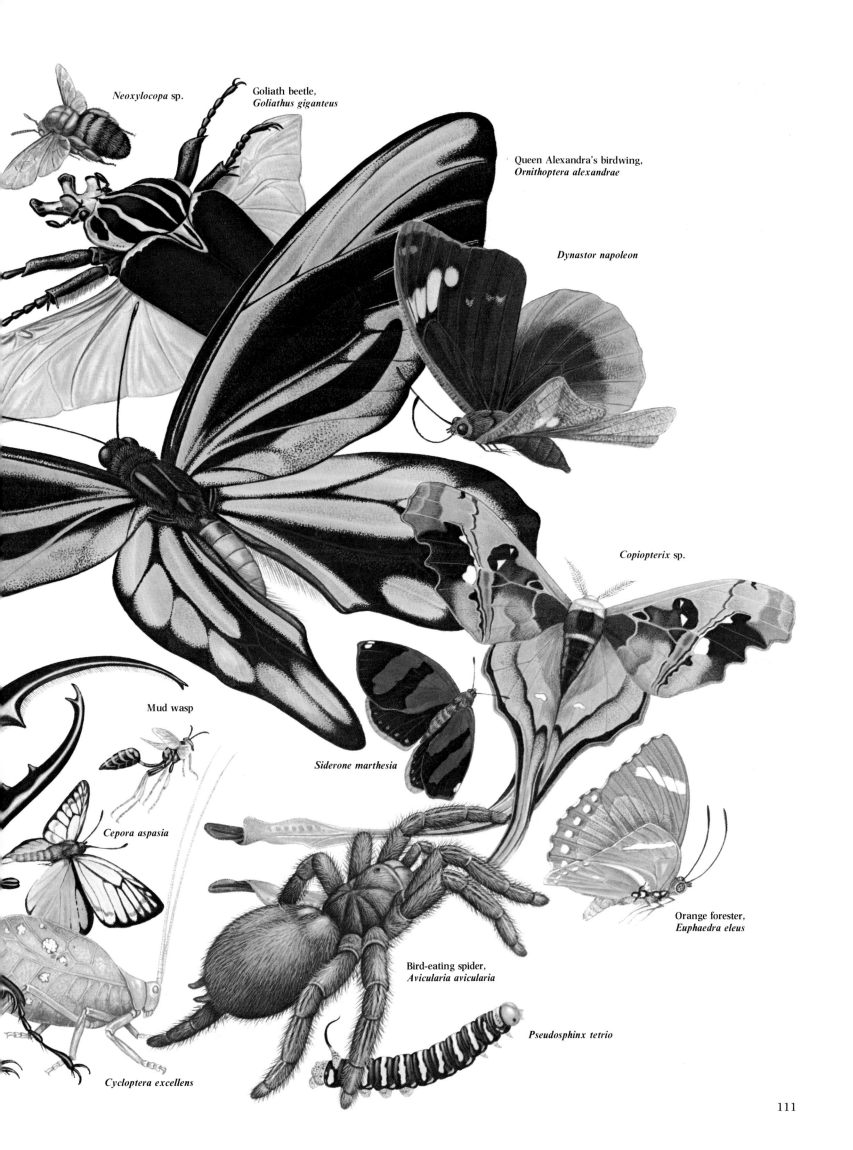

Neoxylocopa sp.

Goliath beetle,
Goliathus giganteus

Queen Alexandra's birdwing,
Ornithoptera alexandrae

Dynastor napoleon

Copiopterix sp.

Mud wasp

Siderone marthesia

Cepora aspasia

Orange forester,
Euphaedra eleus

Bird-eating spider,
Avicularia avicularia

Pseudosphinx tetrio

Cycloptera excellens

High-flying butterflies

Moving in crowds, male butterflies cavort in the sunshine or patrol extensive territories through the upper canopy and emergent layers of the jungle. Many rival or even surpass birds with their bright flamboyant wing patterns. Aircraft pilots flying over the South American jungles have noticed the iridescent blue wings of morpho butterflies far below them, so brilliant are these hues.

The brightness of such butterflies makes them easily recognizable to others of their own species but also obvious to predators. Fortunately, morphos are quick, adept fliers and are difficult to catch. Perhaps such coloration even serves to invite predators—as their attacks are usually unsuccessful, they learn that it is a waste of effort to try and catch morphos.

Butterflies have a distinct larval stage, which is a jawed and usually plant-eating caterpillar, and a resting, non-feeding pupal stage. Adults are fluid feeders, they sip small quantities of nectar. There are also butterflies with less conventional feeding habits. Some heliconids, long-winged South American butterflies, feed on pollen grains. Forest swallowtails, monarch butterflies, and others, are attracted to pools of mammal urine, perhaps encouraged by its high nitrogen content. And *Charaxes* butterflies, native to Africa and Southeast Asia, feed on such large amounts of rotting fruit, faeces and other decaying material that their abdomens become quite distended.

Most butterflies, however, feed at flowers. Swallowtails (family Papilionidae) are drawn to flowers not visited by other butterflies, in particular to red ones. This is unusual since the sensitivity of insects is usually toward the ultraviolet end of the spectrum rather than the red.

Butterfly larvae too are often specific in their choice of food plants. The larvae of some species of *Bematistes* feed only on forest vines, particularly passion flowers. Monarch butterfly larvae restrict themselves to milkweeds.

In their different ways all these forest butterflies make full use of the jungle and the food resources it contains.

Some of the largest and most beautiful butterflies are the birdwings, found only in Southeast Asia. There are 12 species. Rajah Brooke's birdwing, *Ornithoptera brookiana*, lives in the jungles of Borneo, Sumatra and Malaysia. Females have a wingspan of up to 7½in (19cm) and males are slightly smaller. Although primarily a species of the upper layers of the jungle, both sexes may descend to the forest floor in the early morning to feed or drink. Birdwings are rare and much sought after by collectors. Some are bred especially for sale.

Many of the so-called metalmark butterflies spend their lives in the rain forest canopy trees. The common name of these brilliant butterflies refers to the metallic markings evident on the under surfaces of their wings.

Male

Female

Henry Walter Bates (1825–92), British naturalist who explored the Amazon Basin, the first to study the phenomenon of animal mimicry.

Henry Bates had no formal scientific training but was an enthusiastic amateur entomologist and collector. In 1844 he met Alfred Russel Wallace and awakened his interest in the subject of entomology. Three years later the two men, influenced by the ideas of Humboldt, Lyell and Darwin, decided to make their own expedition to South America to collect data that might help solve the problem of the origin of species. They planned to finance their trip by collecting and selling specimens.

In 1848 Bates and Wallace arrived in Brazil and travelled together up the River Tocantin, before separating to explore and collect specimens. Wallace returned to Britain in 1852 but Bates remained in Brazil for eleven years.

Bates collected some 500 species of butterfly and in all amassed specimens of more than 14,000 creatures, mainly insects. Some 8,000 of these were at that time unknown to science.

Bates returned home in 1859, began work on his huge collection and two years later presented his celebrated paper *Contributions to an Insect Fauna of the Amazon Valley*. Described by Charles Darwin as 'one of the most remarkable and admirable papers I ever read', this paper was the first to draw attention to the phenomenon of a particular form of animal mimicry, now known as Batesian mimicry.

In 1863 Bates published his only book *The Naturalist on the River Amazon*—an instant success and still one of the great classics on the Amazon.

The morpho butterflies of South America belong to the family Nymphalidae. They have wonderfully iridescent wings which flash in the sun as they soar over the jungle. Their iridescence is produced by many transparent, strongly reflecting scales, not by pigments.

The green charaxes butterfly, *Charaxes eupale*, is common in the West African rain forests. The female is slightly larger than the male with a wingspan of up to 2¼in (6cm). The adults feed on a strange variety of foods including tree sap, rotting fruit, excrement and even animal carcasses.

A curious resemblance to monkey heads protects the pupae of some lycaenid butterflies, such as *Spalgis lemolea*, from predatory birds. These pupae lie on the upper surface of leaves and from a distance look like bird droppings. When an insectivorous bird approaches more closely to investigate a pupa, the shock of seeing the monkey head image seems to override the reality of the size difference.

The attractive moth *Aurivillius triramis* lives in the West African forests. It belongs to the family Saturnidae which includes many large tropical moths—one with a wingspan of nearly 10in (25cm). Saturnid caterpillars spin strong silken cocoons in which to pupate. The silk made by some species is so fine that it is used for making cloth. Adult saturnids all have distinctive eye-spot markings on their wings. These spots, which resemble the eyes of a larger creature, are thought to startle and deter a would-be predator.

Pupa

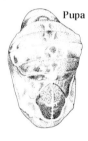

The passion flower butterflies

The brilliant hues and wing patterns of many jungle butterflies can protect them from enemies. Particular patterns advertise the fact that a creature is unpalatable. By trial and error birds have learned to associate these patterns with toxic or distasteful insects and avoid them.

Unpalatability in adult butterflies is usually linked to the feeding habits of the larvae. The larvae of many jungle butterflies feed on plants that contain harmful chemicals but they are able to detoxify and store these chemicals in their tissues. The sequestered compounds are carried on to the adults, rendering them unpalatable also. The chemicals in the plants are of course designed to deter plant feeders, but as insects have a short generation time they can quickly evolve the necessary enzymes to adapt to the plant's chemistry.

Co-evolution of plants and insects is particularly common in jungles. Heliconid butterflies have had a long association with passion flower vines (Passifloraceae). The butterfly lays its eggs on the passion flower; the larvae feed on the plant and acquire poisons from it which make them unpalatable to birds. In the battle to deter the heliconids, new species of passion flower evolve, synthesizing new poisons in the process; in their turn, new heliconid species evolve, able to detoxify the poisons. Many forms of both passion flower and heliconid result. Heliconids adapt to detoxify only the chemicals of their particular passion flower and so are restricted to feeding on that species.

Passion flowers also try other protective devices. Many have additional nectaries which are not inside flowers; some of these nectaries attract ants which then defend the plant from egg-laying butterflies. Others look like heliconid eggs, so when a female heliconid lands on the plant to assess the egg load before laying her own, she is confused into thinking that the plant is already heavily populated. Passion flowers such as the Costa Rican species *Passiflora adenopoda*, have evolved hooked hairs which cover their surface. These hairs trap and puncture the heliconid larvae and cause their death by starvation and bleeding.

Toxic butterflies signal their unpalatability by their patterns. To take advantage of this, a number of different distasteful species have evolved the same basic patterns. This reduces the amount of learning for predators and the losses in sampling for the insects. The phenomenon was first noted by Fritz Müller, a German zoologist, and is called Müllerian mimicry.

Even more cunning are the butterflies which cash in on the advantages by imitating the warning patterns even though they themselves are palatable. Known as Batesian mimicry after the naturalist Henry Bates, this trick is successful only if the palatable species are in the minority. Predators must have a high chance of sampling an unpalatable individual, otherwise the device fails.

There are many instances of butterfly mimicry in the jungle. One complex example involves a heliconid butterfly, *Heliconius nattereri*. The male and female have different wing patterns and therefore have their own separate mimics.

The combination of black, yellow and orange coloration is common among distasteful, forest-dwelling butterflies and, in Brazil, forms the basis for a mimetic complex. *Mechanitis lysimnia*, above, has the same basic pattern as the female *Heliconius nattereri*. It is also a distasteful species and is a Müllerian mimic of the heliconid, presenting predators with a common warning coloration. Like the heliconids, the larvae of *Mechanitis* feed on toxic plants.

Another butterfly which closely resembles the female *Heliconius nattereri* and other species in the mimetic complex, is *Dismorphia astyocha* of the Pieridae family. *Dismorphia* is however a 'sheep in wolf's clothing'. Although it has warning coloration it is harmless and therefore a Batesian mimic of *Heliconius*. It gains protection from predators by its resemblance to the distasteful species—the birds recognize the warning pattern and leave it well alone.

Males and females of *Heliconius nattereri* have different wing patterns which means they must also have different mimics. The butterfly *Aeria olena* is a Batesian mimic of the male.

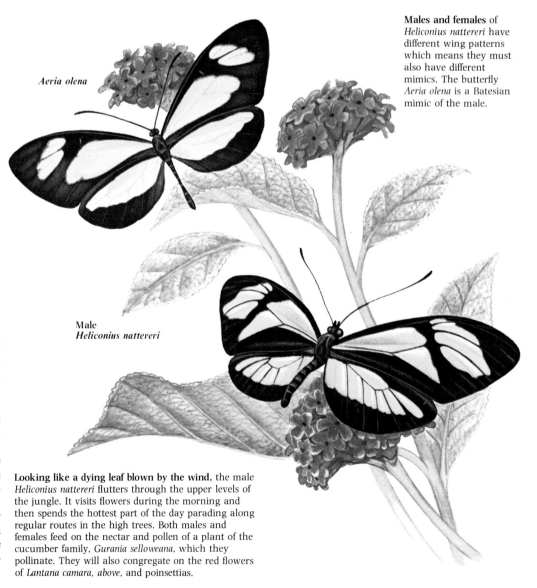

Aeria olena

Male
Heliconius nattereri

Looking like a dying leaf blown by the wind, the male *Heliconius nattereri* flutters through the upper levels of the jungle. It visits flowers during the morning and then spends the hottest part of the day parading along regular routes in the high trees. Both males and females feed on the nectar and pollen of a plant of the cucumber family, *Gurania selloweana*, which they pollinate. They will also congregate on the red flowers of *Lantana camara*, *above*, and poinsettias.

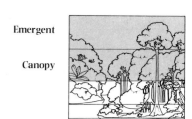

Female
Heliconius nattereri

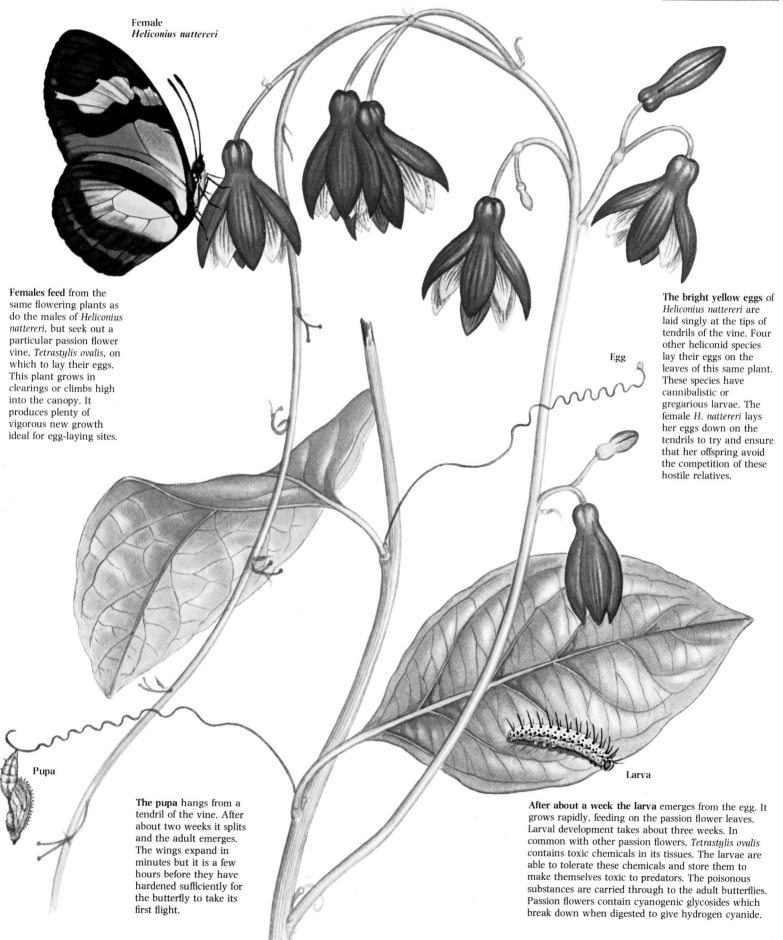

Females feed from the same flowering plants as do the males of *Heliconius nattereri*, but seek out a particular passion flower vine, *Tetrastylis ovalis*, on which to lay their eggs. This plant grows in clearings or climbs high into the canopy. It produces plenty of vigorous new growth ideal for egg-laying sites.

The bright yellow eggs of *Heliconius nattereri* are laid singly at the tips of tendrils of the vine. Four other heliconid species lay their eggs on the leaves of this same plant. These species have cannibalistic or gregarious larvae. The female *H. nattereri* lays her eggs down on the tendrils to try and ensure that her offspring avoid the competition of these hostile relatives.

Egg

Pupa

Larva

The pupa hangs from a tendril of the vine. After about two weeks it splits and the adult emerges. The wings expand in minutes but it is a few hours before they have hardened sufficiently for the butterfly to take its first flight.

After about a week the larva emerges from the egg. It grows rapidly, feeding on the passion flower leaves. Larval development takes about three weeks. In common with other passion flowers, *Tetrastylis ovalis* contains toxic chemicals in its tissues. The larvae are able to tolerate these chemicals and store them to make themselves toxic to predators. The poisonous substances are carried through to the adult butterflies. Passion flowers contain cyanogenic glycosides which break down when digested to give hydrogen cyanide.

115

Insects in disguise

To escape detection by their enemies, jungle insects adopt cunning methods of protecting themselves. Many conceal themselves beneath bark, leaves, stones and vegetation. Others rely on camouflage or disguise because their own coloration, often green or brown, blends into their surroundings. In species such as the stick insects, slow changes of hue enable them to adjust to changes in the background. The glasswing butterflies of South America have transparent wings through which the background is clearly visible.

Since shadows give depth and outline to objects and act as important visual cues to predators, several insects have developed ways of hiding their shadows and thus improving their concealment. Lateral structures in the form of plates, hairs or outgrowths help insects such as caterpillars merge into the substratum. Many other species are flattened and crouch close to the surface they are mimicking.

To offset the shadows produced by the vertical shafts of light in the jungles, some caterpillars are countershaded—the undersurface is a lighter shade than the upper. When viewed from the side, the caterpillars appear flat rather than round.

An insect's outline may also be blurred through disruptive coloration, when bright patches stand out from the rest of the body, which merges into the background. The stripes in caterpillars and grasshoppers commonly have this effect, as well as breaking up an insect's bilateral symmetry.

Ingenious methods of concealment are found in insects which masquerade as commonplace items in their surroundings. Several mimic living, dead or decayed leaves. With their greatly flattened bodies and legs, leaf insects (Phyllidae), for example, are able to imitate a cluster of slightly chewed leaves. Leaf mimics are often further protected by realistic markings of disease patches or bird droppings.

Protective resemblance is also seen in the Membracidae (Homoptera), or treehoppers, plant-sucking bugs of the Central and South American jungles, which have pronotums that may be enlarged to produce a thornlike appearance, or may be knobbed and black, resembling ants. Other structures which are successfully mimicked are seeds by weevils, plant galls by spiders and bird droppings by caterpillars and spiders.

The behaviour of the mimics frequently accentuates the deception. Many remain immobile for long periods, or freeze when danger threatens. Leaf and stick insects gently rock back and forth to simulate movement in a breeze; some butterflies fly hesitantly like falling leaves.

Cryptic species often have a second line of defence which they use when their camouflage has failed. Some species drop to the ground and feign death. Others attempt to startle a predator. When threatened, *Choerodolis rhombicollis*, the leaf-mimicking mantid from Central America, will turn toward its aggressor, exposing the undersurface of its large, flat pronotal shield and thus appear to increase in size. As the mantid lunges toward the predator, it makes a scraping noise by rubbing its forelegs on the pronotal shield.

Stick insects (Phasmidae) have twiglike bodies and can be as much as 13in (33cm) long. Forelegs and antennae can be held forward to fit snugly round the head and disguise its shape.

A New Guinea weevil species, *Gymnopholus*, is camouflaged by lichens, algae and liverworts growing on its back. The upper surface of the insect's back is covered with pits, grooves, hairs and secretions to aid the growth of this covering.

Concealed among the pink flowers, *left*, is a praying mantis, *Hymenopus coronatus*. This Malaysian flower mantis is not only perfectly camouflaged from predators but also attractive to prey. Its mimicry is so good that it is investigated by flower-feeding insects which it swiftly traps.

To appear more fearsome than they are, fulguroids have fat- and air-filled facial outgrowths adorned with eye and teeth markings. The resulting appearance gives the insects their common name of alligator bugs. Fulguroid nymphs, *below*, have tail tufts of fine, white, waxy filaments which can be opened out like umbrellas. The flash of white made by a group of nymphs opening their tails seems to startle predators.

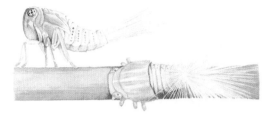

A leaf-mimicking katydid perches among the vegetation which provides its camouflage and its food, *below*. Many katydids (family Tettigoniidae) are leaf mimics. The uncanny resemblance is produced by the insect's laterally flattened body and the enlargement of its forewings. Accentuated veins on the forewings simulate the veining of a leaf to complete the effective disguise.

Brilliance for a purpose

For centuries man has been attracted by the brilliant, jewel-like patterns of many tropical insects. Ancient Indian cultures used insects to decorate ceremonial robes, while more recently the Victorians made collages with bright pieces of insect. Such appealing coloration is produced when some of the wavelengths of white light are removed from the spectrum and the rest are reflected. Specific wavelengths of light may be absorbed by pigments or differentially reflected by the physical nature of the insect cuticle.

In insects the pigments are laid down in the cuticle during its formation, or are deposited in the superficial tissues under fairly transparent cuticle. Pigments are frequently waste products derived from food or from body-building processes which are stored rather than excreted. Carotenoids are the pigments responsible for the yellow-orange-red sequence of coloration seen in some grasshoppers. When carotenoids are combined with blue pigments, greens result. These can be seen in the cryptic coloration of stick insects and many grasshoppers. White, yellow and red are also produced by pterines, pigments which are especially common in butterflies and moths and give the red hue to many insect eyes.

There are certain insects, such as the stick insects, which are able to vary their shade during the day, becoming lighter or darker as the light intensity changes. They lighten by concentrating the pigment in the epidermal cells and deepen their hue by dispersing the pigment.

The other major way in which insects produce patterning depends on the physical splitting of light by surface structures or subcuticular particles. The pearly white of some butterflies is the result of large particles scattering all wavelengths of white light. The brilliant blues of some dragonflies occur when minute particles with dimensions similar to the wavelength of blue light reflect only blue while the remaining wavelengths of red and green are absorbed by a pigment layer beneath the particles.

The metallic or iridescent sheens of many butterflies and plant-feeding beetles are created by microscopic vertical vanes or reflecting layers in the cuticle. The spacing between these structures is such that only certain wavelengths are reflected. When viewed from different angles, the distances between the reflecting layers change and produce different hues.

The advantages of shiny or metallic coloration are not known for certain. Perhaps in the moist jungle conditions, the 'wet look' is more concealing than the matt, pigment-produced effects. Since interference hues change with the viewing angle, they may help an insect escape detection. Another possibility is that the contrast between the area of insect cuticle reflecting light and the rest which does not, serves to obscure the insect's body outline. Whatever the reason for these brilliant metallic hues, they have provided insects with myriad dazzling patterns.

Known as jewel beetles, buprestid beetles, such as *Sternocera* sp. from Southeast Asia, are typically a brilliant metallic green. Buprestids may be up to 3in (7.5cm) long and are day fliers often seen on flowers.

Weevil   Fly

Some Central American weevils have untypically bright markings which give them a strong resemblance to several fly species. By looking alike, weevils and flies are thought to gain some protection. Predators associate the bright patterns with the highly agile movements of both insects and go for easier prey.

This gaudy creature is a pyrgomorph grasshopper, easily identified by its cone-shaped head. The gaudy coloration of these grasshoppers warns off predators. Some pyrgomorphs are distasteful, others have glands that produce unpleasant foams. Winged species may flash brightly patterned forewings to startle predators. These grasshoppers are found in jungles throughout the world feeding on vegetation.

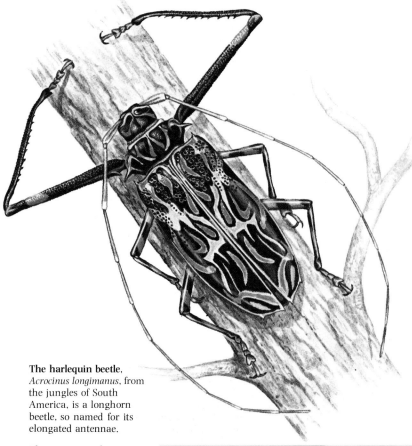

The harlequin beetle, *Acrocinus longimanus*, from the jungles of South America, is a longhorn beetle, so named for its elongated antennae.

The warning coloration of this Costa Rican caterpillar is for good reason. Each segment of the caterpillar's body is armed with tufts of stinging hairs. These hairs are hollow and brittle. If a predator tries to eat the caterpillar it brushes against the hairs, which break and discharge poison from their hollow shafts. An effective deterrent, this poison causes nettle rash in humans at point of contact.

Although Charles Darwin began his career by studying medicine, he had always been a natural history enthusiast and a keen collector, particularly of beetles. At the age of 22, through connections made at Cambridge, he took the post of unpaid naturalist on a voyage of the British naval survey ship H.M.S. *Beagle*. The main objective of the expedition was to map the coast of South America.

The *Beagle*'s voyage lasted five years. Darwin collected thousands of specimens and was continually fascinated by the diversity of life in the South American forests and other areas. His first thoughts on the evolutionary origin of species began while on the voyage.

In 1859 he published his major work *On the Origin of Species by means of Natural Selection*. One of the most influential books of its century, *The Origin of Species* caused a tumult of indignation and scientific interest never to be forgotten.

Charles Robert Darwin (1809–82) British naturalist who revolutionized science with his theory of evolution through natural selection.

The tortoise beetle, *Aspidomorpha miliaris*, from Sumatra, has a transparent cuticle showing an underlying pigment pattern. The pattern resembles that of distasteful ladybirds. The beetle has expanded, flattened wing covers which reduce lateral shadows and merge the body into its background.

Colonies in the trees

To satisfy some of their basic needs many jungle insects adopt a communal way of living. Otherwise solitary individuals may be forced together because suitable food or egg-laying sites are patchily distributed throughout the environment. In other species females build a communal nest in which they rear their offspring. The highest form of communal life, termed eusocial, is found in termites, ants, bees and wasps. In this type a single, long-lived, reproductively active female governs all the activities of sterile individuals of different generations by chemical messages.

Members of this type of colony do not act on their own but as part of a superorganism. The overriding biological force which operates on an individual of any species is the drive to pass on its genes to the next generation. In a eusocial system the workers are sterile, but they continue to care for the offspring of the queen because sister workers share a higher proportion of common genes (75 per cent) with each other than they do with either parent (50 per cent). Thus they are still ensuring the continuance of that proportion of shared genes.

In the jungles many eusocial species, such as stingless bees, are tree nesters. Despite their name these tropical bees are able to defend themselves with well-developed mandibles and a caustic saliva which causes burns and lesions. The wax which they produce is combined with plant resins and sometimes with other materials for use in nest construction.

Honeybees are also tree cavity nesters. In South America domesticated honeybee strains were crossed with a ferocious strain of African honeybee in an attempt to improve the honey yields. Some of the African bee strains escaped, spreading throughout Brazil. The new strains, called killer bees, are so excitable they attack almost any large moving animal. Over 300 people have been killed since the African strain was introduced in 1957.

Arboreal eusocial wasps of the genera *Polistes* and *Polybia* are common throughout jungles of South and Central America; they make hanging nests of a papery material made from chewed wood fragments. Arboreal termites make spherical nests around branches. These are composed of chewed wood and saliva, and have the consistency of brittle cardboard.

Weaver or tailor ants construct miraculous nests of living leaves which are held together with larval silk. The colonies may occupy one or several tree canopies, and contain up to half a million individuals.

Ants, bees, termites and wasps use the materials and niches provided by the jungle trees to great advantage. Their nests have enabled them to establish a degree of control over their environment.

The aggressive and territorial weaver ants, *Oecophylla smaragdina,* live in Southeast Asia. One of the earliest records of biological control of pest species relates to these ants, which were used in A.D. 300 by the Chinese to deal with the insect pests of citrus trees. Weaver or tailor ants construct nests from living leaves which they fold and bind with silk secreted by their larvae. A number of worker ants independently begin pulling at the edges of a selected leaf. Once an ant succeeds at turning over an edge—often the ant at the tip—the others join it and cooperate to fold the leaf. While some ants hold the leaf in position, other workers carrying larvae 'sew' up the edges with the silk from mandibular glands of the larvae. The ants pass the larvae back and forth like shuttles in weaving until the leaf is held together.

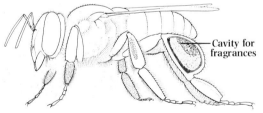

The orchid bees of Latin America have a special relationship with orchid flowers. Male orchid bees, *Euglossa* sp., feed on nectar. They visit orchids not to feed but to gather fragrant scents from the petals with pads on their forelegs. As the bee flies away, the scents are transferred to cavities in the enlarged hind legs. The process is repeated many times. The fragrance of the orchid scents attracts male orchid bees to one another. Groups of male bees form and display competitively for the attentions of females. Female bees are attracted to the groups not by the fragrance but by the brilliant visual spectacle of the glittering males swarming together.

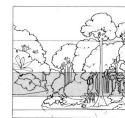
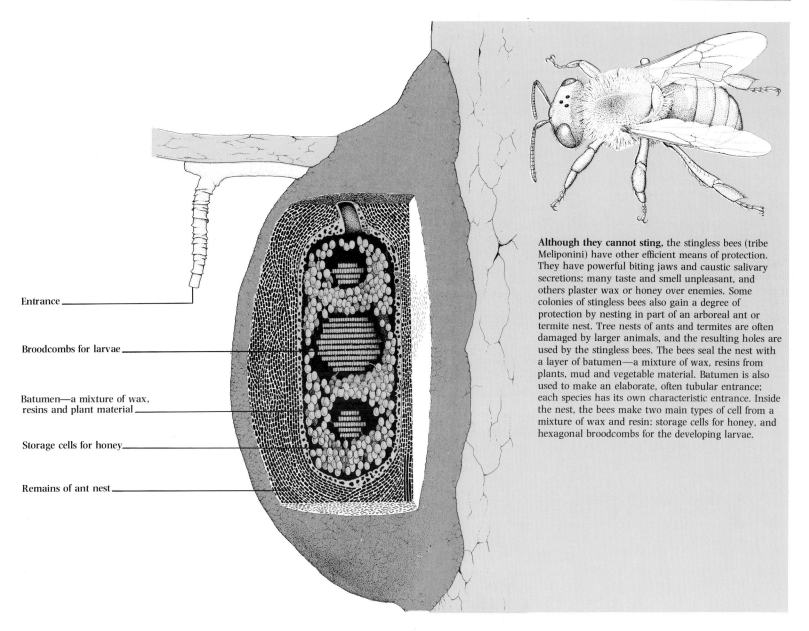

Entrance

Broodcombs for larvae

Batumen—a mixture of wax, resins and plant material

Storage cells for honey

Remains of ant nest

Although they cannot sting, the stingless bees (tribe Meliponini) have other efficient means of protection. They have powerful biting jaws and caustic salivary secretions; many taste and smell unpleasant, and others plaster wax or honey over enemies. Some colonies of stingless bees also gain a degree of protection by nesting in part of an arboreal ant or termite nest. Tree nests of ants and termites are often damaged by larger animals, and the resulting holes are used by the stingless bees. The bees seal the nest with a layer of batumen—a mixture of wax, resins from plants, mud and vegetable material. Batumen is also used to make an elaborate, often tubular entrance; each species has its own characteristic entrance. Inside the nest, the bees make two main types of cell from a mixture of wax and resin: storage cells for honey, and hexagonal broodcombs for the developing larvae.

Covered passageways lead from the termite nest down the trunk and branches to foraging areas. These protect the termites as they travel to and from the nest. If a passageway is damaged it is quickly repaired by workers.

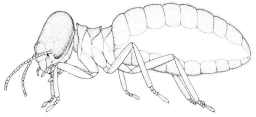

The common forest termite species, *Nasutitermes arborum*, constructs its nest around tree branches. The nest is made from fragments of wood and saliva. Inside it is a maze of irregular passages, but toward the centre is the royal cell containing the termite queen and king. Glands in the enlarged head of the soldier termites secrete a sticky repellent fluid which the soldier can squirt from the 'nose' at enemies. Worker termites have strong, well-developed mandibles with which they chew woody material. The termites cannot themselves digest the cellulose in wood, but have in their guts symbiotic bacteria and protozoa which break down the cellulose into sugars.

The armies of ants

Of all the jungle insects army ants are the most notorious. Because of their nomadic life-style and huge colonies, they are considered the terror of the jungle. A colony of army ants, with up to 20 million stinging, biting individuals, is formidable, but its advance is only about one foot per minute, and so an active animal can easily escape capture.

There are about 240 species of army ants; some known as legionary, or driver, ants. Jungle representatives include *Eciton burchelli*, *E. hamatum* and *Labidus praedator*, indigenous to Central and South America; the genus *Anomma*, restricted to Africa; and the smaller *Aenictus*, found in Southeast Asia and Africa.

Army ants undergo cycles of activity linked to brood development and the reproductive activities of the queen. The presence of young larvae stimulates the workers to form raiding parties for prey. When larval development is complete, there is a surplus of food which makes the workers lethargic. Some of this food is supplied to the queen for egg production and these eggs, in turn, give rise to more larvae which again activate the workers. Thus there is an alternating colony behaviour: a quiescent, stationary, phase and an active, exploratory, nomadic phase.

Unlike other ant species, army ants have no fixed nest. During the active phase they forage during the day, and at night occupy temporary structures known as bivouacs, usually in holes in the ground or beneath fallen trees. Frequently masses of worker ants form the only walls—they link their bodies together to protect the brood and queen deep within.

The nomadic phase is characterized by the raids. At dawn, the temporary bivouac becomes a seething, disorganized mass of ants, from which a raiding party develops. Since army ants are virtually blind, they rely on odour trails for guidance. At the advancing front, individual workers explore small areas of ground, laying down odour trails from their abdominal glands before retreating into the mass of raiders. These guide other workers, which then encounter and investigate new ground before retreating. Behind the raiding fronts follows the rest of the colony, with the smallest workers in the middle of the column and the largest on the flanks. Prey are carried back along the column and collected together in 'booty caches'.

At specific times, the queen produces a special batch of eggs composed mainly of males and a few queens. A group of the workers associates with, and tends, these developing sexuals. The new queens are the first to emerge; the later emergence of the males heralds the galvanization of the workers. They move off in raiding parties, dividing the bivouac in two, with the old queen and her workers going off in one direction and the new queens and some workers in another. When the splinter group bivouacs for the night, only one queen is allowed to enter it. The remainder are sealed out of the new colony by workers and soon die. The winged males have a pre-mating dispersal flight, after which they seek out other army ant bivouacs to find a virgin queen to mate with.

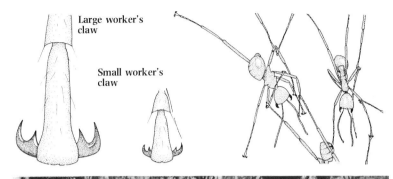

Large worker's claw

Small worker's claw

Using their strong claws, army ants join themselves together to form bivouacs for the night. The formation of the bivouac begins around dusk when some ants attach themselves to a surface by their leg hooks. Other ants then start to link themselves on by their sharp, curving claws.

Hundreds of ants join in the bivouac forming living walls to protect the queen and the developing brood. Within the bivouac, the larvae are tended and fed, and the queen settles with her attendants.

Katydids can be overpowered by army ants, *right*. Such insects often climb up on to vegetation to avoid an advancing column of army ants. When some of the ants also come up to explore the vegetation, the katydid drops off to avoid them and lands among the mass of workers below.

During the nomadic phase when the ants move through the jungle every day, the developing larvae are carried by workers who groom and feed them, *below*. Workers chew morsels of prey into pellets for the larvae.

Small worker 3.9mm   Large worker   12mm

Army ant workers come in several sizes for different tasks. Their long, strong legs enable them to travel rapidly and carry larvae slung beneath them. *Eciton burchelli* workers have particularly enormous jaws, and Amazon Indians have used these tong-jawed ants for 'stitching' deep wounds. The ant is enticed to bite across the wound, drawing the edges together. Its body is nipped off leaving the jaws holding the wound.

Male army ants are larger than workers and wasplike in appearance. They are produced in the colony brood along with potential queens. Males have well-developed eyes, wings, and a large, humped thorax containing flight muscles. These features enable them to fly away from the parent colony, locate another army ant trail and follow it to the bivouac. If this bivouac contains a virgin queen the male ant will then mate with her.

A queen rules the army ant colony. She is wingless, and stouter and stronger than the workers who constantly clean and care for her. Periodically her abdomen becomes enlarged and within a few days she lays between 100,000 and 300,000 eggs. The behaviour of the rest of the colony is synchronized to the queen's reproductive cycle—its stationary phase coincides with her period of enlargement and egg laying.

The plant processers

Beneath the rain forest floor there is a world of constant activity. One of its major inhabitants is the termite, an insect which plays a key role in reprocessing the forest's dead wood and leaf litter.

In the jungles of Southeast Asia and the East Indies, troops of as many as 500,000 workers of the genus *Hospitalitermes* go on periodic forays to restock the nest food stores. They collect lichens, bark-flakes, mosses and other plant materials which they carry back to the nest in their mandibles or guts. A recent study in Sarawak showed that this termite selects specific lichens which may be some distance from the nest, instead of locally abundant material. The chosen lichens are capable of fixing atmospheric nitrogen, and are therefore valuable as a source of amino acids for protein production.

The rain forests of northern Queensland are likewise not immune from the attacks of termites. *Coptotermes dreghorni* destroys valuable trees, while *Amitermes herbertensis* hollows out rotting logs and tree stumps, then fills them with an earthy material in which it constructs its nest.

One neotropical termite species, *Anoplotermes pacificus*, from the Brazilian rain forests, has an unusual link with certain plant roots. The workers construct a large subterranean nest from humus which they have already chewed and passed through their intestinal tracts. Plant roots invade the nest and form a thick mat around it. The termites then chew the tips of these roots; this causes them to develop growths like small cauliflowers, which the termites also eat. What the plant derives from the association is unknown, but its roots die if the termites abandon their nest.

The leaf-cutting ants (*Atta* sp.), cultivate crops of fungi which they nourish with leaves. The ants are the most important defoliating insects of tropical crops, often reducing vegetable patches to leafless stalks overnight. An *Atta* colony, with over two million inhabitants, contains different types of individual. A single large queen founds the colony and produces the eggs. Next in size are the soldiers, with large, almost triangular heads, and huge shearing mandibles. The workers vary in size; the largest ones cut leaf pieces from foliage, which they carry back to the nest above their heads. The smaller workers protect the larger ones from parasitic flies, as well as feeding and caring for the larvae.

The pieces of leaf collected by the workers are cut up, chewed to a pulp and used as a substratum for the fungus. In order for this fungus to decompose leaves, it needs enzymes from faecal secretions of the workers. Both insects and fungi are therefore necessary for each other's continued survival.

Communication in ants is primarily by pheromones, airborne chemical messages which produce particular responses in suitable recipients. In leaf-cutting ants, secretions of the poison gland have pheromonal qualities. When the ants are in distress, they make virtually ultrasonic chirps by scraping together two specialized structures on the abdomen. Fellow workers are able to pick up the chirps as vibrations in the ground. These signals are used to locate workers buried in tunnels, or to assist workers being attacked.

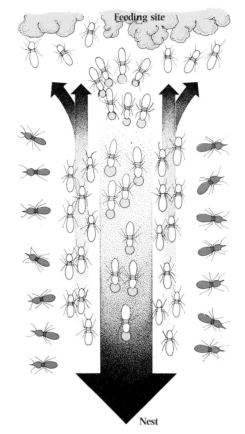

Feeding site

Nest

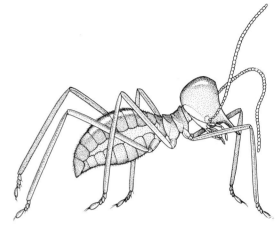

Foraging columns of the termite species *Hospitalitermes umbrinus* are common in the rain forests of Southeast Asia. At the feeding site one group of workers collects lichens, mosses and pieces of bark and wood, while a second group works the food into balls to carry back to the nest. By following odour trails, the workers move in a well-ordered column to and from the feeding area. Homebound workers carrying balls of food occupy the central part of the column, and outward bound workers move at the sides. The feeding site and the column are flanked by soldier termites on guard duty. The head of the *Hospitalitermes* soldier is modified into a long 'nose'. It contains glands which manufacture a sticky, repellent secretion which the soldier can shoot out of its nose at an enemy.

Nests like large, multi-capped mushrooms are built by the East African termites, *Cubitermes speciosus*. The nests are designed to resist heavy jungle rainfall. A nest is started by a king and queen termite who burrow into the ground. From this underground nest, columns are constructed which are then capped. Up to five caps may be added to a column. Inside the structure are many cells connected by narrow openings.

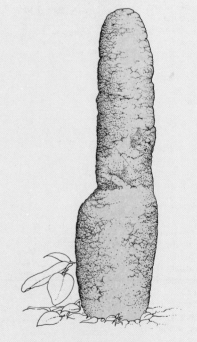

In the jungles of the Ivory Coast are the column nests of the termite species *Thoracotermes macrothorax*. A nest is about 5ft (1.5m) high and is made of soft, chewed humus mixed with saliva. The shape and design allow a large surface area for gas exchange, but make it impossible to control the internal temperature—usually similar to the surrounding air. There are no specialized compartments for housing the king and queen.

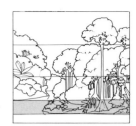

Leaf-cutting ants, of Central and South America, have worker ants of different sizes. As the large workers cut pieces from leaves and carry them back to their nest, they are guarded by small workers—when holding leaves in their jaws the larger ants are defenceless against parasitic flies (Phoridae) which like to lay their eggs on the neck of an ant. The emerging larvae burrow into the ant and kill it. The small worker ants fend off the flies.

After her nuptial flight, a new queen leaf-cutting ant founds a colony. She breaks off her wings and digs a nest about 12in (30cm) deep. In a pouch behind her mouthparts, she has a small piece of fungus, which she has brought with her from her original nest. She places this fungus on the nest floor and manures it with faecal material. She then lays her eggs.

A colony of leaf-cutting ants lives in a huge underground nest with many entrances. In one example almost 23 cubic metres of soil was brought to the surface in six and a half years. A colony may house between one and two and a half million worker ants. Workers tend the fungus garden—they fertilize it with faecal material, gather pieces of leaf, chew them up and put them on the garden, and weed out any alien material. They feed on the expanded hyphal tips which grow on the garden. The many entrances ventilate the nest. Air flows into the nest through the entrances near the nest edge and leaves it through those at the centre.

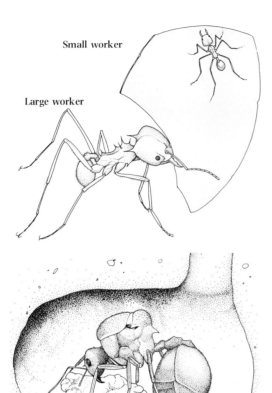

Small worker

Large worker

125

The floor dwellers

Unlike the temperate forests, where leaves fall mainly in the autumn, the jungle experiences some leaf fall throughout the year. Yet there is less debris in the rain forest because its termite population, high temperatures and humidity ensure that the litter is rapidly decomposed and re-used by plants and animals.

This sparse litter layer provides a home for a variety of Cryptozoa, invertebrate animals which live for the most part hidden beneath leaves, stones and fallen logs on the forest floor. Many of these, such as springtails, mites, millipedes, centipedes, snails and slugs, are common in temperate forests too, but there are also some bizarre examples in the jungle.

The Onychophora, or velvet worms, are among the most fascinating. Found throughout the jungles of the world, they are thought to be carnivorous predators, although they will scavenge dead insects. Most velvet worms are only an inch or two long, but *Macroperipatus geavi* from Central America, reaching 5 inches (12.5cm) in length, is the biggest species. Onychophorans have two large slime glands which extend over half the length of the body and open on to two small papillae near the mouth. Should a predator attack, the velvet worm can eject slime. It is not known whether this thickening slime is also used to restrain prey. Velvet worms dehydrate rapidly so need the high humidity of the jungle.

Another cryptozoic group, the land planarians (Platyhelminthes: Terricola), also require high humidity. Concentrated in the jungles of South America and Southeast Asia, they are sometimes established in hothouses, having been introduced on tropical plants. One species, *Bipalium kewense*, was first discovered in the greenhouses of Kew Gardens in London and only later found to be of tropical origin. Often brightly hued, with a ribbonlike body, these nocturnal carnivores glide along, forming a slime trail. They feed by wrapping themselves around their prey, liberally coating it with slime, and then either engulf it or pour digestive enzymes out on to it and suck up the resulting 'soup'.

Although the jungle floor is populated by such large spectacular spiders as the trapdoor spiders (Ctenizidae) and the bird-eating spiders, smaller specialist spiders also flourish there. The ogre-faced spider, *Dinopsis longipipes*, constructs a supporting web on low vegetation close to the jungle floor and over an ant trail. It hangs from this web, using its rear two pairs of legs. In its front two pairs of legs, *Dinopsis* holds a net of teased silk which it dabs at passing ants, picking them off the ground.

Cockroaches, beetles, and crickets as well as a multitude of other insects also inhabit the jungle floor. Some, such as the web spinners (Embioptera), produce silk to construct tunnels in which to live.

The great diversity of insect life in the jungle is partly due to the rich plant flora with which it has co-evolved over millions of years. Some insects eat only certain plant seeds, and, as a result, are usually found beneath the seed-producing tree, eating or killing most of the seeds there. Seeds dispersed away from the parent tree and its congregation of seed-eating insects have a greater chance of surviving, and this is one possible advantage of the wide separation of individual trees of the same species in the rain forest.

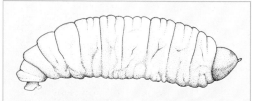

Congo floor maggots, *Auchmeromyia luteola*, live in crevices of the floors of native huts in equatorial Africa. They attack the inhabitants of the huts at night as they lie sleeping on the floor. A maggot emerges, punctures the skin of its victim with its mouth hooks, then sucks the blood avidly. These bites are extremely irritating.

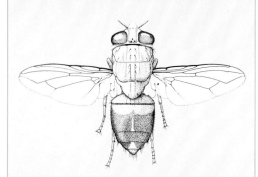

The adult flies of *Auchmeromyia luteola* are a yellowish-brown and about the size of a bluebottle. They are attracted to human dwellings and feed on excrement and decaying vegetation. The female fly lays her eggs in batches of about 50 in the dust of hut floors, often near sleeping mats. The eggs take about two days to hatch and the life cycle lasts ten weeks.

Velvet worms, Onychophora, superficially resemble slugs and live in the jungle where humidity is high. Their fossil records show that they date back at least 500 million years and have changed little since the earliest fossils.

Shy, secretive creatures, scorpion spiders, or amblypygi, are found in all jungles. During the day they hide beneath loose bark, stones or leaf litter on the forest floor, emerging at night to hunt for prey. They move sideways in a crablike fashion, using their long forelegs as antennae to obtain tactile information about their surroundings; the three remaining pairs of legs are used for walking. The scorpion spider's flattened body helps it move easily through the leaf litter.

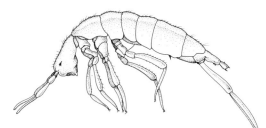

Springtails or Collembola are abundant litter-dwelling animals throughout the world; most feed on bacteria and fungi. The common name comes from a forked appendage at the end of the abdomen which enables the springtail to jump. This tail is held tucked under the abdomen. When released, it springs back catapulting the springtail into the air.

The largest millipedes live in jungles—*Spirobolus* may be almost 1ft (30cm) long. They do not have poison claws like their relatives the centipedes, but can exude or spray caustic secretions from glands in the body segments. These formidable secretions deter predators. Millipedes feed on fallen leaves and plant debris, and play an important role in the decomposition of forest litter. The faecal material of millipedes forms a suitable substrate for bacteria and fungi.

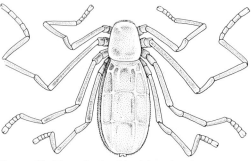

Rare, spiderlike animals, ricinulei need moist surroundings and usually live under damp fallen leaves in the jungles of Africa and Brazil. Their fossil record shows that they date back at least 350 million years to the Carboniferous period when they were quite common. Ricinulei are up to ⅜in (1cm) long with heavy bodies and hinged hoods that protect their mouthparts. They are blind, and use their shortened forelegs to feel their way slowly through the forest.

The trapdoor spider makes a burrow in the forest floor, concealed by a hinged doorway. Using the comblike spines in its fangs, the spider rakes away soil particles as it excavates the burrow. The walls are waterproofed and stabilized with silk and salivary secretions. Alert to passers-by, the spider waits just inside the door of its burrow. If a suitable prey arrives, the spider springs out of the door, captures the victim and drags it down inside the burrow. This trapdoor spider, *Pachylomerus nidicoleus*, lives in the West Indies.

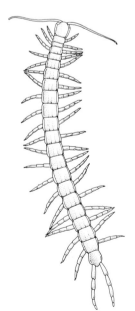

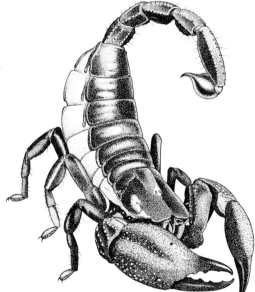

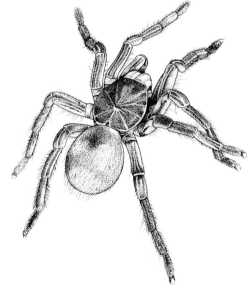

The carnivorous centipedes are equipped with a pair of poison claws and move fast. They prey on insects and small animals. Some of the largest centipedes are jungle species. *Scolopendra* is 6in (15cm) long.

While some scorpions inhabit hot, dry deserts, others such as *Pandinus* and *Palamneus*, prefer the humid conditions of the rain forest and are extremely sensitive to dryness. The Philippine scorpion, *Palamneus longimanus, above*, collects water in its claws, which it drinks or scatters over its body. During the day this scorpion hides in a deep burrow on the forest floor. At night it emerges to search for food, particularly cockroaches, crickets and earwigs.

Land planarians, such as *Dolichoplana striata* from Southeast Asia, are terrestrial relatives of the aquatic flatworms. Up to 2ft (60cm) long, land planarians move by muscular activity and the action of tiny hairs.

The largest living spider, *Theraphosa blondi*, lives in the South American jungles. Its body is about $3\frac{1}{2}$in (9cm) long and it has a leg span of 10in (25cm). This and other bird-eating spiders are collectively referred to as tarantulas. They live under stones, bark and leaves on the forest floor and hunt at night, attacking anything that comes their way. Their size allows these spiders to tackle small reptiles, birds and mammals as well as insect prey.

127

Insects of the waters

Heavy, frequent rainfall ensures that jungles are well endowed with a variety of freshwater habitats for aquatic creatures. Even some insects, normally land-dwelling, have colonized aquatic habitats in the jungle. Of these, the majority must still come to the surface to breathe. The water beetles and water boatmen hold a bubble of air under their wing covers and periodically come to the surface to replenish it. Only a few forms, such as the dragonfly nymphs, possess functional gills.

Many aquatic species in the jungles are similar to those in temperate regions. Male dragonflies are commonly seen winging back and forth along a stretch of water, defending it from other males while waiting for a passing female. They capture small flying insects with their strong, forwardly directed legs and eat them on the wing. Their aquatic nymphs eat not only insects but also small frogs, tadpoles and fish.

Among the water-dwelling beetles, the dytiscids, or diving beetles, are the largest. Both adults and larvae attack a number of small aquatic animals. Diving beetle larvae have large, hollow, curved jaws through which they inject enzymes into a prey. These enzymes digest the prey's tissues and convert them into a 'soup' which the larvae suck back up through their mandibles.

Found in slowly moving water are the giant water bugs, or belastomatids. Voracious carnivores, they stalk their prey through underwater vegetation. When close to their victims, these cryptically hued insects strike quickly and seize prey with their forelegs. Belastomatids have typical piercing bug mouthparts and use enzymes to digest the body contents of their prey.

Belastomatids, though heavy and noisy, are strong fliers. They are often attracted to lights at night, and fly particularly around the time of a full moon. These flights are frequently a prelude to egg laying. Giant water bugs are food for large predators, especially crocodiles, but they are not eaten by fish to any large extent. Cannibalism has been recorded among these carnivorous insects, mainly when food supplies are low.

An important group of aquatic insects, the blackflies (Simuliidae) can cause man considerable misery by their biting activities. The main jungle-dwelling species in West Africa are *Simulium soubrense*, *S. yahense* and *S. sanctipauli*, which are so similar in appearance that they can only be distinguished by analysis of their body proteins.

African blackflies bite during the daytime, rasping a small wound and sucking up the blood which oozes out. They can transmit onchocerciasis (called river blindness in West and Central Africa) a serious human disease caused by the nematode worm *Onchocerca volvulus*. The larval stages of this worm, called microfilariae, are found in the surface layers of the skin and are picked up by feeding *Simulium* adults. The infective larvae which develop from them are deposited in another host when the fly next bites. The developing worms creep through the subcutaneous layers of man's body and eventually congregate with other worms in one spot where they become surrounded by fibrous tissue forming a visible nodule.

Apart from carrying the disease, humans suffer little from the nodules unless they are in the head. The microfilariae then tend to invade the eyes, causing blindness. This gives the disease its common name of river blindness. The larvae of *Simulium* are susceptible to insecticides, and an extensive control programme organized by the World Health Organization is currently in progress in West Africa.

Diving beetles, such as the forest species, *Rhantus pacificus*, are aquatic predators. Their streamlined shape reduces water resistance, and they paddle along with rowing movements of the flattened hind legs. As the beetles breathe air they must return to the surface to replenish air supplies, held as bubbles under their wing covers.

The bizarre diopsid flies have eyes on the ends of long stalks. These stalks unfurl as the adult fly emerges from its pupal case. Although not technically aquatic, the larvae of these strange flies feed on damp rotting plants, and the adults are a common sight in Africa on damp vegetation close to water. Some diopsids are pests on crops such as rice and millet.

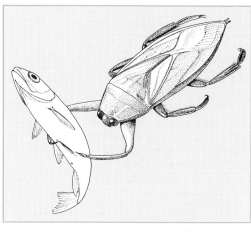

The giant water bug, *Belastoma*, is one of the largest aquatic insects at up to 4¾in (12cm) long. It preys on insects, small fish, frogs and tadpoles, which it attacks and catches with its adapted forelegs. Male water bugs are often used as mobile nests. The female lays her eggs on his wing covers and, during the ten days or so they take to hatch, he cares for them and sweeps debris away with his fringed hind legs. He stays near the water surface, possibly to allow the eggs to obtain enough air.

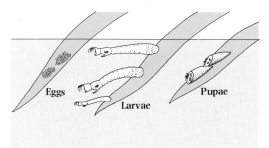

Eggs   Larvae   Pupae

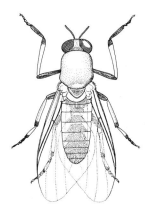

Blackflies are small, blood-sucking flies which carry the parasitic worm *Onchocerca volvulus*, the cause of the widespread and serious disease onchocerciasis. They also carry a number of other diseases which affect birds and animals. The adult fly lays clusters of 150 to 600 eggs on submerged vegetation or rocks in fast-flowing water. These eggs hatch quickly into larvae. Each larva spins a small pad of silk from modified salivary glands and attaches itself to the pad by hooks on its abdomen. Thus secured, they feed by filtering food particles from the water. When they are ready, the larvae spin silken pockets in which to pupate—again under water. The adult flies emerge after a short pupal stage and crawl to the water surface where they mate before flying away.

Several groups of normally aquatic creatures live on land in the jungle. The high humidity keeps them from drying out, and they can exist out of water. Leeches wait on vegetation for passing hosts, and there are also land-dwelling freshwater crabs. These crabs live in flooded burrows and have modified gills for breathing on land. They feed on plants and insects. In the lowland jungles of Sarawak, land crabs are important disposers of plant litter. As these areas are periodically flooded, they are unsuitable habitats for termites and ants; crabs take over the tasks usually performed by these insects and break down the leaves and debris of the forest floor.

The damsel fly, *Megalagrion oahuense*, is excellently adapted to life on land. Its eggs are laid among moist dead ferns, not in water as is usual. The surface of the nymph is covered with fine bristles which hold a layer of moisture and provide a damp surface for gaseous exchange.

The disease carriers

The jungle insects which directly impinge on man, the biting flies (Diptera), not only cause discomfort by their blood-sucking activities but, more importantly, they transmit disease. Both malaria and yellow fever are spread by specific mosquitoes in Central and South America and Africa, while loaiasis is carried by tabanid flies in Africa. In the absence of man, these diseases can cycle in jungle animals.

Mosquitoes require water in which to lay their eggs, and the rain forest provides an abundance of suitable sites. Each type of breeding location has its particular mosquito species. In Africa, some inhabit water-filled tree holes; others prefer leaf axils and a range of species breed in pools on the forest floor. The larvae of most mosquitoes are filter feeders, but those of *Toxorhynchites brevipalpis* are carnivorous and feed on other mosquito larvae which use understorey tree holes.

Adult mosquitoes are highly mobile within the jungle and often take part in daily vertical migrations. Several species, including *Aedes ingrami*, move down toward the relative coolness of the jungle floor during the day and return to the canopy layer at dusk. Although *Aedes africanus* breeds in low-level tree holes, it generally feeds on monkeys living up in the canopy.

Only female mosquitoes are blood feeders, their mates subsist mainly on flower nectar. Jungle females have a range of feeding patterns. Some feed throughout the day, with specific peaks of activity; others are inactive except for short feeding periods, often at sunset. Mosquitoes also feed at specific levels in the jungle. To take a blood meal, the mosquito pierces the victim's skin, then pumps saliva into the wound to prevent the blood coagulating as it sucks. This injection of saliva causes the irritation of a mosquito bite and is also a major factor in the spread of disease, as the infective agents are transmitted in the mosquito's saliva.

Tabanid flies show many behavioural similarities to mosquitoes. The adults lay their eggs in damp regions, and the larvae feed on moist plant debris. Adult tabanids favour open habitats and will feed on humans at river margins or in jungle clearings produced by tree felling.

Loaiasis, caused by the parasitic worm *Loa loa*, is transmitted by African tabanids of the genus *Chrysops*. The adult worm, about two inches long, lives in the connective tissue between the skin and muscles of monkeys and man. The worms move about the body searching for mates, causing some irritation and swelling, particularly at the joints. Although disabling, the disease is not usually fatal. When male and female worms meet, they mate and produce larval worms, or microfilariae, which live in the bloodstream. During the day in man and at night in monkeys, the microfilariae congregate in the blood vessels of the skin and so are in the best position to be taken up by a feeding tabanid fly. The microfilariae grow in the fly and change into a new larval form infective to man. When the fly next takes a blood meal these infective larvae enter the new human host and develop into adults. The adult worms may live for more than ten years.

Yellow fever, a viral disease endemic in equatorial Africa and Central and South America, is inexplicably absent from Southeast Asia. It originates in Africa, producing only minor symptoms in indigenous monkeys and humans. In South America, however, the disease frequently kills its monkey and human hosts.

Yellow fever has an incubation period of five days and for two of these, virus particles are present in the bloodstream. During this short time, mosquitoes taking a blood meal pick up the virus. In man the disease causes vomiting, fever, jaundice and often death.

Early studies of tree-dwelling, jungle insects were severely restricted by the difficulties of observing and collecting insects among the tall trees. A steel tower, built by the East African Virus Research Institute in Mpanga Forest, Uganda, revolutionized such research. Wooden observation platforms were made at 30ft (9m) intervals up the tower, allowing each layer of the forest to be studied at close quarters. Microclimate changes can also be investigated from the tower, and temperature, humidity and wind speeds recorded at each layer.

The tower makes an ideal base for studying the habits of mosquitoes. Lengths of bamboo filled with water and attached to the sides of the tower provide the mosquitoes with egg-laying sites, thus showing at what levels of the jungle different species breed. Human bait has been used to study mosquito biting habits, revealing the heights and times at which mosquitoes feed.

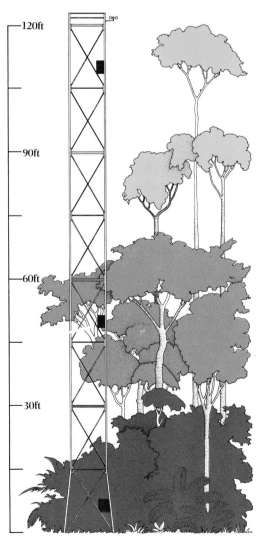

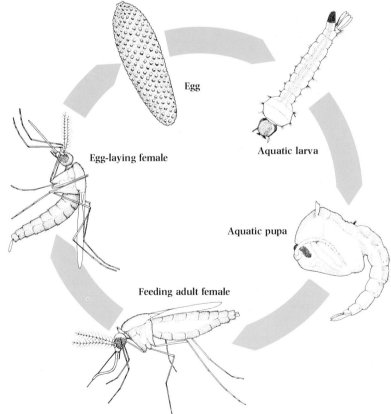

Egg

Aquatic larva

Egg-laying female

Aquatic pupa

Feeding adult female

The female *Aedes africanus* mosquito lays batches of 70 to 100 eggs in pools of water in tree holes. Half the eggs hatch quickly, the others hatch over several months. The air-breathing, detritus-feeding larvae hang from the water surface by siphons through which they breathe. The larvae pupate and the pupae too hang from the water surface. When metamorphosis is complete the adult mosquito emerges from a slit in the pupal case.

Feeding larva

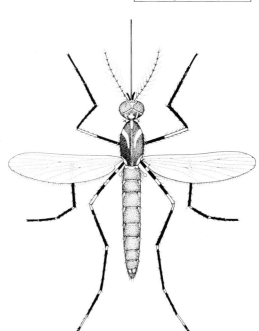

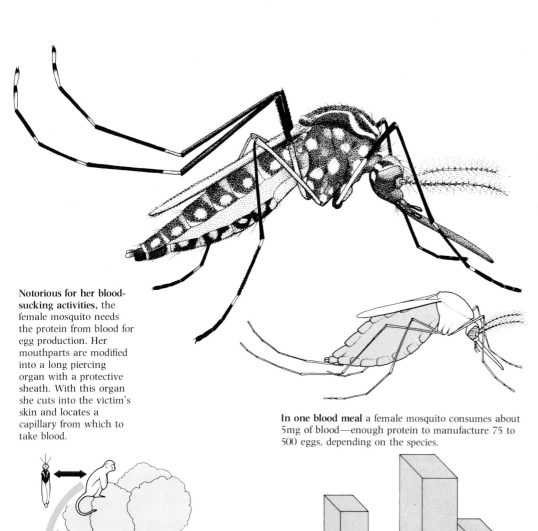

Notorious for her blood-sucking activities, the female mosquito needs the protein from blood for egg production. Her mouthparts are modified into a long piercing organ with a protective sheath. With this organ she cuts into the victim's skin and locates a capillary from which to take blood.

In one blood meal a female mosquito consumes about 5mg of blood—enough protein to manufacture 75 to 500 eggs, depending on the species.

A canopy-dwelling African mosquito, *Aedes africanus* feeds just after sunset on the blood of monkeys sleeping in the canopy.

Yellow fever is present in African canopy monkeys but they are not severely affected by the virus which is cycled between them by the canopy mosquito *Aedes africanus*. In towns the virus is spread from person to person by the *Aedes aegypti* mosquito. As it takes a blood meal the mosquito picks up virus particles from the bloodstream of an infected person. The virus multiplies and invades the mosquito's salivary glands and infects another person when the insect next feeds. The urban and jungle cycles are linked by a third—the rural cycle. Monkeys leave the canopy to feed at banana plantations, where they may be bitten by *Aedes simpsonii*. The mosquito picks up the virus from a monkey and, if it then bites a man, transmits the disease. Man's movement between town and country ensures the continuation of the yellow fever cycle.

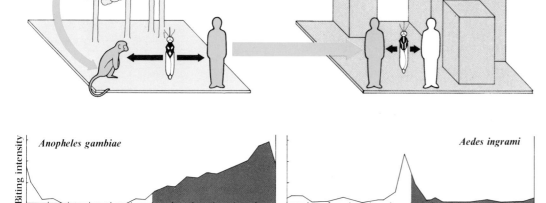

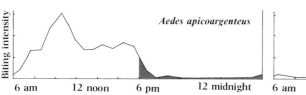

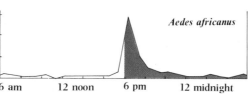

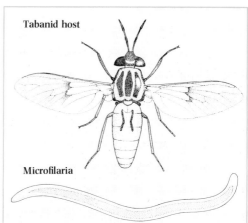

Jungle mosquitoes have distinct daily patterns of activity. Males form courtship swarms around sunset which last from 5 to 35 minutes before the males disperse. Female mosquitoes have specific biting times with different species active at different times. An understorey species, *Anopheles gambiae*, is an important carrier of malaria. It bites during the night, becoming more and more active toward dawn. *Aedes*

apicoargenteus is primarily an understorey species, though also common at other levels. It is active during the day, with a peak of activity around noon. *Aedes ingrami*, an understorey species, has its peak biting period just before sunset, while *Aedes africanus*, a canopy species, is most active just after sunset. The timing of these activity cycles is thought to be linked to light levels.

The blood-sucking tabanid fly, *Chrysops silacea*, lives in the canopy of African forests. Several species of *Chrysops*, or deer flies, transmit the parasitic worm *Loa loa* which lives in man and monkeys and causes the disease loaiasis. The adult worms produce tiny larvae, microfilariae, which live in the bloodstream of the infected individual.

Jungle partnerships

The trees and shrubs of the jungle are a framework on which other plants can live. The complexity of this basic structure provides innumerable tiny habitats, all markedly or subtly different from one another. All possible living space is used.

The base of a large tree trunk, particularly between the buttresses, is dark and damp—an ideal environment for mosses and delicate ferns. The main part of the trunk is a difficult place to colonize, because it is straight, mostly shaded and often smooth, but it is occupied by various orchids and by large-leafed climbers, clinging on by suckerlike aerial roots. The large branches are level and potentially fairly moist with abundant room for plants to attach themselves, and so are conducive to the growth of many epiphytic orchids and bromeliads. These plants accumulate debris to form their own small patch of peaty soil which is also a suitable niche for ants, worms and snakes. The thin outer twigs of the crown, exposed to strong winds, direct sunlight and low humidity, play host to a few orchids and many mosses and lichens which can grow when wet and lapse into dormancy when dry. The tree crown also supports lianas, or large woody climbers, which soar up from the forest floor to hang in loops over the branches of the giant trees.

As well as relationships between dependent plants and their supports, the jungle abounds in relationships between plants and animals. All animals rely directly or indirectly on plant food, and all plants have their own predators, most of which are insects. Most plants produce poisonous or distasteful chemicals to discourage herbivores, but each has its own predators which can overcome these toxins.

Insects do not only prey on plants; they are lured to the flowers for pollen and nectar by hue and scent and, incidentally, carry pollen from one plant to another. In their role as pollinators, insects are joined by birds and bats. Sometimes, as in the case of the fig and the fig wasp which pollinates it, the two organisms are dependent on each other.

One insect group, the ants, are found everywhere in the jungle, but they do not often act as pollinators despite their fondness for sugar. Certain species have developed extraordinary relationships with plants. Some live in the hollow stems of particular trees, feed on plant parts which appear to be produced especially for them, and on the exudations of plant-sucking insects which they have introduced into their nests and look after. In turn, the ants attack any animal which alights on or touches the plant. They may also attack competing plants. Yet other plants absorb nutrients from the debris accumulated by ants in their nest chambers within the plant. Such relationships increase the remarkable diversity of the jungle, but they are also vulnerable to the disruption caused by thoughtless exploitation.

Ants and plants

Ants are everywhere in tropical forests; in the undergrowth, under logs, in bark crevices and all over plants. Some plants have developed mutually beneficial relationships with ants.

In the Central and South American forests, umbrella-shaped trees of the genus *Cecropia* are common colonists of abandoned farmlands, disturbed roadsides and old clearings. They are small, quick-growing trees that increase in height by at least 6 feet (1.8m) each year and live for 20 years at most. The trunk and branches are hollow and divided by partitions, with thin patches in the outer wall. Ants of the genus *Azteca* bite their way into the trunk through these thin patches and establish colonies. They introduce small plant-sucking insects into the chambers and tend them, feeding on the sugary solution which the insects excrete. The plant produces small outgrowths from the leaf bases which are rich in food materials; these are eaten by the ants and fed to their larvae.

Azteca ants are fierce, but do not sting. They attack anyone who disturbs or tries to cut the *Cecropia* in which they live. They also bite through the tips of climbers, which could otherwise smother the *Cecropia* plant.

In Africa, the plant *Barteria fistulosa* provides shelter for large colonies of ants which, in turn, appear to defend it. This small tree grows up to 50 feet (15m) tall and is most abundant in old clearings and disturbed places, but also occurs in undisturbed forest. Its horizontal branches are hollow, and it is these which are occupied by ant colonies.

The ants clear other plants from the area around the tree base by biting off their tips, and attack any animal which disturbs or breaks the tree. Their sting is painful, and its effects can last for a couple of days. The leaves are probably palatable to herbivores; a monkey has been seen feeding greedily from an unoccupied *Barteria*, but it only snatched a single handful of leaves from an occupied tree. The trees are avoided by people clearing forest for farmland—they are well aware of the ants' unpleasant stings. Unfaithful wives were once punished by being tied to *Barteria* plants.

In Southeast Asia, various plants provide a shelter for ants, which then supply the plants with food. The plants concerned are two members of the family Rubiaceae, *Myrmecodia* and *Hydnophytum*; a member of the family Asclepiadaceae, *Dischidia*, and two ferns, *Phymatodes* and *Lecanopteris*. All are epiphytes and, except for *Dischidia*, have swollen rhizomes, or stem bases, which contain hollows; these form whether ants are present or not. They are, however, nearly always colonized by ants, which fill some of the cavities with debris, including insect remains. The nutrients released by this debris as it decomposes are probably taken up as food by the plant.

These relationships are presumably accidental, as it cannot be said that ants deliberately cultivate the plants, even though some of their actions appear remarkably purposeful. As all these epiphytic plants normally have difficulty obtaining sufficient nutrients, the exchange of nest sites for food is an ideal system.

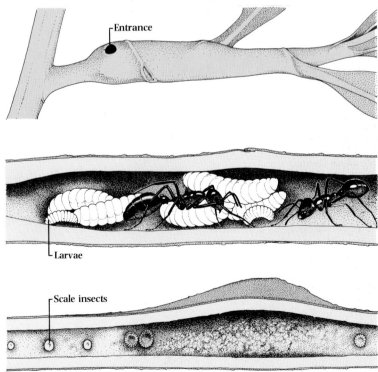
Entrance
Larvae
Scale insects

The hollow branches of *Barteria fistulosa*, a small African tree, may house colonies of ants of the genus *Pachysima aethiops*. Trees with ant colonies are larger and have more foliage than unoccupied trees, and are not laden with climbing plants. The ants remove any insects which might damage their tree, and clear debris from the leaves. They also keep the area around the base of the tree clear by biting off the tips of any other plants growing there.

A queen founds her colony of ants inside a branch of the *Barteria* tree. The larvae are reared there and fed on the secretions of scale insects which also live inside the branches, protected and tended by the ants. Scale insects feed on plant sap, which is essentially a sugar solution but, in order to get enough nitrogen, they must take in more sugar than they need. They excrete the excess which is then used by the ants. The ants also establish fungus gardens in the stems, and eat parts of the fungus. At night the colony retreats into the hollow branches, but during the day the ants wander over the plant and the area surrounding it. If disturbed they will sting, and this seems to protect the plant from grazing animals.

The **quick-growing** *Cecropia* tree springs up in gaps in the forest and by roadsides and clearings. In many, the hollow stems are occupied by ants. The ants attack insects that might damage the tree and also keep it free from lianas. Both these services help the tree to grow fast and enable it to compete successfully with other trees.

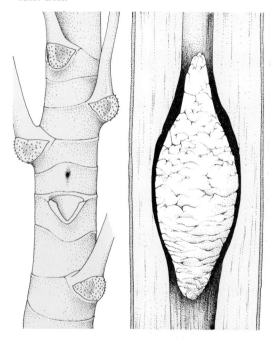

The stem of the *Cecropia* tree is hollow but divided into chambers by cross-walls at the nodes where the leaves arise. The chamber walls have regularly occurring thin spots where the ants can break through. The ants raise their young in the chambers, feeding them on the sugary secretions of plant-sucking bugs which also live there. Outgrowths of the leaf stalk bases, Müllerian bodies, provide the ants with the proteins they need.

Even leaves can make a home for ants. Some of the leaves of the plant *Dischidia* are folded over to form a pouch with a small hole at the base by the leaf stalk. Roots arise from the stem near the stalk and grow into the leaf pouch. Ants of the genus *Iridomyrmex* make nests inside the leaves and fill them with debris into which the roots spread. This debris provides the plant with nutrients which are otherwise scarce in its habitat.

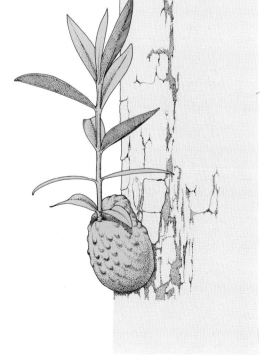

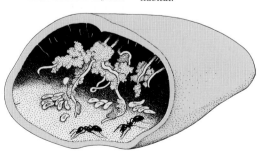

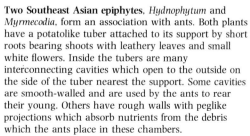

Two Southeast Asian epiphytes, *Hydnophytum* and *Myrmecodia*, form an association with ants. Both plants have a potatolike tuber attached to its support by short roots bearing shoots with leathery leaves and small white flowers. Inside the tubers are many interconnecting cavities which open to the outside on the side of the tuber nearest the support. Some cavities are smooth-walled and are used by the ants to rear their young. Others have rough walls with peglike projections which absorb nutrients from the debris which the ants place in these chambers.

135

The plant pollinators

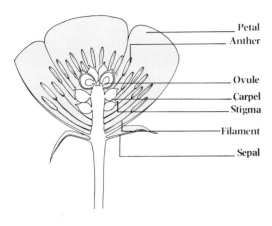

Petal
Anther

Ovule
Carpel
Stigma
Filament

Sepal

The flower houses the reproductive organs of the plant. On the outside, the sepals protect the closed bud and may fall when the flower opens. Inside them, the petals form the main body of the flower and attract pollinators with their bright hues. In the centre of the flower, within the petal case, are the male stamens, made up of the filaments and pollen-bearing anthers, which encircle the female carpels. At the top of each carpel protrudes a 'style' with a sticky stigma for catching pollen, and inside lie the ovaries. Each carpel contains an ovule which becomes a seed when pollinated. The stamens and stigma are usually positioned to reduce the chance of self-pollination and increase the chance of a visiting insect brushing against them. All these reproductive parts take many forms in different flowers.

When a tropical orchid with a six-inch long, nectar-filled spur was first discovered, Charles Darwin predicted that an insect would eventually be found with a tongue long enough to probe the spur. Sure enough, a long-tongued hawk-moth came to light as the flower's pollinator.

Pollination is the transfer of pollen from the male part of a flower to the female part. If the male and female reproductive parts are in the same flower, or on the same plant, self-pollination may occur, and there may be no exchange of genetic material between individuals. If the two are on different plants, cross-pollination takes place and genetic material is exchanged. Pollen produced in the anther borne by the stamen is received by the stigma, part of the female reproductive organ.

For pollination to be effected, many plants rely on physical factors such as the wind. Plants of this type normally produce huge quantities of pollen in relation to the number of ovules to be fertilized, to ensure that some pollen grains reach the stigma by random drift. Since there is little air movement in the lower layers of the jungle, few wind-pollinated plants are found there.

Plants usually enlist the help of other living creatures to pollinate them. Insects are the commonest pollinators, but in the tropics, where there is a constant supply of food throughout the year, bats and birds are frequently involved. Pollinators do not visit flowers to pollinate them, but usually

because they are rewarded with food in the form of pollen or nectar. Nectar is a sugary solution secreted by glands in the flower and often accumulated in special pouches or spurs so that it is inaccessible to all but a few insects. In addition to sugars, some nectars contain amino acids, the building blocks from which proteins are made.

Plants and pollinators are usually adapted to one another. Flowers pollinated by bats open at night, and are either large and strong enough to bear the weight and resist the claws of these flying mammals, or are grouped into dense masses which collectively function in the same way. They have a disagreeable, musty smell, are white or a purplish shade and exude a great deal of sticky and gelatinous nectar.

In the tropics, many flowers are adapted to attract bird pollinators. They open during the day, secrete copious amounts of nectar and are strongly constructed. Although bird flowers are scentless, they are brightly hued, often red and orange, as birds can see well into the red part of the spectrum. Flowers pollinated by hummingbirds are red with protruding stamens and stigma. As a hummingbird hovers in front of a flower and inserts its long bill to reach the nectar, concealed either in a spur or at the base of a tube formed by the petals, both the stamens and stigma touch its head and body. The flower-feeding birds of the Old World, such as the sunbirds and flower-peckers, often perch nearby on

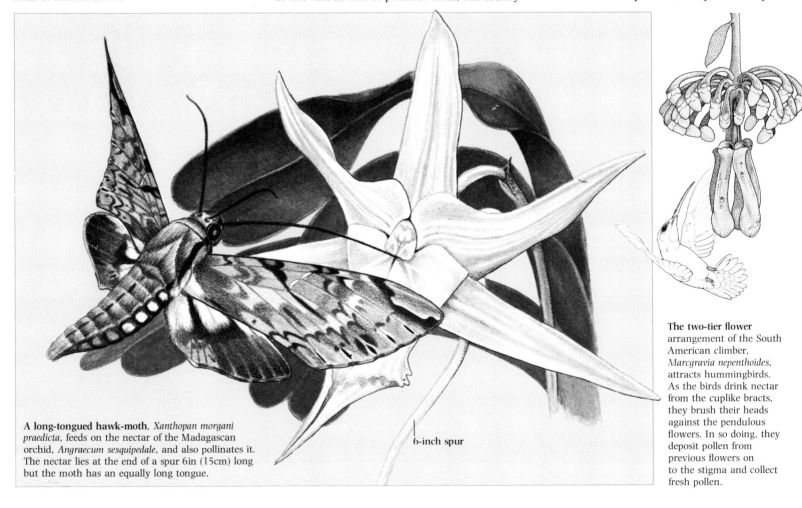

A long-tongued hawk-moth, *Xanthopan morgani praedicta,* feeds on the nectar of the Madagascan orchid, *Angraecum sesquipedale,* and also pollinates it. The nectar lies at the end of a spur 6in (15cm) long but the moth has an equally long tongue.

6-inch spur

The two-tier flower arrangement of the South American climber, *Marcgravia nepenthoides,* attracts hummingbirds. As the birds drink nectar from the cuplike bracts, they brush their heads against the pendulous flowers. In so doing, they deposit pollen from previous flowers on to the stigma and collect fresh pollen.

a bare stem, leaf stalk, bract or flower bud as they feed.

Insect-pollinated flowers show the greatest diversity. Most of these are yellow or blue; a few which appear red to man also reflect ultraviolet, and are seen as such by insects, as they are sensitive to the violet end of the spectrum and beyond.

The simplest insect-pollinated flowers are open-bowl-shaped. They often provide only pollen, and are visited by beetles. Flowers with nectar in shallow spurs or wide tubes attract bees and flies with their relatively short tongues. Some bees, however, use their strong jaws to bite into narrow floral tubes, thus stealing the nectar without pollinating the flower.

Butterflies and moths are the insects most highly adapted to flower feeding. The majority have long, thin tongues which can reach to the bottom of the longest and narrowest spurs. Some butterflies, especially the swallowtails (Papilionidae), regularly visit red flowers and so may be able to see these wavelengths. The night-flying hawk-moths, with their long tongues and their ability to hover in front of a flower while feeding on it, are the insect equivalent of the hummingbirds; the flowers that they pollinate are night-blooming, white, sweet-scented and long-tubed.

Insects and flowers are closely tied to one another; in many cases one could not survive without the other.

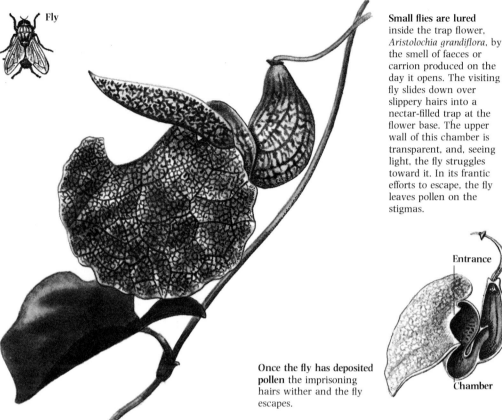

Fly

Small flies are lured inside the trap flower, *Aristolochia grandiflora*, by the smell of faeces or carrion produced on the day it opens. The visiting fly slides down over slippery hairs into a nectar-filled trap at the flower base. The upper wall of this chamber is transparent, and, seeing light, the fly struggles toward it. In its frantic efforts to escape, the fly leaves pollen on the stigmas.

Entrance

Chamber

Once the fly has deposited pollen the imprisoning hairs wither and the fly escapes.

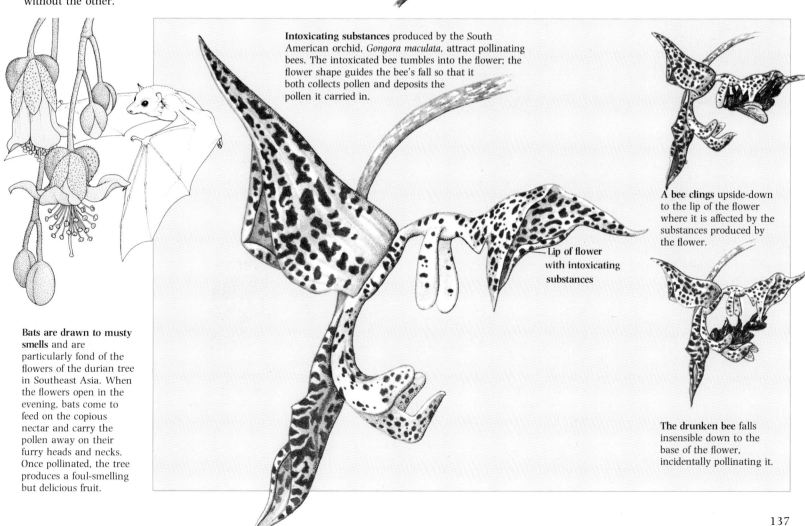

Bats are drawn to musty smells and are particularly fond of the flowers of the durian tree in Southeast Asia. When the flowers open in the evening, bats come to feed on the copious nectar and carry the pollen away on their furry heads and necks. Once pollinated, the tree produces a foul-smelling but delicious fruit.

Intoxicating substances produced by the South American orchid, *Gongora maculata*, attract pollinating bees. The intoxicated bee tumbles into the flower; the flower shape guides the bee's fall so that it both collects pollen and deposits the pollen it carried in.

Lip of flower with intoxicating substances

A bee clings upside-down to the lip of the flower where it is affected by the substances produced by the flower.

The drunken bee falls insensible down to the base of the flower, incidentally pollinating it.

The fig: a life for a life

Fig plants can be of almost any size from small shrubs and root climbers to tall trees. Nearly all contain milky latex. In this species bunches of figs are borne on the trunk.

The tiny flowers of the fig tree are borne in large numbers inside a hollow, more-or-less spherical structure—the fig. The fig has a small opening protected by scaly bracts. The pollination of these flowers, which are quite invisible from the outside, is carried out by a wasp. Each species of fig seems to have its own particular species of fig wasp as a pollinator.

The succulent purple-green figs that make a delicious addition to the dessert bowl are the fruits of the edible or common fig tree, *Ficus carica*, the most familiar representative of a huge genus numbering more than 600 members, almost all of them confined to the tropics. Figs may be shrubs, climbers or epiphytes, but most are trees—often large ones.

Among the biggest figs is the banyan, *Ficus benghalensis*. Roots growing groundward from its branches thicken into 'props', allowing the crown to expand indefinitely. One such tree reputedly has a crown circumference of 2,000 feet (600m). Many figs start life as epiphytes and also send roots down to the ground. These roots grow quickly and the supporting tree is often killed by shade from the fig's crown, by competition from its roots and the tight binding of interlaced fig roots round the trunk.

The india-rubber fig tree, *Ficus elastica*, whose seedlings are ubiquitous houseplants, can be tapped as a low-yield source of impure rubber, and the softened bark of several African fig trees is even used for cloth making, but whatever their form and uses, all figs share a remarkable flower structure. A mass of tiny flowers is borne inside a more-or-less spherical organ—the fig—which has a stalk at one end attaching it to the tree, and a small opening

almost covered in scales at the other.

Fig flowers are of three kinds: male, short-styled female or gall flowers, and long-styled female flowers—a style is a stalk, extending from the flower's reproductive organ which supports the pollen-receiving stigma. Some figs contain all three flower sorts, other species have figs with long-styled female flowers on one tree and those with male and gall flowers on another. All the flowers are very simple.

The way pollen is transferred from male to female flowers is a fascinating evolutionary story, for it appears that every fig species entertains a particular kind of fig wasp, a tiny insect that carries out the pollination process. The development of the fig and the fig wasp are very closely integrated, each depending on the other for its reproduction.

As the fig develops, the female flowers mature first. Attracted by its scent, female fig wasps fly to the fig and enter through the top opening, forcing their way between the scales. This is not easy, for although the fig wasp is tiny, the scales are stiff and pressed tightly together. But with a great deal of persistence, and the asset of a wedge-shaped head, the fig wasp reaches her goal, often losing her wings and part of her antennae in the process.

Once inside, the female fig wasp, possibly with others of her kind, uses her long ovipositor to bore down through the styles of female flowers into the ovary and deposit eggs. As she does so she injects a substance that stimulates gall formation and this incidentally also places pollen on to the stigma of female flowers. The design of female fig flowers is such, however, that the wasp's ovipositor is only long enough to reach the ovules of the short-styled flowers; the long-styled ones are merely probed and fertilized—no egg is laid. So as a result of the attentions of the female wasp, short-styled fig flowers give rise to fig wasp larvae, while long-styled flowers produce a seed.

Next the larval wasps develop and pupate. During this time it seems that they cunningly produce a substance that stops the fig maturing (maturity would mean ripeness and being eaten, an unsatisfactory situation for the wasps). When the pupae are, at last, mature, the male wasps emerge first, seek out female pupae and fertilize them. They then make tunnel holes through the fig wall which, up to this time, has been virtually sealed because the scales covering the entrance cling together even more tightly once the female wasps are inside. The atmosphere inside the fig contains much carbon

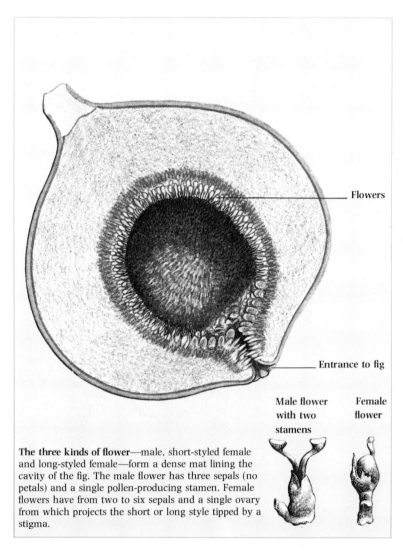

The three kinds of flower—male, short-styled female and long-styled female—form a dense mat lining the cavity of the fig. The male flower has three sepals (no petals) and a single pollen-producing stamen. Female flowers have from two to six sepals and a single ovary from which projects the short or long style tipped by a stigma.

Flowers

Entrance to fig

Male flower with two stamens

Female flower

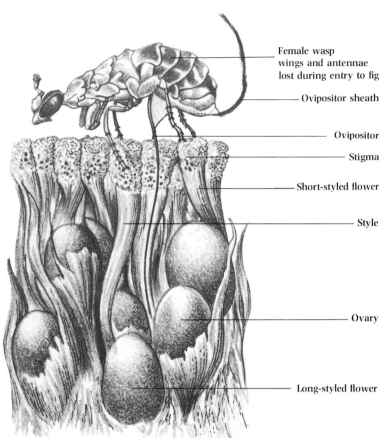

Female wasp wings and antennae lost during entry to fig

Ovipositor sheath

Ovipositor

Stigma

Short-styled flower

Style

Ovary

Long-styled flower

The female wasp must now find and enter a new fig in which to lay her own eggs. With her long ovipositor she inserts eggs into the ovaries of female flowers. She can only reach the ovaries of the short-styled flowers, but as she moves she pollinates all the flowers with the pollen she has brought with her. The pollinated long-styled flowers produce seeds, while the short-styled ones develop galls which nourish the fig wasp larvae. Thus both fig and wasp reproduce satisfactorily.

dioxide (up to 10 per cent compared with 0.03 per cent in air) but this does not impede the males.

Once the males have tunnelled to the surface the carbon dioxide concentration inside the fig falls quickly and this seems to stimulate both the emergence of female wasps and the opening of male flowers. In some figs, including the edible fig, female wasps are coated with pollen from many male flowers. Other species have fewer male flowers, from which the female wasp collects pollen and packs it into special pockets on her body and legs. The female also carries enough stored sperm from her single copulation as a pupa to fertilize all her eggs. Male and female wasps now join forces to bite away the scales at the fig opening, and the females fly off to find another fig at the female stage. The wingless males, their work completed, die without leaving the fig.

Finally the fig ripens, and its many seeds, together with its flesh, are eaten by birds, bats and monkeys. The seeds are dropped or excreted and spread far and wide to develop into new plants. Thus while accomplishing its own reproduction the fig provides an egg-laying site for the fig wasp, nourishment for the wasp larvae, and food for many other creatures.

The wasp larvae develop inside the female flowers. The wingless male wasps emerge first and search for the female pupae. They fertilize the females and then tunnel into the wall of the fig. The tunnels reduce the high level of carbon dioxide in the fig and this reduction stimulates the emergence of the female wasps. The males help the females to bite their way out of the fig and the whole process starts anew.

Female

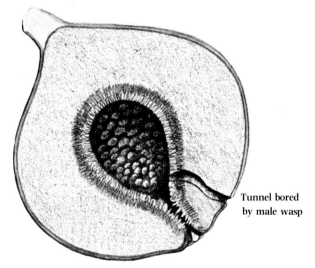

Tunnel bored by male wasp

Male and female fig wasps are strikingly different in appearance. The male is wingless with a long, slender abdomen which is either carried straight or bent forward beneath the head. The female is winged and agile with a long egg-laying tube, the ovipositor. Her wedge-shaped head helps her to push her way through the scales at the opening of a fig.

Wingless male

The network of lianas

Strong enough to support Tarzan, the large, woody climbers, lianas, are a spectacular feature of the jungle.

Starting life as small upright shrubs, most produce long shoots with tendrils which attach themselves to a support. Eventually they extend into the canopy, reaching it via the understorey and lower canopy trees, and sometimes growing up with their supporting trees. Their crowns are large and bind the crowns of adjacent canopy trees together, so that a tree may stay upright even when severed at the base. Should the tree fall, the crowns of neighbouring trees suffer more damage than they would if there were no lianas.

Because lianas are supported by other plants, their stems do not have to be as strong and massive as tree trunks. The stems must, however, be able to support their own weight, which may be considerable; they must be flexible, so that they do not snap when their support sways; and they must be able to conduct all the water that their large crown needs, and all the food, produced in the leaves, essential to support and develop their root system.

Liana stems may be strangely shaped. The wood within them is usually divided into separate strands, with soft food-conducting tissue between. Each stem is able to conduct large amounts of water because it has large vessels in the wood, often big enough to be clearly visible to the naked eye. If a piece of stem a foot long is cut quickly and held upright, the water will run out of the vessels. This water is clear, clean and usually drinkable. The suction exerted by the leafy crown to draw up all this water from the roots is powerful. If a small cut is made in a liana stem, it is possible to hear a hissing sound as air is sucked into the severed vessels.

Lianas do not twine around the trunks of their supporting trees; their stems hang freely, their weight carried by many small attachments in the crown. Normally it is impossible to dislodge any but the smallest lianas by pulling from below. A number of lianas have tendrils, formed from leaves or leaflets. Sometimes these become woody and last much longer than a normal leaf, but for the most part they are continually replaced by new ones.

The stems of lianas may be extremely long. If the support of a liana falls, the stem will lie on the forest floor in a tangle of coils. The crown leaves die quickly in the dense shade, but new long shoots soon appear and work their way up into the canopy. A liana stem can thus be found rising into one tree, then looping down to the ground and rising into a second support. Rattans—the climbing palms from which light furniture is made—carry this to extremes, and stems more than 500 feet (150m) long have been found in Malaya.

Foresters dislike lianas; they compete with the trees for light, and thicken the canopy without contributing anything to the useful crop of the forest. Their tangles are a further complication to the already difficult job of extracting timber.

Many jungle trees are festooned with lianas. The thick, ropelike lianas do not twine around tree trunks, as is often believed, but hang held to the crown of a tree by a mass of tiny attachment devices.

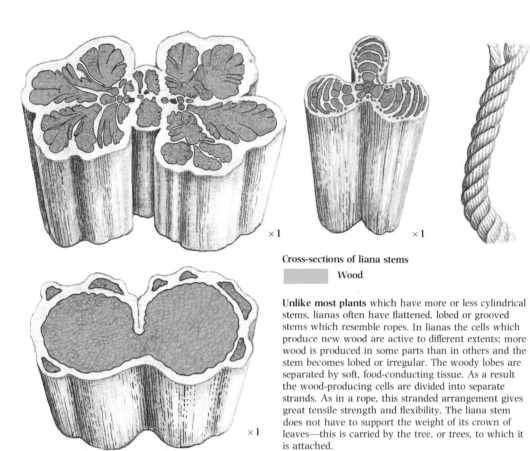

Cross-sections of liana stems

▨ Wood

Unlike most plants which have more or less cylindrical stems, lianas often have flattened, lobed or grooved stems which resemble ropes. In lianas the cells which produce new wood are active to different extents; more wood is produced in some parts than in others and the stem becomes lobed or irregular. The woody lobes are separated by soft, food-conducting tissue. As a result the wood-producing cells are divided into separate strands. As in a rope, this stranded arrangement gives great tensile strength and flexibility. The liana stem does not have to support the weight of its crown of leaves—this is carried by the tree, or trees, to which it is attached.

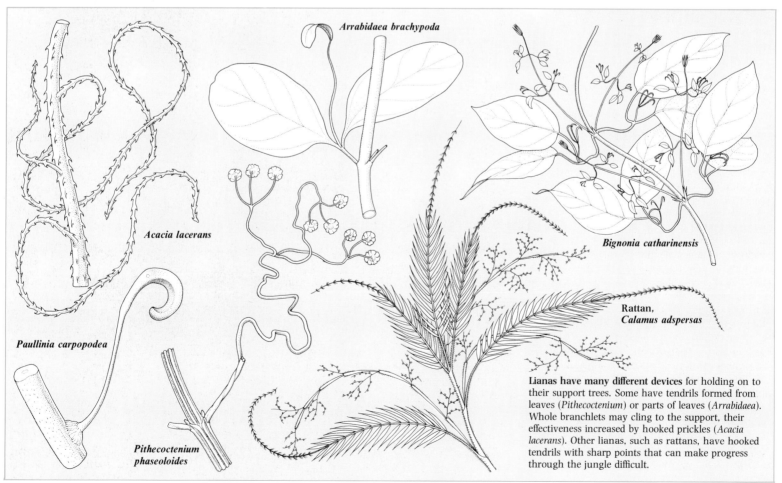

Arrabidaea brachypoda

Acacia lacerans

Paullinia carpopodea

Pithecoctenium phaseoloides

Bignonia catharinensis

Rattan, *Calamus adspersas*

Lianas have many different devices for holding on to their support trees. Some have tendrils formed from leaves (*Pithecoctenium*) or parts of leaves (*Arrabidaea*). Whole branchlets may cling to the support, their effectiveness increased by hooked prickles (*Acacia lacerans*). Other lianas, such as rattans, have hooked tendrils with sharp points that can make progress through the jungle difficult.

Stranglers and climbers

The jungle framework of trees and shrubs is exploited by many other plants for support. Epiphytes grow entirely on other plants, and have no contact with the ground. The climbers, such as the lianas, depend upon other plants for support, but have their own root system in the ground. Stranglers are climbing plants which start life as epiphytes but later become rooted in the ground.

At forest edges, in gaps made by falling trees, and in abandoned clearings, small herbaceous climbers are often abundant, forming dense masses of greenery over other vegetation. The members of the cucumber family (Cucurbitaceae) are particularly common in such sites. They have small yellow male and female flowers which may be borne on separate plants. The fruits usually ripen to red or yellow and are quickly eaten by birds and animals, which then disperse the hard seeds in their dung. Such small, sun-loving climbers enjoy a short spell of rapid growth before the gaps which allow direct sunlight to reach them are closed by the young trees.

To escape the gloom of the forest floor, stem climbers attach themselves to the trunks of the taller trees by short, suckerlike roots. These roots probably absorb water and nutrients from the tree bark surface, as do those of epiphytes. The stem climbers are also known as hemi-epiphytes. A number of them belong to the arum family (Araceae), and are characterized by large, dark-green leaves that have a leathery texture. They may climb high enough to reach the crown of their supporting trees, where they produce larger leaves and flowers, as well as long ropelike roots which hang down and may root into the ground below.

Many of these large jungle climbers such as the Swiss cheese plant, *Monstera deliciosa*, and species of *Scindapsus* and *Philodendron* are handsome and make attractive houseplants. All have spikes of tiny flowers, partly concealed by a hoodlike leafy spathe; in *Monstera* these develop into an edible fruit.

Another group of plants which has no counterpart outside the jungles is the stranglers, the most common of which are the figs (*Ficus*). These plants are found on all the continents. They start life as epiphytes, germinating in hollows in tree crowns where a little soil has accumulated. At first they grow slowly, for there is little water or food for them, but their leathery leaves reduce water loss. Eventually they put out long roots which ultimately descend the trunk of the supporting tree and root into the soil beneath it. Once this occurs, the expanding leafy crown of the strangler starts to shade the crown of the support, while its roots interlace around the supporting trunk and appear to strangle the host. It is probably competition for light in the crown and for water and nutrients underground that finally leads to the death of the support tree, leaving the strangler standing as a hollow trunk.

The destructive habits of stranglers make them unpopular with foresters, who poison them in some regions. This is unfortunate for birds and monkeys as the fruits are a valuable food. At present, most areas of jungle are too large and remote for such treatments to be complete or effective.

A strangling fig starts life up on the branch of a tree from a seed dropped by a bird. The small plant eventually sends long roots down the trunk of the support tree to the ground. The roots make water and nutrients more easily available to the plant and it grows quickly, eventually smothering the original tree. The support tree soon dies.

Quick-growing climbing plants make life difficult for young trees, slowing their growth and even snapping them under their weight. Some, such as *Mormodica charantia, far right,* are at their best in gaps made by falling trees and abandoned clearings. Others are common and conspicuous in undisturbed forest. Root climbers cling to tree trunks by short, specialized roots, just as ivy plants do in temperate woods. Members of the arum family (Araceae) such as *Raphidophora, bottom right,* are large impressive examples. Species of *Peperomia, right,* are smaller stem climbers with attractively patterned leaves.

The prickly, clawing stems of the climber *Acacia kamerunensis, below,* often spring up in forest gaps although this species can also be a large woody liana.

The orchids

Many of the most spectacular flowers and ferns of the jungle are epiphytes—plants that do not root in the soil but make their homes on the surface of other plants, particularly the trunks and branches of trees. These environments are not easy, for they are subject to extremes of temperature, notably in the crown of a tree, and also to enormous variations in the availability of water. One moment plants may be scorching in the sun, the next drenched by a tropical storm. And tree bark does not usually hold much water. Rain flows over its surface and eventually down the tree trunk to the ground. Even after a steady downpour the bark dries out quickly.

One tropical tree can provide a vast range of epiphytic habitats, some more hospitable than others. The outer twigs of the canopy afford little firm base for attachment and are likely to catch the worst of the weather. The tree's main branches, which often spread out almost horizontally from the tops of the boles of large trees within or just below the canopy, are the favourite sites for epiphytes. They offer a nice balance between sun and shade, drought and drowning, plus shelter from wind and nearly all direct solar radiation. The vertical surfaces of the trunk itself are difficult for epiphytes to colonize for they are often in deep shade and, apart from water trickling down from the branches above, are sheltered from rainfall.

Some epiphytes have developed mechanisms for retaining water and soil-forming materials, so making their harsh habitats easier to live in. Others just seem to endure the conditions, taking up water when they can, while resisting water loss and keeping their vital processes going as best they can between times of plenty. The simplest of these plants are the mosses and lichens, which are often common on the outermost tree branches. Mosses and lichens absorb water quickly when rain falls. When dry conditions come they simply shrivel up and remain quiescent until the situation improves. A few more complex plants can also shrivel when dry and resurrect when wetted. One such is the epiphytic stag's horn fern, *Platycerium*, but it is an exception, for most higher plants cannot survive great variations in their water content.

In the tropical forest it is the orchids that have invaded the epiphytic habitat most successfully. Of the 18,000 or so species of orchid about half are epiphytes. Malaysia, for example, which has an area about the size of England or Alabama, has 800 orchid species, most of which are epiphytes. Orchids manage to survive the epiphytic environment by taking up water rapidly when it is available and by restricting its loss during drought.

Epiphytic orchids have thick white roots that spread over the surface of the bark of the trees that lend them support. The outer part of these roots is covered by a layer of dead cells called the velamen. These cells have many small holes in their walls into which water flows with ease. Water-filled velamen cells become transparent and the greenish inner tissues become visible. When the roots are dry the empty velamen cells scatter the light that falls on them and appear white. By reflecting light in this way, and by forming a sort of mat over the root surface, the velamen must also help to reduce water loss from the orchids' roots.

The water absorbed by the cells of the velamen is transported into the living part of the root and from there to the leaves of the plant. The leaves of epiphytic orchids are often thick and rigid, and contain tissue that can both absorb and store a great deal of water. The outermost cells of the leaves are usually covered with a thick waxy layer. This restricts water loss to the small pores on the leaf undersides. The pores open and close in response to light and the water content of the plant, and so give added insurance against dehydration.

Although they live on other plants, epiphytes are not parasites—all they receive from the trees they live on is support. An epiphyte, unlike a parasite, does not obtain any nutrients or water from its tree apart from that arriving in rain, litter or animal droppings, or from what is naturally lost by the tree as its bark is shed. Sometimes the load of epiphytes may be too much for a big branch and it may fall, but this is the end not only for the branch but also for the epiphytes. Precipitated on to the forest floor, they quickly die in its over-moist and lightless environment.

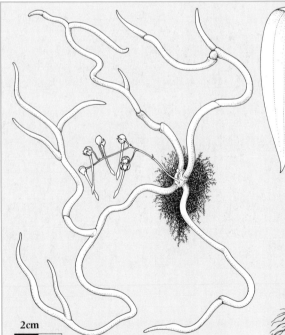

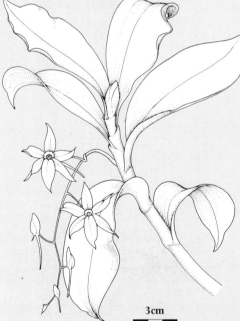

To evade the issue of water loss from their leaves, some epiphytic orchids dispense with them altogether. Such plants have only a short stem bearing scales which are tiny leaf vestiges, flower shoots and many long roots which hang down into the air and spread over the supporting branch. Covering these roots is a whitish, water-absorbing tissue (velamen) transparent enough to let light reach the inner, green, photosynthetic root layers. Orchids that have adopted this form include *Microcoelia, above,* from Africa.

Swollen bulblike stems are common to many epiphytic orchids. These pseudobulbs are solid, not made up of overlapping scales like true bulbs. Every possible gradation in pseudobulbs occurs, from a slight swelling to almost spherical green structures with leaves and flowers sprouting from them. There is also a huge size range from pea-size to the 10ft (3m) cylindrical structures of one Asian species. If detached from the parent plant, pseudobulbs can produce their own roots and shoots.

Extremes of climate are commonplace in the habitat of epiphytic orchids. Their adapted roots allow these plants to take up water quickly when it is available— but how to make it last? The main route of water loss from a plant is via its leaves. Many orchids have thick, often almost cylindrical leaves. The bulk of each leaf consists of cells that can fill with water and act as a reservoir during drought. The outer cell layers of the leaves have thickened waxy layers on their walls restricting water loss.

Huge, spectacular flowers that may last for months if they are not fertilized make many epiphytic orchids extremely popular as cut flowers. The industry of orchid growing and export by air to all corners of the globe is an important part of the economy in many parts of the tropics, particularly Singapore. But whatever man may make of them, all orchids are intended as organs of reproduction and so have hues, scents and designs that attract pollinating insects. Fine examples are *Coelogyne cristata*, *top*, Brassia orchids, *right*, and *Cattleya lawrenceana*, *above*.

Bromeliads and ferns

In their demanding environment, epiphytes take different routes to survival. While the epiphytic orchids rely on their capacity to absorb water quickly when it is available, and can reduce water loss, other plants, including ferns and bromeliads—members of the pineapple family, Bromeliaceae—have overcome the problems in different ways.

In order to live, many epiphytic ferns produce their own little patch of soil in the treetops by accumulating fallen leaves and other debris. This is bound together by the fern's roots and gradually decomposes to a peaty material which can hold much water. Some of these ferns, such as the bird's nest fern, *Asplenium nidus*, of Southeast Asia, and its close African relative, *Asplenium africanum*, have a rosette of long strap-shaped leaves forming a cup within which litter can gather. Others, such as *Drynaria*, have two sorts of leaf. Some are tall, green and produce the plant's reproductive units, the spores. Others are short, stiff, brown and oak-leaf-shaped and help to trap litter.

Another group of ferns with two sorts of leaf is the genus *Platycerium* (stag's horn ferns), often seen as houseplants. Some of the leaves are upright and forked repeatedly like horns, the others are almost circular and remain flat against the trunk of the supporting tree, lying one on top of the other and finally forming a mass of peaty material.

The ultimate step in epiphytic life has been taken by certain bromeliads. Some bromeliads root in the ground like any other plants. Others, including the pineapple, have a normal but rather restricted root system supplemented by extra roots that grow from the stem and absorb water and nutrients that accumulate among the leaf bases. The third group of bromeliads, numbering more species than the other two put together, includes the true tank epiphytes. Anchoring the tank epiphyte to its supporting branch are small roots. The leaf bases are broad and pressed tightly together to form a water-holding tank or cup. The tank's capacity ranges from less than half a pint up to 12 gallons or more.

Tank epiphytes absorb water from their built-in reservoir through umbrella-shaped scales, trichomes, which stand in a little hollow in the leaf surface. When wet they expand and let water into the hollow below the umbrella rim. On drying the leaf shrinks and pulls down the umbrella, sealing off the hollow and preventing water loss from the delicate absorbing cells at its base.

Besides water, much else accumulates in the tank—rotting leaves, old flowers and the droppings of animals and birds that feed and drink at the tank. This debris releases nutrients which are absorbed by the plant and also support a thriving miniature ecosystem. The material is decomposed by bacteria and protozoa. Larger protozoa, tiny crustaceans and mosquito larvae, prey on these and are in turn food for dragonfly larvae. The insects that visit the water are prey for birds, salamanders and frogs.

The flowers of bromeliads are usually bright and attractive or surrounded by striking petal-like bracts. Hummingbirds are common pollinators of bromeliads. At least some of the species have fleshy fruits with seeds surrounded by a sticky pulp which presumably helps to glue the seedling in position until it grows enough roots to attach itself. Their flowers make bromeliads popular houseplants.

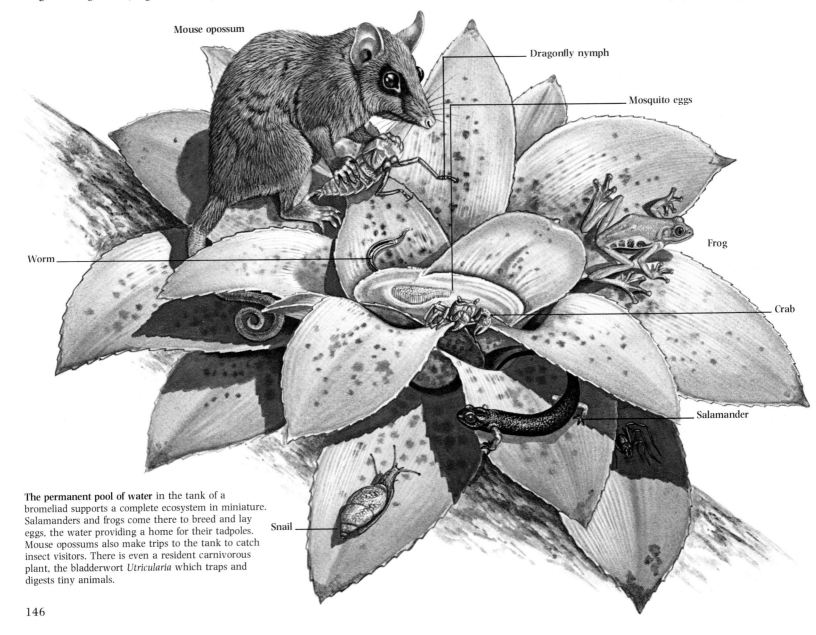

The permanent pool of water in the tank of a bromeliad supports a complete ecosystem in miniature. Salamanders and frogs come there to breed and lay eggs, the water providing a home for their tadpoles. Mouse opossums also make trips to the tank to catch insect visitors. There is even a resident carnivorous plant, the bladderwort *Utricularia* which traps and digests tiny animals.

By creating their own patch of soil, epiphytic ferns ensure supplies of nutrients and water. The bird's nest fern, *above*, relies on a cup-shaped leaf arrangement to accumulate debris; the stag's horn fern has two kinds of leaf: some are upright and forked, others are rounded and remain flat against the tree trunk accumulating peaty soil.

The short roots of many bromeliads serve only for attachment but the plants have leaf bases pressed close together to form a watertight tank which is filled with rain. The plant absorbs water from the tank via special hairs—vital adaptations.

The star-shaped epiphylls are tiny epiphytes which grow on the leaves of other plants. They usually occur in the wettest forests and need constant high humidity. The fact that most rain forest leaves are long-lasting also encourages epiphyll growth. The supporting leaf is shaded from the light by the epiphylls and its lifespan may be reduced.

Man and the jungle

Jungle man is set aside from urban man in one vital respect. To survive within his lush and generally predictable environment, jungle man must conserve his resources—if he should take too much from nature his own future will be jeopardized. This lesson, learned over the centuries, is reflected in the cultural adaptations of the tribes as well as in their religious practices. The size of the tribe, whether it is settled or nomadic, its pattern of marriage and reproduction and whether or not it has warlike and headhunting tendencies, can all be related to the productivity of the environment.

The Punans of Sarawak live in villages of some hundreds of people, in soundly constructed houses. They plant rice and other crops in fields hacked out of the jungle. One group of Punans, however, is forbidden by its religion to cut down large trees. This prevents these people from growing food and building houses, and forces them into a nomadic, hunting and gathering life. Because food gathering is less efficient than food growing, the bands limit their numbers to at most a few dozen. Jungle tribes have an inherent regard and respect for nature. Some of their tribal responses and customs may seem barbaric, but result in adequate food for all.

But jungle life is not idyllic. The infant mortality rate is high and in some areas a baby has only a 50/50 chance of surviving to its second birthday. Motherhood takes a harsh toll and women age prematurely; few live to menopause. A forty-year-old man is an elder of his tribe.

Prior to outside contact, jungle people were, however, remarkably free from fatal diseases, but measles, influenza and tuberculosis spread alarmingly in Amazonia once introduced because the Indians had no immunity to them. For the people living close by the Amazon, Negro and Xingu rivers, repeated contact brought repeated epidemics. The tribes have probably never fully recovered from those onslaughts of disease. Nowadays on the várzea, the floodplain of the Amazon, there are no tribes living exactly as their pre-contact ancestors did, but the details of their customs can be pieced together from the diaries of the early Portuguese explorers.

Exploration, while inevitably leading to the disturbance of traditional ways of life in the jungle, has produced many benefits for the rest of the world. Valuable crops such as rubber, cocoa and oil palm are rain forest plants and there are excellent hardwood timber trees. But in spite of a growing awareness of the value of jungles, their destruction continues. A balance must be found between preserving the rain forest and utilizing its resources efficiently. The rest of the world might learn from the few tribes still living in harmony with the jungle and think of the future before destroying these valuable forests for quick profits.

Living in the rain forest

Over thousands of years, jungle people have become specifically adapted to life in the rain forest. In the last century more change has occurred within their tribes than ever before. In fact, there probably does not exist a single tribe whose jungle adaptations have not been influenced by outside contact. Their previous isolation from the rest of the world has made them vulnerable to relatively trivial diseases such as colds and measles.

The most striking characteristic of jungle people is their small size, which might be a consequence of their low protein and calorie intake. The first six to twelve months in the life of a child are the healthiest from a nutritional point of view, as breast milk is normally plentiful. After the first year the rate of growth slows down, so that full adult height is reached at a later age than is usual in the developed world.

The real hazards of a poor protein diet are seen in pregnancy. American women gain as much as 28 pounds (13kg) during pregnancy; in the Congo women may gain only 11 pounds (5kg) and in the rain forests of Southeast Asia sometimes no weight is gained. In this case, the foetus obtains its nutrients at the direct expense of the mother.

High blood pressure is seldom found in forest dwellers. A typical value for a middle-aged South American Indian male would be $\frac{91}{62}$, for a typical European male $\frac{120}{75}$. Significantly, there is no increase with age in aboriginal people, as occurs in Europeans. This is perhaps partly because few tribes use sodium chloride as a condiment, preferring potassium salts instead. Some tribes, such as the Mundurucú, have recently begun using European salt with their food and are now experiencing increased blood pressure levels.

Compared to North Americans and Europeans, jungle people drink much less and sweat less. Their decreased water requirement can be attributed partly to the higher water content of their food. In addition, the high humidity of the rain forest means that evaporative heat loss is low, and sweating is therefore an inefficient means of keeping cool. Europeans have a higher basal metabolic rate (BMR) than forest dwellers, and so have more excess heat to be dissipated. The slimly built tribesman has little bulk in proportion to his body surface. Therefore his body surface acts as an efficient radiator of heat, and this, coupled with low BMR, reduces the likelihood of overheating.

All jungle tribes are exposed to a wide range of diseases. In the Congo, tribes respond to a high infant mortality rate by increased reproduction, but in Amazonia the onslaught of western diseases is so great that many tribes are steadily decreasing in numbers. Among the pygmies, the level of gamma globulin in the blood is unusually high, which gives them some immunity against malaria. Also, carriers of 'sickle-cell anaemia' (and this may constitute 15 per cent of Congo tribespeople) have some immunity against malaria. In the Congo, where malaria is widespread, the benefits of this immunity outweigh the disadvantages of sickle-cell anaemia.

Every one of these people crossing Brooklyn Bridge, irrespective of ethnic origin, is probably suffering from mental stress. Their physical health is likely to be impaired by an excess of sweet and starchy food and insufficient exercise. Yet, with the aid of medicine, most will live to the age of 70 or more when cancer, heart disease, hardening of the arteries or hypertension will kill them. The Kayapó Indian lives a less stressful life, his mental health is excellent, his pulse and blood pressure are stable and he is physically fit. Nevertheless he is likely to die at about 40 from a disease trivial by North American standards.

With adequate food, jungle people have a high working capacity, particularly in the cool of the early morning and late evening. This is when they concentrate on heavy work such as crushing manioc, *right.* During the heat of the day, they avoid heat stress by resting in the shade of their open houses. Rain forest people are well adapted to humidity; they produce less heat, sweat less and their slight build enables them to lose heat easily. Starvation is rare, but an epidemic can rapidly wipe out a village.

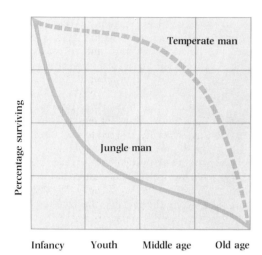

The survival rate of jungle man is significantly lower than temperate man's. Many jungle men die before middle age and one in two babies dies before the age of two.

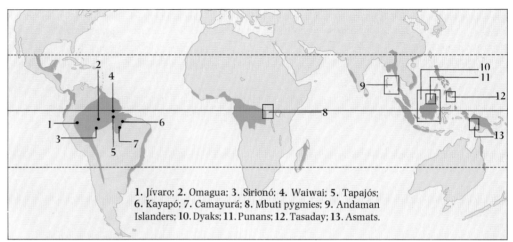

1. Jívaro; 2. Omagua; 3. Sirionó; 4. Waiwai; 5. Tapajós; 6. Kayapó; 7. Camayurá; 8. Mbuti pygmies; 9. Andaman Islanders; 10. Dyaks; 11. Punans; 12. Tasaday; 13. Asmats.

Population densities in jungles are related to the productivity of the ecosystem, and tribes have evolved cultural means of population control. In Amazonia there may be as few as two people per sq km, although there may be ten times this on the fertile várzea. In West Africa the sandy soils can support 30 per sq km but Southeast Asian tribes rarely exceed 10 to 20 per sq km.

Amazonia: the terra firme people

More than two million square miles of Amazonian jungle are supported by impoverished and rain-leached soils. What nourishment there is in these soils is quickly absorbed and stored by the plants. Known as the terra firme, this land is inhabited by a number of tribes which can manage to make a subsistence living from it. The problems facing the Jívaro in western Amazonia, however, are not identical to those experienced by the southern Sirionó or the eastern Kayapó, for differences in annual rainfall pattern, temperature and local flooding demand different life-styles.

All terra firme people spend a great deal of time hunting game and gathering nuts and berries in the jungle, as some items are available year round. Only some tribes, such as the Waiwai and Sirionó, include fish in their diet, because rivers such as the Rio Negro are acidic and hostile to fish.

The hunters shoot peccaries, capybaras, agoutis, parrots and monkeys with long bows and arrows or blowpipes. The tips of the arrows and the blowpipe darts are serrated and coated with a tarlike extract of various toxic plants, such as *Strychnos* and *Chondodendron*, or with the parotid gland extract from the frog *Dendrobates*. The blowpipe is effective up to 120 feet (36m) and is favoured by many hunters because it makes less noise than the bow and arrow.

Despite the small size of terra firme villages (from 25 residents in the Waiwai to 110 in the Camayurá), sufficient food for all cannot be obtained by hunting and gathering. All tribes practise a form of slash-and-burn agriculture in which an area of up to an acre is cleared of trees. The largest trees are felled first, and as they fall they have a domino effect on the smaller trees. Immediately before the start of the rainy season the branches and trunks are burned, and then the 'field' is ready for planting. The tree roots are not grubbed out, and while this makes planting inefficient and difficult, it protects much of the soil from the rain and sun.

Different tribes plant different staples. The Jívaro and Kayapó, for example, plant sweet manioc while the Waiwai and the Camayurá grow the bitter variety which needs careful preparation to make it edible. The Jívaro also grow a small amount of maize, and the Kayapó some sweet potatoes. In the south of Amazonia, where the soils are even poorer than those in the north, the Sirionó are forced to wander in the dry season and exist only on what they can catch and gather. After three years the small fields are abandoned because their yields have fallen, and new ones are created. Within a few years the clearing will again be covered by jungle.

Under this type of agricultural system, the soil is quickly depleted: in the first year a Camayurá village could expect to harvest 18 tons per 2.5 acres; in the second year the yield will drop to 13 tons and in the third year to just 10 tons. Terra firme villages are not permanent structures. As more and more land close to the village is abandoned, the whole village moves to a new site. The Waiwai move once every five years and the Camayurá every ten. If left undisturbed by others, the jungle can then reclaim its former territory.

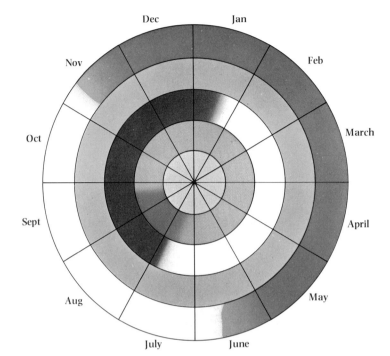

Rainy season

Sweet potato

Yam, sweet manioc

Fishing, Brazil nuts and fruit gathering

Hunting game and tortoises

The annual food cycle of the Kayapó tribe from Brazil is dominated by the rainy season. Before the rains they clear patches of land to plant sweet manioc, yams, and sweet potatoes. Some of these crops are harvested throughout the year, but many fruits, nuts and wild honey are seasonal foods. Small game, tortoises and fish are hunted all the year round.

The Amazonian yam, *Dioscorea trifida,* is the only yam to originate in America. Each plant produces several starchy tubers which grow quickly in newly cleared land. They can be boiled or roasted in a leaf wrapping and have an excellent flavour.

The Brazil nut is an important source of protein and oil to most terra firme tribes, and can be stored. Up to 20 hard-shelled nuts grow inside each urnshaped fruit produced by the magnificent 150ft (45m) jungle tree, *Bertholletia excelsa.*

This land has recently been cleared by the Tukano of Colombia and planted with banana, yam and manioc. The tree roots are left to protect the newly exposed soil from erosion by sun and rain. Such jungle fields are subject to far less erosion than the weed-free soil of advanced agriculture.

Manioc or cassava, *Manihot esculenta*, contains poisonous prussic acid, so needs to be carefully prepared. After being peeled and grated, it is pressed into tubular baskets and squeezed to extract the acid. The floury pulp is then sieved and baked on a griddle to make manioc bread. Washed and heated manioc makes tapioca.

153

Amazonia: the river people

To the people who cluster in villages along the Amazon, the river represents the key to their survival and well-being. Overflowing her banks regularly, she creates a maze of channels, lakes and ponds covering some 24,000 square miles (60,000sq km) of Amazonia. This flood plain is called the várzea.

Although the tribes which live there have to decamp temporarily to higher land when the river is in spate, the advantages of the annual rich deposition of silt to their agriculture are enormous. Their prosperity, *vis-à-vis* the terra firme tribes, is reflected in the large size of their villages (300 inhabitants in the Omagua and up to 2,500 in the Tapajós) and by the fact that they never need to relocate the sites of their villages. The new soil with which these tribal people are presented each year means that not only is the yield per acre of bitter manioc or maize higher than on the best terra firme land, but also that it is maintained at that level.

Several months of abundant food supply, however, are followed by several months of famine. When the great river is at its highest, the surrounding fields are inundated and the game is forced to migrate. Consequently, the várzea tribes have developed techniques for storing food which they harvested during the periods of plenty. Maize and manioc flour are dried and stored on racks or in

atticlike granaries; manioc roots are buried in clamps. Wild rice is converted to wine, and fish and meat are dried or smoked over a fire. The oil from turtle eggs gathered at the time of low water is used as a form of butter. Newly hatched turtles are cooked in *tucupí* (manioc juice and pepper) and stored in pottery jars.

Since the agricultural season lasts only a few months, the várzea tribes must follow a strict schedule of planting and harvesting. If seed is planted too early, rot sets in, and if it is too late the crop may not be ready for harvesting until after the river floods. When two annual crops are required, as with maize, the timing is even more critical. In order to coordinate these activities with fishing and hunting, the village has a chief who not only issues orders but also commands total obedience. To support his commands he calls upon a deity. All várzea tribes have temples where prayers and offerings for a good harvest may be made.

The hunting season coincides with the farming season; small bands of men fan out from the village looking for game. Most prized are the tapir and the peccary—a single specimen will feed several households for some days. Monkeys, parrots and rodents such as the agouti are often hunted by one man, armed only with a blowpipe and curare-tipped darts. Some specialized hunting techniques

have evolved; for duck hunting, a swimmer wears a calabash hat. Since the ducks are used to seeing floating calabashes, they are not alarmed. At an opportune moment, the swimmer jumps from the water and throws a net over the ducks.

Várzea tribes have been more influenced by the Europeans than have terra firme tribes. It is doubtful if any live today exactly as their aboriginal forefathers did. As Amazonia becomes more exploited, the identity of these tropical forest people increasingly fades.

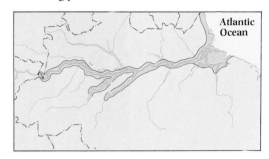

The flood plain of the Amazon, known as the várzea, stretches some 1,500m (2,500km) up river from the mouth. Once a year, the water level rises gradually, driving the people to higher land. The hilliest areas are flooded for only a few weeks in June, while lower regions are under water for nearly six months.

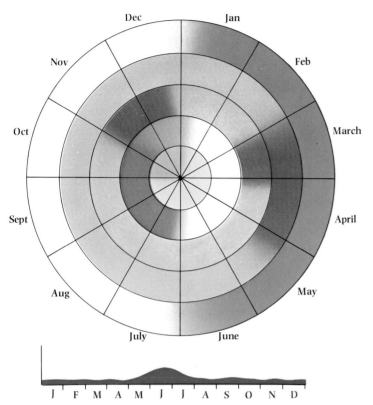

Rainy season

Manioc

Maize

Wild rice

Turtles, eggs, birds, manatees

The level of the river controls plant, animal and human life alike. The high flood (May to July) is a time of scarcity when tribesmen must survive on stored food. When the river is low (October to December) wild plants and animals thrive, providing fruitful hunting and gathering trips. Before the flood rises too far, maize, bitter manioc and rice are harvested. Maize stores well if properly dried. With cobs intact, it is hung on specially built drying racks in the sun.

Maize is one of the most important cereals in the world. It originated in Central America and, as a high yield, nutritious crop, made settled life possible there. The grain is ground into flour.

As the várzea flood-water recedes, wild rice takes root on the lakesides. It is gathered when almost ripe, dried then stored. The grain is ground for bread-making or fermented for wine.

Fish become plentiful as the turbulent waters begin to retreat, and many tribes celebrate with a fishing festival. The Tapajós, Omagua and other várzea tribes are skilled fishermen. Bows and arrows are efficient weapons, particularly for large fish such as the 10ft (3m) long piraiba catfish, but the most productive fishing technique is to poison the water. Crushed shoots and leaves of one of the many narcotic plant species are cast from a canoe. The stunned fish are then scooped up with a hand net made of tucum fibre. Some tribes use basketry fish traps, others have rods and lines. Superfluous fish are smoked and stored on a rack. For even longer storage, some are preserved in turtle or manatee oil in pottery jars. Baby turtles and caimans are captured and kept alive in bamboo corrals until needed for the pot.

Amazonia: a fine balance

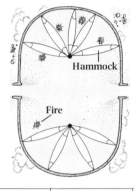

The Camayurá of south Amazonia build thatched houses large enough to accommodate several related families. Hammocks slung between the roof posts and wall leave the centre free for communal activities, and divide men and women. Fires lit between and under the hammocks provide warmth during the night.

The culture of any group reflects its environmental conditions. Since life in the jungle is so harsh for its various tribespeople, the so-called higher forms of culture have not had the opportunity to develop, as they play no part in the survival of the tribes. The cultural patterns that have evolved there, however, are diverse.

This welter of variations in any cultural characteristic means that some tribes will always have the behavioural ability to cope with particular environmental changes. Abortion and the use of contraceptives, for example, are used at characteristically different levels in different tribes to adjust their population sizes in relation to ecological and sociological constraints.

Study of the peoples of Amazonia provides some excellent examples of the adaptability of human culture. On the terra firme, the environment is generally predictable. But the low biological productivity means that village groups must be small and widely spaced if overexploitation is not to occur. As a result, there is much inter-village hatred and warfare. Tribes such as the Jívaro and Mundurucú parade and vilify the shrunken heads of their foes to keep the level of hatred high. Other tribes make flutes out of victims' leg bones, and necklaces of their teeth.

The tribes of the várzea, by contrast, need to be large so that they have enough hands available for planting and harvesting rice and maize when the Amazon subsides. They practise no population control and do not fight among themselves. But they do fight against terra firme tribes, with the objective of taking slaves for work in the paddy fields. Because they experience six months' deprivation during the flooding season, they worship idols in an attempt to obtain better crops during the growing season.

A characteristic of Amazonian tribes is the pre-sence of a headman. He may be leader of one family or household, or of a village or a group of villages. His enormous powers enable him to impose some magic or religious justification for periodic prohibition on various natural resources. His authority is so strictly obeyed that the closed season allows the resources to recover.

The influence of the headman is much in evidence among the Andaman Islanders. Both he and his council, at certain times, limit the number of *Dioscorea* tubers, or hearts of the *Caryota* palm, that the tribe may take. Harsh punishments are meted out to villagers who disobey. Social decisions are taken on a strictly ecological basis—mystical, magical or religious powers vested in the leaders, serve to ensure that the future survival of all is not put at risk by the greedy actions of a few. Natural selection favours the cultural adoption of rituals, such as the display of shrunken heads or the wearing of a supposedly magic mantle, which serve to enhance the authority of the chief.

Cultural practices, then, often keep the level of human exploitation of the environment by jungle tribes in balance with the region's natural productivity. Although outsiders who come to the jungles specifically to plunder their animal life or timber may have sophisticated technology, they sometimes lack any understanding of the natural balance inherent in jungle ecosystems. Jungle man, through cultural as well as physical adaptation, is an integral part of that ecosystem and has achieved a balance with his surroundings envied by resource planners elsewhere.

The main similarities and differences in cultural organization between the tribes living on the terra firme and the tribes of the várzea are indicated on the table, *right*.

Traits	Terra firme Unproductive soil. Regular hunting, fishing and crop production.	Várzea Soils revitalized by annual flood. All food is seasonal. High productivity.
Village characteristics Village population Village permanency	25 to 100+ 6 months to years	300 to 2,500 indefinite
Social organization Household chief Village council Multivillage 　council Slaves	X only in big villages –	X X X X
Occupational specialists Shaman	X	sometimes
Trade Between villages	X	X
Specialized structures Temple/ 　shrine Storehouse/ 　granary	– –	X X
Religion Idols	only in big villages	X
Population control Warfare between 　villages Prenatal 　intercourse taboo Contraception Abortion Infanticide Accidental flooding 　disaster	X X rare rare common –	– – X
Key X characteristic present　– characteristic absent		

Africa: the Mbuti pygmies

From the moment he is born, the pygmy is a child of the forest; it protects him, feeds him and allows him to express himself. He sees it as another mother and father. The pygmy is also aware of the power of the jungle to take away what it usually supplies in abundance, and so he approaches his hunting trips with humility and appeasement. Almost as if it is in sympathy with the pygmies, the jungle seldom withholds game, nuts, berries and fruit.

Scattered over much of tropical West Africa from the Cameroons through Gabon, the Congo, the Central African Republic, Zaire and east to its borders with the Sudan, Uganda, Rwanda and Burundi are almost 200,000 pygmy people. The huge majority have fused with many races of Bantu which migrated southward some two millenia ago, but in the Ituri forest in eastern Zaire there remain about 25,000 Mbuti pygmies who retain a traditional culture and are of relatively pure blood.

The Mbuti are among the world's smallest people. A fully grown man stands 4 feet 6 inches (137cm); a woman 2½ inches (6cm) less. They live in bands of from 20 to 100, and each band has exclusive hunting rights to an agreed territory, which may take eight or more days' fast march to cross.

Some bands hunt with bows and arrows; others hunt with nets and spears. The former go off daily in parties of two or three and shoot monkeys, rodents or perhaps tiny antelope such as the chevrotain. Net hunters go out in much larger bands, which usually include everybody except women in the later stages of pregnancy. Each man has a net, somewhat like a tennis net but up to 330 feet (100m) long. It is a prized possession, handed down from father to son. Made from *nkusa* vine, twisted and knotted, the net needs constant repair. The nets of the oldest men are slung between trees in an area where game is thought to be, with the nets of the younger men forming a wide semicircle. When an antelope is entangled, a spear coated with the plant poison *Strophanthus* is driven into it.

Very occasionally pygmies kill elephants. A small band pursues an elephant and, when they get close enough, one man darts forward and slashes the hamstrings with a razor-sharp spear. Another thrusts a spear deep into its bladder. They then leave the elephant to die slowly. A day or two later the band finds the dead, bloated carcass and, after appeasing the spirit of the beast, they cut it up and carry it back to camp.

For two months of the year wild honey is readily available to the pygmies. This provides the stimulus not only for a change in diet but also for a social reappraisal of kinships. The fragmented groups of bow and arrow hunters come together, and social tensions are eased by the jollity of the large group. Net hunters split up and form different friendships. For both types the resumption of hunting sees new group structures.

Pygmies are mild-mannered people, with no penal system. When a person commits some crime, he is shamed and ridiculed. The doors of his neighbours' huts are moved so that nobody needs look at him. Temporary sight screens, called spite fences, are erected to isolate him further. But memories are short, and it will not be long before he is back in favour. Bands have no chiefs, and all decisions are taken democratically.

Almost every band of pygmies has some trading links with settled Bantu tribes outside the forest. In return for thatching leaves, meat and help with the harvest, the Bantu give the pygmies manioc, bananas, beans, salt and tobacco. The Bantu see the pygmies as slaves, though they use no political or other type of coercion. The pygmies view the relationship as an informal one and often 'liberate' the villagers' portable goods when they return to the forest. But pygmies have no use for possessions and live free, unfettered lives. In times of trouble the Mbuti say they only have to sing their sacred *molimo* songs to alert the jungle to their plight. The power of this simple faith enables them to live in balance with their supportive jungle.

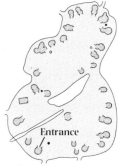

Entrance

A pygmy hut has a domed framework of pliable saplings covered with overlapping tiers of leaves. Women build these simple homes around the perimeter of the camp and maintain the roofs daily to prevent leaks. Huts are grouped according to friendships, and the doorway positions change to indicate current warm or cool relations with a neighbour. Pygmies are relaxed, gregarious people who settle their differences amicably. The centre of the camp is kept open for meetings and social events. During the honey-gathering season, the pygmies perform complex, symbolic dances to thank the jungle for past favours and pray for its future benevolence.

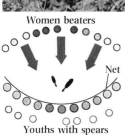

Women beaters

Net

Youths with spears

Women and children beat the game forward into the wide semicircle of nets. The men then spear the entangled prey.

Bow and arrow hunters of Aka are skilled, accurate marksmen, using fire-hardened or metal-tipped arrows. The Mbuti net hunt requires the cooperation of the entire group. A pygmy woman will usually make a net for her son. She shreds the supple parts of the *nkusa* vine and twists it into twine. It lasts years with careful repair.

Southeast Asia: a variety of life-styles

The Kayan of Sarawak build several longhouses in a jungle clearing like other land-Dyak tribes. Village affairs are conducted in the headhouse, where the shrunken heads of enemies were kept in days gone by.

The Punan hunter can slip through the Sarawak jungles as silently as a shadow, even armed with his 6ft (1.8m) long bamboo blowpipe. He can shoot a bird with a wooden dart or a large mammal with a steel tipped dart from 50yd (45m). The darts are often treated with plant poison and the blowpipe may be embellished with a bayonet to kill paralyzed prey.

The stars govern the cycle of the Dyaks' rice crop. When the Pleiades appear on the horizon in June, men start to clear the forest. Three months later, with the Pleiades at the zenith, they sow the precious grain. By the time Sirius passes the zenith in mid-October they know it is too late to sow. After two seasons the soil is exhausted and new fields must be cleared.

To the Dyak tribesman of Borneo, a knowledge of astronomy is as important as a knowledge of the habits of the wild animals upon which he relies for meat. By watching the positions of various constellations he knows the best time to clear new land and plant his staple crop—rice. His economy is based on rice and much of his culture is bound up in ceremonies to ensure a good harvest.

Dyaks are settled people who live in substantial longhouses; their agricultural activity centres on nuclear families, or *bileks*, of three generations. Unlike the rice fields of the settled tribes of the Amazonian *várzea* which are inundated every year, the Dyak fields are not revitalized annually. After two or three years of use, the *bilek* must clear a new patch of four or five acres and leave the old to regenerate naturally. The women and children work hard to remove saplings and undergrowth, while the men take the opportunity of felling the largest trees to display their strength and manhood. In the use of their small hand axes, called *bliongs*, they are highly skilled; in three months they will have cleared a field for planting.

Many of the Dyak tribes (the term Dyak refers to a huge number of distinct peoples) have supplemented rice planting with cucumbers, pumpkins, chillies, manioc, maize and bananas. Some

keep cattle, poultry and pigs, but these appear to be used for trade rather than for home consumption. Dyaks contribute to the western economy by growing rubber and collecting *illipe* nuts, whose pithy kernel is used as a base for cosmetics.

By comparison, the Punans of Sarawak seem very primitive. These people live in the deepest forest and shun the sunlight. They trade bananas and manioc with the Dyaks for patent medicines (which the Dyaks get from Europeans) and, most prized of all, guns. The Punans are unsurpassed hunters and can kill a gibbon with a blowpipe and dart at 50 yards. Some Punans are settled, live in longhouses and grow rice, as do the Dyaks. Others are proscribed from cutting down forest trees by their powerful religion, which not only denies them the strong timbers required for the construction of a longhouse, but also prevents them from clearing fields for rice planting.

While settled Punans may live in villages of more than 200 people, the nomadic bands seldom exceed 40 persons. Like the pygmies of the Ituri forest they believe deeply in the power of forest spirits, and regard thunder as a retribution for having mocked animals. Although they exist by their hunting they make pets of wild piglets and monkeys.

The Dyaks and, to a much lesser extent, the Punans, are a warlike people, who until recently have been headhunters. Dyak village life revolves around the headhouse, in whose roof the grisly tokens of battle are stored. Here, the men hold council meetings and formerly planned battles. For these primitive peoples, headhunting should be viewed as a means of population control, and should be compared with infanticide and sexual continence among the Amazonian Indians.

Hovering on the brink of extinction is the Tasaday tribe, from the craggy southern tip of Mindanao in the Philippines. Discovered for the first time by Europeans in 1966 and not properly observed until 1971, the tribe numbers 24 people. They have no word for war, and no weapons. What tools they have are made of stone. A cave serves as the communal home, and their diet consists of gathered nuts, grubs, palm pith, yams, fruits, frogs, crabs and small fish that inhabit rapidly flowing mountain streams. These peaceful and gentle people have lived for centuries totally unaffected by the advance of civilization. Sadly, the timber companies are already pushing roads through to the Tasaday valley and, unless the strongest of conservation measures are introduced, the world will lose one of its most primitive races.

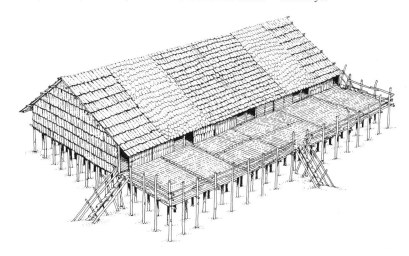

To the Sea-Dyaks or Ibans from the coast and rivers of Borneo, life revolves around one wooden longhouse, which houses an entire village of 14 families. Every *bilek* has its own living room leading off the main gallery which is the social centre and where heads of enemies were formerly displayed. Rice is sunned in the open gallery and stored in bark bins in the loft.

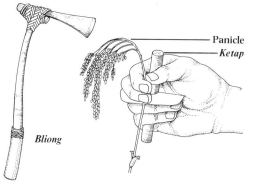

— Panicle
— Ketap

Bliong

Felling the primary jungle is crucial to the Dyak system of agriculture. It demands great skill and a razor-sharp *bliong*, an axe which is reforged every year. Women harvest the rice with the aid of a bladed tool, the traditional *ketap*. A skilled reaper can pluck up to 80 panicles a minute, or one acre in two or three weeks.

The cave-dwelling Tasaday from southern Mindanao live a Stone Age existence, foraging in the jungle for fruit, nuts, roots and the asparagus-flavoured *ubud* palm pith, *above*. Each man needs only spend a few hours a day providing for his family, as fish, frogs, crabs and tadpoles can be swiftly scooped from the fast-flowing streams and supply a healthy amount of protein. Processing *natek* from palm pith is the Tasadays' most advanced form of technology and was taught to them in 1966. The pith is chipped out of the palm trunk, then trampled and washed through a filter of leaves. An orange soup emerges, which, when settled, forms dough. It is baked in bark and is a staple food.

161

The faces of ritual

An early artist's impression of the New Guinea natives encountered by Captain Cook, though exaggerated, is not inaccurate. Cassowary quills in the hair and body paints of ochre, kaolin and charcoal are still used today.

Large shell nose ornaments are worn by the Asmats of New Guinea to enhance their warring image. The *bi pane* is threaded through a hole cut in the nose, and beeswax pressed into the nostrils stops it slipping. This man also wears a dog's tooth necklace and sago palm plaits.

Since the earliest times man has ornamented and decorated his body. The fantastic adornment of some other animals serves two main purposes: first, to enable males to show off to one another, with the most assertive getting the biggest territory or the best perch; second, to attract a mate. Humans paint themselves and mutilate their bodies partly in order to command, and retain, the respect and admiration of their fellows.

But man is a spiritual creature and he alone among all the animals is capable of abstract thought. Thus he is able to apply pigments artistically to his unadorned body, weave grasses and feathers into his hair, design intricate patterns of skin wounds and prepare delicately carved totems in order to ward off evil spirits. Protection from illness can be gained by painting the body; the love of a dead relative can be perpetuated by wearing his jawbone as a necklace. To jungle people ornamentation, decoration, adornment and the superstitious rituals which accompany them are much more than idle frippery. The spiritual protection which such decoration provides and the physical prowess and status it represents are undoubtedly cornerstones of jungle society.

The simplest form of decoration is body painting. Most jungle tribes practise some type of painting, but it is most advanced in the people of the Andaman Islands which lie midway between India and Malaysia. The Andamanese spend many hours each day working geometric patterns in red ochre, yellow ochre, kaolin and charcoal all over their bodies. The ochres are made from burnt soils and are mixed with fat before being applied to the skin with a fine stick—often chewed to make it brushlike—or a fragment of bone. Women often decorate their husbands. A much admired pattern is quickly copied, bringing increased status to the man and wife. Such patterns have no symbolic meaning.

For the Asmats of New Guinea some of their patterns do have meaning. The red lines which they paint around their eyes imitate the red spots which

appear around the eyes of the black cockatoo when it is angry. Certain hues have universal meanings—red usually signifies blood. If a man commits a murder he flees the village and paints himself red. The constant awareness of blood that this creates is considered punishment enough.

Scarification of the body—tiny skin wounds which heal slowly into raised weals—is a well-developed art in the Andaman Islands. An additional function of scarification is to increase the subject's ability to withstand pain. This has obvious advantages to people living in a dangerous environment without medical aid. Other decorative mutilations are the piercing of the nose to insert bizarre ornaments, and the placing of plugs in lips and ears.

The feathers of birds, the claws, teeth and fur of mammals, as well as shells and leaves are used by many jungle people for necklaces, head-dresses and loincloths. The Asmats make necklaces from dogs' teeth, naming each tooth after an ancestor whose spirit they wish to save. The range of imaginative uses of the parts of animals is limitless and there are characteristic patterns among the various tribes. In the onetime headhunting tribes of New Guinea, a young man displayed his bravery, and hence his attractiveness, by wearing the heads of his victims around his waist, attached to a belt. Displays of heads, whether on the victor or in a headhouse,

allowed warriors to purge their fear of death in battle by mocking and vilifying the heads of their former foes.

When European explorers first visited jungles, they brought home fantastic stories of headhunters and cannibals. By the time these stories reached the popular press they bore little resemblance to reality. Headhunting and cannibalism still occur from time to time in the remote areas of Sarawak and New Guinea but are largely things of the past.

Such activities were not indulged in because of hunger, for the jungles usually offer adequate food for those who know how to gather it. They were part of the spiritual world; a victim's severed head kept close to the victor was thought to protect him from the spirit of the victim seeking its revenge. But the victim's strength and courage was honoured by the victor consuming some of his flesh—usually the thigh—and his brains. When a boy took part in the ceremony to mark his initiation into manhood, a victim's head was placed between his legs. This was believed to make the boy grow fast.

In some areas a variation on cannibalism was the practice of a family eating a dead relative's body. To the Asmats and many South American tribes this is an expression of affection and allows the good qualities and life forces of the dead person to survive.

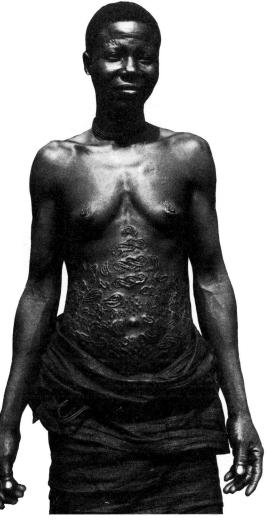

Scarification is a highly developed art among the Andamanese. A superficial skin cut is made with a sliver of quartz, and wood ash is often rubbed into the wound to produce a raised weal. Three rows of scars characterize tribes from the north Andaman Islands. Scarring begins in infancy and continues into adulthood when most of the body is covered. The scarring is thought to improve the appearance and to help the child grow into a strong, healthy adult.

The spoils of a New Guinea headhunting raid are victoriously displayed on a door post, firmly held with rattan fibres. A spirit cannot stand the sight of its own skull and bones so this warrior and his wife hope to ward off the spirit's revenge by exhibiting its remains.

Papuan warriors set out on their headhunting raid well armed with spears, bows and arrows and sharp bamboo knives. Victims were ritually beheaded at specific places where spirits are known to live.

This display of Punan heads on a Dyak gibbet, although abhorrent to western eyes, fulfills a spiritual need for the jungle people. The heads are a reminder that enemies are not unconquerable giants but real people. They are also made objects of ridicule to boost confidence before battle, in much the same way as western people sing denigrating songs about the enemy. The heads are also status symbols, since in these societies, a man's virility depended on his headhunting skills. Some tribes stitch the lips of the head together, to imprison the spirit within.

Fantasies, faiths and fables

Today's travellers are well prepared for their destinations by films and photographs, but to the early explorers who knew nothing of the misty primeval rain forest, it must have seemed an unreal world. The atmosphere of their extraordinary surroundings was bound to stimulate their imagination—and fear—and inspire outlandish tales of what lurked in the dense, dark forests.

The first Spanish pioneers returned from the immense jungles and rivers of South America with stories as fabulous as medieval legends. They told of men whose white hair turned black with old age, men with eight toes or two fingers, others with no neck, a dog's head or one cyclopean eye. There was reputed to be a one-legged tribe who ran like the wind, men whose feet pointed backward to confuse followers, and bat people who lived in holes and only emerged at night. There were beings that were half-fish, half-man, who were conceived by fish, fertilized by the sperm of drowned men. Fossilized bones of extinct giant ostriches and horses were even believed to be the skeletons of human giants. No one really knew what did exist in the jungle, and anything seemed possible.

During his marathon voyage down the Amazon river in 1540, explorer Francisco de Orellana reported seeing a tribe of powerful warrior women reminiscent of the Amazons of Greek mythology—warlike women who killed all male children at birth. Later, another explorer, La Condamine, found green stones in the jungle, said to be the Amazons' rewards to men who gave them female offspring. The stories of these legendary viragos gave the Amazon river its name.

Equally fanciful tales are circulated by the jungle tribes themselves. The inhabitants of the Peten rain forest in Middle America believe it to be haunted by small, elfin people called *dwendis* who have yellow

faces, long arms and hairy bodies; they have pointed heels, and leave deep footprints. The Sisemites, huge monsters that killed men and abducted women, are also believed to haunt the Middle American forests; there have even been reports this century of women being taken by these fiends. Brazilian Indians tell of a legendary tribe who whistle through a hole in their heads and grow coconuts under their arms which they break off, smash open against their heads and eat. Many South American Indians are convinced that malevolent spirits hide in the forest and cause problems such as accidents and disease. These demons make useful scapegoats for any misfortune.

Before anthropologists, archaeologists and palaeontologists determined the scientific truth, the origin of the real inhabitants of the South American rain forests, the Indians, remained a puzzle. There was much conjecture based on both Biblical and classical sources, and on the Indians' physical and linguistic resemblances to other cultures. All believed that they originated from another land, but few agreed on their ethnic roots—Sumerian, Babylonian, Egyptian, Mongoloid, Chinese and Polynesian were among the suggestions.

In 1512 a Papal Bull declared that all American natives were descendants of Adam and Eve, and this sparked off a host of Biblical theories. Some believed that the Indians were related to Ham, whose children were cursed because he had seen Noah's nakedness. Others labelled them sons of Jacob or one of the lost tribes of Israel. In the seventeenth century a Spanish monk, Gregorio Garcia, claimed that the Indians were Jews because they did not recognize Jesus Christ—this idea found apparent support in the similarity of the Spanish words for Jew and Indian: *iudio* and *indio*.

Anthropologists now agree that South Amer-

ican Indians are an independent race of Mongoloid origin, who arrived from Asia less than 20,000 years ago.

In common with all human societies the forest Indians have spiritual beliefs, superstitions and myths which help to explain the earth's natural phenomena. Some have a scientific base. Chac, the rain lord of the Mayans in Middle America, was depicted on temples with a long, curling nose and carrying a thunder axe. To entreat him to bring the heavy spring rains after the regular dry spell in that area, the natives built huge fires of wild rubber. Chac responded to the billowing clouds of black smoke by sending messengers to pour jars of sacred water through the clouds. Today, more advanced societies encourage rainfall by scattering clouds with crystals from aircraft. The crystals precipitate the formation of rain drops; perhaps the particles of smoke acted in the same way.

The Xingu Indians of Brazil have a vast repertoire of Kiplingesque fables which describe the origins of familiar features of jungle life: how the language of the birds was created, how rivers were formed and where the bow came from. A favourite saga tells of the conquest of fire. A man named Kanassa went in search of fire. On the way he met the curassow making a feather head-dress to ward off Indians. Kanassa demanded that all curassows wear elegant head-dresses, which explains why today many have fine crests. Kanassa then met an alligator making a manioc grater. He carried it on his tail, and Kanassa declared that the grater should not be removed; so, all alligators have grater-shaped tails. While crossing a lagoon in a clay canoe, Kanassa passed some ducks in a wooden canoe; they swapped vessels and the clay canoe sank, leaving the ducks floundering. When the ducks realized that they were not sinking they

began to enjoy themselves, and now ducks readily take to water.

Kanassa's ultimate mission was to catch the master of fire, the king vulture. He drew a deer in the earth and hid by the drawing of the deer's hoof. He caught the vulture when it came to feed, and in return for freedom the vulture taught Kanassa the secret of fire.

The pygmies—children of the forest

The people of the African forests, the pygmies, were first featured in Egyptian mythology, and in the Iliad, Homer recounted a tale of a battle between the pygmies and the cranes. Aristotle claimed that pygmy people actually existed, and the Romans accurately depicted pygmies and their huts on Pompeiian mosaics, yet for centuries Europeans continued to think of the pygmies as a legendary race. The findings of a seventeenth century anatomist who, after studying a chimpanzee skeleton, declared that pygmies were definitely not human, perpetuated the myth.

The lively, imaginative Mbuti pygmies are certainly no legend but they do have a large fund of stories and convictions about the jungle. For them the forest is the great life-giver; it is their father, mother, lover and friend, and it both governs and protects them. They even prefer to make love in the benevolent forest rather than in their huts. In times of death, illness or poor hunting, the pygmies believe that the forest is sleeping and not guarding its children. So to awaken and cheer up the forest the pygmies hold a festival of singing and dancing.

Inexplicable little mishaps are attributed to the *keti*—invisible mirror images of the Mbuti. If a pygmy trips, he bumped into a *keti*; if game is scarce, the *keti* hunted it first; if a pygmy dreams, he slipped into a *keti* mirage. The villagers on the fringes of the forest, with whom the pygmies trade, believe that the forest is peopled with evil beings. To encourage the villagers' fear and keep them out of their beloved forest, the pygmies spin yarns about daunting forest spirits. Thus they maintain their role as intermediaries between the forest and the village.

The beliefs of the Southeast Asian tribes

Southeast Asian forest people have their own traditional cultures and beliefs, many of which reflect their jungle surroundings. The Dyaks of Borneo have a sophisticated religion. They believe in Sang Huang, supreme ruler of the seven heavens and creator of the universe, and a host of lesser gods who each have their own earthly duties and a place in one of the heavens. Some need to be pacified or flattered, others demand revenge, which usually requires human sacrifice. The god Gana protects the hunter, and the Dyaks wear feathered headdresses to attract his attention and win his favour.

In Dyak society where many die young, death is thought of as the robbery of man's defences by evil spirits, not the natural result of old age. The type of coffin a man is buried in decides which heaven his soul attains. A sappu wood coffin earns the soul a place in the fourth heaven, provided the corpse is folded so the feet rest on the head—the house of the soul—and can walk the spirit to heaven. To reach the seventh heaven, a man is staked, and buried alive; his soul is flown to paradise by the *tingang* (a bird of paradise) placed on top of the stake.

Countless charms and tokens accompany each stage of Dyak life. A crocodile's tooth blesses a woman with pregnancy—pregnancy is not connected with intercourse by the Dyaks. A newborn baby is given a collection of charms to bring good fortune: a short piece of bamboo to ensure cooperation in tribal life, a piece of a thorny bush placed above his head to catch falling evil spirits, and sesarpat leaves to bestow beauty of face and nature. Charms are also used in Dyak medicine; pain is transferred on to a wooden stick with a carved human head and left in the forest where it disappears.

The beliefs of the Malayan Semang have a similar function to Dyak and Christian religions but differ in detail. Their supreme god Ta Pedn controls a three-layered heaven where fruit trees grow and where the soul returns after death. Ta Pedn's helpers, the Cenoi, inhabit flowers, ripen fruit and speak in a secret language that only the shaman (medicine man) understands.

Theories to explain how the world and man were created also abound in this area. One holds that man was born out of Mother Earth and Father Water, another that man is descended from two white apes—a notion which comes curiously close to Darwin's theory of evolution. The Andaman Islanders believe that Paluga, the storm goddess, created the earth which stands on a huge palm tree growing from a jungle housing the spirits of the dead. The Andamanese live in fear that Paluga will upset their existence by turning the earth upside-down in an earthquake. By doing this she would tip the living into the jungle of death and bring the dead back to earth.

Born of man's unquenchable desire for explanation of life's mysteries and of his restless imagination is this plethora of myths, legends and spiritual convictions. Explorers could let their fantasies run riot on what might be found in the jungle, as no one really knew. For the jungle people themselves their beliefs, often related directly to the forest, help to maintain the order and cooperation necessary to survive in this environment and fill their lives with hope, meaning and tradition.

The forest's harvest

The old way to fell a rain forest timber tree was with an axe. This could take as much as a whole day of hard, skilled work. The giant timber trees often have their crowns tangled together with big woody climbers, as in this example in Guyana. To bring them down, the whole group of trees knitted together in the canopy would have to be felled.

Forests are a renewable resource. Their wise stewardship ensures a perpetual supply of timber and other commodities. They also have an important role in watershed and wildlife management, and as centres for recreation and tourism. The multiple use of forests is most developed in densely populated, industrial parts of the world, but this trend is spreading to the humid tropics as pressure on land and the remaining areas of tropical rain forest increases.

Historically, the exploitation of tropical rain forest for timber falls into two phases. Apart from meeting the needs of local inhabitants, the initial market was for choice cabinet woods—ebony, satinwood and mahogany—and for specialized timbers, such as naturally durable hardwoods, for construction, lignum vitae for ships' thrust bearings, and logwood for the dye haematoxylin. Single trees were felled and dragged by man, mule or buffalo to the nearest watercourse, then floated away. Foresters in the better organized countries, such as Malaya, attempted to stimulate regeneration of these scattered trees in the small gaps created by felling.

Beside specialized timbers there was also trade in the so-called minor forest products—gums, resins, rattans. These were taxed by governments, with foresters responsible for the revenue collection. There were attempts at regulation and prevention of destructive exploitation. In some Asian countries there were even specified revenue rates for large leaves harvested for wrapping material, and for edible birds' nests. Forest industry was on a small scale; many of its benefits were tied to people living in or near the forest.

Since World War II, however, the nature of forest exploitation has changed dramatically. A world market has developed for the paler, lighter, less durable rain forest timbers. Instead of individual, scattered trees, virtually whole rain forests have become marketable. This change has coincided with the development of reliable, heavy machines for road building and log transport, based initially on war surplus equipment. With the 1950s came the invention and perfection of the one-man chain saw. A forest giant could be felled in half an hour rather than half a day. Furthermore, the remaining temperate forest hardwoods became scarce, and tropical timbers were required to take their place.

All these factors led to a rapid attack on the jungle. Foresters often lost control of the exploiters and, instead of being felled in such a way that new trees grew, timber was extracted by means of a 'quarrying' operation that often left behind a low green scrub devoid of regenerating commercial big-tree species—a 'green desert'.

The West African rain forest has been the main source of hardwoods for Europe during this period and is now severely depleted. Nigeria, once a major exporter, has developed an internal market and today is a net importer of timber. In 1980 the lowland rain forests of the Philippines and Malaya are within sight of exhaustion, and by the end of the century there is likely to be little left in the whole region. Much of the timber from Southeast Asia

Present-day exploitation of the jungle can completely destroy the ecosystem, leaving few or no trees standing. Such destruction is encouraged by the buoyant international market for tropical hardwoods, and made possible by modern heavy machinery. Animals and plants specialized to live in the dark, humid interior of the forest, and timber trees with seedlings fitted to this environment, cannot survive this devastation, similar to that caused by a cyclone or landslide. The regrowth forest comprises animals and plants specialized for these different conditions.

goes as logs to Japan, Taiwan and Korea, to be made into plywood and re-exported, mainly to North America. The Southeast Asian rain forests, and to a lesser extent the African ones, have groups of different tree species which produce a single grade of timber. This has made them highly valuable commercially. The South American rain forests do not have similar broad timber groups; the myriad species are more individually distinctive. This is one reason why the Amazonian rain forest has not been so depleted.

For many nations with tropical rain forest, the rapid exploitation has been a boon. It frees land for agriculture and provides a source of cash for national development. But the concomitant problems and the degree of extensive clear felling by big, sometimes transnational, companies with heavy machines have come increasingly to be realized. No longer do local communities gain much benefit. Serious flooding and erosion frequently occur, the forest is no longer a continuing source of minor products, and many species of drug plants and fruit trees disappear following the massive disturbance. Now, once again governments are attempting to regulate timber exploitation with benefit to rural communities.

The regeneration of a forest after trees have been removed involves manipulation of its natural

growth and that of its different tree species. The old mode of exploiting scattered trees created small gaps which were filled by slow-growing, shade-bearing species, including those valuable cabinet-wood species then in demand. Conversely, modern exploitation produces big gaps in the forest which are colonized naturally by fast-growing trees with pale, soft timber. Many of these are commercially valuable.

The forester's job is not to prevent this kind of exploitation but to control it so that damage to the environment is minimized and a new tall forest of useful trees quickly grows. With care, sustained yield of timber is possible. But some forest values are not compatible with such radical exploitation, and can be maintained only by the creation of conservation areas or by logging at lower intensity. It is only in inviolate areas that the full structural complexity and species diversity of virgin rain forest can be preserved. These areas will be refuges for many kinds of arboreal animal, and for plants with potential as fruit and drug species. There is great scientific debate about the optimum size and shape of such conservation areas.

To fell a forest and then manipulate the natural regrowth is not the sole option. Foresters sometimes plant new trees. At its simplest, this plan involves cutting clear lines through a forest and enriching it with a more valuable species. American mahogany, for instance, has been planted in Fiji to create semi-artificial forests dominated by this valuable species. The more extreme step is to create an entirely artificial plantation. Trees grown for fuelwood or pulpwood in artificial plantations in the tropics can reach maturity in five to eight years, but those grown for timber are more likely to need two or three decades. The trees mostly used are pioneer, gap-colonizing species of the natural forest whose characteristics make them ideal: readily available seed, usually with a good storage life; ease of establishment in a harsh, open environment; rapid growth soon swamping weed competitors; and pale, light timber.

The most important tropical plantation species today are some of the tropical *Eucalyptus*, *Gmelina* and the subtropical pines. Plantations grow more timber per hectare per year than does natural forest, and the extra expense of selecting superior stock, fertilizing and pruning can be justified. Excessive enthusiasm in the 1960s led to the clearing of rain forest for plantations. It is now realized that there is a place for both natural forest and plantations, with the latter on degraded sites.

In the future, when fossil fuels run out, the best land-use for large areas of infertile, poorly structured, easily eroded soils in the humid tropics might well be to grow trees, not only for timber, pulp and panel products, but also for fuel and chemical feedstocks. In addition, there will be inviolate natural rain forests and managed, semi-natural ones to provide the economic and other products of these tropical jungles. Hence, there is great interest in the big plantation enterprises currently developing in several parts of the humid tropics such as in Fiji and at Jari in Amazonian Brazil.

The story of rubber

The Indians of South and Middle America were the first to make rubber from the latex of various plants, including *Hevea brasiliensis*, today's major source of natural rubber. Columbus observed them using latex to make bouncing balls and for waterproofing.

When pieces of rubber were first brought to Europe in the eighteenth century they were treated as a curiosity, for raw rubber becomes hard in cold weather and soft and sticky in hot weather. An English chemist found that rubber would erase pencil and put small pieces of it on sale for a few shillings. In 1839, it was discovered that when latex was combined with sulphur in the process known as vulcanization, it stayed tough and firm at all normal temperatures. The uses of rubber multiplied and the development of cars and pneumatic tyres sparked off an enormous demand in the early years of this century.

At first, the need for rubber was met by exploiting the wild trees in the Amazon basin, creating a brief rubber boom in that area. But it became clear that excessive exploitation of the wild trees would soon lead to their extinction. Plantations were therefore planned in tropical Asia to maintain the world's supply. Sir Joseph Hooker, then Director of the Royal Botanic Gardens, Kew, arranged for H.A. Wickham to collect seeds of *Hevea* in Brazil and send them to Kew in a chartered ship. Only 2,800 seedlings were grown from 70,000 seeds, even though they were planted as soon as they arrived in England. Most were later sent, as young plants, by ship to Ceylon. Twenty-two, of which eighteen survived, were sent to Singapore.

In Asia, the plants flourished and produced seed, and so the stock increased. Initially, no one wanted to grow rubber; coffee was the crop of the moment. But at the beginning of the twentieth century, coffee prices fell and the bushes were attacked by disease, while rubber prices were rising fast. By 1910, the 'rubber boom' was at its height. Asia still produces more than 90 per cent of the world's natural rubber. No successful plantations have been established in Brazil because disease, in particular South American leaf blight, kills the young leaves, and eventually the whole tree.

Rubber occurs in *Hevea* as a milky suspension in a watery liquid. Its functions in the plant may be to close wounds against disease entry, and to hinder insect feeding. Rubber trees are tapped by cutting the latex vessels in the bark with a sharp knife; a small cup is attached below the wound to collect the escaping latex. Each tree is tapped every other day. At a plantation, the latex is poured into large tanks to which formic acid is later added. This makes it coagulate, or form solid particles of crude rubber.

Rubber is the most recently domesticated economic crop. *Hevea* needs wet tropical conditions in which to grow, and the great expansion of rubber plantations and rubber production in Asia and, more recently, in Africa, has been at the expense of vast areas of jungle. The flora and fauna of a rubber plantation, although rich, are drastically impoverished by comparison with the rain forest before clearance.

The famous rubber tree, *Hevea brasiliensis*, grows up to 120ft (36m) tall. The tiny, petal-less flowers are pollinated by insects who are drawn to their sweet scent. On each inflorescence, the male flowers outnumber the female by up to 80–1. Each large fruit contains three seeds which are flung out when the fruit dries and explodes.

Cover crops are often grown between the straight rows of plantation rubber trees, to protect the soil from erosion. Trees of five to seven years old can be tapped, and after five years of tapping yield 300 to 1,300 pounds of rubber per acre per year.

La Condamine was an outstanding scientist. Primarily a mathematician, he was also a fine geodesist, map-maker and astronomer, and by the age of 29 was already a member of the French Académie des Sciences. At that time the Académie maintained, in direct opposition to Isaac Newton, that the earth bulged at the poles and flattened at the equator. To settle the dispute, in 1735 La Condamine led an expedition to Peru to measure the meridian of an arc of a degree of latitude to the equator, and so help to establish accurately the shape of the earth.

The task took seven years and was carried out under appalling conditions. The result proved that Newton was right.

La Condamine went on to make the first scientific study of the Amazon on a two-month journey from the River Maranon down the Amazon to the Atlantic. His detailed observations of the Amazon included research into its depth, rate of flow and the probable existence of a natural canal between it and the Orinoco.

One outstanding feature of his stay in South America was his discovery, in 1736, of caoutchouc or wild rubber. He was interested by the elastic and waterproofing qualities of the fluid produced by the rubber tree and made waterproof coverings from latex for his scientific equipment. He sent a specimen back to the Académie and produced a full description in 1751. The first man to bring rubber to Europe, he awoke interest in the material.

La Condamine's other researches in South America included an investigation into curare, a poison extracted from various plants and used as an arrow poison by the South American Indians, and the collection of various botanical specimens including quinine seeds. He published an account of his travels in *A Voyage Through the Inner Parts of South America*.

Charles Marie de la Condamine (1701–75), French explorer and scientist, the first man to make a scientific study of the Amazon.

The prosperous days of the Brazilian rubber boom in the 1890s are recorded in such symbols of opulence as the magnificent opera house at Manaus, *left*, completed in 1896. This gilt and crimson theatre attracted opera singers from all over Europe, bringing status and fame to the area.

Woody xylem

Bark

Latex and phloem vessels

Stone cells

Latex vessels are found in the inner bark, within the food-conducting tissue or phloem. A thin layer of dry corky bark on the outer side of the phloem, protects the trunk from damage by insects or fungi. On the inner side, next to the latex, lies the water-conducting wood or xylem.

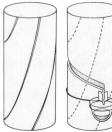

Latex vessels form an anti-clockwise spiral instead of running straight up and down the trunk. To tap the tree, a cut is made on the opposite slant through a maximum of vessels, allowing the latex to flow out into a cup.

A few hours after tapping, the coagulated latex seals the cut. The wound is reopened at the next tapping by taking a paper-thin paring of bark, and the latex flows out along the grooved channel left by the knife blade. The thinner the shaving the longer the tree can be tapped.

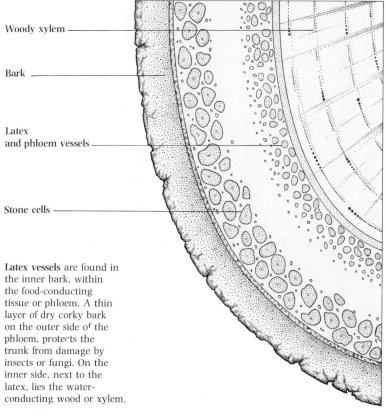

Cocoa: 'the food of the gods'

The cocoa tree is a native of the South American rain forests but has been introduced in other regions by man. It is an understorey tree in the wild and grows to about 15 to 20ft (4.5 to 6m) high. The main trunk is often not more than 4ft (1.2m) high and is generally covered with multi-hued lichens. The tree tends to branch profusely and the weighty pods hang from the main branches and the trunk. A healthy tree bears more than 70 pods a year.

Cocoa first grew wild in South America, probably in the Amazon basin, and was cultivated in Middle America for 2,000 years before the Europeans arrived. According to the legends of the pre-Aztecs, cocoa was of divine origin and an important part of the diet of their plumed serpent god, Quetzalcoatl. It was this divine association that influenced the Swedish botanist Carl von Linné, popularly known as Linnaeus, when in 1753 he classified cocoa as *Theobroma cacao*, *Theobroma* meaning 'food of the gods'.

The Aztecs too valued cocoa and to such an extent that the beans were often used as currency; they continued to serve as an acceptable means for the payment of taxes until 1887.

But despite cocoa's long history of cultivation, it was not until after 1519 when the Spanish conquistador Hernando Cortez arrived in southern Mexico, that cocoa and its products became known to the outside world. The Aztec emperor Montezuma is thought to have entertained Cortez by offering him a delicate preparation of cocoa in the form of a drink which the Aztecs called 'chocolatt'. This was prepared in great secrecy by old women and was often flavoured with vanilla, capsicum peppers, and other aromatic spices. The Spaniards substituted sugar for the peppers and obtained a beverage not too different from today's cocoa drink. Exports to Spain soon began. Maize flour was also added to the beverage to reduce the taste of the high fat content and the drink was a success.

For some years the Spaniards jealously guarded their discovery, but cocoa was sold privately to the wealthy upper classes of Europe. Initial exports from Mexico to Spain consisted of cocoa powder mixed with sugar and spices, but later only the unprocessed beans were exported.

The Spaniards were unable to keep the secret of cocoa to themselves for long, and by the seventeenth century cocoa was one of the most popular and fashionable drinks in Europe. In 1606 Antonio Carlotti, a Spaniard from Florence, acquired a taste for cocoa and introduced it into Italy. He may also have introduced it to France during the reign of Louis XIII; it was then popularized at the French court.

For some years Spain monopolized the cocoa trade and under their control cultivation spread to Trinidad, Venezuela, Jamaica, Haiti, the Philippines and the Celebes Islands. When the Dutch occupied the island of Curaçao off the Venezuelan coast in 1634, the Spanish monopoly ended and the Dutch began to export cocoa to the Netherlands and the rest of Europe.

During the seventeenth century the Dutch and Portuguese introduced cocoa to the islands in the Gulf of Guinea and it was from one of these islands, Fernando Po, in 1878, that cocoa was introduced into Ghana by a Ghanaian migrant labourer, Tetteh Quarshie. This particular introduction gave rise to the great Ghanaian cocoa industry.

From these humble beginnings cocoa production in Ghana boomed and soon became of enormous commercial importance. Today Ghana is the world's major cocoa-producing country, providing more than one-third of the total output. Cocoa is the

nation's financial backbone, accounting for 62 per cent of its total earnings. Ghana's first export of 80 pounds (36kg) of cocoa to Britain in 1891 brought the nation a total of four pounds sterling. By the time Ghana attained independence from Britain in 1960 she was exporting well over 260,000 tons of cocoa beans to European countries and the United States at a value of more than 80 million pounds sterling.

Cocoa pods are harvested by hand rather than by machine—the main harvest usually beginning at the end of the rainy season and continuing through the first half of the dry season. A second, minor harvest follows early in the rainy season. In West Africa the main harvest lasts from October to January; in Trinidad from November to February. The pods are cut off the tree with a sharp knife or machete; sometimes secateurs are also used to avoid damaging the tree trunk. Out of reach pods are cut off with long-handled knives.

The harvested pods are then either cut open with a sharp knife, split with a wooden mallet, or opened by striking two pods together—a highly skilled operation. Beans and pulp are extracted with a wooden spatula and carried in containers to the curing sheds where the process of fermentation begins. Depending on their size, seven to fourteen pods are required to produce one pound (0.45kg) of dry cocoa.

Beans and pulp are fermented in wooden fermenting or sweat boxes, covered with banana leaves. Bacteria and yeasts attack the sweet pulp, turning it into alcohol and carbon dioxide. As the beans die and enzymes are released, the pulp cells collapse; as air enters the mass there is rapid oxidation of the alcohol to acetic acid by the acetobacter bacteria. The beans die as a result of the penetration of alcohol and acetic acid into them. After the first 48 hours the temperature inside the box rises to about 120 degrees Fahrenheit and the beans are turned; 48 hours later they are turned again. The process of fermentation takes some six and a half days but must not be hurried. It is the key to full chocolate flavour.

After fermentation the beans are spread out to dry in the sun. Straw mats or plantain leaves are kept handy to protect the beans from rain storms which disturb the drying and damage the beans. The beans are stirred and turned over periodically with wooden rakes to ensure uniform drying. The enzymic action continues and during a week or two of drying the moisture content is reduced from 56 per cent to 6 per cent. The dry beans are polished either by machines or by dancing on them, when barefoot dancers trample rhythmically on the dampened beans, rubbing them together until they are polished. Many cocoa connoisseurs believe that these 'primitive' methods bring out the best flavours and aromas of the chocolate. The dried and polished beans are bagged and shipped to chocolate manufacturers.

The chocolate industry depends on even-sized beans to achieve maximum roasting effect—an essential stage in cocoa preparations. The roasted beans are cracked to remove their shells and then ground. This substance is either made into chocolate with the addition of other ingredients, or separated into cocoa powder and cocoa butter. Cocoa butter is used in chocolate making and also in cosmetics and suntan preparations. Even the shells of the beans are sold for feeding animals or as manure.

The most intriguing aspect of the cocoa industry is marketing. Generally the cocoa sold in Middle and South America as well as in the West Indies is produced on large-scale plantations, and is purchased by buyers who conduct their business directly with importers in the major manufacturing and consuming countries. In West Africa where most of the world's cocoa is grown, the bulk of the farms are owned by tens of thousands of peasant farmers who send their crops to local buying agents or to collecting stations owned by subsidiary companies of the government. The cocoa marketing boards of countries such as Ghana and Nigeria have established fixed prices to be paid for a load of beans purchased from the farmers. The marketing boards in turn arrange for the transportation and storage of the crop, and for its sale abroad.

The cocoa exchanges or futures markets that operate in primary consumer cities such as London, New York, Amsterdam and Paris, determine the current and future price of cocoa in the world market. Because it is used as a speculative investment, the total amount of cocoa traded in the world's futures markets tends to exceed the actual volume of cocoa produced by the poor peasant farmers who are involved with hard physical labour. The actual producers of these golden trees generally end up with little of the treasure.

The fruit of the cocoa tree is usually referred to as a pod, although botanically speaking it is a berry. Young pods are white, green or red, and ripen to green, red, yellow or purple. Each pod contains between 20 and 70 seeds, or beans which are covered by a sweet, pulpy material. Unless harvested the pods do not fall off the tree or open, so natural dispersal of seeds is carried out by animals. Monkeys, rats and squirrels break open the pods to feed on the sweet pulp and drop the seeds to the ground.

Cocoa grows wild in the jungle understorey but most commercial cocoa is grown on plantations or small farms. Pods are harvested by hand using long-handled knives.

Can the jungle survive?

Tropical jungles, the world's greatest treasure houses of plant and animal life, are doomed. Many are likely to disappear or be drastically changed within the next 20 years. Small remnants will probably survive into the next century on inaccessible mountain slopes or in national parks, but most of the great rain forests, which until not much more than 100 years ago covered about a third of the earth's habitable surface, will soon vanish.

Having survived for millions of years, why are the tropical forests now disappearing so fast, and what will take their place?

To answer these questions it is necessary to look at a few figures and to understand the changes going on in the tropical countries today. Tropical rain forests (as distinct from deciduous forests and the somewhat less complex montane forests) can grow from sea level to about 3,000 feet (1,000m) everywhere in the 'humid tropics'—that is where there is not less than about 80 inches (2,000mm) rainfall spread over enough days in the year for there never to be a long, severe dry season. Locally the soil may be too swampy or otherwise unsuitable for forest to develop, but such areas are small and the total extent of potential forest land in the tropics of Africa, Asia, and America is probably about 14.5

million square miles (38 million sq km).

The area actually covered with forest in fact began to decrease long ago—as soon as men with tools and the ability to make fires evolved. Even the primitive people of New Guinea with nothing more than stone axes were able to clear large tracts of forest and bring about their replacement by grassland. Over the centuries forest destruction has accelerated as populations have grown and tools improved. One reason for the rapid shrinkage of tropical forests over the last forty years is the replacement of hand tools by power tools.

In 1976 it was estimated that only 60 per cent of the potential forest area in the humid tropics was still forest; since then destruction has continued at an ever-increasing rate. According to the FAO, 15 million hectares—rather more than the whole of England and Wales, or the state of Florida—are now being cut down every year; another estimate is that 30 hectares (74 acres) are felled every minute. For several reasons these figures cannot be very accurate. In some countries, for example Indonesia, lowland Malaysia and parts of Amazonia, the present rate of destruction is high; in others, such as the Guianas and parts of Zaire, much forest still survives and less is being cut down at present. To

make firm predictions about the future more reliable information is needed, both about the size of the areas now remaining and the rate at which they are decreasing. Such information can best be obtained by remote sensing (satellite imagery) as has been done in Brazil and Indonesia. But there cannot be much doubt that the world's tropical forests are shrinking fast.

Tropical forests are being cut down because their timber is valuable; for many developing countries it is one of the few sources of foreign currency. But increasingly they are also being cut down to plant crops bringing quick profits, or to grow food.

In the tropics simple agricultural people, such as the Dyaks of Borneo and most of the forest dwellers of Africa and South America, require only small amounts of timber, for firewood, house building and other purposes, but they must destroy areas of forest to grow crops of manioc (cassava), maize and other staple foods. Families clear land, burn the felled trees, and as soon as the wood ash is cool, sow crops.

Contrary to what might be expected from the luxuriant appearance of the forest, the soils are seldom very fertile and when they are exposed to rain and sun they rapidly lose their small store of plant nutrients. For this reason, and because with only simple tools it is difficult to control the rank growth of weeds, after two or three crops have been raised it is more profitable to move on and fell and plant a new patch of forest.

This shifting or 'slash-and-burn' agricultural system is one of the causes of the destruction of vast areas of forest. If an abandoned field is left undisturbed for a few years, the forest recolonizes it, but the new (secondary) forest is for many years different both in its plant and animal species. It probably takes at least 150 years before a secondary forest becomes indistinguishable from a primary or virgin forest. As the secondary forest develops, the soil fertility is gradually restored and the land can be cultivated again. But if it is cleared too soon, as often happens where there is a large population, the soil deteriorates catastrophically and the forest becomes replaced by ferns or poor grassland. In most parts of the tropics much of the remaining forest is now secondary forest of various ages and, especially in Africa, there are large expanses of savannalike vegetation which has invaded the forest because of over-cultivation.

Shifting cultivation does not give a large return for the labour involved and the amount of forest used up. A more permanent type of agriculture would require expenditure on fertilizers and machinery which poor forest dwellers cannot afford Rather than try to improve subsistence farming (apart from rice cultivation on land liable to floods), many governments encourage the planting of oil palms, rubber and other export crops, or of fast-growing pines and gmelina trees which can be made into paper pulp.

Tropical forests usually consist of an enormous number of different kinds of tree growing in a mixture, so that it is uncommon to find many individuals of the same species together. Many of these trees produce hard, heavy timbers; some of them are very durable and some, such as the mahoganies, extremely beautiful. The tropical timbers which find a market are only a small proportion of the thousands of species which exist. The mixed composition of the forest is a great disadvantage from the forester's point of view, as is also the slow rate of growth of many of the most desirable tropical trees; a large hardwood may take several hundred years to reach maturity, compared with the 50 to 100 years needed to grow a usable pine or eucalyptus.

One solution to the problem of having too many kinds of tree is to clear-fell the forest and make all the trees into wood chips which can be exported to industrial countries for paper making. This is being done on a large scale in several tropical countries. Unfortunately, it is not a simple matter to replant tropical forests or to grow the more valuable tree species in plantations. Lumber companies often claim that they will 're-plant the forest' but this involves much more than merely raising and planting out tree seedlings.

If the whole, or at least the greater part, of the world's tropical forest is likely to disappear within

Much of the world's rain forest is steadily being destroyed. Vast areas of jungle are cleared for commercial use—ranches and plantations. Smaller areas are cleared by local people for growing food crops.

the next 50 years or less, what will the consequences be? In fairness it must be said that not everybody will regard them as a loss. To many, tropical forests are dark, wet, uncomfortable places where agriculture is difficult and unproductive in comparison to the temperate farmlands. To South American peasants, depending on small crops of maize and manioc (cassava) for food, the forest is 'green hell' and the sooner destroyed the better. The jungle is also a focus of deadly diseases such as yellow fever and leishmaniasis.

On the other side must be set the final extinction of many thousands of plant and animal species, and the destruction of the most complex ecosystem on earth. There are estimated to be about 155,000 species of flowering plants (including trees) in the tropics and a large proportion are found only in forests. The number of animal species (of which a large majority are insects) is not known, but is certainly many times greater. What is particularly disturbing about this is that we know so little about what we are losing. It is believed that only a sixth of the plants and animals have even been given names; of most of them their characteristics and potentialities for good or evil are practically unknown.

Gums, fibres, rattans, nuts and drugs figure modestly in official reports as 'minor forest products'. Some of these, such as the invaluable drugs curare and L-dopa, and the Mexican vine *Dioscorea* from which the steroids used in manufacturing contraceptive pills are obtained, are of considerable importance. But there may be many still undiscovered useful plants and animals in tropical forests. Little known chemical compounds which in nature probably help to protect them against insect and other predators might be useful as pesticides for crops, or in other ways; we simply do not know the value of what we are so rapidly destroying. As Robert Allen of the International Union for Conservation of Nature and Natural Resources, said, 'Tropical trees, thanks to their constant battle with herbivores, are source books of chemical invention of which man has scarcely turned the pages.' Apart from any material value they may have, many jungle inhabitants, both plant and animal, are among the most beautiful and fascinating in the whole world of nature.

It is not only because of the wealth of organisms they contain that jungles are of enormous importance. All forests affect climate and the composition of the atmosphere by transpiring large quantities of water vapour, moderating the effects of excessive or inadequate rainfall and extremes of temperature. Also, like other vegetation, they absorb carbon dioxide and give off oxygen in daylight and do the reverse in the dark. If tropical forests were all replaced by vegetation of smaller biomass, the percentage of carbon dioxide in the air would increase and the oxygen decrease. There is enough oxygen available, but an increase in carbon dioxide additional to that produced by burning fossil fuels might seriously affect the transmission of heat and cause a worldwide increase of temperature. The environmental effects of forest destruction are extremely hard to measure or predict, but it would be very unwise to ignore them.

However strong the reasons for reducing the extent of tropical jungles, their total disappearance would be a disaster. The case for preserving them on mountain slopes where they protect the soil from erosion, and on soils which are too poor to use for agriculture, is unanswerable and is generally accepted. But the lowland forests are the richest in species and are disappearing the fastest; more lowland forest reserves are urgently needed and must be set aside.

Fortunately there is some awareness that tropical forests are a priceless part of our human heritage, quite apart from their money value as natural resources. National parks and biosphere reserves have been set up in many places; some of these, such as the Smithsonian Institution's Barro Colorado Island in Panama and the Albert National Park in Zaire, are more than 50 years old. These are not nearly enough, and some are not adequately protected from encroachment. But the political and economic problems of conserving jungles must be overcome if our generation is not to be the last to see one of the most splendid and remarkable of earth's natural monuments.

The brink of extinction

Caryota no

Pelagodoxa henryana

Mountain gorilla,
Gorilla gorilla beringei

Helmeted hornbill,
Rhinoplax vigil

Birdwing butterfly,
Ornithoptera paradisea

Gigasiphon macrosiphon

Black caiman,
Melanosuchus niger

White-winged wood-duck,
Cairina scutulata

It is a sad reflection on man's stewardship of the earth that so many species have become extinct in such a short time and that so many others are fighting for survival. At least a couple of hundred mammals and birds have become extinct in the last two centuries and several hundred more are in danger of extinction now. Perhaps as many as 25,000 plant species are seriously endangered. This rate of species loss is probably far greater than existed on earth before man had an impact on the natural world. Because tropical rain forests are the home of so many species of plants and animals, their situation is particularly critical.

There are many arguments for preserving endangered species. One is based on the premise that it is wrong to disturb the complexity of nature and that man, as just one species, has no right to determine the fate of others. A more compelling argument is that each species represents a unique gene pool which may be of value to mankind in the search for new medicines, disease-resistant plant strains or more hardy or productive stock. The avocado, *Persea americana*, suffers from blight on its root stock. In years when the attacks are bad, commercial producers suffer significant losses of income. The caoba tree, *Persea theobromifolia*, from

the Ecuadorean jungle, however, is genetically compatible with the avocado and has blight-resistant roots. But, because so much forest has been cleared for bananas, only 12 specimens of this tree remain in the wild.

Why are some species of animals and plants more threatened than others? Jungles are complex ecosystems, containing a vast number of ecological niches. Orang-utans, gorillas and Sumatran rhinoceroses, for instance, require deep cover and a lot of space, and so these animals are naturally rare. Any clearing of the forest for advanced agriculture disrupts their life cycles, and breeding slows down.

Orang-utan,
Pongo pygmaeus

Glomeropitcairnia erectiflora

Imperial parrot,
Amazon imperialis

Sumatran rhinoceros,
Didermoceros sumatrensis

Lycaste suaveolens

On small islands the ecological niches are especially narrow; forest clearance on the Marquesas Islands has reduced the number of enu, or vehane, palm to just 30 individuals, and on Fiji the vulieto palm to a handful. Many forest trees support epiphytes, particularly orchids and pineapple-like bromeliads. The surge of coffee planting in El Salvador is endangering *Lycaste suaveolens*, a sweet-smelling orchid pollinated by euglossine bees. Destruction of cloud forest in Trinidad, Tobago and Venezuela is hastening the demise of *Glomeropitcairnia erectiflora*, a handsome bromeliad. Forest trees such as the Malayan fish-tail palm and *Areca concinna* from the swamps of Sri Lanka may be extinct within the next ten years.

Natural rarity is not the only reason for supporting conservation measures. A few plants and many animals are used by man to assuage his curiosity or vanity. Rafflesia, with the largest flower in the world measuring 3 feet (90cm) across, is one example sought avidly by tourists in Sumatra and Indonesia, causing many buds to be trampled. A single specimen of one of the birdwing butterflies from Papua New Guinea will fetch hundreds of dollars. Caimans and all the large jungle cats are hunted for their skins and fur, and high prices are paid for the prestigious items made from them.

In the short term, the best course of action to preserve these and other endangered species is to create reserves and establish more international cooperation to regulate trading in these threatened plants and animals. Consumers in both industrialized and developing countries must refuse to buy the skins and feathers of wild animals, for without a market there will be no exploitation. But more importantly, they must persuade their fellow human beings to develop a caring attitude toward those resources which they hold in trust for their children.

Products
of the jungle

Since man's earliest days on earth, trees have provided him with timber to construct his dwellings, household goods, boats, furniture and other necessities of life. From the rain forests of Latin America, Africa, the Far East and Australasia have come some of the world's most beautiful hardwoods, such as mahogany, greenheart, iroko and meranti. These timbers represent the most important forest product both in quantity produced and in commercial value of the crop. Since the 1950s the extraction of the oldest and most valuable trees has been so extensive that the jungles are shrinking in size.

The tropical forests of the world also produce a remarkable variety of minor products, such as spices, resins, gums and aromatic wood oils. In total, these play a significant role in the world commodity market and, most important of all, in the local economies of the producer countries.

From the beginning of recorded history, man has held in high esteem many of the spices, resins, gums and aromatic wood oils which now make up the bulk of the minor forest products. Today, the wood, bark, leaves, flowers and fruits of a great variety of forest trees and herbaceous plants are processed to yield well-known commercial products. Turpentines, derived from a number of different pine species, are used in a range of products, including paints and varnishes, lubricants and inks, and are also valuable raw materials in the chemical industry. The volatile essential oils extracted from forest trees are flavouring and scenting agents in such disparate items as floor polish, baked goods, fly sprays and cosmetics.

Gums and other exudates are basic ingredients in soaps and varnishes, medicines and golf balls, while the spices enhance food throughout the world. The list is almost endless: fibre crops provide clothing, insulation and packing materials; other forest products yield dyes and tanning agents; and in the producer countries, the forest food resources—the nuts, berries and fruits—form an important local food source, and in many areas an additional cash crop. The oil palm, an important source of vegetable oil, is native to West Africa but is now grown commercially in Southeast Asia. It is used by the local peasant farmers, and is also a valuable cash crop sold for manufacturing uses.

The minor forest products fall broadly into two groups: those that are exploited in their natural state, and those whose natural growth characteristics have made intensive plantation cultivation commercially viable. A good example of the former type of crop is rosewood oil, which is distilled from *Aniba rosaeadora*, a tropical evergreen of the Amazon basin. The individual trees are widely scattered, and are often more than 100 miles (160km) from the main river. Consequently, mechanized extraction is not feasible. Highly specialized teams of native woodsmen select trees to fell during the dry season; then the huge logs are floated down the Amazon tributaries to the main river during the flood season. Only the special properties of rosewood oil, and its consequent high value, make such difficult and slow extraction a viable proposition.

In marked contrast, the majority of the spice-bearing trees, and the fibre-yielding crops, are grown under controlled conditions to ensure a constant supply of good-quality produce for local use and for export. The need for research into new strains, new methods of pest control and improved efficiency in utilization is a pressing one if optimum use is to be made of the resource. Yet it is equally crucial that increased exploitation of the minor products should be carefully monitored.

The majority of the products described in the following pages are from the tropical rain forests, but some of particular relevance from tropical seasonal forests are included.

African timbers

The seventeenth century was an elegant age of grand residences with sweeping mahogany staircases and rooms richly adorned with wood panelling. It also marked the beginning of the trade in fine tropical hardwoods, particularly mahoganies from the West Indies and Central America.

By the end of the eighteenth century most of the timber used in Britain and Europe was imported, and a major factor in the growth of this international trade was the search for new supplies of naval timbers. As a result, iroko, the so-called African teak, was much sought after in world markets.

During the nineteenth century, the import timber trade was dominated by the mahoganies and other fine decorative woods. Greenheart, a tropical species used in dock work, was imported from Guyana, and the teak trade started, initially from India and later from Burma and Thailand. The shipment of African mahogany to England began toward the close of the nineteenth century.

Both the quantity and the range of imported tropical timbers rose markedly after World War I, with obeche, agba and opepe from Nigeria, and meranti from Malaysia, growing in importance. This phase of expansion was repeated after World War II, with the West African countries the principal suppliers. These were soon eclipsed, however, by the tremendous growth of trade from Southeast Asia. Timber extraction from the rain forests of South America is now on the increase.

It may prove possible to slow down the intensive rate of exploitation of the rain forests which began in the 1950s. If the population of the tropical countries continues to grow, however, then the forests will suffer as the pressure for agricultural land accelerates. At the same time, the output of timber will decrease from those forests still exploited unless their regrowth is carefully monitored and new trees planted.

Large-scale plantation projects have been started in a number of countries, mainly in an attempt to meet local demand for utility wood, though some also envisage exporting lumber, pulp or paper products. For such projects, the need is for very fast-growing species. In the wet rain forests these include *Pinus caribaea*, *Gmelina arborea* and some of the eucalypts, which should be exploitable 15 to 20 years after planting.

Trial plantations have also been started using some higher-quality commercial species such as *Terminalia*, *Cedrela* and *Aucoumea*, which are expected to have a rotation period of 25 to 45 years. The mahoganies are difficult to grow in plantations because of their vulnerability to attack by shoot-boring insects, but South American mahogany has now been planted in Fiji for commercial use. If such enterprises are not successful, supplies of these fine timbers will almost certainly be greatly reduced by the end of this century.

Sapele
Entandrophragma cylindricum

This very popular and important commercial hardwood is also known as sapelli in Cameroon and in France, by the name aboudikro on the Ivory Coast and as penkwa in Ghana.

The tree occurs widely throughout tropical Africa from Sierra Leone to Uganda and to southern Zaire, but the main source of commercial timber is the West African coastal forest.

The height of the tree is usually in the region of 150ft (45m) but occasionally specimens in excess of 200ft (60m) are found. The diameter is generally about 4ft (1.2m) but may be greater, and the cylindrical bole often rises 100ft (30m) or more. Buttresses are broad and low but are sometimes absent. The tree bears many small starlike flowers of a yellowish-white hue and also cylindrical fruit capsules.

The wood is medium to dark reddish-brown and the grain is interlocked and sometimes also wavy, giving a characteristic striped or roe figure, or occasionally a handsome decorative fiddle-back figure. The texture is fine and the wood is similar in strength to European beech. It is harder and heavier than African mahogany.

The timber is relatively quick-drying but has a marked tendency to distort. It is not difficult to work, though the interlocking grain affects some machining characteristics and requires reduction of the angle of the cutting head. The acceptance of nails and glues is good and sapele takes an excellent polish. The heartwood is also moderately durable. While not as easy to work as African mahogany, sapele is harder, stronger and more durable, but it does have the tendency to move a little in use. The sapwood of this tree is susceptible to the attacks of powder-post beetles and termites.

Sapele is used on a large scale for the manufacture of furniture and plywood and for general joinery and shop fittings. Figured material commands a good price for slicing into decorative veneers. Because of its moderate to high resistance to abrasion it is suitable for use in decorative floorings in both domestic and public buildings, but the tendency to move means that only the best quality, well-seasoned wood should be used. *E. cylindricum* provides one of the most important export timbers from the Ivory Coast, Ghana and Nigeria and is shipped out in huge quantities both as logs and as sawn timber.

Afara
Terminalia superba

Variously known as limba (Zaire region), fraké (Ivory Coast), ofram (Ghana), noyer du Mayombe (France) and korina (USA), *Terminalia superba* is of widespread occurrence in West Africa where it is one of the more common forest trees. It reaches a height of 150ft (45m) or more and has buttresses up to 8ft (2.5m). The bole is often up to 90ft (27m) in length above the buttresses.

The wood is a pale straw shade or yellow-brown (limba clair) but some logs have an irregular darker core with grey-brown to near-black markings which give an attractive figure to the wood, then known as dark limba (limba noir). The main source region of commercial afara is Zaire and western central Africa. The grain of the wood varies from straight to irregular and is sometimes interlocked; texture is moderately coarse but usually even. Weight and strength vary a great deal due to the presence in many logs of 'brittleheart'—very brittle heartwood which greatly reduces the strength of the timber.

Afara dries quickly with very little degrade. It is easy to work, except for wood in which the grain is interlocked, and its blunting effect is slight. Nailing, gluing and staining properties are all satisfactory but the wood is not durable and is attacked by insects and termites. It is exported as complete logs and as sawn timber.

Afara is widely used in the manufacture of furniture—for framing, for table and chair legs and stretchers, for interior joinery and general utility purposes. It is used extensively in the manufacture of plywood and the dark figured variety is often sliced to give a pleasing decorative veneer, similar to walnut in appearance.

Abura
Mitragyna stipulosa

Also known as bahia (Ivory Coast) and subaha (Ghana), *M. stipulosa* is widespread throughout West Africa and abundant in the freshwater swamp forests of southern Nigeria where, because access for heavy machinery is restricted, the timber is extracted mainly by native workers.

The tree is of medium size, reaching 100ft (30m) in height and up to 5ft (1.5m) in diameter, with a clear bole of 60ft (18m) or more. The stem is straight and without buttresses. The wood is uniform pale yellow-brown or pink-brown with some darker streaks. The grain is irregular, usually fairly straight but sometimes interlocked. The wood texture is fine to medium and very even. In strength it rates rather lower than European beech.

The timber dries quickly with very little deterioration and once dried is stable in use. It has good working properties but requires very sharp blades as it tends to blunt the cutters quite quickly. Pre-boring is necessary when thicker-gauge nails are used.

Because it is vulnerable to fungi and to boring insects, abura is not suitable for exterior use, but its uniform nature, ease of working, and stability make it a popular wood for interior work and furniture. It takes glues, stains and polishes well and is consequently widely used for drawer sides, runners, furniture frames and for shop fittings. Its ready acceptance of stains means that it can be matched with more expensive decorative woods, such as walnut, and is therefore widely used for lipping and moulding. Abura is also often used in the manufacture of plywood.

Gedu nohor
Entandrophragma angolense

Known as tiama (Ivory Coast and France), edinam (Ghana) and kalungi (Zaire region), *E. angolense* has a wide distribution in western and central Africa from the Ivory Coast to southern Zaire and eastward to Uganda.

It is a large buttressed tree, mature specimens attaining a height of up to 160ft (50m) and diameter in excess of 5ft (1.5m). The bole is fairly straight and may be 60 to 80ft (18 to 25m) long. The wood is a dull red-brown with an interlocking grain although this does not generally produce a marked figure on the sawn timber. Texture is medium to coarse. Generally the timber of gedu nohor is less attractive than sapele or African mahogany but it may be used as a substitute for these woods. Strength lies about midway between that of obeche and European beech but is inferior to both sapele and utile.

The timber dries fairly quickly but has a marked tendency to distort. Once dried, however, it remains stable in use. The interlocking grain affects the working properties of the timber but if very sharp machine blades are used the wood will take a good finish. Nailing and gluing are satisfactory and the wood takes stains and polishes well, which enhances its usefulness as a general-purpose timber.

Gedu nohor is classed as a mahogany-type timber, exported mainly as logs but also as sawn timber. It is suitable for both interior and exterior use and has been used with success for the deck planking, cabin construction and interior fittings in boats. Other uses of this wood include shop fitting joinery, motor vehicle trims and railway carriage interiors.

African timbers

Utile
Entandrophragma utile

One of the most important African hardwoods, E. utile is found from the Ivory Coast to Uganda and Angola. The main commercial supplies come from the Ivory Coast and Ghana. The tree is one of the true tropical forest giants—commonly reaching 200ft (60m) or more in height with narrow buttresses supporting the towering stem.

The timber is usually reddish or purplish-brown. The grain is interlocked and somewhat irregular, producing a striped figure on quarter-sawn timber, although the stripe is wider and generally less attractive than that typical of sapele.

Drying time is average and some degree of degrade is common due to the extension of shakes (natural splits) and an exaggeration of the twisting common in irregular-grained timbers. Once dried, utile is generally stable and machines to a good finish if sharp tools are used. There is no difficulty with nailing and gluing, or with staining and polishing.

Utile is one of the mahogany-type woods and is used for quality joinery work—window and door frames, furniture, interior work and all types of constructional work where strength and durability are required. Decorative veneers may be obtained from selected logs, but, more important, the strength and durability of utile make it ideal for heavy grade constructional plywood.

Agba
Gossweilerodendron balsamiferum

This species is known also as tola branca or white tola (Angola) and tola (Zaire and France). The distribution of this tree extends from Nigeria to the Congo basin, with Nigeria and Cabinda the most important sources of commercial supply.

G. balsamiferum is one of the largest trees in tropical Africa, commonly 200ft (60m) in height and up to 7ft (2m) in diameter. The stem has no buttresses and the straight cylindrical bole soars upward for 100ft (30m) or more.

The wood is a straw shade or yellow-brown. The grain is straight or slightly interlocked which may produce a striped figure on quarter-sawn timber. The texture is fine and the wood is of moderate strength. In general, it is not difficult to work.

The timber dries quickly with little deterioration but some exudation of resin may occur. After surface filling, staining and polishing properties are satisfactory and the heartwood is rated fairly durable.

Agba is a lightweight, durable and easily worked timber, used widely as a general utility timber and often as an alternative to oak in interior and exterior joinery and in some furniture manufacture. In boat-building it is used for planking and laminated frames. A proportion of the wood exported is peeled for plywood manufacture.

Ayan
Distemonanthus benthamianus

Ayan is of widespread occurrence in West Africa and is locally very abundant. In France the wood is known as movingui, in Ghana as bonsamdua, and in Britain and the United States as either ayan or distemonanthus.

The average height of the tree is 90ft (27m) and average diameter about 2½ft (80cm) although it may attain much larger dimensions.

The wood is lemon-yellow to yellow-brown, sometimes with darker streaking. The grain is often interlocked and sometimes wavy, which can produce an attractive decorative figure on sawn surfaces. The wood is fine-textured and varies considerably in weight.

The timber dries with little degrade and movement in use is small. Some of the timber proves difficult to work because of the interlocking grain and also the presence in the wood of gum and silica. The blunting effect of the silica varies from moderate to severe. Gluing, staining and polishing are all satisfactory once the surface has been filled.

Ayan is commonly used for door frames, window frames and sills, domestic and gymnasium flooring and for cabinet work. A decorative veneer may be obtained from figured logs and the wood is thought to be suitable for the manufacture of plywood. Quantities of large-dimension sawn timber are exported and the wood is also shipped as logs.

Okan
Cylicodiscus gabunensis

C. gabunensis has a wide distribution throughout western Africa and is very common in Ghana, where it is known as denya, and in Nigeria, where it has the name okan.

The tree is one of the emergent forest giants, with a height of up to 200ft (60m). The diameter averages 3 to 4ft (90cm to 1.2m) but trees with diameters up to 8 or 10ft (2.5 to 3m) are known. The buttresses are usually short, above which the cylindrical bole may extend 80ft (25m).

The wood is a greenish-brown, gradually darkening to red-brown. The grain is usually interlocked and the texture of the wood is moderately coarse.

Okan timber dries slowly with a considerable amount of splitting and checking. Because of its hardness and the interlocking grain, it is a difficult wood to work and the blunting effect on cutting tools is quite severe. Pre-boring is invariably required if the wood is to be nailed.

Okan is hard, heavy and durable; consequently its most common use is for the piles and decking of wharf structures. It is also suitable for heavy duty factory flooring although the difficulties in machining count against it to some extent. Some sawn timber is supplied to order for export but the majority is used locally.

Ogea
Daniellia ogea

Daniellia ogea is of common occurrence in southern Nigeria, where it is also known as oziya, ogea and daniellia, and in other parts of West Africa where it is variously marketed under the names incenso, or insenso (Guinea-Bissau) and fara (Ivory Coast).

The tree is 100 to 150ft (30 to 45m) in height with diameter ranging from 4 to 5ft (1.2 to 1.5m) and a cylindrical bole 50 to 100ft (15 to 30m) long, sometimes with very short buttresses.

The wood is pale pink to red-brown with some darker streaks. The grain is slightly interlocked and the texture is rather coarse and woolly. Brittleheart is often found in the core of the tree and the heartwood is generally subject to deterioration. Sound timber rates midway between obeche and European beech in strength.

The timber dries fairly quickly with little degrade although further movement in use is moderate. The interlocking grain and woolly texture may cause tearing on quarter-sawn surfaces and blunting of cutting tools is sometimes a problem. Good results are obtained with nailing and gluing, and both staining and polishing are satisfactory once the surface has been treated with filler.

Ogea is a fairly low grade light hardwood with a wide sapwood, liable to become stained, and vulnerable to attack by powder-post beetles. The wood is also moderately resistant to preservative treatment. It is generally used for cabinet interior work, boxes and packing cases, and rough construction use. In Europe it has been used for the manufacture of plywood, mainly as core stock, and decorative veneers can be taken from selected logs.

Gaboon
Aucoumea klaineana

Although known in the English-speaking countries as gaboon, the name being a derivative of the West African state of Gabon, this timber is also widely known as okoumé. The tree has an unusually restricted range, being found only in Gabon, Equatorial Guinea and the Zaire region, but in its range it grows in great abundance. Gaboon was one of the first tropical hardwoods used by the European plywood industry and remains one of the most important African export timbers.

A. klaineana forms a large tree up to 130ft (40m) in height although fine specimens up to 200ft (60m) have been recorded. The diameter is usually between 2½ and 3½ft (0.8 to 1.1m) but occasionally up to 6½ft (2m). The bole is often slightly curved and 80ft (25m) in length above short buttresses.

The wood has a pink hue, darkening to a pinkish-brown. Grain is often slightly interlocked and may be wavy, and the texture is medium.

The timber dries easily with very little degrade, but in processing the cutter blades must be very sharp and the cutting angles reduced as the wood's blunting effect ranges from moderate to severe. Nailing, gluing and polishing characteristics are all satisfactory but the wood is not very durable.

The prime use of gaboon is in the manufacture of plywood and blockboard. The plywood is light and fairly strong and is used for drawer panels, flush doors, partitions, wardrobe carcasses and the backs of chests. The lack of durability however, makes gaboon unsuitable for use in conditions favouring decay. A small amount of timber is sold as sawn lumber for use in cigar boxes, framing and in the construction of packing cases.

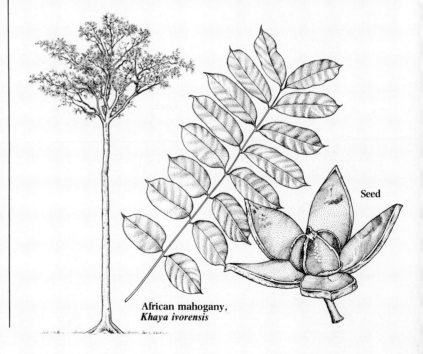

Seed

African mahogany,
Khaya ivorensis

Guarea
Guarea cedrata   Guarea thompsonii

Two species of the genus *Guarea* provide the timber marketed under the trade name guarea. The general name obobo is used in Nigeria, while on the Ivory Coast and in France the name bossé is used. *G. cedrata* may be distinguished in Britain by the name scented guarea and in Nigeria by the name obobonufua. *G. thompsonii* in the same areas may be called black guarea and obobonekwi.

The trees are of widespread occurrence in West Africa and the Zaire region and of the two, *cedrata* is the more common. They grow to a height of about 160ft (50m) and are 3 to 4ft (1 to 1.2m) in diameter. They are buttressed and have long, straight, cylindrical boles.

The wood resembles a pale mahogany, pinkish-brown in hue. The grain is sometimes straight, particularly in the plainer *G. thompsonii*, but is more often interlocked and *G. cedrata* sometimes has a mottled or curly figure. Texture is fine, and *cedrata* has a characteristic pleasant odour which gradually fades.

The timber dries fairly quickly, with little degrade, but there may be some exudation of gum. Of the two, *cedrata* is the more difficult to work because of the combination of gum, interlocked grain and the fibrous nature of the wood. Gluing and finishing properties are good and the wood is very durable.

The guareas are stable and durable timbers of the mahogany type, exported as logs and sawn timber. They are used in the manufacture of furniture, for interior fittings, in vehicle body construction and for the frames and decking of caravans. Resin exudation, however, precludes certain uses; guarea cannot, for example, be used for instrument cases. It is used as a decorative veneer.

Afzelia
Afzelia bipindensis   Afzelia pachyloba

The five species of *Afzelia* are found widely distributed through tropical Africa from Sierra Leone to the Sudan and as far south as Zimbabwe and Mozambique. The commercial timber sold as afzelia is predominantly from two species—*bipindensis* and *pachyloba*—exploited extensively in the forests of Cameroon and Nigeria.

The trees attain a height of 100ft (30m) or more with boles of fairly good form, often with irregular buttresses extending a few feet up the trunk.

The red-brown wood is coarse-textured and has a straight, sometimes interlocked, or irregular grain. The weight is variable, but afzelia is a fairly dense wood, similar in strength to European beech though stronger if used in compression.

The timber dries slowly but with little degrade, and movement in use is small. There are some difficulties in working afzelia and it has a moderate blunting effect on cutting edges. It takes a fine polish if treated first with a filler and the heartwood is very durable and moderately resistant to termites.

Afzelia is a heavy, strong, durable and stable wood of good appearance, exported as logs and as sawn timber. It is used for high-class joinery both indoors and out, particularly for staircases, window frames, counter tops and flooring. It is also widely used for the underframes of road vehicles and railway wagons, and in the manufacture of vats for the chemical industry. It is never used for kitchen draining or work surfaces, laundry equipment or garden seats as the wood contains a strong yellow dye. A small quantity of decorative veneer is produced by slicing from selected figured logs.

Ekki
Lophira alata

This important West African tree is known by a wide variety of names: ekki or bongossi in Cameroon; azobé in parts of West Africa and in Europe; kaku in Ghana and eba in Nigeria. It grows from Sierra Leone to Gabon and is of great commercial importance in Cameroon—the source of the major export supply.

Ekki is a large tree—up to 180ft (55m) in height, and up to 6ft (1.8m) in diameter at the lower part of the bole. The tree is usually without buttresses but sometimes has a basal swelling of the trunk.

The wood is dark-red or chocolate-brown with white deposits in the pores which give a distinctive flecked appearance to the timber. The grain is usually interlocked and the texture characteristically coarse and uneven. It is one of the very heavy tropical hardwoods—similar in weight to greenheart and about 50 per cent heavier than oak.

Ekki dries slowly with severe splitting and some distortion. It is very difficult to work; green wood saws reasonably well but dry wood has a very severe blunting effect on blades. Pre-boring is essential if the wood is to be nailed.

This hard, strong and durable wood is exported in log form and as sawn timber, and finds a multitude of uses in heavy construction work—notably for piling and decking for piers, jetties, harbour works, bridges and wharfs. It is also ideal for heavy duty flooring in factories and warehouses and for the bottom-cladding of railway rolling-stock. It is used for filter presses and frames because of its great strength, but the difficulties in machining limit its use.

Dahoma
Piptadeniastrum africanum

Known also as agboin and ekhimi in Nigeria, and as dabema on the Ivory Coast and in France, *P. africanum* is widespread throughout West, Central and parts of East Africa. It is a large tree, attaining heights of about 150ft (45m) with diameters of from 3 to 4ft (90cm to 1.2m). The bole is cylindrical, 30 to 50ft (9 to 15m) long above the huge buttresses.

The wood is yellow-brown and has an interlocked grain which can produce an attractive striped figure on quarter-sawn timber. The wood is coarse in texture but of comparable strength to European beech.

Dahoma typically dries very slowly and with some material there is a very marked tendency to collapse and distort. Working is often problematic because of the interlocked grain and the fibrous nature of the wood, but blunting of the cutting edges is only moderate.

Satisfactory results are achieved with gluing and nailing and also with the application of stains and polishes if the wood surface is filled.

Dahoma is most suitable for use in the form of large-dimension timber; for veh-

icle bearers and bottom members, for work-benches and for heavy building construction uses—often as an alternative to oak. Small quantities of lumber are exported but the majority of the timber is used in the country of origin.

African mahogany
Khaya ivorensis

The common trade name African mahogany is often prefixed by the name of the place of origin and so may be marketed as Ivory Coast mahogany, Nigerian mahogany and so on. In France the wood is known as acajou d'Afrique or ngollon, while the name khaya is more commonly used in the United States of America and Britain.

Khaya ivorensis is truly one of the great rain forest giants—a magnificent tree reaching 200ft (60m) in height and 6ft (1.8m) in diameter. The buttresses are short and the clear branch-free bole is commonly up to 90ft (27m) in length. It is widely distributed throughout the coastal rain forests of West Africa. Though commercial timber is derived mainly from *K. ivorensis* and *K. anthotheca* from West Africa, other species of khaya are found from Portuguese Guinea to Angola and from the Sudan to Mozambique.

The light and moderately strong wood is reddish-brown, and the interlocked grain produces a decorative stripe or roe figure on quarter-sawn surfaces. Some trees suffer from brittleheart but sound timber lies midway between obeche and European beech in strength.

The timber dries fairly quickly and with little degrade, except for trees in which tension wood is present. There are some difficulties in working mahogany due to the interlocked grain and because of the woolliness caused by tension wood. Nailing and gluing properties are satisfactory and the wood takes staining and polishing well on carefully prepared surfaces. Heartwood is moderately durable but trees and logs may be attacked by forest longhorn beetles.

Khaya is a medium-weight wood of very pleasing appearance, usually of good working properties and stable in use. It is exported as logs and as sawn timber and is used extensively in the production of quality furniture for domestic and office use, for reproduction furniture and for cabinet work. It is widely used in boat-building, for planking, deck-housing and cabin fittings but is unsuitable for steam-bent framing. It can, however, be laminated for use in boat stems and frames and is also used in veneer form for cold moulding. Poorer grades of mahogany, being light and moderately durable, are used in the manufacture of plywood for a variety of uses. Few other woods have proved so versatile and so lastingly popular as mahogany, but this very popularity must place *Khaya* high on the list of those forest trees most threatened by man's over-exploitation of the forest timber resource.

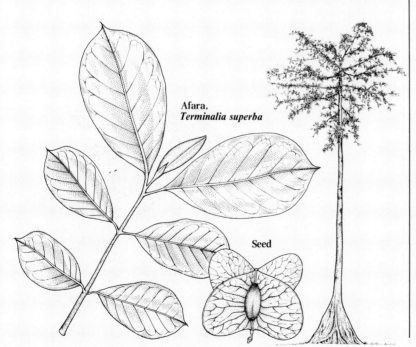

Afara,
Terminalia superba

Seed

South American timbers

Crabwood
Carapa guianensis

Variously known as crabwood (Guyana), andiroba (Brazil), krappa (Surinam), figueroa, and tangare (Ecuador), *Carapa guianensis* is widely distributed in the forests of northern South America and also in the West Indian islands and in Central America as far north as Belize.

It is a large tree, commonly 100 to 130ft (30 to 40m) in height and 3 to 4ft (90cm to 1.2m) in diameter with a straight cylindrical bole, often clear of branches for about 50ft (15m).

Crabwood resembles plain mahogany but does not have its natural lustre. It varies from pale pink to red-brown when freshly sawn, darkening on exposure to dull red-brown. The grain is usually straight, but some material is interlocked, and texture varies from coarse to medium. Crabwood is heavier than mahogany and rather stronger.

The wood dries rather slowly, and there is some tendency to split. It is more difficult to work than mahogany and often splits when nailed unless pre-bored. Gluing, staining and polishing are all satisfactory and the heartwood is moderately durable.

Crabwood is exported to the United States and Europe from Brazil, Guyana and Surinam where it is common. It is used as a substitute for mahogany in furniture manufacture and interior joinery, but it is inferior in appearance.

Mora
Mora excelsa

Mora is one of the important timber trees of Guyana and the Orinoco delta region of Venezuela. It grows to a height of 100 to 150ft (30 to 45m) but is slender, having an average diameter of only about 1½ft (45cm). Large buttresses extending 15ft (4.5m) up the stem give added support, and above them the bole rises clear for up to 80ft (25m).

The wood varies from dark chocolate-brown to reddish-brown and is of uneven and not very attractive appearance. The grain is usually interlocked and irregular and the texture is rather coarse. Mora is another of the heavy woods and is similar in strength to greenheart.

The wood dries slowly and with considerable deterioration in the form of splitting, surface checking and overall distortion. There is also a high degree of dimensional movement even after seasoning. The wood is difficult to work and has a moderate or at times severe blunting effect on cutting edges.

Mora excelsa is used locally for all manner of heavy construction tasks—for framing, piling and decking of wharf and bridge structures and also for house building. The durability and hardness of the timber also make it suitable for use as heavy duty flooring material and for railway sleepers. So far, mora has a limited export market.

Balsa
Ochroma lagopus

Balsa is of widespread occurrence in tropical America but commercial supplies come mainly from trees grown in plantations in Ecuador. The tree is extremely fast-growing and will attain a height of 70ft (21m) and a diameter of 2ft (60cm) in just six to seven years.

O. lagopus has a large proportion of sapwood. It varies from white to oatmeal, often with a yellow or pink tint, and the wood has a marked silky lustre. The grain is straight and the texture moderately coarse but even.

Balsa is the lightest of all woods in commercial use. Its weight is very variable but timber selected for commercial use is generally 1/7th to 1/3rd the weight of an equivalent piece of oak. As would be expected from its very low density, balsa is the weakest of all commercial timbers but its unusual properties, particularly its low thermal conductivity and high sound absorption, make it suitable for a number of uses for which other woods would be quite unsuitable.

The logs must be sawn soon after the tree is felled to avoid serious splitting, and timber is best kiln-dried to reduce splitting and warping. Once dry, however, the wood is stable. The heartwood is perishable and also resistant to preservative treatment.

Balsa is easy to work with thin sharp cutting edges. It does not hold nails well but gluing is satisfactory and, although absorbent; the wood takes stain and polish quite well.

The wood has a high commercial value and is widely used for insulation in cold stores and refrigeration ships. It is used as core material in lightweight sandwich-construction panels, and as a buoyancy material in rafts and lifebelts. Other uses include packaging of delicate objects and a wide range of applications in modelling, toy aircraft manufacture, and theatrical props and scenery.

Purpleheart
Peltogyne spp

The timber marketed as purpleheart, or amaranth, is derived from about twenty species of *Peltogyne* distributed from Mexico to southern Brazil. Commercial supplies of purpleheart come mainly from Guyana and from the forests of the Amazon basin.

The trees vary considerably in size but are commonly 125 to 150ft (38 to 45m) in height with diameters ranging from 2 to 4ft (60cm to 1.2m). Some trees are buttressed and in most there is a clear bole—often 50ft (15m) or more in length. The trees yield logs of more than 3ft (90cm) in diameter.

When freshly cut the wood is a dull brown shade but on exposure to air it quickly changes to a striking purple, which slowly matures to a rich dark red- or purple-brown. The grain is usually straight but may be wavy or interlocked. The texture of this most attractive and distinctive wood also varies from medium to fine.

Purpleheart dries fairly quickly and there is little deterioration; any further movement after drying is small. There are often some difficulties in working due to the high density of the wood and also due to the accumulation of gum on the cutting tools. Blunting of cutting edges may also be severe in some woods. Care is required if the wood is to be nailed but good results are obtained with stains and polishes. Although a heavy wood, purpleheart is not generally as dense as greenheart.

Purpleheart is very strong and very durable and has wide applications in heavy constructional work in bridge and dock facilities. It is also widely used for flooring, for chemical vats, and for filter presses. Despite its exceptional appearance the wood is not much used for its visual appeal beyond a limited use for small turned items and some decorative inlay.

Greenheart
Ocotea rodiaei

The principal source of this outstanding South American hardwood is Guyana, although the tree is also found in smaller quantities in the forests of Surinam and Brazil.

Ocotea rodiaei is a medium to large tree, reaching a height of 70 to 130ft (21 to 40m) and having an average diameter of about 3ft (90cm). The trunk sometimes has low buttresses, and the bole is straight, cylindrical and up to 80ft (25m) in length.

Greenheart varies from light to dark olive-green, sometimes with darker brown or black streaks. The grain is straight or interlocked and the texture is fine and even. It is an extremely heavy timber, half as heavy again as oak, and will not float in water even when completely dry. The strength properties of greenheart are remarkable even when its high density is taken into account.

The timber dries slowly during which time it suffers considerable degrade in the form of splitting and checking, particularly in large sizes. Some difficulties arise in working the wood, partly due to the interlocked grain, and the blunting effect on cutting tools is moderate. The wood is not suitable for nailing but does take a good polish. The heartwood is very durable and resistant to attack by fungi, insects and marine borers.

Greenheart is one of the world's strongest, hardest, heaviest and most durable timbers and consequently commands a high commercial value. It is usually available in large dimensions, up to 12 by 18in (30 by 45cm) and in lengths of up to 55ft (17m). Its unique properties, particularly its resistance to marine borers, make it the ideal timber for lock gates, piles, and a variety of dock and harbour work. Its great hardness suits it for use as heavy industrial flooring and for engine bearers, and its resistance to chemicals makes it an ideal timber for use in chemical vats.

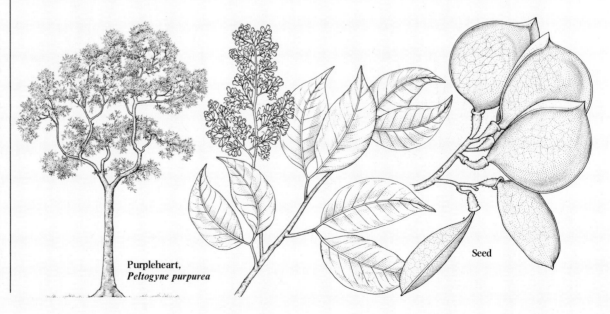

Purpleheart,
Peltogyne purpurea

Seed

Central American mahogany
Swietenia macrophylla

Mahogany is of widespread occurrence in Central America, particularly in Mexico and Belize, and in parts of northern South America including the upper regions of the Amazon basin.

Average height of the tree is 100ft (30m) with diameters of about 4 to 6ft (1.2 to 1.8m). The bole is straight and cylindrical and often rises more than 60ft (18m) above the huge buttresses.

The wood varies from a light red-brown or yellow-brown to a dark red-brown with a characteristic natural lustre. Some wood is straight-grained, but the grain tends more often to be inter-locked, and there are many irregularities which give rise to a range of attractive figures—stripe, roe, fiddle-back, blister, curl and mottle. Texture is moderately coarse but generally finer than the African mahogany. The American maho-gany is very strong for a wood of its weight-range and it is stable in use.

The wood dries fairly rapidly without much checking or distortion. It has good working properties but sharp tools are required with some material in order to avoid creating a woolly surface. The wood takes an excellent polish.

Central American mahogany is a high-class timber and is regarded as superior to other mahoganies. Because of its high cost and limited availability, it is used mainly in the solid form for repro-duction cabinet work and special con-tract work. It is suitable for all types of interior joinery and panelling and is popular for the decking and cabin fittings of quality boats. Further uses are for pattern-making, where fine tolerances and stability are essential, and for instru-ments and instrument cases. Mahogany plywood is made but is seldom seen in Europe. For mass-produced furniture, American mahogany has been largely replaced by the cheaper and more plenti-ful African mahogany.

Sucupira
Bowdichia nitida

Bowdichia nitida is a forest tree of the Rio Negro and lower Amazon regions of northern Brazil. Another commercially exploited species, *B. virgiliodes*, has a natural range extending from Venezuela and Guyana to southeastern Brazil, though this species is a savanna tree of small size and poor form over part of its range.

The high forest trees reach 150ft (45m) in height and 4ft (1.2m) in dia-meter and yield a dark chocolate-brown timber with paler markings which give a striking appearance to flat-sawn surfaces. There is sometimes a striped figure on quarter-sawn timber, caused by the inter-locked or irregular grain. The texture of the wood is medium to coarse. Sucupira is an exceptionally heavy timber having a weight, when dry, approaching that of greenheart. The wood is as strong and hard as would be expected from its high density.

There is little information about the wood's drying behaviour. It is difficult to work because of its great density and interlocked grain, but a satisfactory finish can be obtained with sharp and carefully adjusted cutters. The heartwood is very durable.

Sucupira is best suited for large-scale construction work requiring very little precise machining or complex fabri-cation. Although the wood has an attrac-tive appearance, it is too hard, and too difficult to work, to be suitable for furni-ture and other quality joinery, although it may prove useful in turned work and even as a decorative veneer inlay in cabinet work.

As the demand for very hard, strong timbers continues, and supplies of the more familiar greenheart and ekki come under increasing pressure, it is possible that sucupira may find itself subject to greatly increased attention over the coming years.

Basralocus
Dicorynia guianensis   Dicorynia paraensis

Dicorynia guianensis is of common occur-rence in Surinam, where it is called basralocus, and in Guyana, where it is called angélique or teck de la Guyana. The other species, *D. paraensis*, is a native of the rain forests of the Amazon basin in Brazil.

The tree attains a height of 100ft (30m) or more, and a diameter of up to 5ft (1.5m), with a long clear bole rising above the buttresses.

The shade of the wood varies con-siderably and the darker red timber (an-gélique rouge), which is the dominant commercial type, darkens after drying and takes on a deep red-brown or purple-brown hue. The grain is usually straight or slightly interlocked, giving a striped figure when sawn on the quarter. Texture is medium and the lines of conspicuous vessels within the wood give the timber a distinctive character. It is moderately heavy and somewhat stronger than Euro-pean beech.

Basralocus must be dried very slowly in air as it has a tendency to split, distort and collapse if kiln-dried. Some wood is difficult to work because of its high den-sity and the presence within the wood of silica. Tools tipped with tungsten-carbide are generally used to process dry timber. The heartwood is very durable and is also very resistant to marine borers and to termites.

The timber is exported in log form, large dimension sawn timber, and smal-ler lumber—mainly for use where strength and durability are required, such as in dock and harbour work, and lock gates. The wood is also valued for heavy construction work, bridge decking, boat framing, railway sleepers, barrel and vat manufacture (because of its natural re-sistance to acids) and for flooring. It is popular for boat-building in many Euro-pean countries and the United States of America.

Virola
Virola spp   Dialyanthera spp

Commercial timbers from trees of the genera *Virola* and *Dialyanthera* are sold under a variety of names and form an important export trade from Brazil, Sur-inam, Guyana and Colombia.

Commercial timber is taken from the taller trees in which the clear bole is on average about 60ft (18m) in length above the buttresses and up to 3ft (90cm) in diameter. The heartwood is a pale pinkish-brown and there is very little differenti-ation between heartwood and sapwood. Grain is usually straight, the texture is variable, and the wood—although not decorative—is attractive in appearance, resembling gaboon. The wood is light and consequently it has little structural strength.

The timber dries rather slowly with a marked tendency to split, sometimes with appreciable distortion. However, the working properties are satisfactory; the wood takes nailing and gluing well, and although it is not naturally durable it can be treated with preservatives.

This soft and lightweight timber, if processed with care, is suitable for all general utility purposes, for joinery and mouldings, and for plywood core stock.

Freijo
Cordia goeldiana

The genus *Cordia* has representatives in many tropical countries, but commer-cially important timbers come mainly from West Africa, where they are known as cordia or omo, and from Brazil, notably from the Amazon basin, where they are called freijo or louro.

The Brazilian trees are of medium size, usually up to 100ft (30m) in height and 2 to 3ft (60 to 90cm) in diameter. The wood is yellow-brown, sometimes with darker streaks; although a little lighter than teak it is similar in appearance and is often sold under the name Brazilian teak.

The grain is generally straight and the texture medium-fine. In strength, freijo rates slightly lower than European beech and much the same as true teak.

The timber dries easily with little distortion although there is some ten-dency for the ends to split. Working properties are satisfactory but tearing and lifting of the grain may occur if cutting edges are not kept very sharp. Support is required in end-grain boring, and in the cutting of mortices, to prevent the wood breaking away. Nailing is satisfactory and the wood can be stained and polished well after filling. The heartwood is dur-able but not as durable as teak.

Although similar to teak in appear-ance and in some properties, freijo has not yet been fully recognized in export mar-kets where it is regarded as rather unim-portant. It is used in South America for high-class joinery and furniture manu-facture, in boat-building, and in motor vehicle interiors.

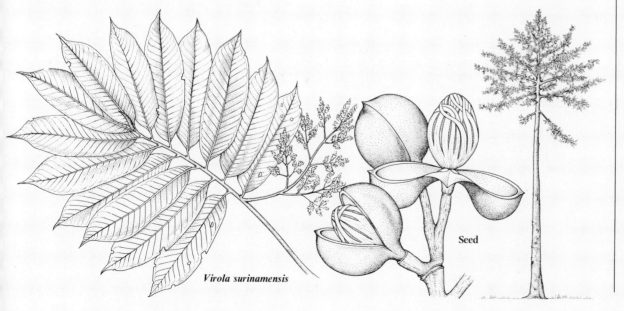

Virola surinamensis

Seed

Southeast Asian timbers

Teak
Tectona grandis

Probably the finest of the tropical hardwoods, true teak is obtained from *Tectona grandis*, native to India, Vietnam, Burma and Thailand—the source countries of the main commercial supplies—and found also in Indo-China and Java.

The tree is very variable in size and in form but the larger specimens may reach 150ft (45m) in height with a stem diameter of up to 8ft (2.5m). In the larger trees, the stem is often fluted and buttressed. The wood is golden-brown or deeper red-brown and may have darker streaking. The texture is coarse and uneven.

Teak dries slowly but with very little deterioration, and is exceptionally stable in use. It is strong for a medium-weight wood but can be difficult to work due to its abrasive character. It is very durable under a wide range of conditions.

Strength, stability and durability combine to make teak one of the most valued of all timbers—particularly in all aspects of shipbuilding. The wood is also prized for high-quality furniture and interior fittings, and its exceptional resistance to acids makes it ideal for laboratory bench tops. The wood is also now often used as a veneer.

Teak has been extensively planted in Sri Lanka, Trinidad and Nigeria, and the timber from Trinidad and Nigeria is at least as strong as Burma-grown teak of the same density.

Amboyna
Pterocarpus indicus

The trade name of this Asian timber was taken from Amboyna Island in the Molucca group from where the original supplies were obtained. The tree is, however, more widely distributed throughout the forests of Malaysia, Borneo and New Guinea.

Amboyna is the Asian equivalent of the padauk timbers of West Africa and is derived from closely related species. The tree is of variable size and usually of rather poor form with widely spreading buttresses.

The timber is golden-brown or red, with straight, interlocked or wavy grain and a rather coarse and uneven texture. The weight is very variable, more so than almost any other commercially exploited timber, and this considerably affects its value.

Sawn timber dries easily, with very little deterioration, and is stable in use. It is said to turn well and to take a very high polish, but working may be difficult due to the extreme variability of the wood. In the countries of origin amboyna is widely used as a furniture timber; in the export market it is the burrs that are of interest. These are shipped to Europe to be sliced into high-quality veneers for use in cabinet-making and other specialist work.

Kempas
Koompassia malaccensis

K. malaccensis is of widespread but sparse distribution in peninsular Malaysia and is also found in Indonesia, Sumatra and Borneo. It is a large tree, up to 180ft (55m) in height and 3 to 4ft (90cm to 1.2m) in diameter with large well-developed buttresses and a straight cylindrical bole of up to 90ft (27m) in length.

The timber is orange-red or brown-red with numerous yellow-brown streaks. Grain is interlocked and sometimes wavy; the texture is coarse but even. The wood contains veins of hard stonelike tissue, sometimes extending for several feet along the grain. Weight is naturally variable, due in part to the extent of the mineral concentrations, but kempas is extremely strong.

Drying presents few problems but the timber is liable to split, due in part to the stony tissue. The interlocked grain and fibrous texture make it a difficult wood to work and it must always be bored prior to nailing. The heartwood is durable and resistant to fungi but is reported to be vulnerable to attack by termites in Malaysia.

Kempas is primarily a heavy duty constructional timber and has a wide range of local applications including, after preservative treatment, use as railway sleepers.

Kapur
Dryobalanops spp

Several species of *Dryobalanops* are sold under the trade name kapur, including *D. aromatica* from peninsular Malaysia and *D. lanceolata* and *D. beccarii* from Sabah and Sarawak.

The trees are very large, often 200ft (60m) or more in height and about 5ft (1.5m) in diameter with up to 100ft (30m) of clear bole rising above well-developed buttresses.

The wood is reddish-brown and very uniform, with a straight or slightly interlocked grain. The texture is coarse but even and gives the wood a generally plain appearance. Kapur is a fairly heavy wood and is stronger than European beech.

The timber is slow to dry and some species have a tendency to split and to distort. It is rather difficult wood to work when dry, partly because of the presence of crystalline silica in some of the cells; this causes considerable blunting of cutting tools and may even require the use of tungsten-carbide-tipped tools.

Kapur is a strong timber, very durable and suited to a variety of uses. It is particularly suitable for heavy constructional uses, such as estate and farm buildings, bridge and wharf decking and industrial flooring. Locally it is used for boat-building and its properties should make it suitable for more widespread use in export markets for exterior and interior joinery, door and window frames, cladding and garden furniture.

White seraya
Parashorea spp

White seraya, which is distinct from the white meranti of Malaysia, is obtained from two species of *Parashorea* and is supplied to the international timber trade from Sabah, as white seraya or urat mata, and from the Philippines where it is called bagtikan.

Parashorea are very large trees, *P. malaanonan* commonly attaining a height of up to 200ft (60m) and diameter of 3 to 5ft (90cm to 1.5m). The bole may be 100ft (30m) long above the massive supporting buttresses.

The wood is a straw shade or pale brown, occasionally with a faint pink hue, and uniform in appearance. The grain is slightly interlocked and produces a broad striped figure on quarter-sawn surfaces. The wood texture is moderately coarse and brittleheart is quite common.

White seraya dries easily and quickly with little deterioration. It is easy to work but requires very sharp cutting edges for good results. Nailing properties are good and the wood takes stains and polishes well after filling. It is rather variable in durability and is vulnerable to attack by beetles.

The most important use of white seraya is for plywood manufacture, but it also has wide general applications in light construction work, interior joinery and domestic flooring. Large quantities of the timber are exported, mainly to Japan.

Sepetir
Pseudosindora palustris

Pseudosindora palustris and a number of trees of the genus *Sindora* are of very wide distribution in Southeast Asia and in places are among the most abundant forest trees. Swamp sepetir, also known as petir and sepetir paya in Sarawak, is a tall tree with a diameter between 2 and 4ft (60cm to 1.2m) and a straight, cylindrical unbuttressed bole.

The wood of *Pseudosindora* is red-brown with darker markings, and is redder and less varied than the Malaysian sepetir obtained from *Sindora*. The grain is straight or slightly interlocked and the texture medium-fine and even.

The timber dries slowly but with little distortion although there is a tendency to split at the ends. Movement in use is small. The interlocked grain affects some working properties and there is a marked tendency for the wood to split when nails are used. Staining and polishing are satisfactory.

Sepetir is a durable and stable wood, fairly easy to work to a good finish. It is therefore suitable for all general joinery and carpentry, and is regarded by many wood technologists as likely to increase in popularity for furniture manufacture and cabinet work. Although at present the wood is exported only in small quantities of selected sawn sizes, it is likely to increase in commercial importance.

Jelutong
Dyera costulata   Dyera lowii

D. costulata is native to peninsular Malaysia, but both *costulata* and *lowii* are found in Sumatra, Sarawak and Sabah. Both species attain spectacular size, often reaching 200ft (60m) in height and up to 8ft (2.5m) in diameter, with straight, unbuttressed cylindrical boles up to 90ft (27m) in length.

The light wood is plain and is sometimes stained by fungi where the stem has been tapped for its valuable latex. The grain is straight and the texture fine and even. The plain appearance of the wood is often marred by slitlike latex channels occurring at intervals along the grain, though these can usually be eliminated during processing.

The timber dries easily and with little degrade but precautions are necessary to prevent staining of the wood. There is no difficulty working the wood to a good finish with hand tools or machine tools and the blunting effect is slight. Nailing, gluing, staining and polishing are all satisfactory, and although the wood is not naturally durable it accepts preservative treatment readily.

Because of its fine even texture, stability and good working properties, jelutong makes a good substitute for yellow pine in pattern-making and the manufacture of drawing boards. Its softness and ability to take a smooth finish make it popular for model making, hand carving and toy making. In much of its natural range the tree is tapped for its milky latex, which is exported for use as a base for chewing gum.

Balau
Shorea spp

Balau (Malaysia) and selangan batu (Sabah) are species of the huge genus *Shorea* which yield timber very similar to the sal tree, *Shorea robusta*, one of the most important timber trees of India. The trees of this group are generally of large size, though variable, and of very good form.

The wood is usually yellow-brown, darkening on exposure to red-brown, and its interlocked grain gives a striped figure on quarter-sawn wood. Most of the sal-type timbers are much harder, and are rated appreciably stronger, than teak.

The timber dries slowly, with very little distortion, but tends to split and suffer from surface checking. Movement in use is moderate. The high density also makes the wood rather difficult to work.

These *Shorea* species produce hard, robust timbers of great importance for structural use in their countries of origin, where they are widely used for bridges, wharf construction, piling, railway sleepers, and for house-building and decking of commercial vehicles. A good deal of the timber is also exported as large-dimension stock for use in dock and harbour work.

Merbau

Intsia palembanica   *Intsia bijuga*

Intsia bijuga has a wide distribution throughout Vietnam, Thailand, Malaysia, Malagasy, the Seychelles, Fiji and New Caledonia. *I. palembanica* is found in Sumatra and Borneo and in Malaysia, Sarawak and Sabah, where most of the merbau timber is produced. *I. palembanica* is a large tree of variable stem form. Boles are about 5ft (1.5m) in diameter, but rather short and often fluted.

The wood is medium to dark redbrown and the grain is interlocked and sometimes wavy, giving a ribbon figure on quarter-sawn surfaces. In strength the wood rates about the same, or slightly lower than, European beech.

Merbau dries fairly quickly and with little deterioration. Shrinkage is low and movement in use negligible. It needs preboring for nailing and the surface must be carefully filled in order to achieve a good finish. The heartwood is rated as durable.

This Asian timber is of good appearance and, like afzelia, is used for varied structural work, high-class joinery, furniture manufacture, panelling and flooring. It is exported to most of the European countries and in particular to the Netherlands.

Keruing

Dipterocarpus spp

Timbers of the keruing type are obtained from more than seventy species of the genus *Dipterocarpus* occurring in parts of India, Pakistan and Sri Lanka, throughout Malaysia, Burma and Thailand, and also in Sumatra, Borneo and the Philippines.

Because of the large number of source species, and their extensive distribution, the nature of the wood varies considerably. The trees range in height from 100 to 200ft (30 to 60m) and from 3 to 6ft (90cm to 1.8m) in diameter. Most have long straight boles, and some species are buttressed.

The wood varies from pinkish-brown to dark brown, sometimes with a marked purple tint. The grain is straight or slightly interlocked and the texture moderately coarse but even.

Keruing dries slowly with a tendency to distort and collapse, and there are problems with exudation of resin if the wood is kiln-dried. Working properties vary. The wood can be machined satisfactorily but the finish is slightly fibrous and the blunting effect moderate to severe, so that use of tungsten-carbide tools is advisable. The timber is reasonably durable.

The timber is widely used as a substitute for oak in frames, flooring, vehicle construction, decking and other shipwork. Use for exterior work is limited as the wood exudes resin if exposed to sunlight. Lighter-weight logs are used in Malaysia for the manufacture of plywood and the wood is exported in this form as well as in the form of sawn timber.

Ramin

Gonystylus bancanus

Ramin, or melawis as it is also known in Malaysia, is found throughout the swamp forests of Malaysia, parts of Sumatra, the west coast of Borneo and the Philippines. It is particularly abundant in the peat swamp conditions of river deltas in Sarawak.

The trees are tall with cylindrical boles 50 to 60ft (15 to 18m) long and averaging 2ft (60cm) in diameter. The stem is not buttressed. The wood is a uniform white or a pale straw shade; the grain is straight or slightly interlocked, and the texture fine to medium and even. Freshly sawn timber often has an unpleasant smell.

Ramin dries easily with little degrade though there is a tendency for the ends to split, particularly in large-sized timbers, and for checking to occur. Movement in use may be quite large. The wood can be worked satisfactorily with both hand tools and machine tools and the blunting effect is quite moderate. The timber will take a good finish, and will accept stain and polish well after filling. The heartwood is not durable and is susceptible to attack by termites.

Ramin is exported mainly as lumber and strips, but logs are available. It is a firmly established utility timber used in furniture industries and for all types of interior joinery, mouldings, panelling of flush doors and even small items such as handles and toys.

Mersawa

Anisoptera spp

The timber is known as mersawa in Malaysia, Sabah, Brunei and Sarawak, and as krabak in Thailand, and is obtained from several trees of the genus *Anisoptera*, widely distributed from Pakistan and northern Burma to the Philippines and Papua New Guinea.

Trees are medium to large in size, reaching a height of 150ft (45m) and often yielding a cylindrical bole 3 to 5ft (90cm to 1.5m) in diameter and up to 100ft (30m) in length.

The wood is pale yellow-brown which darkens on exposure, and the grain is straight or slightly interlocked. The texture is generally rather coarse.

Mersawa dries slowly but without any serious deterioration, and movement in use is not extensive. Because of the presence of silica in the wood, and the interlocking of the grain, the timber is rather difficult to work and has a pronounced blunting effect on tools. It is moderately resistant to fungal attack.

This wood is widely used for general construction work, interior joinery and vehicle construction. Logs selected for straight grain can be used for the manufacture of plywood for tea chests, but mersawa plywood is not to be used for shuttering as it retards the setting of concrete.

Mengkulang

Heritiera spp

Mengkulang is obtained from several *Heritiera* species distributed throughout Southeast Asia, the most common and abundant of which is thought to be *H. simplicifolia*, a medium to large tree, 100 to 150ft (30 to 45m) in height, with a well-formed bole rising above a buttressed base.

The wood varies from medium pink to red-brown or dark red-brown. Grain is usually interlocked, sometimes also irregular, and the texture is moderately coarse. In strength the wood is very similar to European beech.

The timber dries extremely quickly with some tendency to develop surface checks, but movement in use is small. Difficulties in machining often arise from the interlocked grain and the wood has a severe blunting effect on machine tools. Nailing properties are good and the wood takes stains and polishes reasonably well after filling. Mengkulang is not a durable timber and is susceptible to termite attack.

In Malaysia, mengkulang is used as a general utility timber for interior construction, flooring, furniture and boat-building. It is also used locally for plywood manufacture. For export markets it is recommended as an alternative to the heavier types of mahogany for joinery, flooring and other uses. It is exported as sawn timber and as plywood sheets.

Dark-red meranti

Shorea spp

The timber known to the trade as dark-red meranti (Malaysia, Sarawak) or as dark-red seraya (Sabah) is derived from several species of the *Shorea* group, the most important individual species being *S. pauciflora*.

The trees are large—among the tallest of all the rain forest giants—attaining a height of up to 225ft (70m) above the huge buttresses. The wood is a medium to dark red-brown and conspicuous streaks of white resin are a characteristic feature. Grain is interlocked and produces a striped figure on quarter-sawn material.

The timber dries rather slowly with a tendency to distort, while thicker timbers may also show splitting and surface checking. It is not difficult to work, but very sharp cutters are required for machining in order to achieve good results. Nailing properties are good and the timber accepts stain and polish quite well. Dark-red meranti is also moderately durable.

This timber is heavier, stronger, more durable and less variable than the light-red meranti and is both stable and attractive in use. It is exported for use in construction work, interior and exterior joinery, shop fitting and boat-building. Plywood is manufactured from the dark-red meranti timbers and is generally available.

Light-red meranti

Shorea spp

Light-red meranti (seraya in Sabah) is obtained from several *Shorea* species of widespread and common occurrence in Malaysia. The trees are commonly up to 200ft (60m) high with diameters of 3 to 4ft (90cm to 1.5m) and boles 100ft (30m) in length. Some species are buttressed.

The wood varies from a pale pink to medium red. Grain is usually slightly interlocked, giving a broad striped figure on quarter-sawn surfaces. The texture is coarse but generally even.

Drying behaviour varies a great deal between the species; generally the wood dries fairly quickly and with little distortion, but there is a marked tendency to cup. Movement in use is usually small, and the wood gives little difficulty in processing. It takes nails well and can be stained and polished after filling.

Light-red meranti is a useful general purpose timber for light construction work and joinery, for the interior parts of furniture and for the manufacture of plywood. Large quantities are exported to European countries, Japan, Australia and many other markets and the timber is undoubtedly one of the most important export timbers of southern Asia.

Yellow meranti

Shorea spp

Yellow meranti, or yellow seraya is a very pale timber obtained from a dozen or more species of *Shorea* widespread in Malaysia and Sabah. The trees are medium to large but generally not quite as impressive as the red meranti trees. They do however attain heights up to 200ft (60m) with straight cylindrical boles of up to 5ft (1.5m) in diameter. Most of the producer species are buttressed.

The wood varies from dull yellow to yellow-brown and darkens slowly on exposure. The grain is slightly interlocked and texture is moderately coarse. Some trees contain brittleheart, which causes considerable variation in weight and strength.

The timber dries slowly in thicknesses up to 2in (5cm) but with little deterioration apart from a tendency to cup. Larger sizes dry extremely slowly and honeycombing and extension of shakes (natural splits) usually occur. The wood is stable in use, is easy to work, and has only a moderate blunting effect on cutting tools. Nailing is good and after filling the wood will take stains and polishes satisfactorily. One slight disadvantage is that yellow meranti is often disfigured by the presence of tiny wormholes.

Yellow meranti is slightly harder and heavier than light-red meranti and is used for very similar work—light building construction, interior joinery and as a utility timber. In Malaysia the wood is extensively used in the manufacture of plywood, but the majority of export timber is in the form of sawn timber.

Spices

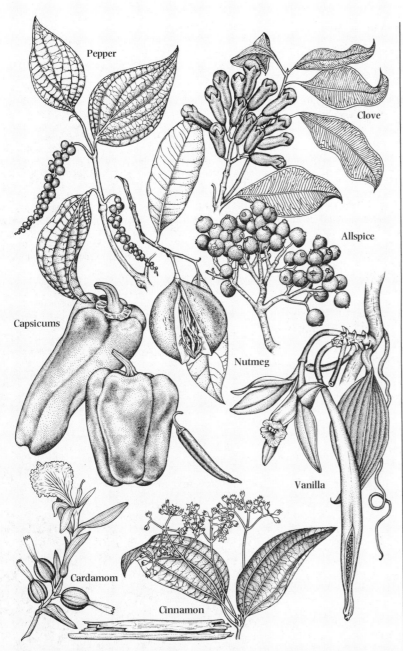

Pepper

Clove

Allspice

Capsicums

Nutmeg

Vanilla

Cardamom

Cinnamon

Along with gold and silver, precious stones and fine cloths, the spices must surely rank among those commodities to which man has attached a very special importance. Rare spices appear time and time again in the written records of the gifts and tributes paid to kings and princes of many lands, while throughout the world, spices and herbs have played an important part in the lore and the secret remedies of the magician and the natural healer.

The quest for new supplies, and for new spices, motivated many of the great voyages of discovery during the 1400s and 1500s as men like Vasco da Gama and Christopher Columbus sought new trading routes by which a Europe hungry for conquest, prestige and material wealth could tap the resources of these distant lands.

In the period from about 1500 until the nineteenth century many of the nations of Europe were in constant conflict as Portuguese, Dutch and British interests in particular struggled to gain the monopoly of the highly valuable spice trade of the islands of the East Indies.

Today it is hardly likely that Portugal and the Netherlands would find themselves at war over the nutmeg tree in the Moluccas; the colonial powers have largely withdrawn leaving production under local control. But the western nations who for many centuries controlled the spice trade are still very much involved, in the provision of financial resources and technical expertise, in the stimulation of research and development, and as the buyers and sellers in an international market which, though formerly based in India, Java, China and the Moluccas, is currently centred on New York, Hamburg, London and Singapore.

Allspice (Pimento)
Pimenta dioica

Pimenta dioica was one of the many plant species described by Dr Diego Chanca, a talented observer and naturalist who sailed with Columbus in 1493 and recorded in detail many hundreds of New World animal and plant species. He described the tree as a medium-sized evergreen with a smooth grey trunk and small aromatic fruits characterized by a subtle flavour rather like a mixture of clove, cinnamon and nutmeg: hence the name allspice. Since the berries were very like peppercorns in shape, they took the name *pimienta* (Spanish = pepper).

The slender, upright tree is native to the West Indies and Latin America. Usually it grows to about 25 to 40ft (7.6 to 12m) in height although it may attain a height of 100ft (30m) in the rain forests of Guatemala, southeastern Mexico and Honduras. Commercial production of allspice is restricted to the New World—to Jamaica, Guatemala, Mexico, Honduras, Belize and the Leeward Islands.

Plantation cultivation starts with the planting of seeds squeezed from the fresh ripe fruit of selected strong trees. After about one year the young trees are taken from the nursery and planted out in temporary shade. After six years the trees are spaced more widely and most of the non-productive male trees (often up to 50 per cent of the total) are removed. In Jamaica the berries are harvested carefully by hand just before they ripen. They are then spread in the sun to dry for seven to ten days before they are cleaned and packed. In much of Central America and Mexico the berries are collected from trees growing wild but the methods used are often crude—the fruiting branches, and sometimes even the whole tree, being hacked down.

Capsicum peppers
Paprika   *Capsicum annuum*
Cayenne   *Capsicum frutescens*
Chilli   *Capsicum frutescens*

The capsicum peppers are members of the nightshade family indigenous to Mexico, Central America, the West Indies and northern South America. They were discovered by the early Spanish explorers who, in their search for further supplies of the popular Asian black pepper, found something rather more piquant.

By 1650 the capsicum peppers were successfully transplanted to Europe, Asia and Africa, and the resilience and the adaptability of the plant soon became apparent. Constant experimentation under different growing conditions has given rise to many varieties, both tropical and temperate, and today more than 90 distinct variants are recognized.

C. annuum is the most widely cultivated of the three types and the many varieties include all the sweet peppers in addition to some of the more pungent ones. *Capsicum* is an annual herbaceous plant, usually growing to a height of about 3ft (90cm) and bearing fruit varying from $1\frac{1}{2}$ to 11in (4 to 27cm) in length. The glossy fruits are very variable in hue, ranging from bright yellow through orange, brown and red to a deep purple. In most of the producer areas the fruits are sun-dried for between 5 and 15 days but some of the more highly mechanized plantations now use hot air dryers which prepare the peppers in as little as 30 hours.

In the past, the capsicum peppers were widely used in the preparation of medicines for the treatment of gout, toothache and stomach pains and for making liniments for the relief of rheumatism. Today their use is restricted to the kitchen where they are popular both for their attractive visual effect and for their pleasing flavours. They are also commonly blended in powder form with a variety of other spices.

Cardamom
Elettaria cardamomum var. *cardamomum*

The cardamom plant is a tall herbaceous perennial of the ginger family, native to southern India and Sri Lanka. Its long leafy shoots may grow to a height of 18ft (5.5m) with one or more flowering stems rising from the base to a height of 2 to 4ft (60cm to 1.2m).

The fruit is a small, oval capsule, $\frac{1}{2}$ to $\frac{3}{4}$in (12 to 19mm) long containing 15 to 20 hard, angular dark-brown seeds.

Until about 1800 the spice was harvested from wild-growing trees in southern India and Sri Lanka. The natural forest was cut down to form a small clearing and the cardamom seeds allowed to germinate. The plot would be cropped until exhausted, when it would be abandoned in favour of a new clearing.

Today the plants are grown from carefully selected seeds or from cuttings and are planted out in light shade in controlled conditions. The plants start to produce after the fourth year and are then productive for up to nine months of the year for a further 10 to 15 years.

The pods are harvested when three-quarters ripe, when they are full and firm but still green, and are either spread out in the sun to dry or placed in artificial drying rooms.

The major part of the world supply comes from the Indian states of Kerala, Mysore and Madras, but in recent years Guatemala has become a significant producer and exporter of the spice.

Traditionally cardamom was widely used in Europe to disguise the unpleasant taste of many medicinal preparations, but its high price today limits its use primarily to the perfume industry. It is also used as a flavouring for tobacco, and in the processed meat industry. In Scandinavia it is a popular flavouring for bread and pastry, and in Arab countries, notably Saudi Arabia, cardamom coffee, known as *gahwa*, is a traditional drink of hospitality. The Middle East accounts for 60 per cent of world cardamom imports.

Cinnamon
Cinnamomum zeylanicum
Cassia
Cinnamomum cassia
Indonesian cassia
Cinnamomum burmanni
Vietnamese cassia
Cinnamomum loureirii

Cinnamon and cassia are two of the oldest spices known to man—and 4,000 years of confusion between the two persists even today. The popular American 'cinnamon toast' should perhaps be called 'cassia toast'—the United States imports three times as much cassia as it does true cinnamon, and most of the cinnamon imported is immediately re-exported to Mexico. Europe has traditionally favoured the more delicately flavoured spice *C. zeylanicum* to the stronger spice derived from *C. cassia*.

Cinnamomum zeylanicum is a bushy evergreen tree of the laurel family and is native to southern India and Sri Lanka. In the wild it grows to 30 or 40ft high (9 to 12m) but in plantation production the tree is rigorously cropped to form a dense bush. The trees are grown from selected seed and two to three years after planting each is cut back to only 6 to 8 selected stems. The bush is then harvested every two or three years when the woody shoots are 6 to 8ft (1.8 to 2.5m) long.

The bark is peeled from the stems with a sharp curved knife and is left in bundles to ferment for 24 hours. The corklike outer bark is then carefully scraped off to leave the clean pale inner bark which, when dried, is the true cinnamon.

Cinnamomum cassia is also an evergreen laurel, slightly larger than *zeylanicum* and native across Southeast Asia to China. Like cinnamon, the tree is cut back to bush form and the preparation of the spice is similar although the fermentation stage is omitted and both branch and stem bark is used. Cassia bark is coarser, thicker, has a more intense aroma and is more pungent than cinnamon.

Both cinnamon and cassia are widely used in powder form for baking, and in stick form in pickling, in the preserving of fruit, and in various mulled wine recipes. The spices were formerly widespread in medicinal use but although no longer used in Europe they are retained in many Indian remedies.

Clove
Syzygium aromaticum

The clove tree is a small, straight-trunked evergreen of the myrtle family, 30 to 40ft (9 to 12m) in height with a characteristic conical shape. It is indigenous to the Moluccas, or Spice Islands, and was certainly known to the ancient Chinese: the spice is mentioned in writings of the Han period of the third century B.C. It was well known in Europe by the fourth century A.D. and has remained popular.

The spice itself is the whole dried nail-shaped flower bud, picked just before the pink-green blossom of the tree opens and turns a deep red. The name derives from the French word *clou*=nail.

Production was originally restricted to the Moluccas, first under Portuguese rule and then, in the seventeenth and eighteenth centuries, under Dutch rule. The Dutch East India Company held a monopoly on the clove trade, with harsh penalties for any unauthorised growing or trading. Today, cloves are produced in the Malagasy Republic, Zanzibar and Indonesia. The trees are propagated from seed and are planted out when two years old. The first crop is taken at 6 to 8 years but the tree does not reach its peak until 20 to 25 years old, after which it may remain productive—even though less prolific—for 100 years.

At harvest time, the branches are pulled down with hooked sticks and the tender buds are gently removed, if they open, or are damaged at all, they are worthless. The buds are gently brushed from their stems against the open palm of the hand and are then spread out on mats or platforms for several days to dry.

The whole clove is one of the most widely used of all spices. But perhaps the most remarkable application of the spice is to be found in Southeast Asia where, in the nineteenth century, Javanese smokers began mixing ground clove with tobacco to form the *kretek* cigarette. This industry is now so big that it employs a labour force of more than 70,000 in Indonesia, and the production of *kretek* cigarettes accounts for 50 per cent of the total world consumption of cloves.

Mace and nutmeg
Myristica fragrans

One remarkable feature sets *Myristica fragrans* apart from all other spice-bearing trees. From its apricotlike fruit, two entirely separate and very distinctive spices are produced.

The nutmeg is a handsome, densely-foliated tree indigenous to the Moluccas and other islands in the East Indies. It is characterized by its dark-grey bark, broad spread, long glossy leaves (very like those of the rhododendron) and small yellow flowers. In plantation conditions the tree grows to a height of about 60ft (18m).

When fully ripe, the lemon-yellow fleshy fruit splits open to expose a brilliant scarlet netlike membrane, the mace, covering a lustrous dark-brown shell within which lies the single glossy brown oily seed, the nutmeg.

Although the nutmeg was probably not known in the ancient world, it was imported into Constantinople from the East Indies in the sixth century and was widely known in Europe by the end of the twelfth century. In 1512 the Portuguese discovered the nutmeg tree in the Moluccas and for nearly 100 years that nation held a monopoly on the spice. The area was subsequently dominated by Dutch influence and later came under British control, during which time the nutmeg tree was transplanted to Penang, then to St Vincent in the West Indies and finally via Trinidad to Grenada which, from the mid-1840s, rapidly became the most important producer area in the Western hemisphere. Today the prime commercial sources are Indonesia, Grenada and Sri Lanka.

The fruit ripens six months after the tree has flowered and in tropical regions harvesting is carried out throughout the year. The fruits are picked with a *gai-gai*—a long pole with sharp prongs at the tip which dislodge the fruit and guide it into a basket. The nut and the enclosing mace are taken from the husk and the thin membrane is carefully detached and spread out to dry for up to two weeks, during which time it fades to a pale brown and takes on a pungent aroma. The unshelled seeds are allowed to dry until they rattle and are then removed from their shells.

In addition to their widespread use as cooking spices, both mace and nutmeg yield valuable essential oils which are used in perfumery and cosmetics.

Pepper
Piper nigrum

The world's most important spice is derived from the small, round berries of a woody climbing vine—native to the Malabar coast of southwestern India but now distributed throughout the tropical region as a cultivated plant of great commercial importance.

Pepper figures largely in the 3,000 year-old Sanskrit medical literature of India and was one of the first articles of commerce between Europe and the Orient. So highly regarded was the spice that in medieval times rents, dowries and taxes were often paid in pepper. The value of the spice as a commodity had a profound effect on European trade in the Middle Ages and was one of the main reasons for Vasco da Gama's voyages in search of a sea route to the Malabar coast in 1498.

Both black and white pepper come from the same plant—the difference in hue and flavour being due to the method of processing. If black pepper is required, the berries are harvested while green (unripe) and are piled up and allowed to ferment for a few days. They are then spread in the sun to dry until they are blackened and shrivelled. Thus the entire peppercorn, including the husk, is used. To produce white pepper, the peppercorns are picked when fully ripe and just about to turn red. They are packed in sacks and soaked in running water for 8 days, after which the softened berries are gently rubbed to remove the husk. The grey inner peppercorns are then dried to produce the white spice.

The vines are trained along young shade trees or support posts and are carefully pruned to prevent over-growth and tangling of the prolific side-growths. Each vine is productive after the third year and has a useful life of 15 to 20 years.

Vanilla
Vanilla fragrans (= *V. planifolia*)
Vanilla planifolia

This large green-stemmed climbing vine with thick smooth leaves and twisting aerial roots, is a member of the orchid family and is native to the dense rain forests of southeastern Mexico, Central America, the West Indies and northern South America. The wild vine may grow to lengths far in excess of 80ft (24m).

Vanilla is unusual in many respects. It is the one outstanding spice produced by the western hemisphere, it is the only commercially significant plant among the 35,000 known orchid species; and it is an exceptionally highly valued commodity, due mainly to the great care, and great length of time, required for its preparation.

The young vines, propagated by cuttings, are supported on live trees and, like the pepper vines, require constant care to control their growth and to maintain a shape conducive to good pollination and efficient harvesting. The long, slender pods, up to 10in (25cm) long and 1in (2.5cm) in diameter, are picked when fully grown but not quite fully ripe. At this stage they have no flavour at all. The pods are dipped in hot water and then 'sweated' and dried—alternately closely wrapped and left to sweat overnight, then spread out in the sun for several hours. This process is repeated many times until the pods are a deep-brown shade and pliable. They are then dried in the sun for several weeks. The whole process takes 5 to 6 months of very carefully controlled, and skilled, management, and hence the crop has a very high cash value.

Vanillin, the major flavouring constituent of vanilla beans, is now produced synthetically, and the synthetic vanillin has replaced true vanilla in most flavouring applications. However, it does not possess the full flavour of true vanilla. Synthetic vanillin is produced from eugenol, which is now obtained from lignin (wood-processing waste). Eugenol was formerly produced from clove leaf and cinnamon leaf oils.

The difficulties experienced in transplanting vanilla from its native area illustrate the complexities of the forest ecosystem. Hernando Cortez brought the flavouring to Europe in 1520 and it gained immediate popularity as an additive to beverages and tobacco. But for three centuries all attempts to produce the spice in new areas failed; the vines would grow but would not fruit. The breakthrough came in 1836 when it was found that the vine was pollinated by a specific bee, and by one type of hummingbird. Failure had been due to a lack of any suitable pollinator. Techniques of hand pollination were rapidly evolved and, using these methods, the vine is now grown commercially in many tropical countries. Today, vanilla is produced in the Malagasy Republic, Réunion, Indonesia and Mexico, entirely by artificial methods of pollination.

Fibres and cane

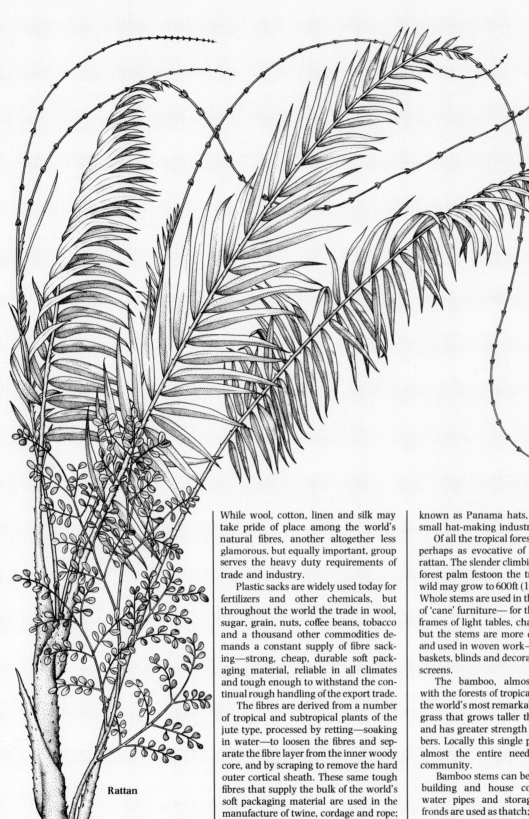

Rattan

While wool, cotton, linen and silk may take pride of place among the world's natural fibres, another altogether less glamorous, but equally important, group serves the heavy duty requirements of trade and industry.

Plastic sacks are widely used today for fertilizers and other chemicals, but throughout the world the trade in wool, sugar, grain, nuts, coffee beans, tobacco and a thousand other commodities demands a constant supply of fibre sacking—strong, cheap, durable soft packaging material, reliable in all climates and tough enough to withstand the continual rough handling of the export trade.

The fibres are derived from a number of tropical and subtropical plants of the jute type, processed by retting—soaking in water—to loosen the fibres and separate the fibre layer from the inner woody core, and by scraping to remove the hard outer cortical sheath. These same tough fibres that supply the bulk of the world's soft packaging material are used in the manufacture of twine, cordage and rope; for the backing cloth used in carpets and linoleum floor coverings; for upholstery tapes and webbings and in heavy duty cable cores.

The palmlike plant *Carludovica palmata*, sometimes called the toquilla palm, grows in the rain forests of Central and South America. The plant reaches a height of 6½ft (2m) in the wild. Fibre from the palm is used for making the hats known as Panama hats, and there is a small hat-making industry in Ecuador.

Of all the tropical forest plants none is perhaps as evocative of 'jungle' as the rattan. The slender climbing stems of this forest palm festoon the trees and in the wild may grow to 600ft (180m) in length. Whole stems are used in the manufacture of 'cane' furniture— for the uprights and frames of light tables, chairs and beds— but the stems are more commonly split and used in woven work—in chair seats, baskets, blinds and decorative panels and screens.

The bamboo, almost synonymous with the forests of tropical Asia, is one of the world's most remarkable plants. It is a grass that grows taller than many trees and has greater strength than some timbers. Locally this single plant may serve almost the entire needs of a village community.

Bamboo stems can be used in bridge-building and house construction, for water pipes and storage vessels. The fronds are used as thatch; the shoots are a popular vegetable. Smaller stems are used in a variety of domestic furniture and utensils and when split may be woven into baskets and mats or reduced to fibres and made into ropes and coarse woven fabrics. Few materials have served so many people, in so many ways, or for such a length of time, as this giant tropical relative of corn, wheat and barley.

Ramie
Boehmeria sp

Ramie is one of the most attractive of the textile fibres and, excluding mainland China for which information is not available, some 93 per cent of the known world production comes from Brazil and the Philippines. The largest consumers are Brazil and Japan but small quantities are also imported and processed in Europe, Indonesia, Taiwan and Korea.

The plant is indigenous to central and western China and like hemp and flax its fibres have been used for many centuries. In China it was the principal source of cloth prior to the introduction of cotton around A.D. 1300 ramie was first described, and named *Rammum majus*, by a Dutch botanist who found the plant growing in the East Indies in 1660. Later the species was more fully described by a Viennese botanist who established the current genus *Boehmeria*.

Commercial exploitation on a large scale was initially held up through difficulties in hand-scraping the fibre, but once these were solved ramie quickly became an important commodity. The plant has a wide range of climatic tolerance though the shallow roots are vulnerable to frost. In temperate areas 2 to 3 crops are taken each year; in subtropical regions, 4 to 5 crops, and in tropical areas, within 10 degrees north and south of the equator, 6 or more crops may be taken. Actual yield per acre is, however, higher outside the tropics.

In China stems are harvested by hand and are first defoliated. The raw bast is then stripped away in ribbons from the woody stem core and the ribbons scraped to remove the outer bark and any gummy material adhering to the fibres. The fibrous ribbons are bleached in the sun or by placing them in a small building where they are exposed to the fumes of burning sulphur.

Small quantities of ramie fibre are produced locally, by hand-scraping, for making fishing lines, nets and cordage and for making hand-loom cloth. Mechanized scraping increases productivity and is generally used where the fibre product is being prepared for export.

Rattans
Calamus spp
Daemonorops spp

Among the handful of tropical plants made familiar by the film-makers of Hollywood, the rattan must surely be the best known. Who has not at some time seen one of the many screen Tarzans hurl himself across a raging torrent suspended from one of these ropelike, woody climbing plants? Foresters dislike rattans, for they complicate the task of felling trees by binding the tree crowns together, but rattans too have their uses.

The rattans of commerce are the stems of various climbing palms, the two main genera being *Calamus* and *Daemonorops*. Climbing higher and higher into the forest canopy, supported by their twisting tendrils of specialized leaf tissue, mature rattans may grow to lengths in excess of 600ft (180m) though more commonly 250ft (75m) is the limit. The principal sources of commercial supplies are the Malay Peninsula, Indonesia, Borneo and China. Smaller quantities are also exported from India and from the Philippines.

Where rattans grow wild near native villages they provide a useful source of income for relatively little effort. Mature stems, at least ten years old, are selected and cut close to the ground. The stem is then dragged to the ground and the last few feet, too soft to be of commercial value, are cut off. The leaves are removed and dried in the sun and then the stems are cut into lengths of about 16ft (5m), made into bundles of about 100 stems and carried to the trading centres. Individual bundles often contain stems from several different species, some of which have a hard surface glaze which must be scraped off to avoid splintering and to allow the rattan to accept paint or varnish. After grading, the rattans are washed, scoured with sand, and then bleached either naturally in the sun or by exposure to burning sulphur.

Where natural wild rattans are not available, or have been over-exploited, the palms may be grown on plantations. The seeds are started in nursery beds and are then planted out in areas where the forest has been cut down and the undergrowth removed. Narrow strips of young trees are left standing to give support to the rattans as they climb. At ten years old, each plant will have produced about 40 stems, 80 to 100ft (24 to 30m) long and as thick as a man's finger. Selected stems are then harvested and each year after that roughly 10 per cent of the stems may be cut.

Where strength is required, as, for example, in furniture-making, the rattan may be used whole, but usually the stems are split. Alternatively the stems may be passed through a machine which removes the bark, leaving the round, compact core intact. The bark may then be split into fine strips for use in woven goods such as baskets, decorative screens and chair seats.

Jute
Corchorus capsularis
Corchorus olitorius

Jute is by far the most important long-fibre in terms of world trade and is surpassed in tonnage only by the world's premier short-fibre crop—cotton. It is the most widely used of the soft packaging fibres, although periodic shortages in supply have led to increased use of synthetic substitutes and to a greater use of alternative natural fibres.

The principal areas of supply are Bangladesh and India—accounting for more than 85 per cent of world production—but the fibre is of increasing importance now in China, Burma, and in Brazil where, although initial attempts at cultivation failed, Indian seed finally proved successful in 1930 in the Manaus—Belem sector of the Amazon basin.

Jute occupies the land for four to five months so that, depending on local conditions, two or three crops are taken in each year. The crop is usually stem-retted, although in some areas the ribbons may be retted after separation from the stem. Generally the stems are tied in bundles and made into a raft; a second layer of bundles is laid across the first at right-angles, and sometimes a third layer is added. The raft is then weighted down with stones in a canal, ditch or pond in about 3ft of water. The retting process takes between a week and a month depending on the acidity of the water, its temperature, its rate of flow and the level of bacterial action.

After retting, the stems are stripped of their bast or phloem layer. The end of a stem is lifted from the water and beaten to loosen the outer layer. A section of the inner core is broken out and discarded, and the operator then grasps the empty section of fibrous sheath and jerks the stem through the water, gradually ripping the fibre away from the woody core. The ribbons are scraped, by hand or by pulling them across a knife edge mounted on a block, and are then dried and baled.

Roselle
Hibiscus sabdariffa var. *altissima*

Roselle is the one truly tropical fibre plant, and one which is rapidly increasing in importance as a commercial product. In ideal conditions roselle will outgrow either jute or kenaf, and since it was first produced commercially in Java in 1938 the fibre has attracted much attention.

The main producing areas are India, Bangladesh, Thailand, Indonesia and Vietnam. Like kenaf, roselle is often retted after the ribbons have been scraped by pulling them across a mounted knife edge of metal or hardwood. In the larger plantations, demand for increased production has led to the development of machines to take over the slow and laborious task of hand-scraping the fibre.

Kenaf
Hibiscus cannabinus

Kenaf is a soft-stem fibre similar to jute, and, along with roselle, is being used increasingly as an alternative to jute. Inconsistencies in the world supply of jute encouraged users to seek alternative fibres, and today kenaf and roselle account for nearly one-third of the total world output of soft packaging material.

The plant probably originated in Africa but the principal producers are China, India and the USSR, although more recently the crop has been introduced successfully into El Salvador, Guatemala and Dahomey, the Ivory Coast and parts of Nigeria.

H. cannabinus is an annual herbaceous plant growing to a height of 3 to 12ft (90cm to 3m). The stems are hand-cut and are usually stem-retted before the fibrous ribbons are stripped away and processed ready for export.

Kapok
Ceiba pentandra
Bombax spp

Ceiba pentandra is indigenous to East Africa, West Africa, Sri Lanka, the Philippines, Indonesia and tropical America. It naturally forms part of the secondary forest flora and is found from sea level to 4,000ft (1,220m) or more. For fibre production, however, the tree is at its best below 1,500ft (450m) in well-tended plantations where it is grown from seed or from stem or branch cuttings.

The tree begins to bear pods in its third or fourth year and is fully productive at about ten years. The pods are harvested when fully ripe and just about to burst open. They change from green to brown and the surface takes on a withered, wrinkled appearance. Mature pods open easily and the silky white floss simply falls out. Immature pods are not picked as the floss is difficult to remove and is of inferior quality. Any immature pods which are dislodged from the tree are spread on the drying floor and left to ripen in the sun before they are opened.

The collected floss is carefully dried in large open-sided sheds, constantly turned to free the lumps and ensure an even exposure to the warm dry air. Gradually the floss becomes fully expanded and dry, and seeds and other foreign bodies are removed. So light and fine is the kapok fibre that the drying sheds are entirely enclosed in small-gauge wire mesh, and the workers turning the floss usually wear masks.

Kapok is a relative newcomer on the international fibre market, having been used commercially for only about 100 years. It has excellent thermal insulation properties and, although slightly inferior to down, it has the advantage of being waterproof and also of not being attacked by insects. The main commercial uses are in insulating and soundproofing applications and in life-saving equipment.

Bamboo
Bambusa spp
Phyllostachys spp

There can be little doubt that bamboo is among the oldest materials used by man—and few natural materials can rival the versatility of this remarkable plant. Its uses range from bridge-building to weaving and from weapons of war to a popular culinary ingredient. The origins of the name bamboo are lost but the plant is mentioned in the writings of Ctesias, court physician to King Artaxerxes Mnemon of Persia in 400 B.C.

The tribe Bambuseae is a member of the huge Gramineae family of grasses—relatives of corn, wheat and barley. All are woody perennials and some giant forms grow to a height of 60ft (18m). The classification of the bamboos is poorly organized; various authorities put the number of species at between 500 and 1000 and the number of genera at 60 or more.

Bamboo is naturally associated in the mind with the hot steaming jungles of Burma and Thailand and the dense forests of southern China. However, more myth than fact surrounded the bamboo until Victorian botanists took an interest in the plants and discovered that these giant tree-grasses were part of a huge family—widespread and by no means entirely tropical.

The bamboo of commerce, however, is the tropical bamboo, the familiar pale yellow or brown cane with its hollow core, characteristic growth rings (nodes) and hard shiny surface, widely used for cane furniture and countless small domestic items from boxes and chopsticks to screens and garden canes.

In the natural state bamboo is an exceptionally fast-growing plant—many species attaining their full height in only six to eight weeks. Three alternative methods are employed in the exploitation of bamboo groves. Selective cutting is labour-intensive, and therefore expensive, but is safe. No damage can be done to the grove. Strip cutting, in which a swathe is cut by machine through the grove, takes out all stems in the machine's path. It is fast, and economical. The third method, clear-cutting, is attractive in the short term but the cleared grove may take 15 years or more to recover fully.

Urena
Urena lobata

The true origins of *Urena lobata* are unknown but the plant is widespread in the tropical and subtropical regions.

Commercial production based on both wild and plantation-grown urena is carried out in Brazil, mainly in the Para region; in Zaire, mainly in Kinshasa province, and in the Malagasy Republic. In recent years trial plantations have been established in Peru, along the tributaries of the Amazon, and in Angola.

Essential oils

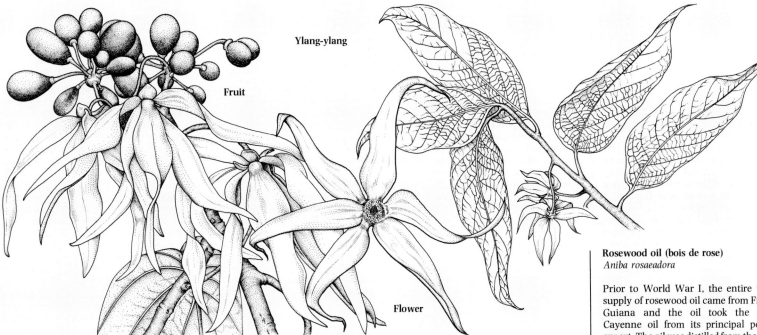

Ylang-ylang

Fruit

Flower

The essential oils are volatile aromatic liquids found in many types of plant tissue. Some are more or less powerful external or internal antiseptics, others have analgesic properties; some are mild sedatives, others act as stimulants; but the main commercial value of the oils today lies in their wide application as scenting and flavouring agents.

Although some oils, for example the citrus oils, may be extracted simply by pressing the fruit, and others, including many of the floral oils, by solution processes, the majority of the commercial oils are extracted from the source material—be it bark, wood, leaf, flower or fruit—by steam-distillation. The process of extraction is a delicate and skilled operation, for many of the oils have an exceptionally complex chemical make-up and some of the constituents are vulnerable to chemical changes during processing, sometimes creating entirely new compounds which may alter the characteristics of the oil. Hence much of the research and development on these oils is directed to ensuring the highest possible standards of purity in the final product and to eliminating causes of deterioration in the period between harvesting and sale.

Oils may be distilled from almost any part of a plant. Bay oil is distilled from the leaves of a tree, and sandalwood oil from wood itself; oil of star anise and the tropical citrus oils are derived from the fruit, nutmeg oil from the seed, and ylang-ylang oil from the flower. In some cases different oils may be distilled from different parts of the same tree.

In terms of capital involved the essential oil industry is small, but at the local level it is an important export currency earner and, indirectly, is of considerable importance to the millions of people worldwide working in manufacturing industries for which these ethereal substances are an essential raw material.

Ylang-ylang oil
Cananga odorata var. *odorata*

Ylang-ylang is one of the most important essential oils and is distilled from the freshly picked flowers of *Cananga odorata*, a tall forest tree native to the Moluccas and found wild, semi-wild and planted in many parts of tropical Asia and the islands of the Indian Ocean. The main producing areas are Malagasy, the Comoro Islands, Réunion and the Philippines.

The tree has an unusually deep tap-root and therefore grows best in deep, loose, fertile and well-drained soil. Plantation trees are planted out from the nursery beds at two years old and are cropped after the fourth year. In the natural state the tree may grow to 100ft (30m) tall but in plantations the trees are cropped to encourage a more lateral growth and to maintain a shape convenient for harvesting the flowers.

Harvesting the flowers demands great care. The blossom is picked by hand in the early hours of the morning when the flowers have their maximum oil content, and only the yellow, fully developed flowers are taken. Bruising must be avoided or the flower turns black and causes fermentation to set in—possibly ruining an entire basket of blossom.

Distillation is very complex and requires expert supervision if the top grades ('Extra' and 'First') are to hold their high commercial value. Ylang-ylang is one of the premier perfume oils; it requires expert handling during the blending process but blends well with jasmine, lilac, gardenia and similar scents, and is one of the key ingredients in many of the French perfumery masterpieces. The entire 'Extra' grade oil is taken by the perfume industry; 'First' and 'Second' largely by cosmetics manufacturers, and the 'Third' grade is used in soap manufacture—usually combined with synthetic aromatics.

Patchouli oil
Pogostemon cablin

About 150 years ago nearly all carpets, rugs and shawls imported from India had a characteristic scent—so typical in fact that for many years the scent itself was widely held to be proof that the merchandise was of Indian origin. But in 1844 a shipment of dried leaves received in London disclosed the source of the scent and very soon French, and other manufacturers, were importing patchouli and using it to very good effect in the promotion of their own woven goods.

Several species of the family Labiatae, or mints, are found in the tropics but only one, *Pogostemon cablin*, yields an essential oil of commercial importance. Patchouli is a herbaceous plant that thrives in the warm damp tropical climate and is best grown on cleared virgin jungle land, as the plant exhausts the soil very quickly. Plantation growth is based on propagation of stem cuttings started in nursery beds and then planted out at four weeks in jungle plots that have been burned off and then allowed to cool for a number of weeks.

The bushy growth quickly reaches 3 to 4ft (90cm to 1.2m) in height, at which point the leaves and young shoots are harvested and spread out to dry in the sun—turned frequently to avoid uneven drying and to avoid too-rapid drying which causes the leaves to crumble with a consequent loss of the oil by evaporation. The main commercial supplies of the oil are from Malaysia, and a small amount from plantations in Brazil.

The dried leaf material is steam-distilled and the resultant oil is then stored for some time to allow its full fine odour to mature. Patchouli is one of the very important perfumery oils. It imparts strength and character to any blend of constituents and has a particularly Oriental character not matched by any other oil.

Rosewood oil (bois de rose)
Aniba rosaeadora

Prior to World War I, the entire world supply of rosewood oil came from French Guiana and the oil took the name Cayenne oil from its principal port of export. The oil was distilled from the hard. heavy pinkish-yellow mahoganylike wood of *A. rosaeadora*, a large evergreen tree common in the vast tropical rain forests of the country. However, reckless and uncontrolled exploitation so reduced the numbers of the tree that the distilleries were forced further and further into the forest regions, and eventually the operation became impossible and the supply of oil virtually ceased.

But by 1932 a new source of rosewood oil had been discovered in the Amazonas and Para regions of the Amazon basin. Here a closely related variety of the tree, var. *amazonica*, was found to be widely distributed. Its wood is grey-yellow with a silky lustre and pleasant odour, and but for minor botanical differences the tree is very similar to its more northerly relative. Initially the same errors were made—primarily that of over-exploitation—but the Brazilian government then introduced cutting restrictions and a requirement that replanting should be undertaken on a one-for-one basis. Nevertheless, exploitation is difficult. Prime trees may be scattered over a wide area, often up to 100 miles from the main river, and so specialist teams are employed by the distillers to seek out suitable trees and cut them during the dry season. The huge logs are then floated down the Amazon tributaries during the months of April to July when the rivers are in flood and the Amazon itself rises 50ft (15m) and floods its banks.

The logs are cut lengthwise and are then reduced to chips by massive fly-wheels armed with sharp blades. The mass is steam-distilled to extract the oil and the pulpy residue is sun-dried and used as fuel for the stills.

Rosewood oil is used extensively by the perfume industry and in many technical preparations, and the oil is also an important source of the main aromatic constituent linaloöl, which is isolated for use in cosmetics and as a flavouring agent.

Eucalyptus oil
Eucalyptus citriodora
Eucalyptus globulus

The huge botanical family of the eucalypts forms nearly three-quarters of the total Australian flora. The genus is typically Australian and although some species are known to be native to New Guinea, Timor and the Philippines, all other areas in which eucalypts are found have been seeded with Australian seed.

Members of the family exhibit great variety in shape and form, from small bushy growths to forest trees of great height, and range from the temperate climate of Tasmania to the dense tropical rain forest of northern Queensland and New Guinea. The eucalypts represent an important natural resource in Australia, for in addition to the essential oils distilled from the leaves of several species, the trees yield good timber, and the wood of a number of species may be processed to yield rutin, used in medicinal preparations, and kinos, a source of excellent tanning material.

One of the most valuable oil-producing trees is the spotted gum, *E. citriodora*, a large tree found in the tropical rain forest of Queensland, especially in the coastal belt.

In its natural form the tree has a tall trunk and small crown, and so estate-grown trees are cropped to encourage a more branching bushy crown, with a consequently higher leaf yield, from which the oil is extracted by distillation. *E. citriodora* is widely used in the perfume industry and forms an important source of the principal constituent, citronella. *E. globulus* leaves yield an oil used in cough medicines and lozenges.

East Indian sandalwood oil
Santalum album

Sandalwood is one of the oldest known perfumery materials and has a recorded history reaching back at least 4,000 years. The oil derived from this aromatic wood was certainly known in Sri Lanka more than 1,000 years ago but was introduced into Europe only within the last century.

The oil is steam-distilled from the coarsely powdered wood of billeted stems and roots of *Santalum album*, a relatively small tree originating in India, Sri Lanka and Indonesia, and also found in Timor and the Celebes. Commercial production of the oil today is mainly from cultivated trees within the original area of distribution, as attempts to introduce the tree to new areas have not been successful.

Wood taken from trees at least 30 years old is sawn, chipped and then coarsely ground before distillation, which produces a soft, pale yellow liquid with a soft, sweet, woody aroma. The oil blends exceptionally well with a wide range of other essential oils and is therefore much in demand throughout the perfume industry.

Oil of cascarilla
Croton eluteria

The spice cascarilla is the ground dried bark of *Croton eluteria*, a small tree or shrub native to the Bahamas.

In finely ground form the bark is used in a number of medicinal preparations, notably in stomachic bitters, which benefit from its warm spicy flavour.

The bark may also be distilled to yield a volatile essential oil characterized by a spicy odour very reminiscent of nutmeg, clove and thyme. This oil is an exceptionally high-priced commodity and is used as a flavouring in very high-quality confectionery and in a number of very popular drinks—notably in aromatic bitters and in Martini.

Oil of lime
Citrus aurantifolia

The lime is probably native to the East Indies, and from there spread to the Asian mainland and to adjacent tropical and subtropical regions. It has been suggested that it reached the west coast of South America (Colombia and Ecuador) via the Pacific Islands, carried by Polynesian seafarers, but a more widely held view is that the lime was introduced to South America in the sixteenth century by Spanish and Portuguese explorers. By whatever route the tree first made its way to the New World, it was a successful emigration and the lime is now distributed extensively throughout the forests of tropical northern South America, Central America and the Caribbean.

In the days of sailing ships the lime was valued for its anti-scurvy properties and hence the earliest lime plantations were developed on the slave routes, first in Antigua and Barbados and later in Dominica and Montserrat. Mexico is now an important lime oil source and Ghana also produces lime oil and juice.

The lime thrives in the Caribbean climate and grows well on the undulating island terrain and particularly on the steep valley sides. Good exposure to the sun and protection from wind are important requirements and therefore plantation trees naturally prove very much more prolific than wild trees, which are usually shaded by taller forest trees. Trees grown from seed are in full production at ten years old and may have a useful life of up to 50 years.

The fruit is picked when fully developed but still green—the fully ripened yellow fruit having a lower oil content. The main products are, in addition to the fresh whole fruit, clear pressed lime juice, lime juice concentrate, distilled oil of lime and citric acid. The chief uses of the lime oil are in the flavouring of non-alcoholic drinks, ice cream, confectionery and sweets, and in the scenting of lower-priced soaps, bath-oils and similar household preparations. Nowadays, the oil is usually a by-product of juice.

Oil of star anise
Illicium verum

The star anise, so named after the delicate starlike shape of its fruit, is a stately evergreen tree found in tropical and subtropical eastern Asia. The slender tree, seldom more than 10in (25cm) in diameter and about 45ft (13.5m) in height, has a white birchlike bark and in shape is similar to the European poplar.

The trees flower throughout the year but the main harvest is taken during the August–October period when the fruits are detached with long poles, or by shaking the tree, or by climbing—the natural form of the tree placing most of the fruiting branches within man's reach from the main stem. Planted trees are first harvested at about 10 years and full commercial production is reached after 15 years, although trees may continue to produce prolifically at 100 years of age.

The fruits are distilled when fresh to yield a delicately flavoured aromatic oil, or may be sun-dried for export as the brown star anise of the drug market. The oil is a major source of anethole, which has a better flavour and odour than the natural oil; it is used in oral pharmaceuticals as a flavouring and as a mild expectorant in cough pastilles; it is a popular flavouring in Mediterranean confectionery and is an important ingredient in absinthe and anisette drinks, and has many further applications as a scenting agent in soaps and cosmetic preparations.

Bay oil
Pimenta racemosa

Bay oil is distilled from the leaves and young shoots of *Pimenta racemosa*, a medium-sized tree native to the West Indies. Commercial production of the oil is centred on Dominica.

The tree grows prolifically in the warm moist climate of the Caribbean Islands and is a common element in the dense rain forest clothing the magnificent volcanic scenery of the islands. A small part of the bay leaf crop is taken from trees growing wild, but more commonly semi-wild plots are created by cutting down the natural forest and undergrowth and encouraging wild seeding from nearby trees. In its natural state the tree grows 60ft (18m) high.

The leaves are usually processed immediately after harvesting and the process of steam-distillation produces a compound distillate. One fraction is heavier than water, the other lighter, and the two are mixed to give the desired oil.

The main consumer of bay oil is the United States and the main user is the perfume industry. The producer areas have benefited greatly in recent years from the tremendous growth in popularity of men's toiletries based on the 'Bay Rum' aroma. Less significantly, the oil is still used to some extent in the preparation of processed foodstuffs, notably in a variety of table sauces.

Oil of petigrain
Citrus aurantium

True petigrain bigarde oil comes from southern France and other Mediterranean countries and is distilled from very carefully selected leaves of the true bitter orange tree *Citrus aurantium* var. *amara*. This oil is, however, extremely expensive and today the bulk of the oil used in the less expensive cosmetics and in soaps is produced in Paraguay.

Originally the sweet orange *Citrus sinensis* and the bitter orange *C. aurantium* were introduced into South America by Spanish Jesuit priests in the seventeenth century. Soil and climate proved ideal in Paraguay and the trees quickly spread beyond the cultivated areas.

The petigrain oil industry was started by a French botanist in 1880 and Paraguay soon became an important supplier to the perfume industry and in particular to the manufacturers of soaps who valued the oil's strong and refreshing smell. The free-growing tree usually has a stout trunk and fully developed rounded crown, but plantation trees, grown from seed, are drastically cut back to keep them in the form of a dense bush. The harvesting of the leaves is made easier this way and leaf-growth is encouraged by the heavy pruning.

A significant proportion of the total crop is taken from wild trees in the forest regions but the methods of collection are crude: branches are simply hacked off and even the whole tree may be felled for the sake of the leaves.

Guaiac oil
Bulnesia sarmienti

The two genuine guaiac woods, *Guaiacum officinale* (Lignum vitae) and *G. sanctum*, are both low on natural oil content and so, rather confusingly, the essential oil marketed as oil of guaiac wood is derived from the heartwood of *Bulnesia sarmienti*, a stunted, crooked and gnarled tree, seldom more than 12ft (3.5m) tall, growing wild and in great abundance in the Gran Chaco—the so-called 'Green Hell' of Paraguay and Argentina.

The trees are cut down, the thick bark and sapwood is removed and the heartwood logs reduced to a coarse dust by flywheel cutters. The dust falls straight into a concrete tank sunk into the ground and partially filled with water—the liquid mass, 25 per cent wood dust and 75 per cent water, forming the charge for the still. The entire still must be kept warm because the oil is naturally solid at room temperature and any drop below its 'flow' temperature would lead to clogging of the still.

The better-quality oil is used in the perfume industry, particularly in rose-scented preparations. Guaiac oil is also noted for its lasting property and hence it is widely used as a fixative for less stable scenting agents.

Gums and resins

The exudates are an important group of natural materials occurring in a large number of tree species in both tropical and temperate regions. Their remarkable properties lend themselves to a wide range of applications from food-processing to the manufacture of golf balls and the waterproofing of fabrics, and from the sizing of paper to the manufacture of items such as chewing gum, paint and varnish.

In the natural state these materials may collect in reservoirs within the tree, or ooze, either spontaneously or in response to some physical injury, from the bark. The gums and resins usually appear as clear, yellow or amber liquids which harden on exposure to air to form translucent lumps or tears, while the latexes flow as opaque milky liquids which eventually harden to a dull grey rubbery mass.

The most familiar exudate, rubber, is obtained by tapping the milky latex of two main producer-trees—*Hevea brasiliensis*, native to the Amazon basin, and *Palaquim gutta*, native to Borneo, Sumatra and the Malay Peninsula. Such is the commercial importance of this forest product that a more detailed treatment of the cultivation and harvesting of rubber is given (pp 168–9).

Copals and dammars

Although tapping is the most widely used method of collection some exudates—notably the dammars and copals—are collected in the form of fossilized or semi-fossilized lumps lying perhaps several feet below ground, having fallen from the tree and been gradually buried. The longer these materials have been in the ground, the higher their quality, and it is quite possible for prime-grade dammar and copal deposits to be found in places where today not a single tree is to be seen.

The copals form a large group of resins characterized by their hardness and high melting points. They are the finest of the natural resins for use in paints and varnishes and are derived mainly from forest trees of the family Leguminosae. Some of the copals are tapped from the living tree but many of the better and more valuable copals are found as fossilized lumps or plates in the earth.

Damar is the Malay word for a resin, or for a torch made from resin, and through years of commercial usage the slightly altered name dammar has been adopted for an important group of Asian resins obtained from trees of the family Dipterocarpaceae.

Unlike the copals, dammars are readily soluble in turpentine and coal-tar hydrocarbons. They are also softer than the copals but are of special value in the making of spirit varnishes because of their solubility and pale hue. They are used for white paper varnishes and white enamels, for wallpapers and interior decorations, and to improve the lustre of cellulose lacquers.

Congo copal
Copaifera demeusei

Since the 1920s Congo copal has been the most highly valued of the African copals. Although some resin is tapped from living trees in the central Zaire basin, the quality is invariably inferior to that of the fossilized copal found up to three feet below ground by native collectors who probe the ground with iron-tipped sticks. The most productive areas are generally found in the marshy forests along the courses of the Congo tributaries, particularly in the Lake Leopold and Stanleyville areas.

Formerly copals were exported from several of the West African coastal states from Sierra Leone to Angola. The source trees also included *Copaifera copallifera* and several species of *Daniellia*, the latter having a very fragrant resin.

South American copal

The South American copals are generally much softer than those of Africa and the East Indies and are consequently of lower value.

Among the several source trees the most important is *Hymenaea courbaril*, a tree also valued for its timber. The tree grows to a height of 100ft (30m) with a straight stem rising above buttress roots. The seeds are enclosed in massive thick-walled pods filled with a sugary resinous pulp, and these nutritious fruits are eaten locally.

The pale yellow or reddish resin of *H. courbaril* oozes from the bark and collects at the base of the tree, often in large quantities, but the ideal collecting spot is at the site of a long-dead large tree; the longer the resin has lain in the ground the harder and clearer it becomes and the higher is its value. Like all copals it has been replaced in many uses by synthetic materials.

East Indian copal
Agathis alba

Unlike most of the other copals, the copal from the East Indies is from one specific tree only. *Agathis alba* is a huge forest tree, up to 200ft (60m) in height, found throughout Malaysia from Sumatra to New Guinea. It is a typical conifer, tall, unbuttressed, straight-stemmed and with a dense conical crown, and is related to the kauri pine of New Zealand.

The gum is collected in fossil form, from accumulations in the branch-forks (where it collects having oozed from cracks caused by storm damage), and by tapping the living tree.

The resin is used locally in the Celebes for making the torches used in night fishing. The copal is softened over a fire and worked into $\frac{1}{2}$in (1.5cm) diameter candles; these are then wrapped in leaves and bound into bundles which burn with a bright, steady flame.

East Indian dammar

Locally the resin is a widely-used raw material. It is applied to boats as a caulking material; it is used in local medicine as a constituent in ointments; it is used in 'batik' work, and is powdered, mixed with wood-dust, and packed into leaves or split bamboo stems for use as an effective torch-light.

Commercially, the most highly valued form is 'Batavian dammar' from western Java and eastern Sumatra. The resin is collected as a dried mass where it has exuded naturally from the bark, and also by tapping healthy trees.

The luxuriant rain forests of Malaysia include many resin-producing species, but the best quality dammar from this region is obtained from *Balanocarpus heimii*, a very abundant though widely dispersed tree and also one of the important timber trees. It is a very slow-growing species and trees which are less than 50 years old are seldom tapped.

The best results are obtained by tapping the upper part of the bole, which is reached by climbing the prolific forest creepers or by hammering bamboo pegs into the sapwood to form a ladder. Several incisions are made in the bark and the tree is then left for several months, by which time the exuded resin has hardened into a characteristic form like a stalactite. The resin is never collected while it is still sticky as this would disrupt the vital hardening and cleaning processes.

Thai dammar

Dammar collection in Thailand is a government-controlled activity. Permits are issued specifying the number of trees each collector may tap and also the size of tree that may be tapped. *Balanocarpus heimii* and the closely related *B. maximus* are two of the main producers but these species are also prized for their attractive and fine-working timbers and many are utilized in the manufacture of quality furniture.

Many species of the genus, *Shorea* and also of the genus *Hopea*, are exploited for their resins although these trees are never tapped—all the resin is collected in the form of natural hardened exudate.

Burmese and Indian dammar

The sal tree, *Shorea robusta*, is one of the dominant trees in the forests of central and northern India. It is an important commercial timber tree and also the source of a light-hued aromatic resin which is used locally as incense, for making torch-lights, and for caulking boats.

Other dammars are exploited for very similar local uses in Burma, the main source trees again being predominantly members of the large genera *Shorea* and *Hopea*.

Pine oleoresin
Pinus spp

Pine oleoresin is a pale gummy fluid, not to be confused with sap, which oozes from the wound when the bark of a pine tree is cut. Turpentine and rosin are obtained either by tapping oleoresin, followed by processing (distillation), or as by-products of the Kraft pulp process. The United States was the major source but the industry is now virtually extinct. Although at present mostly derived from temperate forests, these products are likely to play an increasingly important role in the future commercial exploitation of the world's tropical forests.

In tapping the tree a working face is prepared by taking off the rough outer bark with an axe. A collecting cup and lateral gutters are then fitted at the base of the face, and just above them the first pair of 8in (20cm) long, $\frac{1}{2}$in (1.5cm) deep, angled cuts (streaks) is opened. The oleoresin flows within seconds and is channelled into the cup. After a few days the flow slows and the streak is reopened with a special cutter. The three-pint cup fills in about a month, by which time three or four new cuts will have been opened in a herring-bone pattern, each new cut being about half an inch above the last. In this manner the 32 streaks of a full season's tapping will leave a worked face 16in (40cm) high. The face is then left to heal and a new part of the trunk is opened the following season.

Distillation of the oleoresin involves distilling off the turpentine. The resin remains as a molten residue. The turpentine is used in solvents, paints and varnishes; in the preparation of various oils and greases; in some rubber processes; and most importantly, as a source of raw materials for the chemical industries—constituents of the oleoresin forming the starting materials in the synthesis of many pharmaceutical, perfumery, insecticide and other compounds. The rosin is used in paper size, rubber compounds, adhesives, printing inks and in many other synthetic materials. Annual world production of rosin and turpentine is about $\frac{3}{4}$ and $\frac{1}{4}$ million tonnes respectively. Turpentine is the largest volume essential oil produced in the world.

There are roughly 100 *Pinus* species; all produce oleoresins and many have been tapped commercially—in temperate and tropical areas, and in wild and plantation conditions. As more and more research is carried out into selective breeding, plantation management and methods of improving yields, the development of oleoresin-based industries could become an important factor in the economic growth of the tropical world. Already, some of the truly tropical pines—notably *P. caribaea*, *P. kesiya*, *P. oocarpa* and *P. merkusii*—have shown considerable promise, and several of the subtropical and temperate species show great potential for successful commercial exploitation in tropical rain forest conditions.

Balata
Mimusops globosa

Balata is the coagulated latex of *Mimusops globosa*, a tall, straight-stemmed tree found wild and in abundance in the tropical forests of northern South America. The latex is produced in two forms, from two main source areas.

Sheet balata is produced in the Guianas and Surinam by collectors operating under government licence. Tapping is carried out by cutting a feather-stitch pattern of incisions in the bark, starting at the base and working far up the long unbranching trunk. The milky latex collects in a calabash and is then poured into a shallow tray where it is left to coagulate. Once dry, the successive layers are peeled off, graded, and baled ready for export as sheet balata.

Block balata is the product of the Orinoco valley in Venezuela and particularly of the thickly forested lowland region lying some 100 miles inland from the coast. The area is tropical forest at its most dense. Much of it is unexplored except by the native collectors operating under licence who penetrate the jungle via the mass of interlinking watercourses. Trees along the riverbanks are exploited, but those in the interior are largely inaccessible and this factor, combined with the wasteful method of utilization, has led to an alarming reduction in the number of exploitable trees. As yet no attempt has been made to grow *Mimusops* in plantations but this development is likely to become necessary in the future.

The Venezuelan balata is collected from the tree after it has been felled and the bark scored along each flank of the trunk. The latex is boiled on the spot until it coagulates and is then pressed into the characteristic blocks from which its trade name derives.

By far the most important use of balata is in the manufacture of golf ball covers, no synthetic material having yet proved its equal in toughness, durability and elasticity. The latex is also used to a lesser extent in adhesives (notably for medical plasters), for the waterproofing of fabrics, and for backing cloth used in shoe manufacture.

Gum copaiba (oil of balsam copaiba)
Copaifera spp

Balsam copaiba is the oleoresin obtained from the trunks of several species of *Copaifera*—tall, smooth-stemmed, multi-branched trees that grow wild in the vast tropical rain forests of the Amazon basin and to a lesser extent in Venezuela, Guyana and Colombia.

The oleoresin probably results from the decomposition of parenchyma cells, and cavities within the wood and bark of the trunk enlarge to form reservoirs which commonly hold several gallons of resin. When the stem is tapped, the resin flows as a clear fluid which then thickens and takes on a yellowish hue.

The most important source trees are *C. reticulata* (which accounts for 70 per cent of the Brazilian copaiba) and *C. guianensis* (which accounts for about 10 per cent), several minor producer-trees making up the balance. The major part of the South American output comes from the middle and lower regions of the Amazon basin.

Gum copaiba is collected entirely from wild trees by self-employed native tappers hired season-by-season by the traders and exporters. Good producer-trees may be widely scattered, often days' or weeks' travel from the nearest settlement, but the rewards can be considerable; some of the prime specimens are almost hollow—the trunk like a great vertical pipe containing a vast quantity of resin. Such trees are tapped simply by boring two holes in the trunk, one near the base into which is fitted a bamboo pipe holding a tap, and the other about 20ft (6m) higher. Usually the resin flows easily; if not, a fire at the base of the tree encourages the flow. Most of the tapping is done in the relatively dry season (July to November) as the resin content of the trees is much reduced in the rainy season.

The resin is distilled to produce oil of copaiba—once widely used in medicines but today used chiefly as an odour fixative in soaps, lower-priced cosmetics and technical preparations. The oil has a natural soft scent which masks the harsher tones of many of the synthetic aromatics.

Chicle gum
Achras zapota

The lush jungles of Guatemala and British Honduras may seem an unlikely place to look for chewing gum, but this internationally popular product was once entirely based on the white resinous latex of the sapodilla tree, *Achras zapota*, a native of the forests of Central America.

In Guatemala most of the exported chicle gum is taken from plantation-grown trees, but in Honduras the gum is collected mainly from wild-growing trees found in the more accessible areas of lowland forest. Native collectors, called *chicleros*, work the trees from July to February, often spending the entire season away from their families. Their reward, however, is a relatively high income and a unique status in a country where low income and living standards are the lot of most workers.

Each tree can be tapped only three times during its life and must be left to recover for four years between tappings. A working face up to 30ft (9m) high is prepared by cleaning away loose bark and then cutting a herring-bone pattern of slanting incisions in the bark. The tree usually drains within 24 hours, the viscous fluid flowing from one slash to the next until it collects in a leather pouch attached to the base of the tree at the last cut.

The gum is boiled with water to remove impurities and when judged to be at the right consistency is pressed into wooden moulds lined with leaves. The resulting blocks are stored in caches and then carried by mule or by river to the nearest road for shipment by lorry to the trading centres.

Although a large number of gums, and now many synthetic resins, are used in the manufacture of chewing gum, chicle gum is an excellent base and when mixed with sugar, glucose syrup and the familiar mint or vanilla flavourings, this product of the Central American rain forest is transformed into one of the world's commonest and most popular types of confectionery.

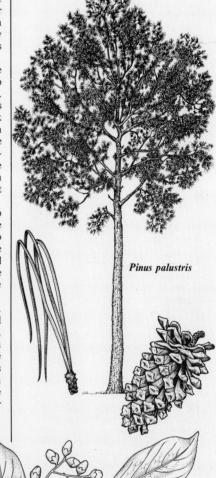

Pinus palustris

Hymenaea courbaril

Agathis alba

Balanocarpus heimii

Pharmaceuticals, tanning agents and dyes

Quite apart from the more obvious forest products—the fruits and timbers, gums and canes, and the spices, oils and dyes—the roots, leaves, stems and flowers of the living forest system represent a vast storehouse of chemical raw materials, comparatively few of which have even been recorded, let alone studied in detail. A single tree might, for example, yield a tanning material from the bark, a dye from the heartwood and a locally important crude drug from the leaves or fruits.

Local practice often provides important clues to the potential value of a plant. The study of vegetable extracts used as dart and arrow poisons by the forest hunters of Africa and South America led to major advances in the use of heart-regulating drugs. The study of fish poisons derived from the Asian climbing plant *Derris* revealed a group of powerful toxins, the most important of which now forms the basis of one of the world's most valuable and widely used insecticides. The drug rauvolfia was used in Indian medicine for centuries and yet only in the last twenty years has its key alkaloid, reserpine, been isolated—providing doctors with an important drug for use in the treatment of hypertension.

The main arguments advanced for the conservation of the tropical forests are that they are the great fixers and regulators of our atmosphere; the primary control on the distribution and stability of our climatic zones, and the last great wilderness 'gene-bank' of animal and plant biology. Perhaps to these should be added the role of the forest as the last great reserve of natural chemicals—most of them as yet undiscovered.

Strychnine
Strychnos spp

Although not nearly so widely used in medicine as it was in the last century, strychnine—a very powerful alkaloid poison—is still in widespread use in the Indo-Malay region as a tonic and stimulant, in the treatment of colic and nervous disorders, and as an emetic. It was formerly widely used in Europe for the treatment of chronic heart disorders, surgical shock and extreme fevers, but advances in medical research proved that there was no firm scientific basis for many of these uses and today the use of the drug has virtually ceased.

Strychnine, however, retains its commercial value as a powerful and effective vermin poison.

The drug is prepared from the dried ripe seeds of the strychnine tree, or snakewood tree, *Strychnos nux-vomica*, a tall straight-stemmed evergreen tree indigenous to the monsoon forests of the western coastal regions of India. In large doses strychnine is a powerful poison, causing death by contraction of the diaphragm and of the muscles of the chest and abdomen. In many parts of Southeast Asia the seeds of *nux-vomica* are used in the preparation of hunting poisons used on the tips of arrows and blowpipe darts.

Diosgenin
(Yam)
Dioscorea spp

Dioscorea is a large genus of annually herbaceous plants distributed throughout the moist tropical zone. Most are characterized by a twisting vinelike growth above ground and large tubers below, some of which—the true yams—are an important food crop.

The yam represents a cheap and plentiful source of carbohydrate food in tropical countries, yet even the best edible varieties must be thoroughly cooked to remove dangerous alkaloids and other toxic compounds. Even the least toxic varieties cause irritation of the throat lining if eaten raw.

Food apart, the yam has many uses. Some species, notably *alata*, are used commercially as a source of starch; some are used for the production of alcohol; others are very rich in vitamins of the 'B' group. The alkaloid dioscorine and the saponin dioscin are extracted from various yams for medicinal use. Dioscorine is abundant in *D. hispida*—and can cause respiratory failure if the yam is inadvertently eaten in large quantity—while *D. deltoidea* is notably rich in saponins, used in the washing of silk and other delicate fabrics and also used throughout the tropics as a fish poison.

Some of the American yam species, *D. composita*, *D. floribunda* and *D. speculiflora*, are used commercially for the production of diosgenin. Diosgenin is an important starting medicine for the production of the birth control pill, sex hormones, anabolic steroids, and a range of corticosteroids used in the treatment of asthma, rheumatoid arthritis and skin disorders.

Ipecacuanha root
Cephaelis ipecacuanha

The drug consists of the dried root of *C. ipecacuanha*, a plant indigenous to the moist tropical forests of Brazil. The plant has also been introduced into Asia with considerable success and ipecacuanha root is now produced commercially in Bengal, Burma and parts of the Malay Peninsula.

The plant produces a slender rhizome bearing tough fibrous roots, many of which become thickened and enlarged, and these form the source of the drug. The whole plant is lifted from the ground with a stick, and after all loose earth has been shaken off, the roots are left to dry in the open air. The root contains a mixture of alkaloids but the most important active agent is emetine, usually making up between 50 per cent and 70 per cent of the total alkaloid content.

Ipecacuanha root is used as an expectorant and emetic but its major application is in the treatment of amoebic dysentery—emetine in concentration of 1 part in 100,000 being fatal to *Entamoeba histolytica*, the amoeba causing the disease.

Strophanthus seeds
Strophanthus kombe

Strophanthus seeds are obtained from a large climbing plant native to eastern tropical Africa in the region of Lake Nyanza and Lake Malawi.

An extract prepared from the seeds is used in the area as an arrow-tip poison, and specimens sent to England in the early 1860s were recognized as an extremely potent cardiac poison. Further investigation resulted in the isolation of the main active constituent, strophanthin, and this was soon accepted by the medical profession as an alternative to foxglove leaves in the treatment of heart complaints.

Like digoxin, the main active agent of the foxglove, the drug slows the rate of the heart-beat, regulates the action of the cardiac muscles and relieves some of the difficulties caused by bad circulation. Unlike digoxin, however, strophanthin does not have a cumulative effect on the body and rarely produces the gastro-intestinal problems which are a troublesome side effect of the use of digoxin.

Reserpine
Rauvolfia spp

Members of the large *Rauvolfia* genus are widely distributed throughout the tropical regions of Asia, Africa and America, but one species in particular has become an important medicinal plant.

For centuries the drug rauvolfia played a major role in the medicine of India and parts of Southeast Asia, but only in the last twenty years has its importance—and particularly the value of its main alkaloid constituent, reserpine—been fully appreciated. It is now widely used in western medicine as a sedative and tranquilizing agent in the treatment of hypertension and chronic mental illness.

The bulk of the supply of reserpine to Europe and America formerly came from India and to a lesser extent from Pakistan, Sri Lanka, Burma and Thailand, but government restrictions in recent years on the export of the crude drug from India led to an urgent search for alternative sources, and today reserpine is being extracted commercially from *R. tetraphylla* in America and from *R. vomitoria* in Africa.

R. serpentina is an erect evergreen shrub, usually about 18in (45cm) high, commonly forming part of the underbrush layer in moist deciduous forest and in the margins of the tropical evergreen forests. *R. serpentina* has proved very difficult to cultivate and the main Indian supply still rests almost entirely on wild plants. The whole plant is uprooted and the stems removed from the root masses which are carefully cleaned of loose soil. Careful handling throughout the collection and drying process is essential as the root bark in particular is rich in the valuable alkaloids.

Quassia
Picraena excelsa

Quassia wood was introduced into the medical world in the mid-eighteenth century as a tonic and stomachic. Although it is now largely replaced by alternative drugs it is still sometimes used as an enema in the treatment of threadworm and as a dusting powder to destroy lice and other parasites.

Initially quassia wood came from *Quassia amara*, a small bushy tree indigenous to northern South America. Later however *P. excelsa*, a lofty bitterwood tree of the West Indies, was found to have very similar properties.

When the tree is felled the trunk and main branches are logged, the bark is removed and the logs are reduced to fine chips or shavings. The shavings are immediately dried in kilns to prevent the growth of moulds which develop rapidly in the moist freshly cut wood.

Today the main use of quassia is as an agricultural and horticultural insecticide in the fight against members of the aphid pest group.

Tuba root/Derris
Derris spp

Plants of the genus *Derris* are mainly woody climbers, distributed throughout the tropics but with their major concentration in Southeast Asia.

The roots of *D. elliptica* and *D. malaccensis* form the source of commercial derris—the raw material from which is prepared a wide range of agricultural and horticultural insecticides, many of which have proved of immense importance in the advancement of tropical agriculture. The two species are grown commercially in Malaysia, Sumatra, Java, Sarawak, the Philippines, Zaire region and to a lesser extent in parts of India.

D. elliptica is a large bushy climbing plant with dense branches and white, pink or red flowers. It is distributed from Chittagong through Burma and Indo-China to Papua New Guinea. This species is the main source of derris.

The roots are harvested after two years when the concentration of toxins is at its highest. Derris owes its insecticidal properties to a group of toxic chemicals called rotenoids—the most powerful of which is rotenone. In parts of southern Asia, derris root is used as a fish poison, one part of the root to 300,000 parts water being sufficient to kill, and in Borneo an extract of the root is used as an ingredient in a potent arrow-tip poison.

Today, derris insecticides are widely used throughout the world for pest control in horticulture, agriculture and in animal husbandry in the form of dusting powders, sprays, dips and aerosols. The agent has been used in combination with pyrethrum against house-flies and also as a moth-proofing agent. When used with animals it is effective against fleas, lice, ticks and a number of other external parasites.

Quinine
Cinchona spp

Some 65 species of evergreen shrubs and trees make up the genus *Cinchona*, most of them indigenous to the forests of South America, particularly to the montane forests of Colombia, Peru, Ecuador and Bolivia. Some species are also cultivated in Java, Sri Lanka, India and Burma and in parts of Africa—primarily for the bark which forms the source of the very important anti-malarial drug quinine.

Four species provide the main commercial supplies of the drug: *C. calisaya* (Peruvian or Calisaya bark), *C. ledgeriana* (Ledger bark), *C. officinalis* (Crown or Loxa bark) and *C. succirubra* (Red bark).

The trees are grown at altitudes between 3,000 and 6,000ft in conditions of high average temperature, constant high humidity and high average rainfall well distributed throughout the year. Virgin forest soil is preferred and the trees, once established in nursery beds, are planted out in strips cleared in the forest with intervening strips of shade trees left standing.

Harvesting begins after about four years although maximum production of the alkaloid content is not reached until the tree is ten to twelve years old. Branches are cut off and discarded and the roots, with about 5ft (1.5m) of the main stem, are taken out, cleaned and the bark carefully stripped off and dried to avoid fermentation setting in. As the alkaloids are formed during descent of the sap, the alkaloid content of the leaves and outer branches is low.

The total alkaloid content is made up of several medicinally valuable alkaloids of which the most important is quinine—extracted in the form of quinine sulphate. This drug is the oldest and still the most effective in the treatment and prevention of malaria and is consequently one of the most important elements in tropical medicine. Quinine also has marked bacteriological properties and until recently was widely used in the treatment of bacteriological infections, including pneumonia. It was also formerly used as a substitute for cocaine as an anaesthetic. A second alkaloid, quinidine, is used in heart treatments.

In addition to the major medicinal uses, quinine is used in soft drinks as a bitter and, with its associated alkaloids, has been used in insecticide preparations. The residual mass left after extraction of the alkaloids has been used in a number of industrial processes including metal working and the manufacture of anti-corrosive paints.

Gambier
Uncaria gambir

Although widely used locally as a drug, notably in the treatment of diarrhoea, in which form it was first introduced into Europe toward the close of the eighteenth century, the medicinal uses of gambier are today insignificant. For a period the material was used as a source of tannin but it has been superseded by synthetic chemicals. Chemicals of mineral origin have now largely replaced the natural tanning materials in modern tanneries.

Gambier is prepared by the careful evaporation of a decoction made by boiling the leaves and young shoots of the climbing shrub *Uncaria gambir*. The plant is native to the Malay Peninsula and to the islands of the East Indies, and gambier production is based, in the main, on *U. gambier* grown in plantations in clearings hacked out of the virgin jungle, generally close to sea level. The first crop is usually taken two years after planting and the plant will continue to yield a good crop for about twenty years.

Cutch
Acacia catechu

Like gambier, with which it has sometimes been confused due to the use, for both drugs, of the name *catechu*, cutch was probably first used for its remedial properties and only later for tanning.

The tree is native to India and Burma where it is valued as a source of high-grade timber. To obtain the drug, the dark-red heartwood alone is reduced to chips and boiled with water. The liquor is then boiled down in iron cauldrons until it thickens, at which point it is poured out onto leaf mats to dry into hard slabs. For the preparation of the valuable tanning material, the bark and sapwood are used—reduced to chips and boiled, and then allowed to stand so that the solid material can separate out of the fluid. Although widely used in the tanning of hides, cutch is also commonly used for the tanning of fishing nets to render them more resistant to deterioration through rotting.

The name cutch is in widespread and fairly loose use for a wide variety of extracts, among which are two more important tanning materials—the mangrove cutch extracts from *Rhizophora mangle* and *Ceriops candolleana*.

Gamboge
Garcinia hanburyi

The commercial dye gamboge is prepared from a natural exudate of the tree *Garcinia hanburyi*, formerly thought to be a variety of the Indian gamboge tree *G. morella* but it has since been recognized as a distinct species.

G. hanburyi, source of the commercial dye, is distributed throughout Thailand, Burma, Kampuchea (Cambodia), the East Indies, Sri Lanka, and parts of southern India.

The exudate is collected by making a spiral cut in the bark and attaching a bamboo cup at the base to collect the yellowish fluid. Trees at least ten years old are selected and the tapping is carried out at the start of the rainy season. The juice is allowed to harden in the cup, usually for about one month, then the container is gently heated and the solidified gamboge is removed as a stick or 'pipe'.

Gamboge is reddish-yellow or brown-orange, forming a deep-yellow emulsion with water. It is highly esteemed as a pigment due to the unique brilliance of its hue and is consequently the prime ingredient in many of the best paints, in golden spirit varnishes used for metals and, in Thailand, in a remarkable golden-yellow ink used on black paper. Perhaps the most familiar use of all to Western eyes is to be found in Burma and Thailand where the dye gamboge imparts its vivid hue to the silken robes of Buddhist monks.

The *Garcinia* genus includes many trees and shrubs distributed throughout the tropical regions of Asia, Africa and the Pacific. Many yield dyes and extracts used in local medicine, and several produce edible fruits; among the latter is *G. mangostana*, the mangosteen, widely regarded as the finest of all tropical fruits.

Sappanwood
Caesalpinia sappan

This small tree or shrub is native to southern India, Sri Lanka, Burma and Malaysia and its rich orange-red heartwood is the source of the dye sappanwood, used in the coloration of silk, cotton and woollen fabrics.

To extract the pigment, the heartwood is reduced to chips or rasped to a coarse powder and then steeped twice in hot water. The deep-orange extract is allowed to ferment in the vat, during which time chemical changes occur in the liquor and the main constituent *brazilin* (yellow) is oxidized to *brazilein* (deep red).

When used with cotton fabrics the dye gives a bright reddish-orange hue; when mixed with indigo for the dyeing of cotton or wool, the blended dye produces rich tones of purple.

Extract of sappanwood also has some remedial properties and the preparation is used medicinally in parts of India for the treatment of dysentery and for alleviating some skin ailments.

The same constituents—*brazilin* oxidizing to *brazilein*—are found in the dye brazilwood produced by a very similar method from the heartwood of *C. brasiliensis*.

Red sanderswood
Pterocarpus santalinus

The small tree *Pterocarpus santalinus*, native to southern India and the East Indies, provides a dyeing agent unusual in the very restricted nature of its use.

Once the thick bark and pale sapwood have been removed, the irregularly shaped billets of dark-red heartwood are reduced to chips or coarse shavings and processed to yield an intense red dye—insoluble in water but readily soluble in alcohol. The sole use of this coloration is in the preparation of alcoholic drinks.

Logwood
Haematoxylon campechianum

The dye derived from the dense heartwood of the logwood tree was almost certainly known to the people of Mexico at the time of the Spanish conquest, for very soon after Cortez' return there are records of the dye being used in Europe.

The tree is native to the mainland of Central America but has also become established throughout the West Indian islands. The wood is exported in the form of heartwood logs and billets—all sapwood and bark being stripped off, as it contains none of the dyeing agents. The outer surface of the wood is dark orange-red varying to purple, while freshly cut surfaces are a rich red-brown. The extraction of the dye follows the same method as most wood dyes; the hard, heavy billets are reduced to chips and then steeped to remove the active principles. It was formerly common for the wood chips to be piled into heaps, moistened and allowed to ferment for several weeks before being placed in the vats. Today, the necessary oxidizing processes can more easily be initiated by the addition of chemicals.

The main use of logwood extract is as a dye for fabrics and for the coloration of ink. The dye is also used in laboratory work as a staining agent in the study of microscopic sections of organic material, notably in the study of cellulose tissues.

Annatto
Bixa orellana

The source of the rich orange-red dye annatto is a small tree, *Bixa orellana*, native to tropical America and widely cultivated in Brazil, Guyana, Mexico and the Antilles. The species has also been successfully introduced into parts of India where it is now naturalized.

B. orellana occurs in two forms, one having white flowers and green seed capsules, while the other bears pink flowers and red capsules. Each capsule contains about 50 seeds, the pulpy covering of which contains the pigment materials. To extract the dye, the seeds are bruised and mixed with hot water, and then left to soak for several days, after which the pigment forms a fine suspension in the liquid. The seeds are then removed and the liquid *brei* is allowed to ferment for about a week; the orange-red dye settles to the bottom of the vat and the excess liquid is drained off. The dye is variously sold as cakes, tablets or as a paste.

Annatto was formerly widely used for dyeing silk and cotton but as the dye is not fast it was overtaken by alternative dyes and particularly the modern synthetic dyes. However, annatto has the advantage of being non-toxic and is therefore still in demand for the coloration of foodstuffs, notably butter, ghee, margarine and confectionery. The dye is also used in polishes, in hair oils and in a wide range of toiletries.

Houseplants

Ever since the Chinese made the first documented gardens in about 2000 B.C., man has been concerned with growing plants for their aesthetic qualities as well as vital providers of food and other materials essential to survival. The art of indoor gardening also has its origins in ancient Eastern culture, but it was not until the 'expedition explosion' of the eighteenth and nineteenth centuries that a wide selection of evergreen tropical plants were adopted for indoor use and found to thrive. Today hardly a home is without some tropical species or another, albeit in conditions far less lavish than the conservatories erected by the Victorians to house their plant treasures.

Many of the plants introduced in a bygone age are still very much in evidence. Brought from China early in the nineteenth century, the *Aspidistra* has proved to be one of the most durable houseplants, hence its common name of cast-iron plant, earned originally from its ability to survive the dark, smoky conditions of the Victorian parlour.

Expeditions to the lush islands of the Malagasy Republic and Southeast Asia in the mid-eighteenth century returned with specimens of the screw pine, *Pandanus*, just one of the many trees reaching 50ft (15m) or more in the wild, but of manageable proportions when grown in a pot. Among tropical jungle trees, many species of the fig, *Ficus*, have proved very successful for greenhouse and indoor cultivation. Best known of them all is *F. elastica*, the ubiquitous India rubber plant. Not all tropical figs are trees—the popular creeping fig, *F. pumila*, is a trailer.

Many splendid members of the arum family (Araceae) were brought from the tropical jungles of South America in the eighteenth century. Most notable of these is the Swiss cheese plant, *Monstera deliciosa*, with its deeply lobed leaves perforated, in mature specimens, with gruyèrelike holes. From the same family come plants with exotic flowers made up of a cloak or spathe surrounding a clublike structure, the spadix, bearing tiny flowers. The bright red cloaks of *Anthurium andraeanum* last for weeks on end. Other aroids include many fine philodendrons, mostly green but in a variety of leaf sizes and shapes on plants of different forms. Above-ground (aerial) roots used for holding on to tree bark are a natural feature of many aroids.

Perhaps the most fascinating of all jungle plants to have reached the living room are the bromeliads, many of which grow naturally as epiphytes on the branches of tropical trees, housing a tank of water within a rosette of leaves. The bromeliad houseplants are rosette-formers, either with bright foliage or complex flowers and bracts—*Aechmaea* is a splendid combination of the two.

Despite the size of the houseplant industry, many of the plants offered for sale in pots are cuttings that actually started their lives as part of a mature tropical tree. Opposite is a selection of easily available examples.

Philodendron
Philodendron bipinnatifidum
FAMILY: Araceae
ORIGIN: tropical South America

A giant tropical species with many fingered, glossy, mid-green leathery leaf blades to 3ft (90cm) long with reddish-brown veins. The leaves have long stalks that radiate from a stout central trunk that can reach 25ft (7m) in time. As in its natural surroundings, and like other *Philodendron* species, this one thrives in peaty, open compost that never becomes excessively dry. Old plants occasionally develop flowers.

Philodendron
Philodendron hastatum
FAMILY: Araceae
ORIGIN: Brazil

One of the finest members of the arum family, with attractive arrow-shaped leaves to 1ft (30cm) long of a glossy dark-green. A fast grower, it needs a big pot to accommodate its stout stems that can attain a height of 15ft (4.5m). These stems are vinelike and do not actually climb but need and will lean against a support. This philodendron can grow best in high humidity—in hot weather its leaves will benefit from being sprayed.

Sweetheart vine, Parlour ivy
Philodendron scandens (= *oxycardium*)
FAMILY: Araceae
ORIGIN: tropical South America

The small, heart-shaped, deep-green leaves, each 5 to 12in (12 to 30cm) long, that give the sweetheart vine its name also make it the most popular houseplant in its family. In the jungle because of its comparatively small size—to about 10ft (3m)—it plays a less prominent role than other philodendrons. Its thin stems can easily be persuaded to climb or trail.

Anthurium
Anthurium andraeanum
FAMILY: Araceae
ORIGIN: tropical America (SW Colombia)

Dark-green oblong leaves, heart-shaped at their base and 1ft (30cm) long, borne on 2ft (60cm) stalks, radiate from the centre of this plant whose main attraction is its flowers. Each exotic bloom consists of a vivid red or rose-pink cloak or spathe, with a waxen almost artificial look, surrounding a clublike spadix bearing tiny flowers. As in the forest, an *Anthurium* demands constant air humidity of more than 50 per cent, a minimum temperature of about 70 degrees Fahrenheit and a position of partial shade.

Swiss cheese plant, Mexican bread fruit
Monstera deliciosa
FAMILY: Araceae
ORIGIN: South Mexico, Guatemala

An unmistakable plant with huge green leaves to 4ft (1.2m) deeply cut along their margins and, in larger specimens, with decorative perforations. On big plants short-lived flowers made up of a big, thick spike surrounded by a white boat-like spathe are followed by fruit richly flavoured when ripe (hence the name *deliciosa*) but stinging the mouth.

White sails
Spathiphyllum patinii 'Mauna Loa'
FAMILY: Araceae
ORIGIN: tropical South America

Superb plants with exquisite flowers, each with a snowy-white spathe, carried on 2ft (60cm) stalks. The spear-shaped leaves about 6in (15cm) long are abundant if the air humidity is high and the temperature around 70 degrees Fahrenheit.

Urn plant
Aechmaea rhodocyanea (= *Billbergia rhodocyanea*)
FAMILY: Bromeliaceae
ORIGIN: tropical South America

Broad silver-grey banded leaves to 3ft (90cm) long overlap at their base to form a natural watertight rosette. The 'urn' at the rosette's centre is a natural water reservoir and indoors must be kept topped up regularly. Flowers, only occurring in older plants, have a brush of spectacular pink bracts from which small bright blue flowers emerge.

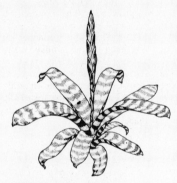

Flaming sword
Vriesea splendens
FAMILY: Bromeliaceae
ORIGIN: tropical South America

Forms a water-holding rosette of deep-green leathery leaves each about 3ft (90cm) long, attractively cross banded in deep purple. From a swordlike flower head made up of overlapping fiery red bracts a small yellow flower eventually emerges, the whole structure measuring up to 2ft (60cm) in length. As in all bromeliads the leaf rosette dies with the flower but new shoots develop at the base.

Rose grape
Medinilla magnifica
FAMILY: Melastomaceae
ORIGIN: Java, Philippines

A spectacular plant for a heated greenhouse with stiff, spreading branches bearing smooth, elliptical boldly veined leaves. Drooping clusters of soft pink flowers, rather like miniature chandeliers, are produced with greatest profusion in summer. It will eventually reach 4ft (1.2m) in height.

Fiddle leaf fig

Ficus lyrata (= *pandurata*)
FAMILY: Moraceae
ORIGIN: tropical West Africa

A dramatic evergreen with huge, dark-green glossy leaves up to 15in (35cm) long and 10in (25cm) wide, each shaped like the body of a violin—hence the plant's common name. Juvenile plants of the species have a single main stem but in time branches radiate from it and provide an important feature of the plant. In the right conditions—light shade, warmth and moisture, with copious water and regular feeding in the growing season, the stem will grow to 10ft (3m) over a period of several years.

Banyan tree

Ficus benghalensis
FAMILY: Moraceae
ORIGIN: India, Sri Lanka

The sacred banyan tree of India is an extremely vigorous and quick grower only suitable for rooms or conservatories offering ample space for development—even outside their native jungle these plants will grow to 20ft (6m) or more. The leathery elliptical leaves attain a length of 8 to 10in (20 to 25cm) and are dark green with ivory-hued veins. Unlike many tropical evergreens the foliage is downy rather than glossy. Choose a large pot at least 1ft (30cm) in diameter for an established plant. Feed the plant frequently when it is in active growth and place it in partial shade.

India rubber tree, Rubber plant

Ficus elastica
FAMILY: Moraceae
ORIGIN: East Asia

One of the best-known indoor, forest plants with a straight, dark stem and thick, glossy, leathery, elliptical dark-green leaves 1ft (30cm) long by 4 to 6in (10 to 15 cm) wide, each unfolding from a rosy-pink sheath. Current favourite among the many commercially bred varieties is the broader-leaved 'Robusta' which is more vigorous than the variety 'Decora' which it has superseded. It will reach a height of 6ft (1.8m).

Joseph's coat, Croton

Codiaeum (= *Croton*) *variegatum* 'pictum'
FAMILY: Euphorbiaceae
ORIGIN: Sri Lanka, India, East Indies

Like the Biblical coat from which it gets its name this species is prized for its brilliant hues. The leathery, glossy, oval or lance-shaped leaves may be all varieties of green, yellow, orange, red, bronze, purple, pink or any combination of these shades. In tropical sun the plants are much more vigorous and their hues much more intense than they are indoors, but they can still reach 3ft (90cm) or more in perfect conditions of high temperature (above 60 degrees Fahrenheit in winter), good light (but not direct sunlight) and meticulous attention to both watering and feeding.

Zebra plant, Maranta

Calathea zebrina
FAMILY: Marantaceae
ORIGIN: Brazil

Growing to a height of 3ft (90cm) zebra plants have wonderfully patterned elliptical leaves each 1–2ft (30–60cm) long that resemble an exquisitely patterned piece of velvet. The 'body' of the leaf is dark green, the pattern composed of bars of yellow- and olive-green extending outwards from the leaf's central vein (midrib). The underside of each leaf is a deep reddish-purple. This plant rarely flowers indoors but in its natural surroundings bears clusters of small white flowers. In ideal conditions—good light but not direct sunshine, even temperatures above 65 degrees Fahrenheit, fast draining peaty soil and high humidity—it will grow vigorously. New plants can easily be obtained by dividing older clumps into sections when they are repotted, cutting through the underground rhizomes.

Kentia palm, Sentry palm

Howea (= *Kentia*) *belmoreana*
FAMILY: Palmaceae
ORIGIN: Lord Howe Island

A feather palm reaching some 60ft (18m) in its home off Australia, but seldom more than 10ft (3m) when its roots are confined to a container. The leaves, each up to 18in (45cm) long, on a stalk of equal length, are made up of narrow, grasslike leaflets. The feathery effect is given by the fanning out of the leaflets and arching of the leaf stalks. The trunk of the palm is a clean shade of green ringed with yellowish scars made by the stalk ends of fallen leaves. Indoors these palms need full sunshine in winter, some shade in summer and a minimum temperature of about 45 degrees Fahrenheit. This is a slow growing species and does best if potted in heavy, humus-rich soil that is never allowed to become waterlogged.

Umbrella tree, Octopus tree

Schlefflera actinophylla
FAMILY: Araliaceae
ORIGIN: Australia, Java, East Indies

A tropical ivy that gets the name 'umbrella' from the way its giant leaves are held. Long-stalked leaves, each made up of 7 to 16 elliptical 1ft (30cm) leaflets spread in an umbrellalike shape are arranged in horizontal tiers. The name 'octopus' comes from the odd configuration of the narrow dark-red flower heads which are followed by tiny deep-purple fruits. The plant will grow to about 10ft (3m) or more indoors.

Screw pine

Pandanus veitchii
FAMILY: Pandanaceae
ORIGIN: Polynesia

The true screw pine, *Pandanus utilis*, is named in the vernacular from the way in which the bases of the leaves twist round the plant's stem. The tough linear leaves of *P. veitchii* are dark green, variegated in yellowish-white along their edges and armed at their margins with wickedly sharp spines. This plant will reach 3ft (90cm) indoors. In the forest, *P. utilis* grows support roots from its stem which act rather like tent guy ropes by keeping it firmly anchored to the ground.

Mother-in-law's tongue

Sansevieria trifasciata
FAMILY: Liliaceae
ORIGIN: tropical West Africa

A stiff rosette of erect sword-shaped leaves, each to 4ft (1.2m) long with mottled horizontal bands of grey-green are incredibly durable and make this *Sansevieria* suitable for situations that few other tropical imports can match. In tropical regions millions of plants are grown annually and then shipped to temperate climates simply as leaves with a piece of rhizome (swollen underground stem) attached, without roots or soil. Rooting is done at the nursery destination and plants grown in very light and warm greenhouses with the principal emphasis on dry root conditions. By a series of breeding programmes the variety 'Laurentii' has been bred with broad yellow leaf margins, and this is the type most commonly seen. There is also a dwarf form 'Hahnii' with triangular 6in (15cm) leaves.

Silhouette plant

Dracaeana marginata
FAMILY: Liliaceae
ORIGIN: Malagasy Republic

Erect, slim, smooth grey stems that can eventually reach 12ft (3.6m) are topped by crowns of leathery, grasslike leaves each up to 2ft (60cm) long. These leaves are a shade of deep glossy green striped in shades of cream and pink or with a narrow outer edge of deep reddish-purple. As it increases in height the lower leaves are shed, leaving V-shaped marks up the stem. The full hues of the leaves will only develop in good light. Other needs are average—but not excess—water. If the plant gets too tall the crown can be cut off and new leaves will grow from the base.

Index

Index

Acknowledgments

The Publishers wish to thank the photographers and agencies listed below for their help in providing material for this book. The following abbreviations have been used: *tl top left, ct centre top, tr top right, cl centre left, cr centre right, bl bottom left, bc bottom centre, br bottom right.*

Cover: Marion Morrison
1 Abril; 2/3 Robert Harding Associates/Photo: R.B. Burbidge; 4/5 Colorific!/Photo: John Moss; 6 Ardea Photographics/Photo: J. Van Gruisen; 8 *Reise des Prinzen von Neuwied in Brasilien*, published by Henry Colburn & Company, 1820; 8/9 P. Morris; 10 A.A.A. Photo/Photo: De Hesse; 11*b* Nigel Press Associates Ltd/Earthsat Data Centre; 12*l* Ecology Pictures/Photo: John Proctor; 12*r* Dr Edward S. Ross; 13 Alan Hutchison Library; 14/15 Dr Edward S. Ayensu; 15*t* Dr Edward S. Ross; 15*cl* Mary Evans Picture Library; 15*c* Mary Evans Picture Library; 15*br A Naturalist on the River Amazon* by H.W. Bates, published by John Murray, 1864; 16 Photo Researchers Inc/Photo: John Moss; 17 all pictures: Mary Evans Picture Library; 18/19 Susan Griggs Agency/Photo: Dr Ivan Polunin; 19 all pictures: Mary Evans Picture Library; 21 Mansell Collection; 22/23 European Space Operations Centre, Darmstadt; 24 Tony Morrison; 26 Dr Michael Lock; 27 Abril; 28/29 Dr Edward S. Ross; 33 Dr T.C. Whitmore; 34 Michael Freeman; 36 Tony Morrison; 37*l* Leslie McGowan; 37*r* Dr T.C. Whitmore; 38*tl* Dr P.W. Richards; 38*tr* & *bl* Dr Michael Lock; 38*br* Dr P.W. Richards; 39*t* Dr P.W. Richards; 39*bl* Dr Edward S. Ross; 39*br* Marion Morrison; 40 Dr P.W. Richards; 41 Dr Edward S. Ross; 43*tl* P. Morris; 43*tr* Royal Botanical Gardens, Kew/Grey Herbarium, Harvard; 43*b* Dr Edward S. Ross; 44 Dr Dransfield; 45*l* Dr Michael Lock; 45*r* Dr Edward S. Ross; 46 Dr P.W. Richards; 47*tl, tr, b* Dr Edward S. Ross; 48 Tony Morrison; 49*t* Dr Edward S. Ross; 49*cl* Dr Dransfield; 49*b* Ding Hou; 50 Tony Morrison; 51*t* Marion Morrison; 51*b* Dr T.C. Whitmore; 55 Ardea Photographics/Photo: Hans & Judy Bestee; 56 Photo Researchers Inc/Photo: Paul Crum; 59 Bruce Coleman Ltd; 60 Jacana/Photo: Philip Barim; 62 N.H.P.A./Photo: Dr Ivan Polunin; 64*tl* Photoresources; 64*br* John Mason; 65 Dr Edward S. Ayensu; 66 Bruce Coleman Ltd/Photo: Jane Burton; 67 Alan Hutchison Library/Photo: Dr Nigel Smith; 69 Biofotos/Photo: Heather Angel; 70 Bruce Coleman Ltd/Photo: Michael Freeman; 71 Jacana; 74 Bruce Coleman Ltd/Photo: Lee Lyon; 78 Michael Freeman; 79*t* Mary Evans Picture Library; 79*c* Yves Lanceau; 80 Tony Morrison; 81 Mary Evans Picture Library; 84 Jacana; 87*t* Jacana/Photo: Ziesler; 87*b* Ardea Photographics/Photo: Peter Steyn; 89*tl* Ardea Photographics/Photo: M.D. England; 89*tr* Photo Researchers Inc/Photo: Walter E. Harvey; 89*b* Jacana/(Collection Varin–Visage); 91*l* Ardea Photographics/Photo: Don Hadden; 91*r* Ardea Photographics/Photo: Trounson & Clampett; 92 N.H.P.A./Photo: Roy D. Mackay; 94 Michael Holford Photographs/Photo: Ianthe Rathven; 95 Bruce Coleman Ltd/Photo: Joseph van Wormer; 96 Bruce Coleman Ltd/Photo: Bruce Coleman; 97*l* Bruce Coleman Ltd/Photo: Rod Williams; 97*r* Bruce Coleman Ltd/Photo: Francisco Erize; 100 Jacana/Photo: Ziesler; 101*l* Photo Researchers Inc/Photo: F. Gohier; 101*r* Photo Researchers Inc/Photo: A.W. Ambler; 102*l* Jacana/Photo: Jean-Michel Labat; 102*r* Ardea Photographics/Photo: P. Morris; 103 Ardea Photographics/Photo: Avone Tilford; 104 Ardea Photographics/Photo: Adrian Warren; 105 Ecology Pictures/Photo: M.P.L. Fogden; 106 Photo Researchers Inc/Photo: John J. Bangma; 107*t* Bruce Coleman Ltd/Photo: E.R. Dawson; 107*b* Bruce Coleman Ltd/Photo: Mike Price; 108 Dr Edward S. Ross; 112 N.H.P.A./Photo: Stephen Dalton; 113*tl* Bruce Coleman Ltd/Photo: Walter Schmidt; 113*tr* Mansell Collection; 113*b* Dr Edward S. Ayensu; 116*t* Bruce Coleman Ltd/Photo: G. Ziesler; 116*b* Dr Edward S. Ross; 117*t* Kjell B. Sandved; 117*b* Ardea Photographics/Photo: Su Gooders; 118*t* & *b* Dr Edward S. Ross; 119*t* Kjell B. Sandved; 119*b* Bruce Coleman Ltd/Photo: Peter Ward; 120*t* John Mason; 120*b* Oxford Scientific Films; 121 Jinny Johnson; 122*t* Dr David J. Stradling; 122*b* Oxford Scientific Films; 123 Oxford Scientific Films/Animals Animals/Photo: Raymond Mendez; 125*t* & *b* Oxford Scientific Films; 126/127 Oxford Scientific Films; 128 Vision International/Photo: Anthony Bannister; 129*t* Bruce Coleman Ltd/Photo: H. Rivarola; 129*b* Bruce Coleman Ltd/Photo: M.P.L. Fogden; 132–133 Bruce Coleman Ltd/Photo: M.P. Kahl; 134 Sean R. Edwards; 135 Dr Edward S. Ayensu; 138 Dr Edward S. Ross; 140 Dr Edward S. Ross; 141 Marion Morrison; 142 Tony Morrison; 143*tl* & *tr* Biofotos/Photo: Heather Angel; 143*bl* Dr Michael Lock; 143*br* P. Morris; 145*tl* Dr Dransfield; 145*r* N.H.P.A./Photo: James H. Carmichael Jr.; 145*bl* Ardea Photographics/Photo: Adrian Warren; 147*tl* Dr T.C. Whitmore; 147*r* Bruce Coleman Ltd/Photo: M.P.L. Fogden; 147*bl* Kjell B. Sandved; 148/149 Susan Griggs Agency/Photo: Victor Englebert; 150*bl* Susan Griggs Agency/Photo: Richard Laird; 150*br* Susan Griggs Agency/Photo: Victor Englebert; 151 Alan Hutchison Library/Photo: Moser/Tayler; 152 Alan Hutchison Library/Photo: W. von Puttkamer; 153 Alan Hutchison Library/Photo: Moser/Tayler; 154 Photo Researchers Inc/Photo: Claudia Andujar; 155*t* & *b* Alan Hutchison Library/Photo: W. von Puttkamer; 156*tl* Alan Hutchison Library/Photo: W. von Puttkamer; 156*tr* Alan Hutchison Library; 157 Robert Harding Associates; 158 Explorer/Photo: Guy Philippart de Foy; 159*tl* Dr Edward S. Ross; 159*tr* & *b* Alan Hutchison Library; 160*l* Photo Researchers Inc/Photo: Victor Englebert; 160*tr* Alan Hutchison Library/Photo: Moser; 160*br* Robert Harding Associates; 161 Photo Researchers Inc/Photo: Toby Bankett Pyle; 162*tl* BBC Hulton Picture Library; 162*r* Picture Researchers Inc/Photo: Robert W. Hernandez; 163*tl, cl, b* Royal Anthropological Institute Photographic Collection; 163*tr* BBC Hulton Picture Library; 163*cr* Mansell Collection; 164*tl* & *tr* Mary Evans Picture Library; 165*tl* & *tr* Mary Evans Picture Library; 166 Explorer/Photo: M. Moisnard; 167 P. Morris; 168 Dr Michael Lock; 169*tl* Tony Morrison; 169*tr The Great Navigators of the 18th Century* by Jules Verne, published by Sampson Low, Marston, Searle & Rivington, 1880; 169*b* Dr Edward S. Ross; 170*t* & *b* Ann Ronan Picture Library; 171 Alan Hutchison Library; 172 P. Morris; 173 Alan Hutchison Library/Photo: W. von Puttkamer

The authors contributed text as follows:

Dr T.C. Whitmore: 8–21, 26–27, 166–67

Dr Michael Lock: 22–25, 30–51, 132–47, 168–69,

Dr D.M. Stoddart: 28–29, 52–83, 88–93, 98–103, 148–63, 174–75

Dr Bryan Turner: 84–87, 94–97, 104–31

Professor P.W. Richards: 172–73

Professor E.S. Ayensu: 170–71

Products of the Jungle (pp 176–95) was compiled by Martyn Bramwell with the assistance of:
Director, Librarian and following staff members of the Tropical Products Institute, London: Dr Clinton Green, Dr K. Jewers, Dr Cyril Jarman; and at the Tropical Products Institute, Culham Laboratory, Oxfordshire: A.E. Chittenden and Dr Simon Robbins.
Timbers: Fred Hughes, Department of Forestry, University of Oxford.
Houseplants: William Davidson, House of Rochford.

Additional artwork was provided by:
Tony Graham, Arka Cartographics Limited, Harry Clow, Ingrid Jacob and Alan Suttie.

The Publishers received invaluable help during the preparation of **The Life and Mysteries of the Jungle** from:
Ruth Binney, Keggie Carew, Marsha Lloyd, John Porter and Alison Tomlinson, who gave editorial assistance;
Ann Kramer, who compiled the index; Barbara Anderson; Barbara Bentley of Survival International; Robert DeFilipps of the Office of Biological Conservation, Smithsonian Institution; Candy Lee; Nigel O'Gorman; Joyce Pope; Royal Botanic Gardens, Kew.

Typesetting by Servis Filmsetting Limited, Manchester
Origination by Gilchrist Brothers Limited, Leeds

Copyright © 2012 by NordSüd Verlag AG, CH-8005 Zürich, Switzerland.
First published in Switzerland under the title *Jagd auf den Lebkuchenmann*.
English text copyright © 2012 by North-South Books Inc., New York 10016.

First published in the United States, Great Britain, Canada, Australia, and New Zealand in 2012 by North-South Books, Inc., an imprint of NordSüd Verlag AG, CH-8005 Zürich, Switzerland.

Designed by Christy Hale.
Distributed in the United States by North-South Books Inc., New York 10016.
Library of Congress Cataloging-in-Publication Data is available.
ISBN: 978-0-7358-4086-7 (trade edition).
1 3 5 7 9 • 10 8 6 4 2
Printed in Germany by Grafisches Centrum Cuno GmbH & Co. KG, 39240 Calbe, April 2012.

FSC
www.fsc.org
MIX
Paper from
responsible sources
FSC® C043106

The Gingerbread Man

Béatrice Rodriguez

NorthSouth
New York / London

Once upon a time, a little old woman and a little old
man lived in a cottage. One day the little old woman made

a gingerbread man. She gave him currants for eyes and cherries for buttons. She put him in the oven to bake.

The little old woman and the little old man were very hungry
and wanted to eat the gingerbread man. As soon as he was baked
the little old woman opened the oven door.

The gingerbread man jumped off of the cookie tin and ran out of the open window, shouting, "Don't eat me!"

The little old woman and the little old man ran after the gingerbread man. "Stop! Stop!" they yelled.

The gingerbread man did not look back. He ran on, saying, "Run, run, as fast as you can. You can't catch me. I'm the gingerbread man!"

Down the lane he sped when he came to a pig.

"Stop! Stop! I would like to eat you," shouted the pig.

The gingerbread man was too fast. He ran on, saying, "Run, run, as fast as you can. You can't catch me. I'm the gingerbread man!"

A little farther on he met a cow. "Stop! Stop! Little man,"
called the hungry cow, "I want to eat you."

Again the gingerbread man was too fast. He sped on down the road, saying, "Run, run, as fast as you can. You can't catch me. I'm the gingerbread man!"

The cow began to chase the gingerbread man, along with the pig and the little old woman. But the gingerbread man was too fast for them.

It was not long before the gingerbread man came to a horse.
"Stop! Stop!" shouted the horse. "I want to eat you, little man."

But the gingerbread man did not stop. He said, "Run, run, as
fast as you can. You can't catch me. I'm the gingerbread man!"

The horse joined in the chase. The gingerbread man
laughed and laughed, until he came to a river.

"Oh no!" he cried. "They will catch me. How can I cross the river?"

A sly fox came out from behind a tree.

"I can help you cross the river," said the fox. "Jump on to my tail, and I will swim across."

"You won't eat me, will you?" said the gingerbread man.

"Of course not," said the fox. "I just want to help."

The gingerbread man climbed on the fox's tail. Soon the gingerbread man began to get wet. "Climb onto my back," said the fox. So the gingerbread man

did. As he swam, the fox said, "You are too heavy. I am tired. Jump onto my nose." So the gingerbread man did as he was told.

No sooner had they reached the other side than the fox tossed the gingerbread man up in the air. He opened his mouth, and—*snap!*— that was the end of the gingerbread man.

Gingerbread Man Recipe

Ingredients for a Gingerbread Man:

2 cups flour

1 heaping teaspoon of baking powder

¾ cup sugar

1 pinch of salt

1 egg

1 T. honey

1 t. cinnamon

1 t. mixed spice (pumpkin pie spice)

3 T. milk

½ stick of butter (4 T.)

For the decoration:

Raisins

Preparation:

Combine the flour, baking powder, sugar, and salt with the egg, molasses, cinnamon, mixed spice, and milk. Cut the butter into small pieces and distribute evenly into the batter. Mix well.

Preheat the oven to 350° F.

On a lightly floured surface, roll the dough out to 1/4-inch thickness. With the help of a stencil or a cookie cutter, cut the dough into a gingerbread man shape, and decorate with raisins.

Place the gingerbread man on a cookie sheet with baking paper.

Bake for 15 minutes at 350° F

Remove, cool, and watch closely to be sure that the gingerbread man doesn't jump off of the cookie sheet!